A Not-So-Special Relationship

Edinburgh Studies in Anglo-American Relations

Series Editors: Steve Marsh and Alan P. Dobson

Published and forthcoming titles

The Anglo-American Relationship
Steve Marsh and Alan P. Dobson

The Arsenal of Democracy: Aircraft Supply and the Anglo-American Alliance, 1938–1942
Gavin J. Bailey

Post-War Planning on the Periphery: Anglo-American Economic Diplomacy in South America, 1939–1945
Thomas C. Mills

A Not-So-Special Relationship: The US, the UK and German Unification, 1945–1990
Luca Ratti

Reagan and Thatcher's Special Relationship: Latin America and Anglo-American Relations
Sally-Ann Treharne

Tacit Alliance: Franklin Roosevelt and the Anglo-American 'Special Relationship' before Churchill, 1933–1940
Tony McCulloch

The Politics of Diplomacy: U.S. Presidents and the Northern Ireland Conflict, 1967–1998
James Cooper

Jimmy Carter and the Anglo-American 'Special Relationship'
Thomas K. Robb

The Congo Crisis: Anglo-American Relations and the United Nations, 1960–1964
Alanna O'Malley

edinburghuniversitypress.com/series/esar

A Not-So-Special Relationship

The US, the UK and German Unification, 1945–1990

Luca Ratti

EDINBURGH
University Press

To my mum and dad

Edinburgh University Press is one of the leading university presses in the UK. We publish academic books and journals in our selected subject areas across the humanities and social sciences, combining cutting-edge scholarship with high editorial and production values to produce academic works of lasting importance. For more information visit our website: edinburghuniversitypress.com

© Luca Ratti, 2017

Edinburgh University Press Ltd
The Tun – Holyrood Road
12(2f) Jackson's Entry
Edinburgh EH8 8PJ

Typeset in 11/14 Sabon by
Servis Filmsetting Ltd, Stockport, Cheshire

A CIP record for this book is available from the British Library

ISBN 978 0 7486 4565 7 (hardback)
ISBN 978 0 7486 8014 6 (webready PDF)
ISBN 978 0 7486 8016 0 (epub)

Contents

Acronyms and Abbreviations

BAOR	British Army of the Rhine
BTO	Brussels Treaty Organization
CDU	Christian Democratic Union
CFE	Conventional Forces in Europe
CFM	Council of Foreign Ministers
CIA	Central Intelligence Agency
CPSU	Communist Party of the Soviet Union
CSCE	Conference on Security and Cooperation in Europe
CSU	Christian Social Union
EC	European Council
ECSC	European Coal and Steel Community
EDC	European Defence Community
EEC	European Economic Community
EFTA	European Free Trade Association
ERP	European Recovery Program
ESC	European Security Conference
EU	European Union
EURATOM	European Atomic Energy Community
FCO	Foreign and Commonwealth Office
FDP	Free Democratic Party
FRG	Federal Republic of Germany
G7	Group of 7
GDR	German Democratic Republic
IMF	International Monetary Fund
INF	Intermediate-Range Nuclear Forces
IRBM	Intermediate- Range Ballistic Missile
MBFR	Mutual and Balanced Force Reductions
NAC	North Atlantic Council
NATO	North Atlantic Treaty Organization
NPT	Non-Proliferation Treaty

NSC	National Security Council
OEEC	Organization of European Economic Cooperation
SA	Supplementary Agreement
SALT	Strategic Arms Limitation Talks
SDI	Strategic Defense Initiative
SEATO	South East Asian Treaty Organization
SED	Socialist Unity Party
SNF	Short-Range Nuclear Forces
SOFA	Status of Forces Agreement
SPD	Social Democratic Party
Stasi	Ministry for State Security
TASS	Telegraph Agency of the Soviet Union
UN	United Nations
USSR	Union of Soviet Socialist Republics
VE Day	Victory in Europe Day
WEU	Western European Union
WTO	Warsaw Treaty Organization

Introduction

'The special relationship between the United States and the United Kingdom is enduring, and the United Kingdom's membership in NATO remains a vital cornerstone of U.S. foreign, security, and economic policy'
(Barack Obama, 24 June 2016)

'The events of 1989 and 1990 in Germany symbolize what can happen when partners cooperate and trust each other'
(Angela Merkel, 3 October 2014)

'Some nations that were then and are now Germany's allies did not support the idea of unification'
(Vladimir Putin, 18 March 2014)

'The top priority for American foreign policy today in Europe should be the fate of the Federal Republic of Germany'
(Brent Scowcroft, 20 March 1989)

'I don't want to see us decoupled from Europe; I don't want to see us pull out of Europe'
(George H. W. Bush, 16 December 1989)

Germany's unification in October 1990 was one of the most momentous events in European history in the second half of the twentieth century. Its unique historical value stems from the highly symbolic and emotional significance of the events that made the unification of the two German states possible. German unity ended the Cold War in Europe, which for forty years had divided Germany and the continent. It knocked down the remaining vestiges of the bipolar order that had emerged at the end of World War II and drew back the Iron Curtain, accelerating the process leading to the collapse of communist regimes across Eastern Europe and to the disintegration of the Union of Soviet Socialist Republics (USSR) in December 1991. At the same time, it marked the demise of the logic of limited sovereignty and the rise of self-determination and liberal democracy in the former Soviet bloc, ushering in a dramatic acceleration in the process of Europe's political and economic integration and triggering the beginning of NATO's post-Cold War transformation and enlargement.

This revolutionary process occurred first and foremost as a consequence of widespread political and social discontent across the Soviet bloc. The East German people's action against their own rulers also played a dramatic role. It began in May 1989 when, inspired by the new Soviet leadership's reforms and by the growth of democratic movements in neighbouring Poland, Hungary and Czechoslovakia, a truly peaceful popular revolt undermined and overwhelmed the dictatorial regime, which had ruled Eastern Germany since the late 1940s with ironclad support from Moscow. Throughout the summer and early autumn of 1989 popular demonstrations overcame political calculations. Although these dynamics were followed closely in the West, until the late spring of 1989 decision-makers in Britain and the US struggled to predict a sudden breakdown of the Cold War structure of international politics in Europe. Furthermore, whereas Washington encouraged demands for change in East Germany and Eastern Europe, in many European capitals they raised fears that the Soviet bloc's collapse might result in widespread disorder and political instability. It was only a few months later the decision-makers of the time came to terms with the results that had been created by popular demand. Then, they skilfully laid the foundations of a new security architecture in Europe, endeavouring to defuse a wide range of potential problems that could have arisen as a result of the crisis in the Soviet bloc and particularly because of German unification. The legacy of those transformations continues to exert a powerful influence on dynamics in Germany and Europe today and on relations between the US and its NATO allies.

In November 2014, on the twenty-fifth anniversary of the Berlin Wall's collapse and a few months after the Russian Federation's annexation of Crimea, Germany's Chancellor Angela Merkel praised the carefully crafted political and diplomatic arrangements that had enabled the peaceful transition in Eastern Europe in 1989 and German unification in October 1990. She remarked how her country's 'peaceful fight for freedom' might be used 'to resolve many of the problems facing Europe and the world today'.[1] Merkel, who grew up in the German Democratic Republic (GDR), praised the courage of the East Germans for making possible the fall of the Berlin Wall and eventually unification. Nonetheless, she also evoked the complex political arrangements that preceded unification. She emphasised how German unity became possible, by convincing the allies and the Soviets alike that a unified Germany would not undermine European security. Merkel's words celebrated a historic achievement for Germany and a masterpiece of East–West diplomacy: in 1990 the Western allies agreed that a united Germany would remain a member of the North Atlantic Treaty Organization (NATO) and the European Union (EU), and German–Soviet relations were raised to a new level.

In contrast to this narrative, only a few months before Merkel's speech, the Russian Federation's president, Vladimir Putin, provided a different and cruder interpretation of those events. His words sounded like a dire reminder of Germany's difficult path towards unification and of Moscow's persistent grievances about how this process was carried out by the West. While Merkel portrayed the events of 1989–90 as a positive lesson, Putin recalled the hostile attitude to a united Germany of a number of allies of the Federal Republic of Germany (FRG), in spite of a formal commitment to unification.[2] Their lack of enthusiasm for a unified Germany reflected fears that had never dissipated about German nationalism and power, which dated back to memories of the two world wars. The fact that unification coincided with the fiftieth anniversary of the Western front's collapse and of the Battle of Britain in 1940 was still alive in the minds of the day's decision-makers.

After the fall of the Berlin Wall in November 1989, German unification less than a year later was a major, if not the most remarkable, milestone towards dismantling Cold War politics in Europe. The dynamics that were unleashed by this process continue to retain major political and strategic significance today. NATO began an ongoing process of determining its new place and role in the post-Cold War world; the European Communities moved towards closer economic and political integration, despite the uncertainties of a number of member states; and the Soviet bloc and the USSR neared their final disintegration and collapse. The purpose of this book is to clarify some aspects of that complex transformation and different perspectives on German unification, by investigating the role in it of the Anglo-American 'special relationship'.

Washington and London played a fundamental role in Germany's post-War governance from the Potsdam Conference in 1945 to unification. However, there were frequent differences between them.[3] Anglo-American relations are much debated in international history: numerous contributions to the literature investigate and discuss particular aspects of what the British, and rather less the Americans, call the 'special relationship'. Winston Churchill, who liked to remind people that he embodied Anglo-American union in his parentage, figured prominently in the construction of the narrative of a special bond between Washington and London. In the late 1940s, often through close cooperation between the Attlee and Truman administrations, the European status quo was consolidated with the US commitment to Europe in the guise of the Truman Doctrine, the deployment of Marshall Aid, the Berlin airlift and the creation of NATO. Nonetheless, in the months immediately following the conclusion of the War in Europe, London's policy towards Germany diverged from American preferences. This was the case again in the early 1950s in the aftermath of the inception of détente in East–West relations. Thereafter, the eruption of extra-European tensions in the late 1950s and early 1960s shifted the focus away from Germany somewhat. Then, ironically, during the 1980s when Margaret Thatcher and Ronald Reagan revived the special relationship, the crisis of Soviet rule in the East rekindled Anglo-American differences over Germany. These differences reflected deeper dynamics in Anglo-American ties and the adaptation of the Anglo-American relationship to a fast-evolving international dynamics. German unification marked a fundamental transition in the US's and Britain's places in the world. While Washington emerged as the only superpower and secured an important role in post-Cold War Europe, Britain's international status changed from being a key ally of the US to that of a power confined on the edge of Europe and confronting a 'profound sense of purposelessness'.[4] These dynamics had a major impact on British political debate and indirectly contributed to a deep reconsideration of the

United Kingdom's international role and complex relationship with the European Communities.

The Anglo-American special relationship in the twentieth century has been and continues to be the subject of numerous analyses and reflections.[5] However, when it comes to the German question, the theme of Anglo-American relations has been dealt with mostly within general studies on the international and European dimensions of unification or in monographic analyses of US and British policy towards Germany.[6] The aim of this book is to fill a gap in the literature, by looking at the special relationship through the prism of British and American policies towards Germany. In particular, the book debates whether the special relationship influenced US and British views of Germany from the summer of 1945 to the autumn of 1990. Ultimately, the smooth conclusion of negotiations about unification has been one of the most successful endeavours of Western diplomacy. The historical significance of that is certainly not inferior to those of the negotiations which in April 1949 led to the signing of the North Atlantic Treaty. However, whereas in the Cold War's early stages the British played a major role in NATO's inception, German unification was certainly not the product of a joint Anglo-American initiative. In contrast, this book's underlying thesis is that of a 'not-so-special' and, at times, conflicting relationship, which was shaped by different strategic priorities as well as by diverging historical memories and perceptions of Germany.

The first Anglo-American differences date back to the Potsdam Conference. Then British endeavours to preserve a degree of cooperation with Moscow were forestalled by a firm American stance. As East–West relations deteriorated, nuances in Anglo-American policies persisted. After a bold Western response to Moscow during the first Berlin crisis, in the early 1950s Washington and London shared a common interest in securing the FRG's commitment to the West. Nonetheless, when it came to German unity it was a different matter. Washington supported the idea of a united Germany, provided it was democratic and a full member of the West. In contrast, although not opposing unification in principle, the British maintained a much more cautious attitude. An even greater difference arose after Stalin's death in 1953 and the consequent thaw in East–West relations. Now, the White House and Whitehall manifested remarkably differing views of the German question. Whereas US rhetoric towards Eastern Europe, including

East Germany, focused on liberation of the captive nations, Britain – led once again by Winston Churchill after the Labour parenthesis of Clement Attlee – repeatedly attempted to establish dialogue with Moscow and to consolidate the balance of power in Europe. Washington strongly disapproved and refused repeated calls by Churchill for a summit meeting with the Soviets.

The situation was further complicated by prevailing views in the FRG. Bonn saw the question of relations with the Soviet Union and its satellites almost exclusively as an aspect of its unification policy. Nonetheless, the promises embodied in the Bonn/Paris Conventions of 1952/4, which solved the thorny issue of West German rearmament, had not committed the allies to German unity per se. They only committed them to a united Germany that was democratic and integrated into the West. At the same time, the Bonn/Paris Conventions ruled out unification on Soviet terms, or a neutral Germany of the kind that Stalin had envisaged in 1952 and which the Soviet leadership floated around until the FRG's integration into NATO in 1955. These promises laid down the preconditions for the West's consent to unification and contained the seeds of the solution eventually arrived at in 1990. However, they also acted like a Western veto. Ultimately, a united, liberal and democratic Germany remained inconceivable as long as Europe was divided. Nonetheless, for most of the Cold War the stalemate in East–West relations allowed the US and Britain, despite not always holding identical views, to proclaim solemnly their commitment to German unity, 'without any serious expectation of being called to account'.[7]

Changing Anglo-American attitudes were sometimes in step but frequently they were not so, and that created difficulties for their German policies and their own relationship. In the Cold War's initial stages there was no Anglo-American urgency to discuss unification. However, from the early 1950s US attitudes were much more sympathetic towards a united Germany than those prevailing in Britain. Divergences between London and Washington first surfaced at Potsdam, where the British Labour government of Clement Attlee had sought to preserve cooperation with Moscow. They persisted after the formation of two German states in 1949. When the East Berlin population revolted against Soviet occupation in 1953, Britain displayed an ambivalent attitude, formally supporting the East German people's claim to self-determination, while silently approving of the Kremlin's repression of the protest. In contrast, Washington, although unwilling to risk military confrontation with Russia, never regarded the preservation of a Russian presence in Germany as an American interest or a Western priority. West German membership of NATO and the Warsaw Pact's establishment in May 1955, consolidating Europe's balance of power, partially laid to rest these differences. At the same time, they confined to mere hypothetical speculation any discussion about German unity until Mikhail Gorbachev's *perestroika* and *glasnost* in the second half of the 1980s provided a new lifeline for aspirations to self-determination. Then, as the prospect of unification increased, different strategic priorities, historical memories and perceptions of the German question resurfaced quickly, generating tensions in the special relationship.

After hesitating initially, the Republican administration of George Herbert Walker Bush endeavoured to grasp the historic opportunity provided by the Soviet bloc's crisis. Washington now aimed to bring about unification, on the condition that a united Germany would remain a committed member of NATO and the European Communities. In contrast, the British, like other European nations, reacted with concern and a degree of hostility to the prospect of a united Germany.[8] London emphasised gradual rather than overnight change, treated demands for German unity as being premature and insisted that unification should come about only after a long period of transition. Furthermore, in the British view, the issue of German unity should not be settled only among the Four Powers that had assumed a special responsibility for Germany at Potsdam, rather negotiations should include the NATO allies and should take place within the wider context of the Conference on Security and Cooperation in Europe (CSCE). Ultimately, Whitehall demanded a comprehensive settlement and detailed arrangements with Moscow and Germany's eastern neighbours. While reflecting a concern about the need to balance a united Germany, Britain's repeated attempts to allow the Russians a residual say in German affairs caused discomfort across the Atlantic. Despite some US officials, particularly the US president's national security advisor, Brent Scowcroft, being initially sympathetic to British concerns, London's repeated calls for reasonable periods of transition were interpreted in Washington and Bonn as a code word for its preference for a divided Germany.[9]

Between late 1989 and the spring of 1990 British policy towards

Germany remained a source of irritation in the White House. Margaret Thatcher endeavoured to seek an arrangement with the Russians and attempted to play upon French fears of German domination in Europe. However, US decision-makers often bypassed the British. Washington preferred to deal bilaterally with Bonn and the Kremlin. On some issues, the Americans also privileged Paris over London, supporting President François Mitterrand's demands for deepening European integration. Not even the more conciliatory views of professional diplomats within the Foreign and Commonwealth Office (FCO) could allay British concerns. Thatcher's fears were reinforced by her lack of trust in the West Germans and difficult personal relationship with Kohl. In his joint memoir with Scowcroft, Bush makes no mystery of the antagonism between Kohl and Thatcher, recalling that in May 1989 Mitterrand told him that Kohl's derogatory expression for Thatcher was the term 'that woman'.[10] Not only did Thatcher and Kohl have an 'incompatible chemistry', but they also had a different perception of history, including contrasting ideas on Europe, nationalism and security policy; a problem which was aggravated by German unification.[11] Only after a long diplomatic fight that lasted until late spring 1990, resulting in a considerable decline of British influence in the US, did Whitehall align its views with those of Washington.[12] The dynamics of this process undermined Anglo-American solidarity and increased British reservations about European integration.

However, the Anglo-American schism over Germany and the White House's disregard for British views did not result in a crisis of the special relationship. Irrespective of the outcome over Germany, Whitehall viewed the special relationship as too important to allow any one issue to significantly damage it. Recognising that London could not strike a deal with the Russians because of the Americans, Thatcher set her losses aside and firmly supported the maintenance of a strong American presence in Europe. Nonetheless, she also promoted closer Franco-British ties in order to contain the strength of a newly unified Germany.[13]

The solution finally arrived at in the summer of 1990 met US preferences. However, it was only 'a second best' for Britain. Different evaluations of Germany's role in the European Communities, and its relationship with NATO, the USSR and the countries of Eastern Europe remained cogent indicators of persistent Anglo-American divergence. Throughout the unification debate the Bush administration endeavoured not to isolate the Germans, often at the expense of the special relationship. In contrast, Whitehall resented the FRG's endeavours to minimise Four Power rights and Bonn's reluctance to discuss political and military issues in advance with the allies before putting them to the Russians. Britain's views revealed a number of concerns about Germany's future reliability. London feared that, with the achievement of unity, 'Germany will not simply be the Federal Republic plus, but a different entity'.[14]

While exposing a deep-rooted distrust of the Germans, this attitude also reflected Britain's relative comfort with the Cold War structure of international politics. Anne Deighton, one of the most eminent scholars of British policy towards Germany, has emphasised how a political and military balance that divided Europe, ensuring a strategic truce between East and West, was seen after the War as the best option for Britain. While the British possessed a degree of leverage over developments in Germany, they had virtually none over the states of Eastern Europe and accepted Moscow's influence over this area as a fait accompli.[15] Britain's limits were evident in successive diplomatic ploys: the percentages agreement that Churchill had negotiated with Stalin in 1944 to create a balance of power in south-eastern Europe;[16] the British search for an arrangement with the Soviets at Potsdam; and Whitehall's ambivalent response to demands for change in the East in the early 1950s. However, after the advent of détente in East–West relations and the German states' integration into the two rival alliances, this search for an arrangement with Moscow was consolidated by successive British prime ministers who, regardless of their party affiliation, made it a central feature of the United Kingdom's German policy. Thatcher, like Macmillan and many of her predecessors, was not only driven by strategic concerns, but genuinely endeavoured to defuse superpower tension.[17] However, while London's value for the Kremlin stemmed from its ability to influence US and Atlantic positions, the dynamics of 1989–90 considerably diminished Whitehall's influence in Europe.

US support for and British hostility to German unification were symptoms of a persistent tension in the special relationship. The origins of the Anglo-American friction over Europe date back to the immediate post-War years. While in the Cold War's early stages Washington had viewed Germany's political and economic rehabilitation as a fundamental step towards European reconstruction and the establishment of a partnership with Western Europe, the US government now perceived a united Germany as the gateway for the preservation of a preponderant American role in Europe and for the deepening of integration on the continent. In contrast, while not objecting to Germany's economic and political reha- bilitation, London struggled to identify a role for itself in the US strategy and in European politics first during the 1950s and then in the transition from the Cold War to a post-Cold War world. Like Britain's preferences for an arrangement with the Russians, London's complex relationship with European integration also dates back to the Cold War's early stages, when this process had started in earnest. As the Soviet bloc disintegrated, the United Kingdom's ambivalence towards Europe, and the hostility to European integration of large sectors of British society, deprived Whitehall of an important tool for exerting influence on both the US and Germany at a crucial historical moment. Hence, German unification was an additional chapter in Britain's estrangement from plans for deeper integration in Europe; and a British govern- ment that was unable to influence European outcomes also had limited value for the Americans.

The result of such an attitude was to diminish Britain's influ- ence in Washington at a time when, following the conclusion of quadripartite rights and the reduction in British forces in Germany, Britain had lost some of its 'special advantages'.[18] After allied legal rights in Germany were terminated, the legitimacy of Britain's permanent seat in the UN Security Council was also questioned.[19] London now found it increasingly difficult to exert any significant or lasting influence on Washington or Berlin. Only when the British aligned themselves with American views, and provided support to the US in a largely uncritical way, did the remnants of a special relationship survive – including on the German question.[20] Furthermore, the theme of Britain's relations with Europe created fractures at the very heart of the British government and public opinion. One of their outcomes was to lead to Thatcher's fall from power during the Paris CSCE summit in November 1990 that, following the coming into force of the 'Two plus Four Treaty' between the two German states and the Four Powers, 'set the seal on German unity'.[21] Ultimately, those fractures re-emerged a quarter of a century later, when the British people were called to vote on their country's relationship with Europe in a 2016 referendum.

Nonetheless, although German unification seemed to undermine Britain's hopes of preserving the special relationship, in the following years London's relations with Washington rapidly recovered from the incomprehension and misunderstandings of 1989–90. The embattled dynamics of European integration and British readiness at the beginning of 1991 to provide support to the US in the Persian Gulf fast rekindled Anglo-American relations. Hence, while stumbling in Germany, solidarity between Washington and London was restored by the fluctuating dynamics of the post-Cold War international system. The British also benefited from Germany's complex path towards a new international role, which did not allow Bonn to contribute troops to the campaign in Kuwait or to claim a lead role in the process of creating a European security and defence identity. Ultimately, Whitehall's support for the US in operation 'Desert Storm' provided, in the face of German reticence for a military solution, a new lifeline to the special relationship, allowing Thatcher to claim that Britain was back as the real 'partner in leadership'.[22] Nonetheless, in the following years London's reservations towards European integration continued to grow in intensity, overshadowing US endeavours to preserve a vibrant transatlantic relationship in the post-Cold War world. How these complex matters unravelled from the mid-1940s to the early 1990s is the detailed subject of this book.

Notes

1. The text of Merkel's speech is available at <http://www.bundesregierung.de/Content/DE/Rede/2014/10/2014-10-03-merkel-tdde.html> (last accessed 21 September 2016).
2. Putin's address on 18 March 2014 to State Duma deputies, Federation Council members, heads of Russian regions and civil society representatives in the Kremlin is available at <http://eng.kremlin.ru/news/6889> (last accessed 21 September 2016).
3. For most of the Cold War Western diplomacy made an indistinct use of the terms 'unification' and 'reunification', although they referred to different solutions for ending Germany's division. Reunification technically implied a return to the borders of 1937, including former German territory beyond the Oder–Neisse line, such as Eastern Prussia and the city of Königsberg, farther Pomerania, Eastern Brandenburg and Silesia. In contrast, unification referred

only to the territory of the two German states that were established in 1949. At the end of 1989 the FRG's chancellor, Helmut Kohl, initially used the term *Wiedervereinigung* – 'reunification' – in a ten-point plan for unification. However, he then carefully avoided using the *'wieder'* ('re') part ever again. See William Safire, 'On Language; Unify or Reunify?', *The New York Times*, 25 February 1990; *Documents on British Policy Overseas* (hereafter *DBPO*), Series III, vol. VII, *German Unification, 1989–1990* (London: Her Majesty's Stationery Office, 2009), p. ix, fn. 2; *DBPO*, Series III, vol. VI, *Berlin in the Cold War, 1948–1990* (London: Her Majesty's Stationery Office, 2009).

4. William Wallace, 'British Foreign Policy after the Cold War', *International Affairs*, vol. 68, no. 3, July 1992, p. 424; Christopher Coker, 'Britain and the New World Order: The Special Relationship in the 1990s', *International Affairs*, vol. 68, no. 3, July 1992, p. 409. Both quoted in Jarrod Hayes and Patrick James, 'Theory as Thought: Britain and German Unification', *Security Studies*, vol. 23, no. 2, 2014, p. 401.

5. Among the major contributions on the special relationship in the twentieth century are Donald Cameron Watt, *Succeeding John Bull: America in Britain's Place, 1900–1975* (Cambridge: Cambridge University Press, 1984); William Roger Louis and Hedley Bull (eds), *The Special Relationship: Anglo-American Relations since 1945* (Oxford and New York: Oxford University Press, 1986); Ritchie Ovendale, *Anglo-American Relations in the Twentieth Century* (Basingstoke: Macmillan and New York: St. Martin's Press, 1998); Christopher John Bartlett, *'The Special Relationship': A Political History of Anglo-American Relations since 1945* (Harlow: Longman, 1992); David Dimbleby and David Reynolds, *An Ocean Apart: The Relationship between Britain and America in the 20th Century* (London and New York: Random House, 1988); John Baylis, *Anglo-American Defence Relations 1939–1984* (London: Macmillan, 1984); John Baylis (ed.), *Anglo-American Relations since 1939: The Enduring Alliance* (Manchester and New York: Manchester University Press, 1997); Jonathan Hollowell, *Twentieth-Century Anglo-American Relations, Contemporary History in Context* (London: Palgrave Macmillan, 2001); Antoine Capet and Aïssatou Sy-Wonyu (eds), *The 'Special Relationship': La «relation spéciale» entre le Royaume-Uni et les Etats-Unis* (Rouen: Université de Rouen, 2003); Alan P. Dobson, *Anglo-American Relations in the Twentieth Century: Of Friendship, Conflict, and the Rise and Decline of Superpowers* (New York: Routledge, 1995); Alan P. Dobson and Steve Marsh (eds), *Anglo-American Relations: Contemporary Perspectives* (London and New York: Routledge, 2013).

6. See, for example, R. Gerald Hughes, *Britain, Germany and the Cold War: The Search for a European Détente 1949–1967* (London and New York: Macmillan, 2007); James McAllister, *No Exit: America and the German Problem 1943–1954* (Ithaca, NY: Cornell University Press, 2002); John P. S. Gearson, *Harold Macmillan and the Berlin Wall Crisis, 1958–1962: The Limits of Interest and Force* (Basingstoke and London: Palgrave, 1998); Heinrich Bortfeldt, *Washington, Bonn, Berlin: die USA und die deutsche Einheit* (Bonn: Bouvier, 1993). A partial exception is a chapter by Daniel Gossel in a collective volume, which addresses the role of the special relationship in fostering the FRG's Western integration during the Cold War. Daniel Gossel, 'Zur Innenarchitektur der westlichen Allianz: Die sicherheitspolitische Integration der Bundesrepublik als Aufgabe und Problem der Special Relationship zwischen den USA und Großbritannien (1945–1965)', in Michael Wala (ed.), *Gesellschaft und Diplomatie im transatlantischen Kontext* (Stuttgart: Steiner, 1999), pp. 273–90.

7. *DBPO*, III, VII, p. x.

8. For a broad account of European approaches to unification see Frédéric Bozo, Andreas Rödder and Mary Elise Sarotte (eds), *German Reunification: A Multinational History* (London and New York: Routledge, 2017).

9. On Scowcroft's views see Bartholomew Sparrow, *The Strategist: Brent Scowcroft and the Call of National Security* (New York: PublicAffairs, 2015), pp. 301–13, 368–84.

10. George H. W. Bush and Brent Scowcroft, *A World Transformed* (New York: Alfred A. Knopf, 1998), p. 77.

11. Alan Watson, 'Europe's Odd Couple', *Prospect*, no. 10, July 1996, available at <http://www.prospectmagazine.co.uk/features/europe soddcouple-germany-britain-thatcher-kohl-conflict> (last accessed 27 September 2016), p. 49. See also Yvonne Klein, 'Obstructive or Promoting? British Views on German Unification 1989/90', *German Politics*, vol. 5, no. 3, 1996, p. 412.

12. Britain's ultimate decision to align with the US is explained by realist theory of international relations as an example of 'wave of the future' bandwagoning; this type of bandwagoning occurs when second-rank powers align with a first-rank great power that is forging a new international order. Although initially attempting to preserve the status quo and to counter unification by balancing with other powers, the British embraced American preferences in order to avoid isolation, grudgingly acknowledging that a united Germany and the resulting European order represented the 'wave of the future'. For an analytical definition of 'wave of the future' bandwagoning see Randall L. Schweller 'Bandwagoning for Profit:

Bringing the Revisionist State Back In', *International Security*, vol. 19, no. 1, 1994, pp. 96–8. See also Tsuyoshi Kawasaki, 'The Rising Sun Was No Jackal: Japanese Grand Strategy, the Tripartite Pact, and Alliance Formation Theory', in Jeffrey W. Taliaferro, Norrin M. Ripsman and Steven E. Lobell (eds), *The Challenge of Grand Strategy: The Great Powers and the Broken Balance between the World Wars* (Cambridge and New York: Cambridge University Press, 2012), p. 227. For an eclectic explanation of British conduct, blending together realist structures and normative motives, see Hayes and James, 'Theory as Thought', pp. 399–429.

13. Margaret Thatcher, *Downing Street Years* (London: Harper Perennial, 1993), p. 791. Quoted in *DBPO*, III, VII, p. xv.

14. *DBPO*, III, VII, doc. no. 238, Weston to Mallaby, p. 470.

15. Anne Deighton, 'Germany and East-Central Europe, 1945–1990: The View from London', in Mark Kramer and Vit Smetana (eds), *Imposing, Maintaining, and Tearing Open the Iron Curtain: The Cold War and East-Central Europe, 1945–1989* (Lanham, MD: Lexington Books, 2014), pp. 211–12.

16. In October 1944 Britain's prime minister had flown to Moscow to discuss political arrangements with the Soviet leadership, reaching an agreement that partitioned Hungary, Yugoslavia, Greece, Bulgaria and Romania into spheres of influence. British predominance was recognised in Greece and Moscow's influence acknowledged over Romania and Bulgaria. Hungary and Yugoslavia were equally divided. Nonetheless, Soviet Foreign Minister Vjačeslav Molotov subsequently changed percentages in Hungary and Bulgaria in the USSR's favour, exposing the Kremlin's disregard of British views. Martin McCauley, *Origins of the Cold War, 1941–1949* (Harlow: Pearson Longman, 2008), doc. no. 7, p. 126. See also R. Gerald Hughes, *The Postwar Legacy of Appeasement: British Foreign Policy since 1945* (Bloomsbury: London, 2014), p. 23.

17. Ilaria Poggiolini and Alex Pravda, 'Britain in Europe in the 1980s: East & West. Introduction', *Journal of European Integration History*, vol. 16, no. 1, 2010, pp. 10–12.

18. *DBPO*, III, VII, doc. no. 242, Mallaby to Weston, p. 490.

19. Klein, 'Obstructive or Promoting?', p. 408.

20. Britain's role was played down by West German accounts of unification. In his *Bundestag* speech of 23 August 1990 Kohl expressed 'warm thanks' to Germany's Western friends and partners for their support, making a special and explicit reference to 'the three Allies', which for decades had ensured the Federal Republic's freedom, and adding that Germany was and would remain part of the 'Western community of values' and would serve 'as an equal partner' in a united Europe. Kohl personally thanked Bush, stating that the US

president had shown himself 'a true friend of the Germans', and reassured Mitterrand that 'the fraternal bonds between the German and French peoples would remain at the heart of the foreign policy of a united Germany'. Any reference to Thatcher's role was instead indicatively omitted. See Deutscher Bundestag, Plenarprotokoll 11/221, 23 August 1990, available at <http://dip21.bundestag.de/dip21/btp/11/11221.pdf> (last accessed 27 September 2016). British reservations about unification were also evoked by Merkel in her 2014 speech, available at <http://www.bundesregierung.de/Content/DE/Rede/2014/10/2014-10-03-merkel-tdde.html> (last accessed 21 September 2016).
21. *DBPO*, III, VII, p. xxxiv.
22. Thatcher, *Downing Street Years*, p. 769. See also Lori Maguire, 'Introduction', in Lori Maguire (ed.), *The Foreign Policy Discourse in the United Kingdom and the United States in the 'New World Order'* (Newcastle upon Tyne: Cambridge Scholars Publishing, 2009), p. 12. For a defence of the argument that the US still does have no better ally than the United Kingdom see also Alan P. Dobson and Steve Marsh, 'Anglo-American Relations: End of a Special Relationship?', *The International History Review*, vol. 36, no. 4, 2014, pp. 673–97.

Part I   The Special Relationship and the German Question during the Cold War

This book is organised into two main sections. The first discusses Anglo-American views of the German question from the Potsdam Conference until Gorbachev's election to general secretary of the Communist Party of the Soviet Union (CPSU) in March 1985 and the embrace of *glasnost* and *perestroika*. The second section focuses on the dynamics of 1989–90, debating Anglo-American approaches to the German question at the Cold War's end.

The first section includes three chapters. The first focuses on the German question from the Cold War's early stages until West German rearmament. The second discusses Anglo-American policy towards Germany during European détente. The third evaluates Anglo-American perceptions of dynamics in Germany following Gorbachev's reforms in the second half of the 1980s.

More specifically, the first chapter debates Anglo-American views of Germany in the context of a deteriorating relationship with Moscow. It focuses on the Potsdam Conference, the Marshall Plan, the Berlin blockade, the 1953 East Berlin riots, West German rearmament and membership of the Atlantic Alliance in 1955. During the early stages of the Cold War the US and Britain endeavoured to integrate Germany into the Atlantic and European structures, but British policy was influenced by London's attempt to preserve a great power status and by fresh memories of the two world wars.

The second chapter focuses on Anglo-American views about Germany during détente. It debates the evolution in Anglo-American policies, their approaches to the Berlin crisis of 1958–61 and the evolution of the FRG's grand strategy from Western integration to *Ostpolitik*. It also discusses Anglo-American perceptions of the FRG's policy towards the GDR or *Deutschlandpolitik* until the signing in August 1975 of the CSCE Final Act at the end of the Helsinki conference. While the US and Britain formally maintained a commitment to German unity, during détente a certain Anglo-American consensus consolidated that the country's division would be a long-term feature of European politics. Thirty years after the conclusion of the War, a number of Anglo-American officials interpreted the signing of the CSCE Final Act as a durable, if not permanent, arrangement of the European status quo rather than a potential first step towards unification, as it was seen in Bonn. The chapter also debates how US and British views of the German question evolved in the second half of the 1970s, following the rapid deterioration in East–West relations which was brought about by the Euro-missiles crisis, conflicting approaches to the CSCE's third basket and human rights issues, and the Soviet invasion of Afghanistan in December 1979. In the early 1980s both Washington and London were reassured by Bonn's commitment to NATO, while the FRG also attempted to preserve dialogue with both the Soviet Union and the GDR.

Ultimately, the third chapter focuses on the impact of Gorbachev's election to the CPSU's leadership in March 1985 on Anglo-American views. While both the US and Britain greeted *glasnost* and *perestroika* with enthusiasm, in the eyes of Anglo-American decision-makers, unification remained more an aspiration of the Federal government than a realistic solution for Germany. Nonetheless, as the new course in the Kremlin gradually brought the German question back onto the international agenda, Anglo-American strategies began to drift apart and Washington largely dictated policy. However, as noted elsewhere, while that was temporarily damaging for Anglo-American relations, it did not fatally damage the special relationship. Understanding the nuances of why that was so is also an important underlying theme of this work.

1 The US, the UK and the German Question from the First Cold War to Détente (1945–1961)

The special relationship and Germany from Potsdam to the Federal Republic's establishment

'We should have lost the one factor which might hold us and the Russians together, viz., the existence of a single Germany which it would be in the interest of us both to hold down'
(Ernest Bevin, 3 May 1946)

'The UK stood for a united Germany, not a dismembered or divided Germany'
(Ernest Bevin, 22 January 1948)

'Neither the West nor the East could or should tolerate a united Germany under any circumstances'
(Robin M. A. Hankey, 14 May 1948)

Anglo-American views of Germany at Potsdam

This first chapter examines Anglo-American views of Germany from the Potsdam Conference, which opened on 17 July 1945 and ended in August with an agreement between the Three Powers, establishing quadripartite rights and responsibilities through France's association, to the FRG's inclusion into NATO in May 1955. Although US and British views were powerfully influenced by the dynamics of their relationship with the Soviet Union, in the early stages of the Cold War there was not a consolidated Anglo-American consensus about Germany. The East–West structure powerfully shaped almost every aspect of Anglo-American policy in Europe, making Germany's unification for a number of years a remote possibility. Furthermore, both US and British decision-makers ostensibly pursued national strategies, which were not always inspired by a shared vision about Germany's place in the post-War order. From the early stages of the Potsdam Conference US decision-makers endeavoured to constrain Soviet influence and after 1948 they favoured West Germany's rehabilitation and rapid integration into the Western security system. In contrast, Britain was driven by the concern to preserve its world standing and by a persistent distrust of the Germans. As a result, London initially attempted to preserve a degree of cooperation with Moscow and only gradually supported American initiatives to restore West German sovereignty.

The Potsdam Conference – convened ten weeks after Admiral Karl Dönitz signed the Third Reich's act of surrender on 8 May 1945 – was the first chapter in a long story of failed Anglo-American and Soviet endeavours to reach an arrangement on Germany. However, East–West disagreements there quickly turned the German question into one of the most pressing and intricate issues of the emerging post-War settlement in Europe. At Potsdam the political and military divergences that had overshadowed relations between the US and Britain on the one side and Moscow on the other during the War deepened. With the Anglo-Americans and the Soviets unable to overcome their respective diffidence, the German question rapidly took centre stage in East–West relations.[1] Despite its heavy and unconditional defeat, Germany retained the potential to tip the balance of power to one side or the other. As East–West solidarity rapidly eroded and turned into animosity, the German problem emerged as a potent combination – as John Lewis Gaddis points out – of two distinct but related concerns, 'how to avoid the danger of a resurgent Germany itself, on the one hand, and the threat of a Germany on the wrong side in the Cold War, on the other'.[2] These concerns decisively influenced US, British and Soviet strategies and conduct, also deeply affecting Anglo-American relations and their post-War dynamics.

Despite earlier and pressing concerns about arrangements in Asia, in the aftermath of the War the Truman administration quickly came to view Germany's future as the most critical and decisive question of the post-War order. The issue of Germany and its new international role was also a pressing theme in the British political debate. As relations with the Soviets began to deteriorate, decision-makers in Washington and London saw no obvious and immediate response to the German dilemma. Nonetheless, as a result of Germany's strategic value and economic potential, the German question had a central role in the definition of the post-War international system. It also deeply impacted on Anglo-American relations. In addition, its fate was of crucial importance for those common principles, including the renunciation to territorial aggrandisements, the right to self-determination and the disarmament of aggressor nations, which Franklin Delano Roosevelt and Winston Churchill had enunciated in the Atlantic Charter in August 1941 despite different geopolitical priorities. Given its centrality for the post-War international settlement and the growing importance it assumed throughout the Cold War, the German question also became one of the main indicators of the state of health of the Anglo-American special relationship.

Establishing an administration for post-War Germany was not the story of a happy Anglo-American marriage. At the end of the War there was no unanimous view of the German problem, but rather conflicting viewpoints in the US and Britain on how to deal with Germany. For example, there was a strong consensus in London to keep the Soviets on board, but that was not a sentiment shared by Washington, or at least not for very long. The main difference lay in Britain's determination to prevent Germany's full political and economic recovery. Nonetheless, hostility towards Germany was not just the prerogative of the British and was initially also widespread in the US. To a certain extent, Washington's views about disempowering Germany were initially bolder than those prevailing in London. A number of influential figures both in the US Democratic administration and in the British Conservative government shared a common conviction that the best solution was to keep Germany in a state of weakness in order to avoid future threats to world peace and stability.

In 1944 prominent members of the Roosevelt administration had endorsed a plan aimed at partitioning and deindustrialising Germany. Assistant Secretary of the Treasury Harry Dexter White and Secretary of the Treasury Henry Morgenthau devised the plan. The Morgenthau Plan advocated Germany's partition and its transformation into a mainly agricultural country. A number of leading personalities within the Roosevelt administration, including Secretary of State Cordell Hull and the US president's confidant, Harry Hopkins, were initially sympathetic to the plan. However, Morgenthau's ideas were vigorously opposed by Secretary of War Henry L. Stimson, who was sceptical about the plan's practical implementation and feared the political and strategic consequences of creating a power vacuum in the heart of Europe. Stimson denounced the risk of economic chaos not only in Germany but in Europe as a whole and criticised the proposal as a 'Carthaginian peace' in reference to the city-state of Carthage, which had been flattened by the Romans following the Third Punic War in 146 BC.[3] Hull's ideas also gradually shifted against the plan and towards those of Stimson. Officials in the State Department had a pragmatic view of the German problem and almost unanimously favoured the prospect of a united rather than a partitioned German state. However, Washington was determined to limit Moscow's influence in Europe and believed that the West should exclusively control Germany's industrial heart, without any Soviet participation.

Nonetheless, until his death in April 1945 Roosevelt had hoped to cooperate with the Soviets and had been much less hostile to Moscow than had Churchill, who believed that a balance of power along traditional lines was the best way to deal with Stalin, maintain British influence in key areas of Europe and avoid any interference in the affairs of the British Empire.[4] At the Yalta Conference in February 1945 the US president had agreed to Soviet access to the resources of the Ruhr and economic reparations from Western areas on the basis that the German economy should be treated as a 'whole'. Washington had treated the British as a 'junior partner' in the negotiations, eliciting a Soviet assumption that 'after 1945 America would adopt a mediating role between Britain and the Soviet Union'.[5] Only following the assumption of the presidency by Henry Truman did the administration's views gradually move closer to those of the State Department and become much less forthcoming towards Moscow. Nonetheless, the new US president was inexperienced in foreign affairs, wanted to avoid open confrontation with Moscow and initially pledged himself to the achievement of his predecessor's post-War goals.[6]

Truman did not reverse the course of US policy before the beginning of the Potsdam Conference. It was the behaviour of Soviet military forces in their zone of occupation that, creating an overall impression of chaos and anarchy in Germany, triggered a shift in US policy and shaped American preparation for and conduct at Potsdam in July and August. The central figure in determining American policy at the conference was Truman's newly appointed Secretary of State, James F. Byrnes. Until then the prevailing view at the State Department had been that the entire German economy must be treated as a single unit. However, its new head was deeply committed to a solution based on separate Western and Soviet zones of occupation in order to avoid the danger of Soviet influence spreading throughout Germany. This view was particularly relevant for the issue of War reparations: whereas American and British thinking prior to Potsdam had always conceptualised Germany as a single unit, at the conference Byrnes endorsed a settlement which economically divided the country into western and eastern zones. Economic relations between the zones would largely consist of trading excess German industrial capacity from the West for food from the East. Whereas Washington did not wish Germany's division to become permanent and as a purely intellectual proposition the US government favoured a united over a partitioned Germany, Byrnes's strategy pursued two main objectives: first, to prevent future conflicts among the allies over Germany and the problem of reparations; and second, to make sure that the Soviet Union would have no influence in the western zones or in any plans for an international control of Germany's industrial powerhouse, the Ruhr region. Until Potsdam Truman had appeared willing to continue Roosevelt's policy of not being seen to 'gang up' with Britain against the USSR. Prior to the conference Washington had rejected attempts by Eden to arrange a meeting with Byrnes. The British and the Americans also remained divided on other key issues, including Moscow's attempts to secure a trusteeship of Tripolitania, an Italian colony in North Africa, which Churchill saw as a major threat to vital British interests. The Americans were unwilling to protect British positions in the Mediterranean and remained suspicious of British imperialism.[7]

Nonetheless, for Germany it was a different matter. Although Truman had envisaged an international control of the Ruhr, neither Byrnes nor the president was willing to even discuss Soviet proposals at Potsdam, as they felt that any arrangement put forward by Moscow would lead to a dangerous extension of Soviet influence into the heart of Western Europe.[8]

However, British views about Germany were more conciliatory towards the Kremlin. Both the British Treasury and the Foreign Office vigorously opposed Byrnes's zonal reparations plan, which had been developed without London's involvement and virtually eliminated any hopes of cooperation with Russia in Germany's economic administration. The British felt utterly insulted by US disregard for their preferences. Even before Churchill and Foreign Secretary Anthony Eden had departed from Potsdam on 25 July to find out the results of elections in Britain, Byrnes had made it clear that British views on Germany were of limited significance for him.[9] Although London controlled the mineral resources of the Ruhr, the US foreign secretary did not discuss the zonal reparations plan with the British before presenting it to Molotov. Successive attempts by Whitehall to convince the US secretary of state to abandon it were also unsuccessful. As the Foreign Office's permanent undersecretary, Alexander Cadogan, wrote in his diary, the numerous ways in which the British were sidetracked at Potsdam suggested that it would be more pertinent to refer to the 'Big 2 1/2' rather than the Big Three.[10]

In stark contrast to the strategy pursued by the US government, Britain's primary objective at Potsdam had been to gain the trust of the Soviets in order to make Moscow a willing partner on the German question.[11] This had been a central feature of British strategic thinking throughout the War, at least since Eden's visit to Moscow in October 1941, and following the signing of an Anglo-Soviet treaty of alliance in May 1942. British officials were not in favour of dividing Germany into separate economic zones and vigorously opposed Byrnes's plan, as they felt that it would 'make it impossible to administer Germany as (a) unit'. Some FCO officials wanted to move along with the American blueprint but the preference for preserving cooperation with the Russians ran across party differences in Britain. The new Labour foreign secretary, Ernest Bevin, remarked in May 1946 that Germany's division should not be easily accepted by the West because 'we should have lost the one factor which might hold us and the Russians together, viz., the existence of a single Germany which it would be in the interest of us both to hold down'.[12]

Anglo-American containment and the Bizone

Contrasting viewpoints at Potsdam on how to administer Germany economically reflected deeper differences in the Anglo-American camp. They also revealed Britain's inability to influence US views. Although the British remained in control of the Ruhr, the US secretary of state would repeatedly propose deals to Molotov without any prior consultation with London. Most American policy-makers in 1946 were not yet thinking ahead to the creation of a separate West German state, let alone the rearmament of the German population within Western controlled areas. However, the White House was moving away fast from the views that had inspired the Morgenthau Plan, the basic philosophy of which had never convinced Truman and his staff. Only when relations with Moscow deteriorated did Britain's importance in the American strategy increase. In Churchill's case the search for an arrangement with the Kremlin had marked a journey from bitter foe of Stalinism to parley with the strongest power on the continent and to 'active connivance' with Soviet domination of Eastern Europe. However, in early August 1945 failure to reach a compromise with the Soviets led the new Labour cabinet of Clement Attlee to make the decision to stand firm against Stalin.[13] The radical change in Britain's attitude was a consequence not only of American leadership but also of worrying dynamics in the Soviet zone.

In early 1946 the prospect of a fusion of the socialist and communist parties in the part of Germany under Soviet occupation fuelled alarming expectations in the West. As one Foreign Office official noted, 'this decision in fact means that we can kiss goodbye to democracy on the Western pattern for what is practically half of pre-War Germany which politically is now being reduced to a Balkan level'.[14] For both Washington and London the fusion had a tremendous political significance that extended well beyond the eastern zone. As one British official remarked, the most depressing fact about the events in the Soviet zone was that, less than nine months after the end of the War, it was now an imperative to actively consider Germany 'as a potential factor in power politics'.[15] While vindicating Byrnes's zonal plan and determination to exclude the Kremlin from any control of the Ruhr, the Soviet-orchestrated fusion between the socialists and the communists undermined Britain's hopes for a deal with Moscow. It also led to a reconsideration of Whitehall's attitude towards French plans for detaching the Ruhr from Germany: although the British had favoured a unitary economic administration of Germany, until then Bevin had been willing to make an exception for the Ruhr in order to foster close cooperation with Paris.[16]

Reactions to Soviet conduct were particularly robust in Washington and reflected growing hostility towards the Kremlin's strategy and objectives. In March 1946 the Truman administration's deep-seated concerns had been further reinforced by George Kennan's 'long telegram': according to the US deputy chief of mission in Moscow, in light of the broader expansionist objectives pursued by the Soviet leadership, the Kremlin would consent to the creation of a united Germany only if the German state was placed completely under its influence.[17] The American response to what were perceived as Soviet designs aimed at expanding Moscow's influence, while subjugating Germany and Europe, was immediate and firm. In May 1946 the US military governor for Germany, Lucius D. Clay, announced that all further work on dismantling plans for purposes of reparations in the American zone would be suspended. This announcement, which also reflected a degree of frustration with French conduct, implied that there would be no more delivery of reparations until the German problem was solved. The Americans were thus trying to deny the Soviets a free hand in their zone of occupation.

While the gap between American and Soviet views continued to grow, in May 1946 Bevin concluded that the West should not easily accept the division of Germany.[18] The foreign secretary was particularly alarmed by the prospect of losing Germany. In an analysis for the cabinet he emphasised that the country's outlook was neither wholly eastward nor wholly westward looking, warning that 'on the whole the balance of advantage' seemed to lie with the Russians.[19] His fears were also justified by the lack of any long-term commitment to Europe by the US. Nonetheless, any remaining British hopes for a deal with the Kremlin abruptly collapsed in the summer. At the second session of the Paris meeting of the Council of Foreign Ministers (CFM) in July 1946 Molotov brutally rejected Byrnes's offer of a disarmament treaty directed against Germany. Moscow's foreign minister also denounced the Western powers' programme of 'Morgenthauism' towards Germany, partition and separation of the Ruhr.[20] Byrnes's response to Molotov was the proposal to merge the American zone with any other zone willing to treat Germany as an economic unit on the basis of the Potsdam agreement. The American reaction to Soviet accusations was a tactical move aimed at disrupting Moscow's objectives and its propaganda in Germany. The Americans were far more determined than the British to proceed with an Anglo-American agreement and exclude the Russians. However, Bevin continued to express deep reservations about a strategy that committed London to a clear division between East and West Germany. Nevertheless, having lost any hopes for a comprehensive deal with the Soviets, the British, who had previously contemplated organising their zone on a unilateral basis, now accepted the US proposal, triggering the formal preparations for the establishment of 'Bizonia'.[21]

The creation of 'Bizonia' was coupled with a decision to suspend the reparation settlement. While undercutting prospects for an arrangement with Moscow, it increased for the US and Britain the need to extend a hand of reconciliation to the Germans. In a September 1946 speech at Stuttgart, later renamed the 'Speech of Hope', the secretary of state countered Moscow's efforts to portray itself as the sole defender of German unity and prosperity. Byrnes officially declared that Washington would oppose the separation of either the Ruhr or the Rhineland from Germany or the maintenance of any control that would subject these areas to outside domination or manipulation. The Stuttgart speech publicly distanced Washington from the legacy of the Morgenthau Plan. It also contained the first official admission that US forces might be maintained on the continent beyond the limit of two years that Roosevelt had indicated at Yalta in February 1945. Byrnes reassured German public opinion that the US would not support France's partitioning designs and sent a firm admonishment to the Kremlin. He also suggested that Germany's eastern borders had not been finalised yet and that some adjustments might still be made to the boundary with Poland.[22] The speech triggered critical reactions in Paris. The French minister in Washington, Armand Bérard, referred to it as 'a move in the direction of a centralized Germany, a move which the French had to deplore'.[23] Nonetheless, Byrnes's words were heartily approved of by the British, who by then had stopped supporting French requests to saw off the Ruhr from Germany. Less than two weeks later, on 19 September, in Zurich, Churchill spoke of 'the re-creation of the

European family' with a 'spiritually great Germany', working in partnership with France and other European nations.[24]

Although by the end of 1946 some in Whitehall had not abandoned the pursuit of a unitary solution for Germany within the context of a balance of power deal with the Russians, Anglo-American determination to proceed to the reconstruction of the Western areas increased in the following months. The events of that autumn and, particularly, the harsh winter, which caused dreadful hunger in Germany and a high number of civilian deaths, played a key role in completing an all-out reversal of American policy from 'Morgenthauism' and the deindustrialising designs of two years earlier. They also thwarted any remaining British hopes for an arrangement with Moscow. Both Washington and London feared that the problem of food, housing and other basic shortages in Western Europe might create a breeding ground for further communist expansion. By late spring 1947 the reversal in Anglo-American policy was complete. For quite understandable reasons, new US Secretary of State George Marshall did not say a word about Germany's place in the American strategy when he announced a massive programme of economic aid for Europe in his famous speech at Harvard on 5 June.[25] Nonetheless, in the following months the White House and the State Department accelerated negotiations with the British over administrative reforms in 'Bizonia'. Washington and London also agreed to an increase in the permitted level of production of the German steel industry.[26] In a new Anglo-American strategy, which was vigorously prodded by Britain, Germany's complete economic rehabilitation was now seen as a crucial step towards Western Europe's economic reconstruction and political stabilisation.

The Dunkirk Treaty and the Brussels Pact

The convergence between US and British views accelerated as disagreements with the USSR increased. Formal discussions over Germany with the Soviets at the London CFM in December 1947 were dominated by the reparations question. The deteriorating relationship with the Kremlin allowed Bevin to make sure that Moscow would not participate in the US-engineered European Recovery Program (ERP).[27] Furthermore, post-conference discussions between the three Western powers set in motion the process that culminated in the creation of the North Atlantic Treaty in

April 1949 and in the formation of a separate West German state in May. The connection between the establishment of a West German polity and the formation of a Western military alliance under US leadership became obvious in the first few months of 1948. It represented one of several key aspects of Anglo-American policy in Europe.

Nonetheless, as in the case of negotiations with Moscow on economic reparations, on this issue too it was the Americans who took the lead, overcoming persistent French and British resistance. At the Anglo-American discussions that were held in London in January 1948, with the purpose of fostering transatlantic security cooperation, US officials established a firm connection between Germany, European unity and the creation of a Western security system. British attitudes were cautious and a source of concern for American negotiators. Unlike the case in Washington, the British viewed the bilateral Treaty of Dunkirk, which Britain and France had signed in February 1947, as a first step towards potential German participation in a Western security endeavour.[28] In contrast, according to American officials, the Dunkirk model, in light of its anti-German character, was not the proper way to proceed because it would make it harder to bring Germany into the system in the future.[29] Furthermore, the formula of bilateral agreements directed against Germany also reflected the strategy employed by Moscow in Eastern Europe since 1945 in order to establish its bloc.[30]

While the French were very anxious about the risks they were taking by going along with the US on the rapid formation of a West German government, let alone any prospect of West German rearmament, the British were more sympathetic to American arguments. Nonetheless, London continued to maintain a degree of caution. A number of reservations persisted in Whitehall, particularly on the issue of a prospective rearmament of Germany's Western sectors. In January 1948 Bevin proposed the formation of a West European Union of states under American leadership with the aim of overcoming US resistance to a close military partnership with the Western Europeans. The foreign secretary described his proposal as a 'sprat to catch a whale'.[31] At the end of the month, he restated in the House of Commons that 'the UK stood for a united Germany, not a dismembered or divided Germany'.[32] As had been the case at Potsdam, British concerns were neglected by the US government, which privileged the fast establishment of a West German state and was willing to leave the door open for its eventual participation in any future European security system against the Soviet Union.

After the failure of the Four Powers' conference in December 1947, in January a conference on Germany between the three occupying Western powers and the Benelux states was convened in London. On the eve of the conference, Marshall instructed the American ambassador to France, Jefferson Caffery, to inform French officials that it was time for them to drop their concerns about an 'outmoded and unrealistic' potential German threat.[33] As had already become apparent in discussions on the Ruhr's destiny, the French were even more sensitive than the British to the idea of a separate West German state. Paris feared the prospect of a resurgence of the German threat and the provocation of a Soviet military reaction that would be utterly catastrophic to both France and the rest of Western Europe. According to Lewis Douglas, American ambassador to Great Britain and head of the US delegation at the conference, reassuring the French on the general security question, in the case of a conflict with the Soviet Union, was the key to making further progress on Germany, 'There is little doubt that if the French were assured . . . that we would fight on the Rhine . . . [they] would relax in their attitude regarding German industry and reconstruction.'[34] During the negotiations Douglas, whose concern to allay French apprehensions was shared by Marshall, informed the French that it was 'very unlikely that American forces would be withdrawn from Germany . . . until the threat from the East had disappeared'.[35]

It was Moscow's East European conduct that cemented Anglo-American views and narrowed persistent differences with the French. The Czechoslovakian coup of February 1948 plunged East–West relations into a crisis atmosphere, convincing London of the need to proceed in Germany without the Russians and making French resistance appear negligible. Bevin remarked that Moscow was 'actively preparing to extend its hold over the remaining part of continental Europe and subsequently, over the Middle East and no doubt the Balkans and the Far East as well'.[36] The events in Czechoslovakia gave operational impetus to Western plans for the creation of a separate West German state and to aspirations to build a security system with the US.[37] In the House of Commons debate on 1 March 1948 Attlee stated that Britain's aim was 'to bring Germany back into the family of nations, unified on a democratic basis as Western civilisation understands the term'.[38] In the same month, Britain, France and the Benelux countries concluded a mutual assistance pact that bonded its members together for fifty years through the establishment of the Brussels Treaty Organization (BTO). However, this endeavour was more symbolic than substantial and lacked the capacity to counter the almost three million men that Moscow still maintained under arms. The most the BTO's handful of divisions could achieve in the face of a Soviet ground attack would be to buy time in the hope of an eventual US intervention.[39] On the same day on which the treaty was signed Truman stated in Congress, 'I am sure that the determination of the free countries of Europe to protect themselves will be matched by an equal determination on our part to help them protect themselves.'[40] France was worried about the immediacy of a Soviet threat to Europe but faced Anglo-American determination to move swiftly in Germany. On 16 June the French National Assembly, despite resistance from the Gaullists and the communists, agreed by a very narrow margin to support the convening of a constituent West German assembly no later than 1 September 1948. Paris also agreed to unite its occupation zone with the Anglo-American Bizone. Its conditions were that the Saarland would be financially merged with France and that the Ruhr would become subject to international control.[41]

The Berlin Blockade, the North Atlantic Treaty and the FRG

Moscow's reaction to Western initiatives in Germany was immediate. The conclusion of the London conference and the announcement of currency reform in the western zones on 18 June prompted the Soviet leadership to declare a blockade of all communications between Germany's Western areas and Berlin. The blockade was implemented within the space of a week of the French National Assembly's vote. The Kremlin's aim was to force the West to reconsider the decisions that had just been taken in London about Germany. The Soviet move on Berlin, following the association of Germany's Western areas to the ERP, tested Western unity. It elicited a strong US response. Washington was determined not to allow Stalin any meddling into Western undertakings and to prevent any concessions being made to Soviet pressures. Secretary of State Marshall immediately excluded any deals that would have involved a suspension of the London decisions in exchange for a Soviet lifting of the blockade.[42] British officials were also determined not to give in to Soviet coercion. Whitehall's firmness was evidence of how, with the evaporation of the prospect of any broader East–West agreement along traditional spheres of influence, Soviet conduct had contributed to cement Anglo-American views.

In the summer of 1948 the majority of Foreign Office officials had become sceptical about the prospects of ever resolving the Berlin situation and argued against the merits of a general settlement with the Soviet Union. Uncertainties about the orientation of German public opinion contributed to reinforce Britain's support for Washington's initiatives and new resolve to proceed in Germany without the Russians. As the head of the German Department in the Foreign Office put it, in light of the deteriorating East–West relationship, the risks involved in counting on the Germans 'to cast their lot with the West rather than the East were deemed to be too great to be left to chance'.[43] In July 1948 General Robertson, deputy British military governor for Germany, had proposed the formation of a unitary German government and the withdrawal of occupation forces to Germany's periphery. Robertson believed that there was little chance of the Germans turning to Moscow, as the Russians had badly damaged their reputation with their repressive policies in Germany. However, the response to the plan was lukewarm, although Kennan's summer proposal for a general settlement with the Kremlin and for the creation of a united Germany elicited even more negative reactions in the State Department.[44] Fresh memories of the War and persistent distrust of the Germans contributed to reinforcing London's support for the creation of a separate West German state.

Unlike a few months earlier, many in Britain now firmly rejected the prospect of a united Germany altogether, let alone an agreement with Russia. The prevailing view was that, while the risks associated with a united Germany might be more manageable at some point in the distant future, 'neither the West nor the East could or should tolerate a united Germany under any circumstances'.[45] US and British reluctance to negotiate with Moscow was reinforced by the increasing interaction between Anglo-American representatives and part of the German political elite in the Western areas of occupation. The former Cologne mayor and leader of the newly formed Christian Democratic Union (CDU), Konrad Adenauer, consistently reminded Western officials that negotiations with the Kremlin might lead to the abandonment of the London programme and discredit those West Germans who welcomed closer ties with the West.[46] US officials in the occupied areas firmly rejected the idea of a compromise with Moscow; newly appointed Director of German and Austrian Affairs Robert Murphy and Military Governor for Germany Lucius Clay were far from convinced that a German settlement was in the West's interest. They firmly opposed the idea that the US should consider getting out of Germany, while keeping the door open to an all-German solution that would involve an agreement with the Soviets. Their views were particularly instrumental in influencing the position of new Secretary of State Dean Acheson, who replaced Marshall at the helm of the State Department in January 1949.

Negotiations between the Anglo-Americans and the French towards the creation of a West German state fast accelerated in the first months of 1949. By the first week of April, after meetings in Washington between Acheson, French Foreign Minister Robert Schuman and British Foreign Secretary Ernest Bevin, the three Western powers had reached significant agreement on all the questions that had been deadlocked for months. French uncertainties were finally overcome when the US clarified its willingness to commit to a treaty of alliance. Growing Western unity had an immediate impact on Soviet conduct. In early May 1949, after the signing of the North Atlantic Treaty on 4 April between the US, Canada, the BTO members, Iceland, Portugal, Denmark, Norway and Italy, the Soviets agreed to lift the Berlin blockade in exchange for a meeting of the CFM.[47] Nonetheless, the British were concerned about the implications of new negotiations with Moscow. London made sure that agreement from the West Germans would be secured before talks were resumed; as Bevin put it, he aimed to have the West Germans 'in his pocket' before talking with the Russians.[48] By the time the Paris CFM meeting was convened in May 1949, a rather strong Anglo-American consensus had emerged on the merits of a divided Germany. The White House presented the Kremlin with an extensive lists of requests: no further consideration of reparations, no Soviet participation in the Ruhr, no Four Power treaty on German disarmament until the final peace treaty, Soviet relinquishment of any ownership of plants in the eastern zone and a proposal to Moscow to renounce its claim to the Kaliningrad Oblast in Poland's favour as compensation for an adjustment along Poland's western frontier. They appeared intentionally aimed at preventing a settlement with the Russians being reached.[49] By then the prevailing view in the US and Britain was that a divided Germany would pose lesser risks to Western interests than a unified one might do.

On 23 May the Federal Republic was established in the *Länder* under US, British and French occupation, formally sealing Germany's post-War division. The following day a constituent charter came into force for the everyday organisation of the new state. The charter was given the name of Basic Law in order to emphasise its provisional character. The Basic Law was intended to remain in effect only until unification and the adoption of a nationwide constitution. Hence, its jurisdiction extended only to FRG territory. The preamble to this provisional constitution called upon the entire German people 'to achieve in free self-determination the unity and freedom of Germany'. Article 23 stated that in the other parts of Germany the Basic Law should be put into force upon their accession to the Federal Republic. Article 146 specified that the document would cease to have validity on the day a new constitution for the whole of Germany came into force.[50] While the Soviets loudly protested against Anglo-American conduct, a fair amount of evidence suggests that Stalin himself welcomed an American military presence in Europe as a way of restraining Germany.[51]

The Federal Republic's Western integration: the Anglo-American allies and German rearmament

'Germany cannot be allowed to develop political conditions or a military status which would threaten other nations or the peace of the world. That means there will be no German army or air force'
(John J. McCloy, 6 February 1950)

The question of West German rearmament

Following the signing of North Atlantic Treaty in April 1949 and the FRG's establishment in May, West German rearmament rapidly gained priority over unification in Anglo-American strategies. Negotiations on West German rearmament consolidated cooperation between London and Washington. However, they proved a fundamental source of tension in East–West relations. Furthermore, while the need for a West German contribution to European security was acknowledged by all members of the alliance, its practical modalities rapidly turned into a bone of contention between the Anglo-Saxon powers and the French. Washington and London now regarded the FRG's rapid economic reconstruction and political and military integration into an Atlantic security system as a fundamental Western priority. In contrast, the Kremlin perceived the newly established West German state's rehabilitation and rearmament as a fundamental strategic and potentially a military threat. As far as the French were concerned, although having accepted Anglo-American views and renounced demands for a separation of the Ruhr from West Germany, Paris regarded talks of German rearmament as premature. Nonetheless, Paris was unable to stop the debate. Demands for a West German military contribution to the West's containment policy arose in the first place as a result of deteriorating relations with Moscow. The Czechoslovakian coup of February 1948, the Berlin blockade in late spring and the first Soviet atomic bomb explosion in August 1949 fuelled Western distrust of the Russians and vindicated concerns about the immediacy of a Soviet threat. However, it was the eruption of the Korean War in June 1950 which, dramatically exposing the conventional military imbalance in Europe, broke the deadlock, becoming the tipping point of the West's strategy towards Germany. Korea had a formidable impact on German rearmament and on America's response to Soviet policy. After the explosion of hostilities in Eastern Asia, Anglo-American diplomacy resolutely prioritised West Germany's rearmament rather than the pursuit of a unitary solution for Germany.

Nonetheless, on this issue also it was the Americans who took the lead and set guidelines; for a variety of reasons, including the British public's almost unanimous disapproval of the idea of German rearmament, Whitehall followed American initiatives. While in Britain it was politically expedient to avoid the issue, speculation about US plans for German rearmament had already been ripe in the aftermath of the signing of the North Atlantic Treaty. However, these concerns became pressing only after the outbreak of the Korean War. In the meantime, the Truman administration's priority had been furthering the FRG's economic and political integration into the West, rather than strengthening NATO's ground forces in Europe through an immediate German contribution. Before the eruption of the Korean conflict, Secretary of State Acheson had been determined to keep German rearmament out of any military discussions and continued to remain sincerely opposed to the prospect of a rearmed West German state throughout 1949. Furthermore, French domestic politics made it very difficult to move forward: both the French government and public opinion were reluctant to contemplate any significant modification in the occupation regime.[52] Paris initially fought the German rearmament tooth and nail. However, by early 1949 French military officials were already beginning to contemplate the possibility of rearmament.[53] Furthermore, the French were aware that the Americans held most of the cards and that the Germans might not be kept down forever.[54]

Washington acknowledged French apprehensions. However, Acheson was equally convinced that Germany's political integration into the West could not proceed at too slow a pace. Nonetheless, until early 1950 the official American position remained one of substantial caution. It was formalised by US High Commissioner John J. McCloy in a speech in Stuttgart on 6 February upon his return to Germany after consultation with the White House and the State Department. On this occasion, McCloy stated that the German people should take an increasingly active part in Europe's political and economic reconstruction. However, he concluded that, 'Germany cannot be allowed to develop political conditions or a military status which would threaten other nations or the peace of the world. That means there will be no German army or air force.'[55]

Positions in the United Kingdom were more varied and reflected a concern that Germany's full rehabilitation might end up damaging British interests. In November 1949 then opposition leader Churchill had called for a West German contribution to European defence, although not in the form of a 'national German army'.[56] Despite Churchill's public endorsement of German rearmament even before the eruption of hostilities in Korea, there were nuances within the British Labour government. Prominent Labourite Richard Crossman and key cabinet ministers Hugh Dalton and Aneurin Bevan were firm critics of the idea.[57] However, Foreign Secretary Bevin was convinced that a German military contribution was necessary and inevitable though Whitehall was wary of the potential effects of rearmament on relations with France and public opinion. On 28 March 1950 in the Foreign Affairs debate in the House of Commons Churchill spoke in favour of German participation in the defence of Western Europe, but Bevin declared that the US, Britain and France had set their face against the rearming of Germany.[58] Whereas Bevin's words appeased the ideological views of a number of the Labour Party's members, London's uncertainties also reflected a concern that the United Kingdom might be threatened by Germany's full rehabilitation in its role as a 'special ally' of the US in Europe and middleman in East–West relations.

In a memorandum on Anglo-American relations prepared in April 1950, FCO officials expressed the concern that German rearmament, if combined with increased US assistance to continental Europe and with the assumption that the United Kingdom might not represent a safe flank or even a firm base for an eventual campaign of liberation, 'would not only gravely jeopardize United Kingdom security in time of war but would also deprive her of any appreciable influence in European affairs in time of peace'. According to FCO officials, the most likely result would be a Europe dominated politically and economically by Germany. One additional consequence of this situation was described as the even more unpleasant possibility of an agreement between Russia and Germany on 'spheres of influence' or on other accommodating lines. The paper also acknowledged that the Anglo-American partnership would for some time inevitably remain an unequal one. However, FCO officials concluded that the inequality need not be burdensome if the two countries were working in close relationship with the other signatories of the North Atlantic Treaty.[59] These considerations confirmed that while London acknowledged the importance of a German contribution to the West's policy of containment, the British, unlike the Americans, feared the consequences of Germany's return to centre stage in European politics.

The German question, European integration and conflicting Anglo-American views before the Korean War

Conflicting evaluations of the impact on German rearmament on the European balance of power continued until the eruption of hostilities in Korea. The British government's favourite option was to maintain West Germany in a position of manifest inferiority and to pursue its integration into the West outside of the framework provided by the North Atlantic Treaty. A brief prepared on 24 April 1950 by the FCO for the British delegation at the Tripartite Foreign Ministers' Conference on Germany in London identified the Federal Republic's entry into the organisational structure of the West as one of Britain's fundamental objectives. Nonetheless, it also invoked a closer political and economic association of the US and Canada with Western Europe and deeper American involvement on the continent as a means of controlling Germany and consolidating European cooperation. The paper acknowledged that one of the advantages of associating Germany with the Atlantic community as a whole would be 'to offset the preponderance of her population and industrial power in Europe alone'. However, FCO officials suggested that the first step towards providing an antechamber for Germany's entry into the West, in a non-military capacity, should be to bring it into the Council of Europe, which had no military significance and carried no responsibility of any kind for defence. The successive step should be Germany's gradual association with subsidiary organisations that may be set up under the North Atlantic Treaty. The British hoped that in this way the awkward questions connected with German adherence to the treaty itself could be avoided, at least for some time.[60] Rather than moving forward on the rearmament issue, London was particularly concerned to emphasise the special relationship with the US and to set up a political framework that would allow the FRG's integration into the West without upsetting the French or threatening Britain's self-perceived special position.[61]

The concern to preserve a special role for Britain shaped Whitehall's positions in discussions with the Americans before the London conference of the foreign ministers of the Western powers. In the bipartite meeting with their US counterparts that was held in the Foreign Office on 25 April 1950 British delegates took great care to stress that the United Kingdom should be regarded as a power with world interests and not merely as a potential unit of a federated Europe. On this occasion, Britain's representatives also stressed that it was vital to obtain West Germany's participation in the Council of Europe first and that Germany could only be rearmed when 'she was a full partner in the Atlantic system, for under this system she would be under the same measure of control and common planning as all the other members'. Furthermore, according to the British viewpoint, it would have been unthinkable 'to rearm Germany until French strength had been greatly revived', as it was only after the French were in a strong position in the Atlantic system that the Germans could be allowed in.[62] On the following day a brief prepared for the United Kingdom delegation to the conference recommended that the British delegates should avoid raising the subject of German rearmament in the discussions. The brief also instructed that, were the subject to be raised by another delegation, the British attitude should be that there was no need 'to discuss the question in its short term aspect, since all three Powers are understood to be in agreement as to the impossibility of an early re-establishment of German Armed Forces, and that any discussion of the long-term aspect is premature'.[63] There were, however, important nuances within Britain's political and military elite. Whitehall's caution was not shared by British defence planners, who were keen to strengthen Western defences.[64] While acknowledging that immediate rearmament would be imprudent on political grounds and therefore impracticable in the short term, in the spring of 1950 Britain's chief of staff made it clear that the successful defence of Western Europe against an eventual Soviet attack could only be assured with Germany's participation. British representatives in Germany also displayed a more forthcoming attitude towards rearmament. At the end of April, the United Kingdom High Commissioner Ivone A. Kirkpatrick, in response to a Foreign Office request for views, had answered that he favoured the creation of a German gendarmerie, although preferring the 'first overt step [for that] to be a request from Federal Government'.[65]

The British debate about West German rearmament had a broader echo for the special relationship. It confirmed that London was unwilling to take the lead in Europe's integrationist moves. Hence, it caused disturbance in Anglo-American relations. British preference for the special relationship and refusal to take a lead in the European project caused anxiety across the Atlantic. They also strengthened in the eyes of American decision-makers the need to find an alternative in the form of a rapid rehabilitation of West Germany under the leadership of France or, if necessary, under the US lead.[66] The US government was much more forthcoming towards West German rearmament. Furthermore, discussions with West German leaders significantly influenced American views. Although the Germans were ostensibly prohibited from even talking about military issues, Adenauer had let American officials in the FRG know on several occasions that he was in favour of a German defence contribution to Western security. In July 1949 the chancellor had told officials from the Office of Military Government that he 'favoured admitting Germany to the Atlantic Pact' and the inclusion of German soldiers in a European army.[67] McCloy's cables from Germany during this period played a fundamental role in convincing the administration of the benefits of this and contributed to forging American policy on this issue.[68]

However, convincing the Americans about the need for rapid rehabilitation of the Germans was not the chancellor's only concern. Crucial to Adenauer's strategy was also a thorough reconciliation with France. In March 1950 the FRG's chancellor suggested the formation of a Franco-German union as a foundation for a United States of Europe.[69] This initiative was considered, however, by the French, with the exception of the Gaullists, as both out of place and premature. The fact that it was at first coupled with the question of the Saar made it particularly unpalatable to Paris. Although the allies had diverging preferences about the practical modalities of rearmament, Soviet misconduct bridged the gap between the American, British and French views. The signing of a Sino-Soviet treaty of alliance in February 1950 and Soviet military preparations in Austria had already reinforced Western concerns. Nonetheless, at the beginning of April 1950 the State Department, although convinced of the urgency of bringing Germany closer to the West, was divided on whether this should be through expansion of the North Atlantic Treaty or, as suggested by Britain, greater use of the Council of Europe. On 13 May 1950 the London conference of the foreign ministers of the Western powers led to an agreement to set up a study group in London to review the occupation statute, while safeguarding the possibility of a peaceful reunification.[70] However, by the end of the month West German membership of the Organization of European Economic Cooperation (OEEC) – the body that had been set up two years earlier with the aim of coordinating Marshall Plan aid – or of the Council of Europe were deemed in Washington to be inadequate steps for promoting Germany's rehabilitation and integration into the West. As a result, proposals were considered for increasing the Federal government's authority and tying it to the Atlantic Pact.[71] A more favourable attitude to German rearmament was emerging in other members of the alliance also. At the end of April Danish Foreign Minister Gustav Rasmussen, while acknowledging French apprehensions, had suggested that a controlled measure of German rearmament was in the interest of France as well as of that of Belgium, the Netherlands and Denmark.[72]

In contrast, British views remained more cautious and favoured the Federal Republic's gradual admission into the Western defence system. The solution now contemplated by the Foreign Office was Germany's adherence to the BTO as the obvious regional subsidiary of the North Atlantic Treaty. This was seen in London as a convenient compromise between Britain's initial preference for the FRG's participation in the Council of Europe and pressures for Bonn's immediate rearmament. The FRG's membership of the BTO would give partial satisfaction to American expectations. However, it would keep West Germany in a position of manifest inferiority and hence would not upset the French and the Soviets. Nonetheless, the pace of events rapidly overcame Britain's calculations. As late as 6 May Kirkpatrick had remarked that the US delegation in London opposed the idea of German rearmament at present.[73] However, his judgement failed to appreciate the rapid pace of dynamics in Europe. By late spring France's prime minister, Georges Bidault, and his foreign minister, Schuman, fearing being outflanked by Washington, were trying to gain the initiative in the process of West German political rehabilitation and insertion into the emerging Euro-Atlantic structures. The French had accepted the principle of a West German contribution to the defence of the West. However, Paris now advocated as a precondition the creation of a highly integrated NATO structure, including the appointment of a supreme commander and the establishment of a combined military staff.[74]

Furthermore, French officials were also advocating economic integration between the FRG and France. In May 1950 Schuman proposed the pooling of Franco-German coal and steel production under the joint supervision of a European High Authority. Adenauer's warm reception of the plan, with its promise of permanently ending Franco-German animosity over the Ruhr, was far more than the Americans could have possibly hoped for.[75] Nonetheless, the French government's initiative also confirmed persistent divergences in Western views as well as Britain's reluctance to play a leading role in European integration. While London's ambassador to France, Oliver Harvey, greeted the plan's role in replacing 'repressive institutions' with cooperative enterprises, from the outset there reservations abounded in Whitehall about the French proposal. Unlike the Americans and the West Germans, the British had not been given advance notice of the French initiative. Furthermore, London saw no compelling reason to devise a new European mechanism that would control a potentially powerful West German state. Whitehall also feared that Schuman's idea concealed an attempt to gain the initiative in determining the pace of Germany's economic recovery.[76] In contrast, the Truman administration reacted with particular enthusiasm. For the US government the French proposal was consistent with American preferences and approach to European integration since the days of Marshall's economic aid to Europe.[77] As such, it offered a practical solution to end a dangerous impasse in the consolidation of Washington's containment policy.

The Korean War and the Acheson Plan

Schuman's proposal allowed Paris to gain the initiative, at least for some time, and galvanised the US government. However, it was the eruption of the Korean War on 25 June 1950 that dramatically brought to the fore issues related to Western defence and Germany's integration within it. Hostilities in the Far East reinforced Western perceptions that current policies were inadequate, particularly following Moscow's successful testing at the end of August 1949 of an atomic bomb in Kazakhstan, which had shattered the American nuclear monopoly. The Korean War had an immediate impact on the debate about Germany's place in the Atlantic system, re-establishing Western momentum in the Cold War. North Korea's aggression against the territory of the Republic of South Korea increased Washington's determination to proceed with the FRG's Western integration, triggering a sudden acceleration in US efforts to bring about West Germany's rapid rearmament. At the same time, it temporarily sidetracked Anglo-French concerns, giving the upper hand in London and Paris to those who championed the lifting of political restrictions against the Federal Republic. The American military establishment had been particularly active in supporting rearmament during the period between the North Atlantic Treaty's signing and the eruption of the Korean War. However, it is likely that without the increase in East–West tension brought about by the North Korean army's crossing of the provisional border along the 38th parallel, Anglo-French early inclinations for a deferral of German rearmament would have predominated in the immediate future.[78]

Initiatives at rearming Germany had been debated well before the eruption of hostilities in the Far East. Nonetheless, the Korean conflict had a formidable psychological impact on Western evaluations of the situation in Europe. One of its immediate consequences was to increase a sense of vulnerability in the West German populace, which persisted even after the fear of an imminent invasion from the East had receded. At the same time, it strengthened support for Adenauer's security policies and generated a vast consensus that West Germany had to be rearmed as soon as possible. Ultimately, it allowed the chancellor to negotiate much more favourable conditions for the FRG's integration into the Western security system. US Secretary of State Dean Acheson and Paul Nitze, who had succeeded George Kennan at the head of policy planning, had already highlighted the need for major policy adjustments before the Korean War. Their concerns had been illustrated by the drafting of the National Security Council (NSC) document (NSC-68) in April 1950, which called for a massive build-up of the US military and its weaponry.[79] While the authors of NSC-68 had not proposed German rearmament specifically, the American military establishment had been stepping up pressure on the State Department to alter its policy on Germany. Nonetheless, it is doubtful that Truman would have approved the massive expansion of the military budget envisioned by the authors of NSC-68 if the War in the Far East had not started. Initially, a number of US officials strongly opposed NSC-68's recommendations. Secretary of Defense Louis Johnson, and Soviet experts such as Kennan and late President Franklin D. Roosevelt's personal interpreter, Charles Bohlen, argued that the US possessed a military advantage over the Soviets and could contain the Kremlin's ambitions through political and economic measures rather than purely military ones.[80]

There were persistent concerns in the White House that rearmament might have harmful effects on the development of democracy in Germany and bring to a standstill French progressive policies towards the Federal Republic. However, in the aftermath of the North Korean invasion the arguments in favour of rearmament rapidly won over the hearts and minds of US decision-makers. By the end of July Acheson had convinced Truman that the question henceforth to be addressed was no longer whether to rearm Germany, but rather how to do so; also to avoid the risk of being outflanked by the British on the most crucial issue for Western security.[81] Truman had been irritated by reports that the British were stirring up the Germans on the rearmament question and speculated that London's motivation for raising the issue was to destroy Western European unity by frightening the French.[82] Acheson was also concerned by reports of British activities and instructed McCloy and Douglas to tell the British that they were 'seriously misinformed', if they believed that the US would support any arrangements that they worked out with the Germans.[83]

Nonetheless, while by the summer the US political elite saw Germany's rearmament as inevitable, there remained conflicting viewpoints in Washington about its practical modalities. A major concern of State Department officials was rearmament's implications for the role of the US in Europe, as other Western European allies might demand that Washington offset the reconstitution of a German army by increasing its military presence on the continent. This view suggested that a fundamental US interest was to promote European integration alongside rearmament, as closer cooperation in Europe would avoid the establishment of a formal linkage between the constitution of a West German defence force and a surge in the American presence on the continent. For this reason, the State Department initially privileged a European institutional framework as the most viable way in which Germany could be safely rearmed. In contrast, the prospect of a European solution was not endorsed by the US military establishment, which felt that German rearmament should take place, albeit in a controlled fashion, under the auspices of NATO. This belief was so strong that, according to the joint chiefs of staff, the dispatch of additional American forces to Europe or the appointment of a supreme commander for NATO should be deferred until the other members of the alliance had given their full consent to rearmament. Chairman of the Joint Chiefs of Staff Omar Bradley stated clearly to his British counterparts that if the French could not be persuaded of the opportunity of this solution, 'they would simply have to be pressured into going along'.[84]

Under increasing pressures from US military planners, on 12 September Acheson first presented the American plan to the British and French foreign ministers at a meeting at the Waldorf Astoria Hotel in New York. Then he put forward the US blueprint to the other West Europeans at the New York meeting of the North Atlantic Council (NAC). The plan consisted in a package deal that linked the feasibility of US troops' commitments to the FRG's rearmament.[85] However, the secretary of state was only partially able to convince the French and the rest of the NATO allies to make a formal commitment to rearmament. Not even the promise of additional American forces in Europe and the appointment of a supreme commander could overcome resistance to the prospect of a German military contribution to the defence of the West.[86] Even the British were cautious and far from convinced that the time was right to begin establishing German military units. Doubts and reservations remained particularly strong among members of the British Labour government and party. Having received explicit instructions that forbade acceptance of the principle of rearmament before he left for New York, Bevin feared the risk of alienating the French, placing the Germans into a strong bargaining position and possibly provoking Moscow into action before Western military strength had been re-established.[87]

While not opposing rearmament in principle, Bevin favoured a compromise solution between the prospect of no immediate progress on the Federal Republic's Western integration and that of straightforward rearmament. The foreign secretary wanted the allies to create an effective federal gendarmerie, a police force composed of 100,000 volunteers that would counter East German *Bereitschaften*.[88] Only US pressure and warnings that Washington would not bolster its commitment to Europe without acceptance of rearmament led Bevin to drop his plans for a West German gendarmerie and convinced his cabinet to endorse Acheson's proposal. A long work of persuasion by Bevin and by the Foreign Office was then necessary to convince Labour cabinet members that the benefits of the American plan outweighed British and European misgivings. An implicit shift in the American attitude from liberation to defence with the development of NATO's first strategic concept between October 1949 and April 1950 also contributed to reassuring the British.[89] Following London's endorsement of Acheson's proposal, in October Britain's military establishment greeted the stationing of additional US forces on the continent as a demonstration of commitment far bigger 'than we could have ever hoped for'.[90]

Nonetheless, while the US commitment to Europe assuaged Britain's concerns, Anglo-American intentions continued to be hindered by persistent French resistance. While Paris was not that far apart from London and Washington on fundamentals and accepted the basic premises of Western strategy, French decision-makers endeavoured to place some limit on what the Anglo-Americans were doing in Germany in order to salvage as much of the control regime as possible. Furthermore, although accepting in principle the need to arm the FRG, French leaders were constrained by domestic political opposition and continued to hold back largely as a result of internal political calculations. Despite being far more sympathetic to Acheson's arguments than many of his fellow cabinet members, including Defence Minister Jules Moch, Foreign Minister Schuman responded to the American proposal that no French government could remain in power if it sanctioned the rearmament of Germany, and suggested that the question be postponed until French public opinion could be swayed. He concluded that if the French government was forced to take a stand on this issue and make a decision before French public opinion was ready, 'everything might go wrong'.[91]

French decision-makers and diplomats at the Quai d'Orsay were particularly sceptical that the Anglo-Americans would be able to control Germany after it was rearmed. They stressed that West Germany, being primarily guided by an interest in unification, once it had recovered a degree of strength and freedom, might seek to detach itself from the alliance and threaten to go over to the East, if the West was not ready to support it; or alternatively, that Bonn would eventually drag the rest of the alliance into an aggressive war against the Soviet Union for the restitution of its eastern provinces.[92] Some of these arguments were not altogether incompatible even to British thinking. Britain's ambassador to the United Nations (UN) and future ambassador to Paris, Gladwyn Jebb, was particularly sympathetic to French fears. A few years later he remarked that if the Germans resolved to 'use their twelve divisions in an effort to come to terms with the Soviet Union we should not, I suppose, be able to say that we were not warned'.[93]

The Pleven Plan, Stalin's note and the European Defence Community

It was not long before Anglo-American pressures for German rearmament elicited an alternative French proposal. Facing increasing pressure from Washington and London and believing that the British had betrayed them for the sake of their special relationship with the Americans, the French now responded with a counterproposal of their own.[94] In October 1950 new French Prime Minister René Pleven called for the establishment of an integrated European army, consisting of small battalions, under a common military and political authority. All participating countries would be allowed to maintain their defence ministries, general staff and certain independent armed forces. West Germany, being permitted to establish only battalion level units of 800–1,200 soldiers, would be the only and obvious exception.[95] Nonetheless, the plan was not very popular among allied military officers and political leaders. To Marshall, who was now back in the office as secretary of defence, it appeared as a 'miasmic cloud', while Churchill dismissed it as a 'sludgy amalgam'.[96] While acknowledging French sensitivity, the US was also determined to avoid dangerous delays and devise a solution that would be acceptable to Bonn. Acheson was well aware that the French counterproposal did not meet West German consensus and believed that the plan was impracticable in its present form.

Reactions in the FRG to the French initiative largely confirmed American expectations; Adenauer immediately instructed one of his advisors to inform Schuman that he was very disappointed with the discrimination against the Germans contained in the plan.[97] The chancellor was also disappointed by the lack of any provision for American participation and leadership and believed that German rearmament could not be postponed until the institutional framework for a united Europe was in place. In a speech to the *Bundestag* on 8 November, he welcomed the plan as a contribution to European integration. Nonetheless, being aware of American priorities and in light of the situation in the Far East, Adenauer also suggested that discussions about the French proposal should not be allowed to stand in the way of more immediate measures aimed at improving Western defences against the USSR.[98] The chancellor also sought to exploit increasing East–West tension to obtain a number of concessions from Washington and London, which would allow him to overcome domestic opposition and win popular support for rearmament. Among those were a replacement of the occupation statute by a system of contractual arrangements, a reduction in the occupation costs, an immediate halt to dismantling of German factories and an end to war crimes trials.[99] Adenauer was able to exploit the psychological impact of the Korean War to bolster his position at home and within the West. Ultimately, by allowing the Federal government to extract maximum concessions from the allies, hostilities in the Far East paradoxically produced the effect of delaying significantly the moment when German troops finally regained operational capability.[100]

The dynamics of events in the Far East continued not only to shape US policy towards Germany but also to expose persistent tension within Western strategies, including between the Americans and the British. With the conflict in Korea draining US military manpower and delaying the dispatch of reinforcements to Europe, and the disastrous American retreat from the Yalu River on the North Korean border with China in late November, Acheson was convinced to work out an acceptable compromise with the French that would allow him to appoint Dwight D. Eisenhower supreme commander before the situation in Europe deteriorated even further.[101] The American proposition came in the form of a plan put forward by Charles Spofford, the US representative on the NAC, and envisioned the immediate raising of German troops up to the level of 'nationally homogeneous regimental combat teams'.[102] Furthermore, in exchange for France's acceptance of German rearmament, the US secretary of state not only agreed to appoint a supreme commander but also promised to support French efforts to organise a European army conference in Paris.[103] While the Spofford Plan was formally accepted by the NAC in late December, the second concession made by Acheson to the French provoked outcry in Britain.

Washington's decision to back French demands for a European defence arrangement met with Whitehall resistance and infuriated Bevin, who regarded a European army as a threat to Western unity and a potential 'cancer on the Atlantic body'.[104] The foreign secretary was worried that the French had a realistic chance of success. However, Bevin's concerns were not shared by the Ministry of Defence. British military planners argued that London should not fear American support for a European army, as it remained highly unlikely that the French could be successful in their efforts.[105] While the Americans favoured more progress over the terms of rearmament between the West and the Federal Republic, the British, having secured Eisenhower's appointment as supreme commander and being concerned about the prospect of provoking Moscow's reaction before additional American forces had been dispatched to Europe, were now content to protract negotiations with the Germans for as long as possible.[106] The fundamental dispute remained whether Germany would be rearmed on an essentially national basis within NATO or within a supranational European framework. However, Britain was not isolated in expressing scepticism about a European army. London's reservations were also shared in Bonn: before the Spofford Plan was adopted, Adenauer, under strong domestic pressures from the Bavarian Christian Social Union (CSU) and from the Free Democratic Party (FDP), had publicly announced that he would not rearm under the discriminatory conditions agreed to by the allies. The chancellor insisted on political and military equality for Germany and excluded any solution based on the formation of small regimental combat teams and the entire concept of a European army, as the French understood it.[107] Among the French proposal's toughest opponents was Franz Josef Strauss, the young chairman of the Union parties' Defence Policy Working Group and future defence minister of the FRG. West German critics of the European Defence Community (EDC) demanded the removal of discrimination against Germany and the restoration of the German soldiers' honour as prerequisites for rearmament.[108]

The French cabinet's announcement of the Pleven Plan in October 1950 and the ensuing debate on the EDC highlighted persistent divisions on the issues of Germany's Western integration and rearmament not only between the Anglo-Americans and the Germans on the one side and the French on the other but also between the US and Britain. The plan provided the French with a tool 'of self-protection against American pressure' and with an opportunity to prevent the formation of a national German army and defence cadres. Nonetheless, by making it clear that there was no alternative to a protracted US military presence in Europe, as long as Germany remained divided and the Soviet Union posed a threat to European peace and stability, the French proposal also had the unintended effect of bolstering British arguments and reinforcing the special relationship.[109] London did not stand in the way of Paris and tentatively encouraged other West European governments to support the EDC. However, Whitehall feared the practical implementation and federalist leanings of the French proposal, which might have undermined NATO's role in Europe. In the House of Commons Bevin highlighted British concerns, stating, 'Europe is not enough; it is not big enough, it is not strong enough, and it is not able to stand by itself. It is this great conception of an Atlantic Community that we want to build up.'[110] In a report to the Defence Committee in November 1950 the foreign secretary explained that Britain could not afford to allow 'the European federal concept to gain a foothold within NATO and thus weaken instead of strengthen the ties between the countries on the two sides of the Atlantic. We must nip it in the bud!'[111]

Britain's reservations about the Pleven Plan further increased following the Conservative Party's return to power in October 1951. In the following months Whitehall's support for European integration quickly turned into more a matter of rhetoric than reality. A cabinet memorandum of November 1951 identified the defence of the Empire and the Commonwealth, along with the consolidation of the Anglo-American special relationship, as the main priorities for Britain's international strategy. Europe was now viewed as a second theatre of operations. Churchill, in light of Britain's growing nuclear vulnerability and an intensification of the communist insurrection in Malaya, was determined to avoid provoking Moscow on the issue of a European army. The new Conservative cabinet regarded the French project as impracticable in light of its supranational aspects and drew a clear distinction between cooperation within Europe and a European federation. With London excluding any curtailment in British sovereignty, at the end of November Foreign Secretary Eden announced at a press conference in Rome that British troops would not participate in a European defence force. Nonetheless, Britain's refusal to play an active role in plans for European military integration initially caused much disappointment across the Atlantic: President Eisenhower later remarked that he used 'every resource, including argument, cajolery and sheer prayer to get Winston to say a single kind word about EDC'.[112]

While London's reservations dealt a fatal blow to the proposed European army, the dynamics of the Cold War soon allowed the British to regain the initiative on the issue of West German rearmament. A deteriorating military situation in Korea following the Chinese offensive of November, West German resistance to the Pleven Plan's discriminatory conditions and French reluctance to endorse the Spofford Plan, together with prevailing attitudes among the other members of the alliance now all favouring a West German contribution to Western defence, increased

American insistence on a rapid solution to the question of the FRG's rearmament. They also allowed London to claim a crucial role in settling one of the most controversial issues among the Western allies. After Chinese forces had crossed the 38th parallel in Korea, in December Mao presented, following Moscow's approval, his terms for an armistice to Washington. The Chinese advance in Korea led US threat assessments to reach their highest level of urgency and the joint chiefs of staff to ponder whether the conflict in the Far East might be the anticipation of a global war between the US and the Soviet Union.[113] While French decision-makers had attempted to impose precautionary and discriminatory conditions upon West German rearmament, they were unable to win enough support for their proposal from the other members of NATO. Being mainly concerned with economic reconstruction and unwilling to make the necessary sacrifices in terms of national sovereignty that would have been required to rearm West Germany within a truly supranational framework, most West European governments were now all supporting rearmament. Furthermore, the Europeans did not share Eisenhower's basic assumption that the presence of American forces on the continent should be seen only as a temporary and transitory solution. Finally, although Acheson was still contemplating a pure European solution as late as early summer 1951, other American officials doubted whether a Western European army would be strong enough to balance Soviet power.[114]

With the debate on West German rearmament approaching a dangerous stalemate, it was a Soviet attempt to balance the Asian stick with the European carrot that narrowed differences in the Western camp. Determined to resist endeavours at rearming Germany, in 1951 Stalin attempted to play the card of unification to stall Western initiatives. His hope was that the prospect of unification might undermine Adenauer's endeavours at rearming Germany and inserting it into the Western alliance. The Soviet leader prompted East Germany's prime minister, Otto Grotewohl, to formulate two proposals for direct negotiations between the two German states on the question of unification. They were raised under the motto of 'Germans at one table'. Nonetheless, both proposals were rejected by the Federal government, which after consultation with the Western powers made their acceptance conditional upon free elections in the GDR. The American stance was firm. Acheson's reaction to Grotewohl's initiatives was to instruct McCloy 'to do everything necessary to block them' and to tell Adenauer that, while the US welcomed 'ultimate' unification, anything that the East German leadership favoured would jeopardise West German 'freedom' and European integration.[115]

However, Western rejections of East German proposals did not dissuade Stalin. On the contrary, it prompted the Kremlin to intensify its propaganda campaign against West German rearmament. On 10 March 1952, only two weeks after NATO's Lisbon Conference, which had reaffirmed the need for West German rearmament and called for ninety-eight divisions and 7,000 combat aircraft to be available at thirty-day notice for deployment in Europe by 1954, Moscow tabled a formal 'peace note' to the three Western allies. The Soviet proposal stated that the Kremlin would agree to unification if the Oder–Neisse border were recognised as final and if a unified Germany were to remain neutral.[116] In an attempt to forestall further Western steps towards West German rearmament, Stalin also suggested that allied troops leave Germany within one year, with the country regaining its full sovereignty.[117] The 'peace note' also included elements aimed at appealing specifically to German public opinion, such as an end to de-nazification, the removal of all occupying forces within a year, unification and the creation of a national army. The fundamental condition imposed by the Soviets was that the government of a united Germany should not join any alliance directed against any party that had been a member of the War coalition against the Third Reich.[118]

The Kremlin's proposal was regarded as a bluff by the Western allies. Rather than disrupting Western plans, it had the effect of strengthening Bonn's commitment to integration in the Atlantic security system and allied determination to rearm the FRG. Adenauer's firm belief remained that the safest route to unification lay not in negotiations with the East but in fostering the FRG's integration into the West. From the American perspective, the Soviet proposal appeared as an attempt to jeopardise Bonn's Western integration and the debate on European defence cooperation.[119] According to Acheson, it threatened 'the emergence in Europe of a new era in which international relations would be based on cooperation and not on rivalry and distrust'.[120] By the end of March the allies, with the chancellor's support, were countering East German and Soviet diplomatic pressure, engaging Moscow in a battle of notes and making the Kremlin's commitment to holding free all-German elections, under the supervision of the UN, a precondition for negotiations.[121] Rather than dividing the West, Stalin's proposal reinforced American determination to devise a strategy that would finalise the Federal Republic's political and military integration into the Alliance and work out a compromise between the British and the French. In April, also as a result of US insistence, Whitehall agreed to enter into a technical association with the EDC and to sign a number of agreements that were designed to reassure Paris.[122] On 26 May the Western powers and the Federal government went ahead with the signing in Bonn of the contractual agreements, which ended the occupation status and restored German sovereignty. On the following day, the treaty establishing the EDC between France, the FRG, Italy and the Benelux countries and a protocol between the United Kingdom and the EDC providing for mutual military assistance were signed in Paris. Nonetheless, this proved no ultimate solution to the problem of German rearmament. The link between the coming into force of the Bonn agreements and the EDC's ratification now left the entire issue of Germany's political and military rehabilitation under the potentially precarious condition of French ratification of the treaty.[123]

The Western European Union and West German rearmament within NATO

The problems associated with the linkage between the Bonn contractual agreements and the EDC became evident in the first months of the ratification debate. In France a tide of objections to the loss of national sovereignty and fears that the deal would not provide a sufficient degree of control over the FRG strengthened the front of those who opposed German rearmament. The elections of January 1953 were followed by the formation of a new coalition in which Bidault replaced Schuman as foreign minister. Unlike his predecessor, while not opposing the EDC, the new head of French diplomacy favoured an attenuation of its supranational features and feared that European integration might weaken France's position in the international pecking order.[124] In the next two years, no French government could obtain the necessary majority in the National Assembly to secure the EDC's ratification. Britain's feelings about the EDC also remained cool. While the Americans were irked by French hesitation, Britain remained wary of the federalist drift that was favoured by Italy and the Benelux states, which feared France's hegemonic position in Europe. In late December 1951 Italian Prime Minister Alcide De Gasperi had proposed to insert article 38 into the French proposal, which foresaw a future federal structure, bringing the European Coal and Steel Community (ECSC) and the EDC together.[125]

In order to counter the prospect of federal integration in Europe Whitehall now endeavoured to design an alternative framework to the EDC, whose supranational aspects had been a central part of the stalemate on rearmament. In March 1952 Foreign Secretary Eden proposed that the various Western European communities come together under the umbrella of the Council of Europe. Many perceived the plan as an additional British attempt at sabotaging European integrationist schemes.[126] However, London's new initiative benefited from political dynamics in the FRG and France. The resounding electoral victory scored by the Christian Democrats in the second West German general elections in September 1953, following Adenauer's first visit to the US in April, confirmed that, despite the Social Democratic Party's criticism of rearmament, the chancellor enjoyed the support of the overwhelming majority of West German public opinion. The re-election of Adenauer, who had been treated in Washington as an equal friend and ally, initially buoyed new US Secretary of State John Foster Dulles's hopes for a forthcoming ratification of the EDC.[127] Nonetheless, the French remained hesitant. It was their attitude that drove the final nail into the EDC's coffin. The decision of new French Prime Minister Joseph Laniel to postpone the debate within the National Assembly until after the next presidential elections, which were scheduled for December, caused serious alarm in Washington and convinced the Americans of the gravity of the situation in Europe.[128] The French decision elicited similar concerns in London. However, it also provided an important opportunity for the British to regain the initiative. At the British-requested Bermuda Conference from 4 to 8 December 1953 – the first tripartite summit between the Anglo-Americans and the French since the end of the War – Churchill complained to new US President Eisenhower that, as a result of French uncertainties, 'the West had wasted three years in futile negotiations' and suggested that the allies should reconsider the idea of rearming the Federal Republic and allowing its entry into NATO.[129]

By causing serious alarm in Washington, France's delaying attitude boosted Britain's role in the US strategy. At the same time, it allowed Whitehall to prevent the risk of further integrationist moves in Europe. Frustrated by the lack of progress on the EDC, in a speech to the NAC on 14 December Dulles hinted at the risk of an 'agonizing reappraisal' of American policy, if the question of Germany's Western integration remained unsolved, warning the Europeans about the risk of a reduction in the US political and military presence on the continent.[130] While many in Europe dismissed the secretary of state's threat as a 'calculated bluff', Churchill and Eden viewed it as an opportunity to play upon American fears and increase Britain's standing in Washington at the expense of the French. During a visit to the White House in June 1954, Britain's prime minister and his foreign secretary stressed the need to act with the 'real elements of strength in the West', as there was a risk that – if measures were not taken soon to restore West German sovereignty – the Soviets might be able 'to pull the Germans across the line'.[131] On 30 July the US Senate voted unanimously to restore West German sovereignty, even without French ratification of the EDC. Thirty days later, on 30 August the French National Assembly's decision to put off further debate on the subject ended the agony of a European army. It also triggered disappointment and a wave of anti-French feeling throughout Western Europe and in the US.[132] While in Bonn the vote was interpreted as anti-German, the Americans did not waste any time in making it clear to the allies that West German rearmament, sovereignty and equality of rights had to be achieved as soon as possible.

France's rejection of European military integration had left the problem of German rearmament unsolved and sounded the death knell of a federal Europe. However, it had also cleared the ground for Whitehall's endeavour to devise an alternative plan that would be acceptable both for Paris and Washington. After having secured the support of the Benelux countries and the Italians, in September Eden advanced a proposal for a resurrection of the 1948 BTO with France, Belgium, Luxembourg and the Netherlands and the creation of the Western European Union (WEU) as a substitute for the EDC. According to the British proposal, the WEU would be established through a revision of the original BTO and its subsequent enlargement to the FRG and Italy. The new organisation would ensure common European control of German rearmament without raising all of the supranational complications posed by the EDC. After Dulles indicated a willingness to restate the same assurances that the United States had provided for the EDC, Eden was also willing to make specific guarantees about the maintenance of British forces on the continent.[133] More specifically, London agreed to station a British army and a tactical air force in Germany for fifty years, as requested by the French.

Whitehall's commitment to retaining military forces in Germany at a set level for as long as the situation made it necessary ended a long-standing tradition of British policy and proved crucial for resolving a dangerous stalemate on West German rearmament.[134] On 23 October the signing of the Paris protocols, by amending the 1952 Bonn Relations Convention, finally brought to an end West Germany's occupation status. At the same time, the Paris agreements of 1954 modified and completed the Brussels Treaty, allowing the accession of the FRG and Italy to the WEU. By establishing West Germany's sovereignty and providing an institutional framework for its military integration into the West, the Paris protocols ended the long and hard-fought discussions about West German rearmament. The final step of this complex process was the FRG's inclusion into NATO on 9 May 1955.[135] While Dulles regretted the lack of a supranational provision in Eden's solution, the chances of success of Britain's initiative had been eased by the fact that the framework proposed by Whitehall was West Germany's favourite option. Adenauer's acceptance of the same restrictions and force levels within NATO that had been originally envisioned under the EDC made it much easier for London to overcome French reluctance and for the new government of Pierre Mendès France to consent to direct West German membership of the alliance.[136] Whitehall's crucial role in devising a solution to Germany's rearmament contributed to bringing an end to a potentially divisive issue within the West, while consolidating the notion of a special Anglo-American relationship in the Cold War's early stages. The solution designed by Britain also secured another important strategic advantage for the Anglo-American allies in light of a fast-evolving situation within the Soviet bloc following Stalin's death in March 1953. The FRG's membership of NATO and the creation of the WEU temporarily postponed any discourse about unification, for which there was little immediate appetite in either Washington or London.

The special relationship and Germany before and after the 1953 East German riots

'There will always be a German problem and a Prussian danger'
(Winston Churchill, 6 June 1953)

'We all support a united Germany, each on its own terms'
(John Selwyn Lloyd, 22 June 1953)

Washington, London and Germany after Stalin's death

The debate about the FRG's sovereignty and rearmament had highlighted in the early 1950s the persistent fears within the two blocs about the prospect of the restoration of a powerful German state in the heart of Europe. This concern had been one of the main motivations behind the Kremlin's issuing of a 'peace note' in March 1952, which made German unity conditional upon its neutral status in East–West relations. Nonetheless, a path to German unification that might lead to the creation of a unified and neutralised German state encountered firm opposition in both Washington and London. The US and Britain feared that a united and neutralised Germany might undercut Western security. However, they equally excluded the prospect of challenging Soviet domination in the Eastern half of the country.

The cautious Anglo-American response to the East German riots of the summer of 1953 was additional proof that, contrary to US public diplomacy statements, the West did not consider 'rolling back' Soviet power in Eastern Europe as a viable option.[137] Eisenhower and Dulles, despite a bellicose electoral campaign in 1952, emboldened by the slogan of the 'liberation' of the 'captive nations', had been absorbed by developments in the Far East and by the debate on West German rearmament. The president and the secretary of state struggled to devise an effective response first to Moscow's peace campaign, then to Stalin's death in March 1953 and finally to the Korean armistice in June 1953. The administration was particularly fearful that a more conciliatory attitude on the part of the new Soviet leadership and a reactivation of Four Power talks might threaten West European military integration and undermine Adenauer's position in the Federal Republic. After Stalin's death the White House attempted to balance its overall scepticism with a more conciliatory approach. However, in his 'Chance for Peace' speech of 16 April 1953 Eisenhower made any détente in US–Soviet relations dependent upon tangible concessions from Moscow, such as free elections in Eastern Europe or the signing of an Austrian peace treaty.[138] As far as the question of Germany was concerned, only lower-level officials contemplated the possibility of discussions with the Kremlin. Furthermore, as long as the issue of rearmament remained unsolved, US efforts were mainly directed at staving off Moscow's initiative for a Four Power conference or a foreign ministers' meeting.[139]

Unlike in the US, British views were more conciliatory about the prospect of negotiations with Moscow. A concern to prevent a further deterioration in relations with the East was now prevailing in London.[140] While being determined to finalise Bonn's Western integration, the British government only partially shared US diffidence towards the Kremlin's overtures. Many in Whitehall observed with anxiety mixed with hope the implications of the ongoing power struggle in the Soviet Union. Unlike their counterparts in Washington, the British also feared their country's vulnerability to atomic warfare and the consequences of resurgent German nationalism. Churchill himself, though initially uncertain about Soviet motives, had been more inclined to explore the potential opportunities that had been created by Moscow's openings and by the change of leadership in the Kremlin. The prime minister had made it clear that Britain was willing to contemplate high-level talks with the new Soviet leadership. On 11 May 1953, following the publication of an article in *Pravda* on 25 April that had restated Moscow's willingness for talks on Germany, Churchill made an appeal in the House of Commons for a new 'Locarno treaty' in order to reconcile Soviet security with the freedom and safety of Western Europe.[141] According to Churchill, the first inevitable step of this process of reconciliation would have been the Federal Republic's acceptance of Germany's Eastern European frontiers.[142] The British prime minister reiterated his proposal in a speech to Parliament on 16 May, advocating the convening of a conference 'on the highest level' and 'without delay' in order to usher in 'a generation of peace'.[143] Churchill's statements reflected a significant difference from American views about long-term dynamics in Germany and their implications for relations between the two blocs. Before being laid low by a stroke on 26 June, Britain's prime minister had even come to regard a reunited, neutralised Germany as a political prospect. On 6 July in a letter to acting Foreign Minister Lord Salisbury Churchill had remarked on the German people's persistent aspiration to unity, concluding that the fact that 'there will always be a German problem and a Prussian danger is something we must not lose sight of'.[144] These were views that were only partially shared in Washington. In the summer conflicting reactions to the East Berlin riots confirmed these differences in Anglo-American approaches.

The US, the UK and the East German riots of June 1953

Churchill's determination to ameliorate relations with the Soviet Union did not imply that London was willing to contemplate a deal with the East and fast-track Germany's unification. The British continued to prioritise relations with Washington and to work for a consolidation of the West over the prospect of an arrangement with the Kremlin on the German question. There was also no appetite in Whitehall for a confrontation with Moscow in the name of German unity. British reluctance to challenge Soviet domination in the East became evident in the summer of 1953. On 17 June the GDR was shaken by the erup-tion of riots and protests which, while confirming that Soviet-style communism had not made any dent in East Germany, alarmed the Kremlin and neighbouring communist leaders that spill-over effects from the GDR might precipitate similar out-breaks in their own countries.[145] The events of the summer of 1953 led Moscow to abandon, at least temporarily, any plans for liberalising East Germany's internal policies, and secured the leader of the East German Socialist Unity Party (SED), Walter Ulbricht, unconditional support from the Kremlin. They also confirmed for the Soviet leadership the need to reinforce the GDR diplomatically and economically. In the West, the uprising and the resultant surge of nationalism intensified the American commitment to Adenauer and his policy of Western integration and bolstered the prospects of the CDU and its coalition partners in the September 1953 federal elections. However, the riots con-firmed Anglo-American reluctance to confront the Soviet leader-ship on the issue of Germany. The Eisenhower administration initially appeared to lack an effective response to the uprising and, in order to avoid what was deemed an unnecessary escala-tion, it eschewed any options of military intervention to support the demonstrators. The only immediate US initiative was the development of a psychological warfare strategy that was aimed at capitalising on popular discontent in the GDR.

Meanwhile in Britain, after Eden's biliary tract surgery on 10 June and Churchill's major stroke on 23 June, there was even more reluctance to contemplate either support for the rioters or a bolder response to Soviet actions. Whitehall feared that the uprising might damage prospects for negotiations with the Kremlin at a time of increasing European nuclear vulnerability, following Moscow's new nuclear test series and the explosion of the USSR's first thermonuclear device in the summer of 1953. Furthermore, London was worried by the impact on East–West relations of Washington's new vigorous containment policy in the Pacific and Indochina, where the Americans had begun to support the French against the Vietnamese revolutionary forces. Dreading the prospect of a Soviet nuclear attack, London excluded an unconditional alignment with US policy and attempted to get back to business as usual in dealing with Moscow.[146] The British government provided no assistance at all to the East German rioters and sought to contain the US's mild endeavours to aid the uprising. London reacted with indifference when Moscow's repressive response succeeded in putting the demonstrations down.[147] In a memorandum to a Foreign Office diplomat Churchill asked whether the Kremlin should have allowed 'the eastern zone to collapse into anarchy and revolt', concluding that he had the overall impression that Moscow had 'acted with considerable restraint'. On 22 June Selwyn Lloyd – then a junior Foreign Office minister – made Britain's views about Germany crystal clear. In a confidential memorandum to the prime minister he explained that 'a divided Germany is safer for the time being. But none of us dare say so openly because of the effect on German public opinion. Therefore, we all support a united Germany, each on his own terms.'[148] At one point, the British government even blocked the issue from being raised at the UN.[149] While contradicting US liberation rhetoric, on which the expectations of many rioters had been based, the Anglo-American restrained response to the uprising reflected a concern that the riots had undercut the West's agenda for Germany, throwing unification to the forefront of the FRG's election campaign, while giving new momentum to calls for Four Power talks. As reported by US High Commissioner for Germany James Bryant Conant, in addition to strengthening 'the feeling that something must be done to unify Germany', the riots had also created a new expectation that 'something can be done'.[150]

The cautious Anglo-American response was approved of by Adenauer, but it caused disappointment in large sectors of West German public opinion. While the chancellor was convinced that any open East German insurrection would be met by the Kremlin with sheer force and avoided any encouragement of violent revolts, many West Germans, also as a result of a misunderstanding of allied commitments towards Bonn, developed a feeling of betrayal towards the West, reproaching the non-intervention policy of the Anglo-Americans.[151] At the beginning of July West German remonstrations prompted a partial evolution in the US attitude. While the British were determined to eschew confrontation with Moscow, the Eisenhower administration feared that public criticism of Western inaction, as well as of Adenauer's reserved response, could bring about 'a terrible let-down' for the US, which might seriously affect the American position in Germany and also that of the chancellor himself. It was to counter this prospect that the White House quickly acknowledged the need for a more positive and active response to events in East Berlin. The American partial change of attitude came in the form of a large-scale food programme for East Germany. While demonstrating continuing US concern for the East German people's plight, this initiative was aimed at forcing Moscow onto the defensive and at undercutting the Soviet Union's peace campaign. The food relief programme further exacerbated East German anger towards the communist regime and the Soviets. It also weakened Moscow's German policy, while boosting support for Adenauer and his policy of Western integration in the FRG in the months preceding the federal elections. Nonetheless, as Ostermann poignantly puts it, rather than devising a strategy that could liberate East Germany, the American response was at best a 'superb exercise in double-containment'.[152]

The programme was officially announced on 10 July by publication of an exchange of letters between Adenauer and Eisenhower. Distribution commenced on 27 July: East Berliners could collect the food at various distribution centres in the Western sectors of the city, which were still accessible from the East. The food relief campaign forced the East German regime onto the defensive, extending the atmosphere of crisis across East Germany, and proved that the West was still interested in the destiny of the Germans that were living behind the Iron Curtain.[153] As one American official put it, the aid had proved to the East Germans that the West existed and had given them hope that some day also the East would be free.[154] At the same time, the food programme contributed to Adenauer's electoral success in September. That success came, however, at the cost of weakening Anglo-American solidarity. US food assistance exposed broader Anglo-American differences regarding the appropriate level of hostility the West should show to the Soviets. The British were aghast at the level of anti-communism in the US and believed that the Americans were indulging in 'exaggeration' and 'hysteria'. London rejected the anti-communist crusade of Republican Senator Joseph McCarthy and the arguments and techniques McCarthyism employed to counter dissent. Instead, Whitehall privileged a sober and more restrained attitude to addressing the communist threat.[155]

The food programme confirmed that, while Britain was an indispensable partner for the US on the question of West German rearmament, when it came to German aspirations to self-determination, British priorities differed from those of Washington. Rather than grasping the opportunity to launch a diplomatic offensive against Moscow, Whitehall had been concerned by the events and had favoured 'get[ting] things back to normal as fast as possible' and 'letting the Russians save face in East Germany'.[156] British officials criticised the food programme as a unilateral American initiative, which might endanger West Berlin's security and trigger a new crisis in East–West relations. British High Commissioner Ivone A. Kirkpatrick expressed the concern that the 'present plan might result in [the] city being cut off and even Berlin communications with [the] West being cut off' and complained that the project had been 'untidily and hastily handled'.[157] Similar concerns were shared in France. The French, like the British, had been increasingly worried about the implications of the food programme on the situation in East Germany and the security of West Berlin. Paris favoured a 'policy of watchful waiting' throughout the crisis. On one occasion the French Commandant Pierre Manceaux-Démiau sarcastically asked whether, if the food aid resulted 'in cutting [off] the city, ... this [would] be serving [the] best interests of [the] West Berliners'.[158] Washington was aware that both Britain and France remained 'nervous about the matter'.[159] As President Eisenhower was later informed, British High Commissioner Kirkpatrick 'at the last moment . . . nearly prevented the initiation of the program because he felt the risks were far too great'.[160] London's sceptical reception of the programme reflected an overall irritation with what was perceived as a unilateral US effort which left the British, as a Foreign Office official put it, 'in quite bad odour' with the Americans on Cold War matters.[161] Divisions within the West and the sharp Anglo-American disagreement were recognised on the Soviet and East German side, somehow diminishing the impact of the food aid.[162] By the end of September, the Federal government, which had not been exhaustively consulted when the programme was launched, was also pressuring for a 'visible stop' in food distribution, fearing that the programme might provoke a violent Soviet response in East Berlin.[163] Later that autumn, as the East German regime tightened control over the population and prevented people from receiving the aid, the White House admitted that political rollback in Eastern Europe was not immediately feasible.[164] Faced with mounting British, French and West German criticism, the Eisenhower administration, fearing the risk of endangering negotiations on West German rearmament, ultimately opted to abandon the food assistance programme.

Eden's Plan on German Unification

The US response to the East German uprising revealed persistent differences in the Anglo-American camp about their relationship with the Soviet Union and political dynamics beyond the Iron Curtain. Whereas the US publicly bolstered resistance to Soviet power in Eastern Europe, the food programme contradicted Britain's views regarding the appropriate level of hostility the West should show to the communists. It was also perceived in London as proof of American disregard for British concerns. US food aid had fuelled expectations of Western support for political dissenters in the East. However, Washington had failed to devise a strategy that would give operational significance to the vague notions of rollback and liberation and that would empower the West with a response to all contingencies. As a result, though considered in Washington a political success and a potential model for future operations, the food programme was ultimately undermined by anxieties within the administration and fears among the allies of 'pushing too far'. Furthermore, the American reaction to the uprising had made it evident that the Republican slogan of 'liberation' of the 'captive nations', which had taken centre stage in the 1952 presidential campaign, was of little appeal to Britain and France and devoid of any operational significance.[165]

Ultimately, the food programme implicitly acknowledged the Soviet political and military grip on East Germany. Yet, it undermined any residual chance of negotiations with the Kremlin and deepened Germany's division, relegating any residual ambition to raise the issue of unification – which had been one of the hopes of the June 1953 rioters – to a distant and uncertain future. Whereas American policy had proved unable to undercut Soviet influence on Eastern Europe, in August 1953 Moscow's successful testing of a hydrogen bomb led in the following autumn to a reconsideration of US defence strategy. Washington now adopted a new national security posture: the resulting 'New Look' acknowledged the limits of US financial capabilities and advocated extensive reliance on nuclear weapons and air power to deter Soviet expansionism, laying the foundation for the doctrine of 'massive retaliation'.[166]

The US government's new strategic approach further highlighted the difference in Anglo-American policies towards the USSR. While the Americans aimed at discouraging a Soviet attack on Western Europe through the threat of a devastating nuclear strike, Britain feared Moscow's military capabilities and disliked Washington's tendency to overlook its concerns. The British government was particularly doubtful about American intentions and steadfastly endeavoured to promote negotiations with the new leaders in the Kremlin. At the end of January 1954, at the Berlin foreign ministers' conference, the Anglo-American leaders had got on quite well but Whitehall had resented Britain's standing as the junior partner in the special relationship. Furthermore, Eisenhower had worried the British with talks of using nuclear weapons in the Far East and with his reference to the USSR as the 'same old whore' in a new dress.[167] At the conference Eden submitted a five-point plan for German reunification, which envisioned free elections throughout Germany, the convocation of a national Assembly after the elections, the drafting of a constitution and preparation of peace treaty negotiations. Subsequent steps would be the formation of an all-German government, responsible for negotiating a peace treaty, its signature and entry into force. Eden left open the prospect that a united Germany would choose freely its foreign policy in the form of either association with the West or with the East or neutrality. The foreign secretary also clarified that the allies would be prepared to be parties to a security pact with the Soviet Union and a united Germany. The overall agreement would be placed under the authority of the UN and each country could declare itself ready to go to the assistance of the victim of aggression.[168]

However, the plan revealed the limits of prospects of dialogue with Moscow on Germany. It received an outright rejection from the Kremlin, whose reply came in the form of an alternative Molotov Plan in February, which restated long-held Soviet positions, including a Pan-European security treaty, Germany's reunification and its neutralisation. The US was excluded from the original draft treaty. Together with the People's Republic of China, Washington was confined to the role of mere observer. The plan was rejected by the West, prompting Moscow to announce at the end of March two amendments to the proposed treaty: first, its expansion to the US; second, a request by the USSR to be admitted into the Western alliance, if NATO renounced its original military nature and was willing to turn into an effective Pan-European organisation. Nonetheless, the allies rejected the Kremlin's note on the ground that Soviet participation would be incompatible with the alliance's democratic character.[169]

The Americans were doubtful about the plan and London's search for an arrangement with the Soviets.[170] In contrast, Washington's main interest lay in securing the signature and ratification of the Paris agreements and West German membership of NATO. While Eisenhower's main concern remained to counter Soviet propaganda and finalise West Germany's rearmament, Churchill continued to press for negotiations with the Kremlin in the belief that Moscow would welcome peace to avoid nuclear confrontation and develop its domestic economy. On 15 October Churchill mentioned to Dulles during an informal dinner in London the possibility of a trip to Moscow alone or with Eden. The US secretary of state coldly replied that, while Britain's prime minister 'was of course free to go alone', he would not be acting in any way as a representative of the United States. Dulles, who had travelled to the British capital to attend a trilateral meeting with the British and the French, also stressed that the perception of the United Kingdom functioning as a middleman between the US and the Soviet Union would have 'undesirable effects' on Anglo-American relations elsewhere.

Churchill's views about East–West relations met with opposition not only in Washington but also in his own cabinet. Lord Salisbury feared that an opening to Moscow without the White House's consent would damage the special relationship. Eden, despite having supervised the plan's drafting, shared the same concern and believed that no decision should be taken until US views had become clearer. Nonetheless, despite the widespread diffidence towards Soviet intentions, Churchill was able to convince the allies to issue an invitation to Moscow to attend a Four Power foreign ministers' meeting on Germany.[171] Britain's prime minister also continued to raise the issue of a meeting with the new Soviet leadership in his final visit to Washington in June 1954. Then, in the midst of the Geneva conference, he tried again to convince the US president to agree to a summit with the Russians. At a luncheon in the White House he told congressional leaders that conferences of this kind were vitally important, remarking that, 'jaw-jaw is better than war-war'.[172] Nonetheless, despite conflicting perceptions of the Kremlin's strategy and levels of pressure they could apply to the Soviets without provoking them, a common stance united Anglo-American approaches: a reluctance to risk an open confrontation with the Kremlin in the name of German unity.

The special relationship and Germany from 1955 to the second Berlin crisis

'If I had to choose between a neutralized Germany and a Germany in the [Soviet] bloc, it would be almost better to have it in the bloc'
(John Foster Dulles, 9 May 1958)

'We have in a sense had the best of both worlds, because we have been content with the division of Germany, since there was no way of changing it; at the same time, we have been able to make suitably soothing noises about the desirability of reunification'
(Oliver Wright, 1963)

The German question after rearmament, Suez and Vietnam

The FRG's ratification of the contractual agreements of Bonn and Paris on 5 May 1955 and its admission into NATO four days later ultimately brought negotiations on German rearmament to an end. They also drove the final nail into the coffin of an East–West arrangement on a united Germany. The Kremlin's immediate reaction came on 14 May through the establishment of the Warsaw Treaty Organization (WTO). This multilateral treaty of alliance between Moscow and its satellites, popularly known in the West as the Warsaw Pact, further strengthened the GDR's integration into the Soviet bloc. Since then the question of Germany's unification lost centre stage in East–West politics, falling further down the list of Anglo-American priorities. Having secured a German contribution to Western defence, both the Eisenhower administration and the British government, which since April 1955 had been led by Anthony Eden, were now content that as long as Soviet domination of Eastern Europe remained unchallenged they would not be called to account for their commitment to striving for a united Germany. After the FRG's admission to NATO Dulles believed that fundamental American preconditions for unification had been met. However, the Geneva foreign ministers' conference that opened in July 1955 rapidly dissipated any prospect of a fast track to German unification.[173] While the two German states' inclusion into the two rival alliances consolidated Europe's status quo, in the second half of the 1950s the special relationship came under pressure from fast-changing dynamics that bore no immediate relationship to Germany. The acceleration of decolonisation and Soviet penetration in Africa and Asia rekindled long-standing Anglo-American divergences about the post-War international system. In 1956 a joint Anglo-French military intervention against Egypt, on the pretext of preserving the security of the Suez Canal, crudely exposed the limits of American support for Britain's ambitions. Washington firmly opposed Whitehall's attempt to reoccupy the Suez Canal, pressed for an immediate ceasefire and subsequently demanded the complete withdrawal of Anglo-French forces from Egypt. The Americans perceived the enterprise as a last remnant of European imperialism, which would provide Moscow with a cover for its repressive actions in Hungary.[174] While Eden's political career was ended abruptly by the consequences of the expedition, after Suez superpower competition shifted away from Europe and Britain's international status underwent a major downgrade.

The embarrassment suffered in Egypt made evident the

illusory nature of London's great power status, causing a sense of national decline in the United Kingdom. By highlighting the limits of British means, the Suez crisis augmented Whitehall's determination to strengthen ties with Washington, although American policy had been instrumental in bringing about Britain's humiliation over Suez. Nonetheless, Eden's successor, Harold Macmillan, did not immediately grasp the realities of Britain's declining international influence. Upon becoming premier in January 1957, Macmillan was slow to realise that Britain was losing global status, and he was haunted by the fear of decline and of supervising 'the erosion of Britain's international position'. His main priority became to bolster ties with Washington. Macmillan actively sought an early personal meeting with Eisenhower in an attempt to revive the special relationship after the Anglo-American schism over Suez.[175] London's successful testing in the Pacific of its own hydrogen bomb in May 1957 provided the impetus to deepen nuclear cooperation. This objective was achieved through the 1958 Anglo-American mutual defence agreement. For its part, the Eisenhower administration was willing to reinforce bilateral ties with London in the hope that US nuclear assistance would allow Whitehall to retain conventional forces in areas of the world where Washington had limited military capabilities.[176]

For a number of reasons, the German question, unlike in the US and France, was now relegated to the margins of the British political debate. First, with a new overriding concern about the maintenance of the special relationship, strengthening ties with the Americans was now perceived in London as fundamental in order to balance Moscow's growing military prowess. Whitehall also hoped to achieve more coordination on policy on the German question with Washington.

Second, Britain had growing balance of payments problems, the impact of which was augmented by its persistent extra-European commitments, particularly in Africa and Asia. By the late 1950s a number of officials within the Treasury and the Colonial Office began questioning the assumption that the United Kingdom had no other choice than to maintain its overseas commitments. Nonetheless, there were nuances in the views of British officials, as some were critical of an excessive reliance on the special relationship and questioned the desirability of putting all of Britain's eggs in one basket.

The Ministry of Defence and the Foreign Office initially resisted demands for a reduction in military obligations east of Suez. However, those demands had dramatically increased by the time of Macmillan's second term in 1959.[177] Ultimately, after the end of the communist insurrection in Malaya in 1960, the Foreign Office started to prepare the ground for the withdrawal of British forces, which were stationed east of the Canal. Britain's exclusion from plans for European economic integration also contributed to the impending sense of decline. Whitehall's failure to create an alternative free trade area through the establishment of the European Free Trade Association (EFTA) in 1958 and then to act as a bridge between the European Economic Community (EEC) and EFTA led to a gradual reorientation of British policy towards Europe. London now began to look at EEC membership as a solution to its economic problems.[178]

Third, Suez reinforced the British interest in a consolidation of the status quo in Europe and in working out an arrangement with Moscow. Strategically, a divided Europe was seen in London to provide international stability. This preference was made evident by Whitehall's unsympathetic response to the 1953 East German uprising. A weak conception of Britain's ties with the states of Central and Eastern Europe further undermined any remaining ambition to challenge Soviet power there. London discarded bids for fundamental political and economic reform in Poland and Hungary. The British were convinced that efforts to prompt revolts behind the Iron Curtain were futile, unless backed by Western support.[179]

Poland elicited strong interest in Britain, as a result of its size and geographical position between East Germany and the Soviet Union. However, London's response to the Poznan riots and Polish events of 1956 was sceptical if not pessimistic. No significant reaction was seriously contemplated in Whitehall. In contrast, the advice of Foreign Office specialists focused on how to treat Poland in the continuing context of its collocation in the Soviet bloc.[180] Moscow's brutal suppression of the Hungarian Uprising also did not elicit a bold British reaction. Although Eden had complained about the Kremlin's contravention of commitments undertaken in 1945 and the denial of free elections, the cabinet's response was cautious. Having devoted energy and resources to the Middle East, London was unwilling to get involved in Eastern Europe. The Soviet repression of the Hungarian protest traumatised British public opinion. Nevertheless, Whitehall was so preoccupied with Suez that Hungary was hardly discussed.[181]

These distinctive features of Britain's place in East–West relations took priority away from Germany. However, in the late 1950s the German question also ceased to be a major concern for the US government. Moscow's successful repression of the 1956 Hungarian Uprising caused outcry in Washington but helped freeze the European status quo further. Failure to stop the Kremlin's brutal repression confirmed the fictional nature of the White House's liberation rhetoric. Furthermore, during his second presidential term Eisenhower had to face both an increase in Soviet influence in the Middle East and the psychological effects of the launch of *Sputnik* in 1957, which indicated Moscow's potential for developing inter-continental ballistic missiles capable of delivering nuclear bombs to the US. The administration's foreign policy was additionally complicated by developments in Indochina. Washington and London, fearing the consequences of a French withdrawal, had agreed on the need to bolster the French-backed government in South Vietnam. Neither Eisenhower nor Dulles had paid much attention to Indochina in previous years. However, the US president, having brought hostilities in Korea to an end, was now determined to show firmness elsewhere in Asia. For their part, the British feared that a Western defeat in Indochina would render their posture in Malaya untenable. Nonetheless, despite their common interest in supporting the French, by 1954 Whitehall and the White House had developed conflicting assessments of the situation in Vietnam. While the US covered all French costs there, following the Viet Minh's encirclement of the Dien Bien Phu garrison in January, at the Berlin conference Eden pursued a negotiated settlement. His ambition was to facilitate French ratification of the EDC and to consolidate Britain's role in East–West relations. The resultant Geneva conference talks between May and July, where the British found themselves in closer agreement with the French, triggered a severe crisis in Anglo-American relations. The signing of the South East Asian Treaty Organization (SEATO) in Manila in September only partially reduced Anglo-American differences over Indochina, as Washington moved swiftly to back Ngo Dinh Diem's regime through the deployment of military advisors, much to the disquiet of Britain.[182]

Inevitably, Germany temporarily ceased to be a major concern for Washington and London. Formally US and British decision-makers continued to restate their commitment to German unity. However, the German question now took a lower priority than it had done in the earlier part of the decade. Both the White House and Whitehall continued to support the FRG's claim to the exclusive representation of the German people. This legal stance had been reasserted by Bonn through the embrace of the Hallstein doctrine in 1955. The new posture was named after law professor and Federal Republic State Secretary Walter Hallstein, but was the brainchild of Wilhelm G. Grewe, assistant secretary of state for political affairs in the Foreign Ministry. The doctrine posited that the Federal government was still, as before, the only free and lawfully constituted authority in Germany, alone holding a right to represent the entire German nation. As a result, it would not maintain diplomatic relations with any state that recognised the East German regime. The only exception would be the Soviet Union, which had established diplomatic ties with the FRG following Adenauer's visit in September 1955, despite the grave reservations of the Americans, who had warned Bonn that diplomatic relations between Bonn and Moscow would legalise Germany's division.[183]

However, while being supported by the CDU and the CSU, the doctrine was never popular with the Social Democratic Party (SPD). Its first application came in October 1957: when Yugoslavia established diplomatic relations with the GDR, Bonn broke ties with Belgrade and suspended reparations payments. Whitehall did not welcome West Germany's strong reaction to Yugoslavia's recognition of East Germany but Dulles convinced British Foreign Secretary Selwyn Lloyd that a softer attitude would cause damage to the entire Western camp.[184] In the following years, London and Washington avoided initiatives that could upset the Federal government and question the legitimacy of its claim to the Eastern territories. Britain also used its influence in the Commonwealth to discourage members from establishing diplomatic relations with the East German state.[185] Nonetheless, by the end of the 1950s Whitehall had become increasingly unwilling to strain relations with newly independent countries in Africa and Asia to bolster Bonn's claim to the exclusive representation of the German people. At the same time American views about Germany were evolving rapidly. With US attention and resources shifting rapidly towards Vietnam, Washington began to embrace détente in Europe. Adenauer had made détente conditional upon progress towards unification in the belief that faced with Western strength Moscow would eventually be compelled to compromise. However, the Americans were now increasingly frustrated by Bonn's intransigence on the issues of relations with the GDR and Germany's eastern border with Poland.[186]

The US, the UK and the German question in the second half of the 1950s

By the end of the 1950s the German question was losing centre stage in East–West politics and superpower competition was shifting gradually outside of Europe. Two interrelated phenomena were fundamentally altering the Cold War structure of international politics: the rise of the non-aligned movement and the emergence of the Sino-Soviet split. Washington now feared Soviet penetration in the Middle East and South East Asia, while Moscow endeavoured to preserve stability within its bloc and was wary of China's emerging ambitions and endeavours to reach out to non-aligned countries.[187] However, while Germany's situation remained a persistent source of concern for Washington and its allies, neither the Americans nor the British considered unification or the restitution of the Eastern territories a priority. Hence, they began to encourage Bonn to gradually open up to the East and to a less intransigent stance on the border question. These dynamics also affected the evolution of the special relationship.

Whitehall played an important role in ushering in détente with Moscow and with the CPSU's new first secretary, Nikita S. Khrushchev, who at a closed session of the twentieth party congress in February 1956 had denounced the crimes of Stalin's dictatorial rule. In a sense, in the second half of the 1950s British policy on the German question came to be inspired, not by a 'pragmatic' consolidation of the status quo, but by a real desire to institutionalise a system that was seen in London as the best possible option given the harsh reality of Britain's relative decline.[188] Already in 1955 the former high commissioner and first British ambassador to the Federal Republic, Frederick Hoyer Millar, had remarked that, while Whitehall wished to do nothing that might prejudice Western rights and responsibilities, it was in its interest to persuade the Germans that there were numerous issues, such as trade, travel and cultural exchanges, on which Britain and the FRG would both gain from dealing with the Soviet Union. However, while the British should 'gladly let the West Germans take the burden of dealing with the Russians' off their shoulders, London should do nothing to encourage Bonn to make a deal with Moscow on the issue of unification.[189] Furthermore, officials at the Foreign Office believed that the Soviet leadership was likely to continue to weigh the risks very carefully before accepting unification, even on Moscow's terms.[190] There was also a growing consensus among the British political elite that on certain issues, such as the recognition of the Oder–Neisse line as Poland's Western border, the Federal Republic should eventually be prepared to compromise. Sir George Clutton, Britain's ambassador to Warsaw, believed that recognition of the Oder–Neisse line would free the West from an embarrassing 'academic and legal concept'.[191] Some Foreign Office officials perceived Bonn's acceptance of the new frontiers as a first step towards undermining the cohesion of the Soviet bloc.[192] This was likely to be facilitated by Polish disregard of East German guarantees and interest in securing a deal with Bonn on the border question. Although in July 1950 the GDR had solemnly recognised the Oder–Neisse line as the permanent border between Germany and Poland in the Treaty of Zgorzelec, the Polish section of the border town of Görlitz, the Polish authorities regarded the GDR's commitment to the Oder–Neisse only as a 'stopgap measure', the significance of which had been undermined by the West's refusal to acknowledge the border.[193]

By the end of the 1950s the combined effect of Moscow's penetration in Africa and Asia, the psychological impact of a successful Soviet rocketry and space programme and a developing budget deficit, despite a modest surplus in 1956 and 1957, were also making their impact felt on the American approach to détente. These dynamics now also influenced US perceptions of the German question. While the consistent refrain from Washington was a reiteration of Four Power rights, many in the State Department were critical of Bonn's demands for a return to the borders of 1937, which would overturn the Oder–Neisse line. A number of American officials even contemplated the possibility of reaching a deal with the Soviets on the border question and East German statehood in exchange for guarantees on Berlin. Polish-American organisations, such as the Polish American Congress and the Polish Western Association of America, lobbied

US congressmen and State Department officials to recognise the Oder–Neisse line.[194] However, the White House made no movement in this direction. While encouraging the Federal government to revise its Eastern policy, both the US and Britain refrained from making concessions to the East until Bonn was prepared to accept them. The Federal government was not indifferent to Anglo-American suggestions but was cautious of admitting this publicly. As early as May 1956 West German foreign minister, Heinrich von Brentano, during a visit to London had acknowledged that the realisation of Bonn's claims to the Eastern territories was problematic and suggested that one day the Federal government might have to renounce those claims in order to achieve unification. However, London remained sceptical about a deal between Bonn and Moscow on the issue of unification. British representatives in the FRG believed that there could be no effective concession that the Federal government could make to obtain unification, because the Soviet Union already had what it wanted, namely control of both the GDR and the Eastern territories.[195]

Nonetheless, whereas unification was not an immediate priority for both London and Washington, important differences persisted in Anglo-American approaches. These divergences were confirmed by the March 1957 Bermuda conference. This meeting had been convened to reassert Anglo-American relations after the Suez crisis and prevent another rift between Washington and London.[196] The US president had made an important symbolic gesture by meeting Macmillan on British territory, sparing Britain's prime minister a humiliating meeting in Washington. The conference resulted in a restatement of the special relationship and presented a united Anglo-American front in public. Washington undertook to assist Britain's nuclear programme and to station sixty Thor intermediate-range missiles in Britain.[197] In his diary entry of 21 March, Eisenhower described the meeting as 'by far the most successful' since the close of World War II. However, things were not in harmony concerning Germany.[198] As discussions turned to Europe, British Foreign Secretary Selwyn Lloyd expressed the view that the West should 'grasp the nettle' and accept the idea of another meeting with the Russians, in order to make sure that its viewpoint on German unification was explained. Dulles in response emphasised that a meeting per se would not necessarily be an asset.[199]

The British position was complex and to a certain extent contradictory. During the 1958 Berlin crisis, following Moscow's threat to conclude a separate peace with East Germany if the West did not recognise the GDR according to international law, on the surface London supported a firm response to the Kremlin. Whitehall made it clear that under no circumstances should the West withdraw troops from Berlin. In the British view, the allies should have been ready – as they had promised in October 1954 – to consider any attack on West Berlin as an attack on the alliance and, if necessary, to resort to force with all the consequences that such a choice would imply.[200] Nonetheless, while Britain's diplomacy was vocally robust here and, at least on the surface, supportive of West German interests, in private conversations Macmillan now emphasised the weakness of the Western position and endeavoured to promote a dignified retreat from the capital of the former Reich as well as dealings with East Germany.[201] Whitehall was also the only major Western government to support the idea of disengagement: a March 1958 British plan called for the creation of a nuclear-free zone in Germany and for the withdrawal of non-German troops. Macmillan's plan of 'limited disengagement' foresaw a 'thinning-out' of military build-up on either side of the Iron Curtain and, ultimately, the prospect of general, controlled disarmament, especially in the nuclear field. Washington was particularly critical of the plan, on the grounds that disengagement would be highly destabilising, as the presence of Anglo-American troops in Germany served 'as a restraint on the possibility of any independent German action'. Adenauer opposed the plan and derided the prospect of East–West flexibility as an illusion.[202]

Nonetheless, US and West German scepticism did not dissuade Britain's prime minister. Macmillan also revived Churchill's efforts for a summit with the Soviets and conceived of an independent role for Britain, embarking in February 1959 on the first visit by a Western leader to the Soviet Union since 1941. This decision caused grave reservations in Washington and Paris and met with the firm opposition of the West Germans.[203] Britain's prime minister stressed in cabinet talks that he would embark on 'a reconnaissance not a negotiation'. However, he was prepared to discuss Western rights in Berlin and even to deal with East Germany in order to pacify Moscow.[204] Macmillan's visit to the USSR triggered one of the most serious crises in Anglo-German relations. Adenauer feared that the British might be tempted to make hasty concessions to the Kremlin. Ultimately, only a direct intervention by Eisenhower and the Foreign Office success-fully prevented the prime minister from seriously considering the prospect of recognising East Germany upon his return from the Soviet capital.[205] By appeasing Khrushchev, the prime minister pursued different objectives simultaneously: to counter a growing domestic opposition, to present himself both at home and abroad as a paladin of détente and finally, to make one last attempt to prevent the deployment of nuclear weapons on German soil.[206] Furthermore, Macmillan wanted the allies to regard his Moscow meeting as a preliminary encounter before the 1960 East–West summit. However, a number of Britain's professional diplomats, including Britain's ambassador to Paris, Gladwyn Jebb, were par-ticularly pessimistic about the chances of a Four Power summit.[207]

Only the White House's firm opposition forced the prime min-ister to desist from his plans. In his Washington and Camp David meeting with Macmillan in March 1959, Eisenhower insisted that the West make no concessions over Berlin unless as part of an overall agreement for German unification.[208] US pressures caused concern in Whitehall that the chances of a Berlin settle-ment 'were being prejudiced by too rigid an insistence on progress towards the reunification of Germany'. Furthermore, the prospect of unification remained anathema for many in Britain. Cabinet discussions in May noted that 'a substantial number of people in this country would prefer that Germany should continue to be divided, at any rate for some years to come. The strength of this opinion shall not be overlooked.'[209]

Vice President Richard Nixon's Moscow trip in July and Eisenhower's invitation to Khrushchev to visit the US, without prior consultation with Whitehall, highlighted once more Britain's limited room for manoeuvre between the two superpowers. The president's invitation to the Soviet leader gave a new bilateral tone to East–West negotiations, bringing about a crisis of con-fidence in Anglo-American relations.[210] Whitehall was disap-pointed by US neglect of the special relationship. The British were also slow to appreciate the degree of US support for the emerging EEC and the extent to which it was damaging London's stand-ing in Washington. After the limited success of EFTA, Whitehall was not well placed to resist American pressure for Britain's full association to the European Communities. Macmillan was ready to accommodate Washington's demands. The Commonwealth's declining importance for British influence in the world and

Macmillan's March 1960 Skybolt nuclear deal with Eisenhower made it difficult for the prime minister to resist Washington's pressure.[211] However, foreign policy issues did not affect public support for the Conservative Party in Britain. The elections of October 1959 had marked a third consecutive victory for the party of the prime minister, further increasing its majority over the Labour Party. In the aftermath of this electoral success Britain's prime minister also briefly contemplated the idea of an alliance with France in a bolder European role for Britain and a turn away from Washington. His strategy rested on the unlikely eventuality of enticing de Gaulle with a nuclear offer.[212] Discussing Germany in 1959 with the French president, Macmillan said that, although he trusted Adenauer, 'with some other Germans one could not be quite sure'. De Gaulle concurred with the British prime minister that 'one could never be sure with the Germans'.[213] Nonetheless, Whitehall stopped short of endorsing the French president's unilateral recognition of the Oder–Neisse line, which de Gaulle had announced at his first press conference as new head of state on 25 March 1959. On that occasion, the French president had declared to a tense audience of about 600 from the media that Germany's unification should be conditioned on acceptance of the present frontiers 'in the North, the South, the East and the West'.[214]

By the end of the 1950s American evaluations of Germany's situation were also evolving rapidly, increasing support for a deal with Moscow and for an accommodation between the two German states. In 1958 Dulles confided to a group of US diplomats, 'If I had to choose between a neutralized Germany and a Germany in the [Soviet] bloc, it would be almost better to have it in the bloc.'[215] On 13 January 1959, following Soviet Deputy Premier Anastas Mikoyan's visit to the US, the secretary of state suggested that free elections might not be 'the only method by which reunification could be accomplished'. Then, in a press conference he indicated that the West might consider some form of German confederation.[216] These views reflected the intensifying American interest in furthering détente. One of its main consequences was a decline in Washington's readiness to defend both the status of West Berlin and West Germany's claims to the Eastern territories. The Eisenhower administration's official stance continued to be based on the premise that the West should not 'agree to any permanent and compulsory division of the German nation, which would leave Central Europe a perpetual powder mill'.[217] Nonetheless, on 27 May the US president and Macmillan agreed that unification 'would have to come in a step by step process in which the two sides of Germany would themselves have to exhibit a clear readiness to be conciliatory and reasonable'.[218]

However, with a new incoming president in the White House, the change in US policy accelerated even more dramatically. In 1960 relations between Washington and Moscow suffered a severe setback following US acknowledgement that an American U-2 reconnaissance plane had been shot down over the USSR on 1 May. The incident heavily affected the East–West summit and led Soviet premier Nikita S. Khrushchev to cancel an invitation to Eisenhower to visit Russia.[219] Nonetheless, the election of John Fitzgerald Kennedy in November triggered a thorough review of both US defence plans, through the adoption of the novel strategy of 'flexible response', and American policy towards Germany and Berlin. Adenauer's personal preference for Nixon did not help Germany's cause in Washington. Kennedy abandoned demands for unification and frustrated Adenauer by excluding the FRG from allied contingency planning about Berlin and Germany.[220]

The Democratic administration also implemented important institutional and personal changes in the conduct of American foreign relations. These transformations resulted in an increase in the White House's weight at the expense of the State Department. Those that had been actively involved on the German question and were generally more sympathetic to the Federal government's views gradually lost influence in the formulation of US policy.[221] These changes also heavily affected the US stance on Berlin. Running somewhat counter to emergent thinking in Washington, in July 1961 the ambassador to the Federal Republic, John Dowling, had suggested that if another revolt in East Germany broke out, the US should not 'stay on the side-lines'.[222] However, according to the new prevailing discourse in the State Department, the US did not want to see another revolt in East Germany. More specifically, Washington did not want to exacerbate the situation and run the risk that an uprising in East Germany might lead to wider conflict, even East–West warfare, in Central Europe. According to the State Department's view, as much as the Soviets wanted to reach a settlement on the West Berlin problem – as they were sitting on 'top of a volcano' – the US 'would not like to see revolt at this time'.[223] A low consideration of Britain's determination to defend

Western positions also contributed to softening the American attitude on Berlin. Whitehall had rallied to the American side after the Bay of Pigs fiasco of April 1961 and during the Cuban missile crisis Kennedy had actively sought Macmillan's advice. However, the new administration doubted whether, despite its strong rhetorical support for Western rights, Britain could actually be relied upon in the crunch.[224] Rather, the Americans now focused on practical ways to avoid a further deterioration of the situation in Berlin. The State Department's Policy Planning Staff formulated some ground-breaking proposals, including a tacit freeze on the status of Berlin, acceptance of the Oder–Neisse line, support for a West German policy of active engagement towards Eastern Europe through the negotiations of non-aggression pacts and encouragement of closer relations between the FRG and the GDR, including the possibility of officially recognising the East German state.[225] These proposals reflected the new administration's reluctance to endanger East–West relations in the name of Bonn's claim to the Eastern territories and fundamental acceptance of the status quo in Germany.

The US, the UK and the Berlin Wall

The development of such ideas occurred against a backdrop of deteriorating East–West relations, specifically centred on Berlin. As the crisis intensified, the evolution in the US position consolidated further and was spelled out by Kennedy in a landmark televised address on 25 July 1961. On this occasion, the US president restated that Berlin was not part of East Germany, but a separate territory under the control of the allied powers, whose right to maintain a presence in West Berlin and access across East Germany derived from the War, something that had also been repeatedly confirmed by the Soviets. At the same time, Kennedy acknowledged Moscow's historical concern about the situation in Central and Eastern Europe, declaring that the US believed that arrangements could be worked out to meet those concerns. He also stated that Washington was ready to have the legality of Western rights in Berlin submitted to international adjudication.[226] On 30 July the president's words were echoed by the chairman of the Senate Foreign Relations Committee Senator James William Fulbright's televised suggestion that closing the Berlin escape hatch to the West for East Germans unhappy with their circumstances could be a subject for negotiations over West Berlin. Fulbright clarified that 'if the Russians . . . chose to close their borders, they could without violating any treaty' and that the East Germans had 'a right to close their borders'. Such US comments caused outcry in the Federal government and among the authorities in West Berlin. At first West Berlin Mayor Willy Brandt found it hard to believe what Fulbright had said.[227] The US ambassador to Moscow, Llewellyn Thompson, supported Fulbright, saying that he believed that it was to the West's 'long-range advantage that potential refugees remain in East Germany', as this was likely to reduce Soviet pressure on West Berlin. According to the ambassador, not only the Americans but also the West Germans considered it to be to the West's 'long-range advantage that potential refugees remain [in] East Germany'.[228] Thomson's view was shared by a number of State Department officials who thought that Washington should avoid any action that could exacerbate the problem, as another revolt in East Germany was not in US interests 'at this time'. Nonetheless, the US stance on Berlin was not monolithic: American opinion was divided between those who felt a closer personal and emotional involvement with Germany, such as McCloy, Clay and, US Ambassador to the Federal Republic, George McGhee, and favoured a bold response to Soviet and East German threats, and those, such as Kennan and Fulbright, who approached the Berlin question from a broader Cold War and non-Eurocentric perspective and were less inclined to risk complications with the Soviets over what they perceived as a mainly regional problem.[229]

Although the West German government had not encouraged the flow to the West, in order to minimise East–West tensions and avoid the costs of absorbing the refugees, by the summer of 1961 three and a half million, or one in six, East Germans had defected from the GDR. Many of those had crossed over the border from East into West Berlin. During the first two weeks of August 1961 the flow from East Germany continued to increase steadily, with over 1,100 refugees arriving in West Berlin and West Germany daily. On 9 August over 1,600 refugees from East Germany and East Berlin registered at the reception centre at Marienfelde in the US sector of West Berlin. The SED leaders were now utterly concerned about the psychological and material impact of the flow on the other sixteen million inhabitants of East Germany and East Berlin. They reacted by implementing plans for the construction of a barrier to cut off West Berlin from surrounding East Germany and East Berlin: this was the infamous 'Berlin Wall'.[230] Although condemning in public the Wall's erection, senior US officials continued to perceive a long-term advantage from limiting the flow of East German refugees. Secretary of State Dean Rusk perceived the Wall as potentially contributing to the stability of East Germany and thereby to a gradual easing of tension over West Berlin. Whereas on 13 August the secretary of state issued a statement condemning the sector border closures as a 'flagrant violation of the right of free circulation throughout the city', he also noted that the actions taken by the East Germans, while violating Berlin's Four Power status, were not aimed at 'the allied position in West Berlin' and did not touch on 'vital interests' of the US. In other words, according to Rusk, it was important to 'draw a line between what was vital to our interests and [what was] important but not worth risking the precipitation of armed conflict'.[231] A few days later, during a meeting of the Berlin Steering Group, the secretary of state further explained the Wall was not a 'shooting issue'. At the same time, Rusk speculated that the Wall's erection might help solve the Berlin crisis, as a more stable GDR would make the Soviets more relaxed about the West Berlin problem.[232]

Washington's cautious reaction to events in East Germany – eight years after Moscow's brutal suppression of the East Berlin riots – dented any remaining West German hope that the West's public commitment to unification might at some point translate into concrete political initiatives. It also dealt an irreparable blow to West German confidence in allied determination to prevent West Berlin from being swallowed by the Soviet bloc. According to the US ambassador to the Federal Republic, Walter Cecil Dowling, the situation in West Germany was not overly concerning. However, there was a 'crisis of confidence' in West Berlin: the US would need to take 'dramatic steps' to improve the 'psychological climate' there.[233] The concern about the Wall's impact on West Berlin's morale was confirmed in a Central Intelligence Agency (CIA) report of 17 August, which highlighted how West Berlin's population was becoming 'increasingly restive over the lack of prompt Western countermeasures'.[234] In the following days, the administration attempted to remedy the emotional shock and loss of morale caused by allied inaction at the border closure, dispatching Vice President Lyndon B. Johnson and a US army combat brigade to West Berlin. Johnson's visit and the deployment of additional troops initially made the morale problem less severe. Nonetheless, the positive impact of these measures was quickly undercut by East German threats against Western air access to West Berlin. Furthermore, the nature of these initiatives was mostly symbolic. In the eyes of the Federal government and of the West Berlin authorities they appeared to confirm that the US government was, after all, content with the current state of affairs.[235]

In Britain, despite the lack of a vibrant debate on unification, the prevailing view was that the German right to self-determination could be realised only within the framework of reconciliation between East and West. The Berlin Wall's erection further strengthened this perception. However, it also confirmed that London was inadequately prepared and lacked a clear strategy towards Germany beyond a repetition of the refrain that the only feasible path to unification rested in ending the continent's division. Whitehall viewed the crisis over the capital of the former Reich as a distraction from more pressing international issues and saw little gain and potential danger in maintaining a firm attitude on Berlin and on the issue of East Germany's recognition. A few weeks before the Wall's erection Foreign Secretary Alec Douglas-Home had suggested acceptance of the Oder–Neisse line and recognition of the GDR in exchange for Soviet acknowledgement of the Western presence and access rights to West Berlin.[236] When construction of the Wall began Macmillan, who was on holiday in Scotland, did not return to London. Britain's prime minister thought the GDR had been compelled to act and wrote in his journal, 'there is nothing illegal in the East Germans stopping the flow of refugees'.[237] Nonetheless, Whitehall sent some armoured trucks and an additional division with the US battle group in response to Kennedy's plea. Macmillan looked at the Berlin question in relation to other issues in East–West relations rather than on its own merits. Having fought and been wounded in World War I and lacking a personal rapport with Adenauer, Britain's prime minister displayed a fundamental ambivalence which was the consequence of 'deeply inculcated mistrusts and indeed aversions' towards Germany. At the same time, he concentrated on relations with the Kremlin to the detriment of those with the Federal Republic.[238] In a sense, Macmillan interpreted the feelings of a vast segment of the nation towards Germany and, in many respects, reflected Thatcher's later ambivalence on the issue of unification. London was in favour of negotiations with the Soviet Union, opposed drastic counter-measures to the East German action and perceived its military activities in West Berlin in a symbolic light. After the Wall's construction Whitehall found it more important for the West to negotiate without suffering a loss of face or being accused of weak compliance. Furthermore, although London was determined to defend the West's presence in Berlin, the British, like the Americans, believed that Bonn should be prepared to make a number of concessions to Moscow. These included acceptance of the Oder–Neisse line, a degree of recognition of the GDR, renunciation of political ties with West Berlin and a clarification of its commitment not to manufacture nuclear weapons.[239]

Washington, London and the Oder–Neisse

By the early 1960s an overall consensus had emerged in Anglo-American perceptions of the German question. On the surface, the Americans and the British continued to support unification and the Federal government's claim to the exclusive representation of the German people. At the height of the Berlin crisis, the State Department concluded that the complex problems of German unity should not be addressed in a 'piecemeal' fashion, thus trying to reassure the West Germans that unification was still a viable goal.[240] However, both Washington and London now believed that, sooner rather than later, Bonn might have to come to terms with the loss of the Eastern territories and the existence of another German state. American diplomats now endeavoured to bring about a change in Bonn's position on the border question that undercut their commitment to unification. The new US approach also called for a reconsideration of West Germany's relations with Poland. Washington publicly argued that a solution to the border question must await a final peace settlement. However, the Kennedy administration continued the momentum that had begun during the second term of Eisenhower's presidency of encouraging the FRG to be more forthcoming on Polish concerns. Kennedy, whose election had been warmly greeted by Polish-American associations and by the Polish people, who tended to see him as a champion of the working classes and as sympathetic to the Polish cause, faced growing pressure from Congress, Polish-American organisations and academics to grant recognition to the Oder–

Neisse. Cautiously, US decision-makers began to contemplate the possibility of pressuring the West German government to recognise the Oder–Neisse line. Acceptance of the border was now seen in Washington as a contribution towards closer relations between Poland and the West and a number of American senators began to consider the prospect of unilateral recognition of the Oder–Neisse line. In September 1961 Republican Senator Claiborne Pell drafted a lengthy memorandum, which was followed by a senate intervention, during which he emphasised that the US should treat the German question as a whole rather than attempt to settle the Berlin problem separately, as neither the Americans nor the Soviets could retreat on Berlin. The Republican congressman also urged recognition of the Oder–Neisse border as a way to 'wean Poland from the Soviets'. The prospect of unilateral recognition of the German–Polish border was formally discussed by the US ambassador to Poland, John Cabot, in an air-gram from Warsaw of April 1963. However, the diplomat conclusively advised against such a move.[241] Nonetheless, US views continued to evolve rapidly. Washington now expected more flexibility in Bonn's policy on the German question. As one Policy Planning Council paper from 1965 remarked, the Federal Republic would need 'at some point . . . to make a clean cut statement recognizing Poland's present Western frontier . . . It is fantasy to pretend that this "concession" can be held out as a bargaining counter in some eventual negotiation on a final settlement' for Germany.[242]

In the early 1960s the FRG's institutional consolidation and economic development contributed to a further evolution of Anglo-American views. Domestic political dynamics in West Germany also played a role. In November 1959, at their annual congress in the Bonn suburb of Bad Godesberg, West Germany's SPD renounced Marxist dogmas and embraced liberal democracy and a market economy. The convention transformed the Party's programme, turning the SPD into a moderate and pragmatic political force. Bad Godesberg also marked an evolution in the Party's approach to foreign and defence policy. In the early 1950s the Social Democrats had favoured direct negotiations between Bonn and East Berlin and opposed the FRG's integration into the Atlantic Alliance. Their concern was that rearmament would deepen Germany's division. Nonetheless, in a historic *Bundestag* speech on 30 June 1960 its deputy chairman, Herbert Wehner, now committed the SPD to rearmament and NATO membership with the aim of making it an acceptable governmental force.[243] Undoubtedly, the consolidation of the balance of power in Europe and the remarkable growth of West Germany's economy contributed to shape the SPD's views. During the so-called economic miracle, popularly known as the *Wirtschaftwunder*, between the late 1950s and early 1960s industrial production tripled and unemployment sank in the FRG. For a number of years West Germany's gross national product rose at a dramatic rate.[244]

Economic growth consolidated West German democracy and the FRG's international status. However, it became a source of potential conflict with Britain and later the US, contributing to undercut further Anglo-American support for Bonn's claims to the exclusive representation of the German people and to the lands east of Oder–Neisse.[245] With Britain plagued by balance of payments difficulties and a rise in inflationary pressure, London now sought the FRG's support for its EEC membership bid. Whitehall also demanded an increase in the West German contribution for the costs of its troops in the Federal Republic in the belief that the United Kingdom carried a disproportionate share of Western defences.[246] Washington was aware of Britain's difficulties and continued to favour its entry to the EEC. On 5 December 1962, former US Secretary of State Dean Acheson exposed US views and blatantly played down Whitehall's great power ambitions in a famous West Point Speech. He remarked:

> Great Britain has lost an empire and has not yet found a role. The attempt to play a separate power role – that is, a role apart from Europe, a role based on a 'special relationship' with the United States, a role based on being the head of a 'commonwealth' which has no political structure, or unity, or strength ... This role is about to be played out. Great Britain, attempting to work alone and to be a broker between the United States and Russia, has seemed to conduct policy as weak as its military power.[247]

The French too were aware of Macmillan's difficulties; after a December 1962 Rambouillet meeting with the British prime minister, de Gaulle flatly told his information minister, Alain Peyrefitte, 'England's back is broken'.[248]

In the following months both domestic and international dynamics apparently confirmed these views. After de Gaulle's veto in January 1963 of London's application to the EEC, Macmillan resigned in October, officially because of ill health. The new government was led by former Foreign Secretary Douglas-Home, who was firmly anti-communist, acted in the shadow of an impending general election and was not best placed to exploit an atmosphere of détente.[249] In these circumstances, German unity could hardly be a major concern for Whitehall. As Douglas-Home's private secretary, Oliver Wright, poignantly remarked,

> We have in a sense had the best of both worlds, because we have been content with the division of Germany, since there was no way of changing it; at the same time, we have been able to make suitably soothing noises about the desirability of reunification.[250]

Nonetheless, some concern persisted in London about developments in the Federal Republic. Whitehall distrusted the West German Social Democrats and feared that if able to form a government after the next federal elections, the SPD could press the Western allies hard to confront the Russians with proposals towards unification. International dynamics and developments within the FRG also impacted heavily on American perceptions of the German question. At a time of increasing involvement in Vietnam, the new administration led by Lyndon B. Johnson showed no appetite for a new confrontation with Moscow in the name of German unity. Washington now endeavoured to convince the Christian Democratic leadership in Bonn that it was beneficial for the West to pursue a more dynamic détente policy.

In December 1963 Johnson used his first meeting with new West German Chancellor Ludwig Erhard to encourage the Federal government to adopt a more conciliatory stance towards the Soviet bloc.[251] The FRG looked to be a viable and successful state in its own right with no need to acquire further land. Hence, its claims to the exclusive representation of the German people and to the Eastern territories appeared in Washington as anachronistic and only justified by domestic political calculations and by the demands of the organisations of the expellees.[252] American views were particularly strong on the issue of Poland's Western border. Writing to Washington in 1966, the US ambassador to the Federal Republic, George McGhee, concluded, 'there are no Germans east of the Oder–Neisse line. Germany does not need *Lebensraum*.' One year later a State Department official remarked that the Oder–Neisse line had become 'one of the most pressing issues of concern in Washington'.[253] These views confirmed the American interest in favouring an accommodation between the Federal Republic and its eastern neighbours, including the GDR, in order to promote better relations between the two blocs.

Notes

1. For an extensive account of the Potsdam Conference and its impact on East–West relations and Germany see Michael Neiberg, *Potsdam: The End of World War II and the Remaking of Europe* (New York: Basic Books, 2015). See also Herbert Feis, *Between War and Peace: The Potsdam Conference* (Princeton, NJ: Princeton University Press, 1960).
2. John Lewis Gaddis, *We Now Know: Rethinking Cold War History* (New York: Oxford University Press, 1997), p. 116. Quoted in McAllister, *No Exit*, p. 4.
3. Quoted in John Dietrich, *The Morgenthau Plan: Soviet Influence on American Postwar Policy* (New York: Algora Publishing, 2002), p. 45.
4. John Baylis, *The Diplomacy of Pragmatism: Britain and the Formation of NATO, 1942–1949* (Basingstoke: Macmillan, 1993), pp. 33–4.
5. For a very detailed analysis of how British opinions were ignored by the US at Yalta and Potsdam see John E. Farquharson, 'Anglo-American Policy on German Reparations from Yalta to Potsdam', *English Historical Review*, vol. 112, no. 448, 1997, pp. 904–26 (quotation on p. 925). See also Filip Slaveski, *The Soviet Occupation of Germany: Hunger, Mass Violence and the Struggle for Peace, 1945–1947* (Cambridge: Cambridge University Press, 2013), p. 130, fn. 7.
6. McAllister, *No Exit*, p. 61–2.
7. Baylis, *The Diplomacy of Pragmatism*, pp. 35–6, 39–40.
8. McAllister, *No Exit*, p. 86.
9. McAllister, *No Exit*, p. 88.
10. David Dilks (ed.), *The Diaries of Sir Alec Cadogan, 1938–45* (New York: G. P. Putnam and Sons, 1971), p. 778. Quoted in McAllister, *No Exit*, p. 88.
11. On British policy at Potsdam see *Documents on British Policy Overseas* (hereafter *DBPO*), Series I, vol. I, *The Conference at Potsdam, July–August 1945* (London: Her Majesty's Stationery Office, 1984).
12. Ernest Bevin, 'Policy towards Germany', 3 May 1946, CP (46)186, CAB 129/9, PRO. Quoted in Marc Trachtenberg, *A Constructed*

Peace: The Making of the European Settlement, 1945–1963 (Princeton, NJ: Princeton University Press, 1999), p. 70, fn. 17.

13. Hughes, *The Postwar Legacy*, pp. 23–6. On the evolution of British policy towards Germany in the months after the Potsdam Conference see *DBPO*, Series I, vol. V, *Germany and Western Europe, August–December 1945* (London: Her Majesty's Stationery Office, 1990).

14. Minute by A. A. E. Franklin, 7 February 1946, in Rolf Steininger (ed.), *Die Ruhrfrage 1945/46 und die Entstehung des Landes Nordrhein-Westfalen: Britische, Französische und Amerikanische Akten* (Düsseldorf: Droste, 1988), p. 487. See also Victor Rothwell, *Britain and the Cold War, 1941–1947* (London: Jonathan Cape, 1982), pp. 310–11.

15. C. O'Neill, 'German Communists and Social Democrats in Berlin and the Russian Zone', 13 February 1946, in Steininger, *Die Ruhrfrage 1945/46*, p. 514.

16. Until the autumn of 1944 France had not featured in Anglo-American plans for Germany. The French were not invited to Yalta and Potsdam and had little influence in the construction of the post-War European order. Nonetheless, the Anglo-Americans and the Soviets kept Paris informed on the course of the conference. Hereafter, France would be included in the CFM and the Reparations Commission. William I. Hitchcock, *France Restored: Cold War Diplomacy and the Quest for Leadership in Europe, 1944–1954* (Chapel Hill, NC: University of North Carolina Press, 1998), pp. 49–50.

17. The 'long telegram' is published in *Foreign Relations of the United States* (Washington, DC: Government Printing Office) (hereafter *FRUS*), 1946, vol. 6, *Eastern Europe, the Soviet Union*, pp. 696–709. Kennan was convinced that a united Germany would emerge only under complete Soviet control and shared Byrnes's belief that it would be counterproductive to run the country as a single economic unit. See Kennan to Secretary of State, 6 March 1946, *FRUS*, 1946, vol. 5, *The British of Commonwealth, Western and Central Europe*, pp. 516–20. Quoted in McAllister, *No Exit*, p. 110.

18. McAllister, *No Exit*, pp. 117–18.

19. See Ernest Bevin, 'Policy towards Germany', 3 May 1946, CP (46)186, CAB 129/9, PRO. Quoted in Trachtenberg, *A Constructed Peace*, p. 59, fn. 93.

20. McAllister, *No Exit*, p. 115.

21. CAB 128/6, C.M. 46, 15 July 1946, *Cabinet Papers: Complete Classes from the CAB and PREM Series in the Public Record Office*, series 3 (Marlborough: Adam Matthew Publications, 1996). Quoted in McAllister, *No Exit*, pp. 115–16, fn. 139.

22. The speech is reprinted in US State Department, *Germany 1947–49: The Story in Documents* (Washington, DC: Government Printing Office, 1950), pp. 3–8.
23. Quoted in John Gimbell, *The Origins of the Marshall Plan* (Stanford: Stanford University Press, 1976), p. 125.
24. The text of Churchill's speech is reproduced in Trevor C. Salmon and Sir William Nicoll (eds), *Building European Union: A Documentary History and Analysis* (Manchester: Manchester University Press, 1997), pp. 26–8.
25. George C. Marshall, 'European Initiative Essential to Economic Recovery', 5 June 1947, *The Department of State Bulletin*, vol. XVI, no. 415, pp. 1159–60.
26. McAllister, *No Exit*, p. 132.
27. On the evolution of British perceptions of Soviet policy towards Eastern Europe see *DBPO*, Series I, vol. VI, *Eastern Europe, August 1945–April 1946* (London: Her Majesty's Stationery Office, 1991).
28. John Baylis, 'Britain and the Dunkirk Treaty: The Origins of NATO', *Journal of Strategic Studies*, vol. 5, no. 2, 1982, pp. 236–47; Sean Greenwood, 'Return to Dunkirk: The Origins of the Anglo-French Treaty of March 1947', *Journal of Strategic Studies*, vol. 6, no. 4, 1983, pp. 49–65; Bert Zeeman, 'Britain and the Cold War: An Alternative Approach. The Treaty of Dunkirk Example', *European History Quarterly*, vol. 16, no. 3, 1986, pp. 343–67.
29. Kennan to Secretary of State, 20 January 1948, *FRUS*, 1948, vol. 3, *Western Europe*, p. 8.
30. Vladimir O. Pechatnov and C. Earl Edmondson, 'The Russian Perspective', in Ralph B. Levering, Vladimir O. Pechatnov, Verena Botzenhart-Viehe and C. Earl Edmondson (eds), *Debating the Origins of the Cold War: American and Russian Perspectives* (Lanham, MD: Rowman & Littlefield, 2002), p. 110; Jonathan M. House, *A Military History of the Cold War, 1944–1962* (Norman: University of Oklahoma Press, 2012), p. 230.
31. John Baylis (ed.), *Anglo-American Relations since 1939: The Enduring Alliance* (Manchester and New York: Manchester University Press, 1997), p. 38.
32. Foreign and Commonwealth Office (hereafter FCO), *Selected Documents on Germany and the Question of Berlin, 1944–1961*, presented to Parliament by the Secretary of State for Foreign Affairs (London, 1961), p. 103. Quoted in Colin Munro, 'Britain, Berlin, German Unification, and the Fall of the Soviet Empire', *Bulletin of the German Historical Institute*, vol. 31, no. 2, November 2009, p. 52.

33. The conference was organised in two sessions that were held between February and March and between April and June respectively. Secretary of State to Embassy in France, 19 February 1948, *FRUS*, 1948, vol. 2, *Germany and Austria*, pp. 70–1. Quoted in McAllister, *No Exit*, p. 145.

34. Douglas to Secretary of State, 2 March 1948, *FRUS*, 1948, vol. 2, p. 123.

35. Douglas to Secretary of State, 6 March 1948, *FRUS*, 1948, vol. 2, p. 138.

36. Quoted in Vojtech Mastny, *The Cold War and Soviet Insecurity: The Stalin Years* (New York: Oxford University Press, 1996), p. 43.

37. For the significance of the Soviet takeover of Czechoslovakia on British policy towards Germany see Deighton, 'Germany and East-Central Europe', pp. 215–19.

38. Quoted in Munro, 'Britain, Berlin, German Unification', p. 52. See also Adolf M. Birke, *Britain and Germany: Historical Patterns of a Relationship* (London: German Historical Institute, 1987), p. 26.

39. Michael Creswell, *A Question of Balance: How France and the United States Created Cold War Europe* (Cambridge, MA: Harvard University Press, 2006), p. 11.

40. Quoted in Sally Rohan, *The Western European Union: International Politics between Alliance and Integration* (Oxford and New York: Routledge, 2014), p. 22. See also John Baylis, 'Britain, the Brussels Pact and the Continental Commitment', *International Affairs*, vol. 60, 1984, pp. 615–30.

41. Frank Roy Willis, *The French in Germany, 1945–1949* (Stanford, CA: Stanford University Press, 1962), pp. 50–5.

42. *FRUS*, 1948, vol. 2, pp. 946–50.

43. FO 371/70628, Note by Patrick Dean about the Robertson Plan, 2 September 1948, p. 81.

44. McAllister, *No Exit*, pp. 160–1.

45. FO 371/70587/C3653/71/18, Statement by former cabinet secretary Robin M. A. Hankey, 14 May 1948, p. 59. Quoted in McAllister, *No Exit*, p. 161.

46. McAllister, *No Exit*, p. 159.

47. McAllister, *No Exit*, p. 165; Mastny, *The Cold War*, p. 65. See also *FRUS*, 1949, vol. 3, *Council of Foreign Ministers; Germany and Austria*, pp. 694–751.

48. See Douglas to Secretary of State, 25 April 1949 and Bevin to Secretary of State, undated (circa 1 May 1949), *FRUS*, 1949, vol. 3, pp. 730, 749–50.

49. See 'U.S. Position at the Council of Foreign Ministers', 15 May

1949, *FRUS*, 1949, vol. 3, pp. 895–903. Quoted in McAllister, *No Exit*, p. 168.

50. Basic Law for the Federal Republic of Germany, 23 May 1949, *Federal Law Gazette*, p. 1, BGBl III 100–1. See also John J. Metzler, *Divided Dynamism: The Diplomacy of Separated Nations: Germany, Korea, China* (Lanham, MD: University Press of America, 2014), p. 3; Kay Hailbronner and Marcel Kau, 'Constitutional Law', in Matthias Reimann and Joachim Zekoll (eds), *Introduction to German Law* (The Hague: Kluwer Law International, 2005), p. 53.

51. Caroline Kennedy-Pipe, *Stalin's Cold War: Soviet Strategies in Europe, 1943 to 1956* (Manchester: Manchester University Press, 1995), pp. 38–9. This opinion is not shared by George Kennan. Around the fiftieth anniversary of the Berlin crisis, the veteran US diplomat remarked that the Soviet leader 'would have paid a higher price than most people think to get the American forces out of Germany'. George Kennan, 'A Letter on Germany', *New York Review of Books*, 3 December 1998, p. 20. Quoted in McAllister, *No Exit*, p. 169, fn. 159. For Stalin's post-War approach to the German question see also Mastny, *The Cold War*, pp. 24–5, 40–5.

52. On the French perception of, and opposition to, West German rearmament see Linda Risso, *Divided We Stand: The French and Italian Political Parties and the Rearmament of West Germany, 1949–1955* (Newcastle upon Tyne: Cambridge Scholars Publishing, 2007).

53. Georges-Henri Sotou, 'France and the German Rearmament Problem, 1945–55', in Rolf Ahmann, Adolf M. Birke and Michael Howard (eds), *The Quest for Stability: Problems of West European Security 1918–57* (London: Oxford University Press, 1993), pp. 487–512. See also Michael Creswell and Marc Trachtenberg, 'France and the German Question, 1945–55', *Journal of Cold War Studies*, vol. 5, no. 3, 2003, pp. 5–28.

54. Jean-Baptiste Duroselle, *France and the United States: From the Beginnings to the Present* (Chicago: University of Chicago Press, 1978), p. 191.

55. John J. McCloy, 'The Future of Germany: Part of a Great World Problem', *The Department of State Bulletin*, vol. XXII, pp. 275–9. Quoted in *DBPO*, Series II, vol. II, *The London Conferences, January–June 1950* (London: Her Majesty's Stationery Office, 1987), doc. no. 38, 26 April 1950, p. 139, fn. 2.

56. David Clay Large, *Germans to the Front: West German Rearmament in the Adenauer Era* (Chapel Hill, NC: University of North Carolina Press, 1996), p. 42.

57. Norrin M. Ripsman, *Peacemaking by Democracies: The Effect of*

State Autonomy on the Post-World War Settlements (University Park: Pennsylvania State University Press, 2002), pp. 192–3.

58. *Parliamentary Debates, 5th ser., House of Commons*, vol. 473, col. 324 and no. 18, n. 2.
59. The paper was originally submitted to Bevin in an earlier form on 24 August 1949. On 23 April the foreign secretary agreed that the paper could be used for general guidance of officials at their preliminary bipartite and tripartite talks. *DBPO*, II, II, doc. no. 27, 22 April 1950, pp. 81–7.
60. *DBPO*, II, II, doc. no. 30, 24 April 1950, pp. 95–106 (quotation on p. 105).
61. Anne Deighton, 'Three Ministers and the World They Made: Acheson, Bevin and Schuman, and the North Atlantic Treaty, March–April 1949', in Jussi Hanhimäki, Georges-Henri Soutou and Basil Germond (eds), *The Routledge Handbook of Transatlantic Security* (Abingdon and New York: Routledge, 2010), pp. 7–9. See also David Gowland, Arthur Turner and Alex Wright, *Britain and European Integration since 1945: On the Sidelines* (Abingdon and New York: Routledge, 2010).
62. *DBPO*, II, II, doc. no. 33, 25 April 1950, pp. 115–20 (quotation on p. 117).
63. *DBPO*, II, II, doc. no. 38, 26 April 1950, p. 138.
64. For the view of British military planners on the question of West German rearmament see Spencer Mawby, *Containing Germany: Britain and the Arming of the Federal Republic* (New York: St. Martin's Press, 2000), pp. 20–40.
65. The High Commissioner also emphasised that this would not be hard to elicit since 'we have indeed already had various hints' from the West Germans. *DBPO*, II, II, Calendar to doc. no. 38, 26 April 1950, p. 141.
66. Deighton, 'Three Ministers and the World They Made', pp. 10–12. On London's reluctance to support European cooperative schemes see also David Gowland and Arthur Turner, *Reluctant Europeans: Britain and European Integration 1945–1998* (Harlow: Longman, 2000).
67. Department of Army cable CC 9192 of 18 July 1949, attached to RG 59, 862.00 (W)/7-1849, NA. Quoted in McAllister, *No Exit*, p. 175.
68. Thomas A. Schwartz, *America's Germany: John J. McCloy and the Federal Republic of Germany* (Cambridge, MA: Harvard University Press, 1991), pp. 124–30.
69. Konrad Adenauer, *Memoirs 1945–53* (London: Weidenfeld & Nicholson, 1966), pp. 244–8. Quoted in *DBPO*, II, II, doc. no. 44, 27 April 1950, p. 173.

70. Declaration by the Foreign Ministers of Great Britain, the US and France, London, 13 May 1950, in Carl Christoph Schweitzer, Detlev Karsten, Robert Spencer, R. Taylor Cole and Donald P. Kommers (eds), *Politics and Government in Germany, 1944–1994: Basic Documents* (Providence, RI and Oxford: Berghahn Books, 1995), doc. no. 1, pp. 117–18.
71. *DBPO*, II, II, 1950, Calendar to doc. no. 40, 19 April–4 May 1950, p. 150. See also James Reston, 'U.S. Seeks New Way to Tie Bonn Regime to Atlantic Group', *The New York Times*, 26 April 1950.
72. *DBPO*, II, II, 1950, Calendar to doc. no. 40, p. 150.
73. *DBPO*, II, II, 1950, Calendar to doc. no. 40, p. 150.
74. Creswell and Trachtenberg, 'France and the German Question', pp. 17–18.
75. McAllister, *No Exit*, p. 183.
76. Gowland and Turner, *Reluctant Europeans: Britain and European Integration 1945–1998*, pp. 40–8.
77. Harvey to Younger, 16 June 1950, *DBPO*, series II, vol. I, *The Schuman Plan, the Council of Europe and Western European Integration, May 1950–December 1952* (London: Her Majesty's Stationery Office, 1986), pp. 182–6 (quotation on p. 183).
78. McAllister, *No Exit*, p. 173.
79. *FRUS*, 1950, vol. 1, *National Security Affairs; Foreign Economic Policy*, pp. 237–92.
80. McAllister, *No Exit*, p. 184. See also Robert R. Bowie and Richard H. Immerman, *Waging Peace: How Eisenhower Shaped an Enduring Cold War Strategy* (New York and Oxford: Oxford University Press, 1998), p. 28.
81. Memorandum of Conversation by Acheson, 31 July 1950, *FRUS*, 1950, vol. 3, *Western Europe*, pp. 167–8.
82. See Truman's memos in *FRUS*, 1950, vol. 4, *Central and Eastern Europe; The Soviet Union*, pp. 688–9.
83. Acheson to McCloy, 21 June 1950, *FRUS*, 1950, vol. 4, pp. 689–90. Quoted in McAllister, *No Exit*, p. 185.
84. Lord Tedder to Chiefs of Staff, 6 September 1950, in *DBPO*, Series II, vol. III, *German Rearmament, September–December 1950* (London: Her Majesty's Stationery Office, 1989), calendar 2i. Quoted in McAllister, *No Exit*, p. 188.
85. Samuel F. Wells, Jr., 'The Korean War: Miscalculation and Alliance Transformation', in Jussi Hanhimäki, Georges-Henri Soutou and Basil Germond (eds), *The Routledge Handbook of Transatlantic Security* (Abingdon and New York: Routledge, 2010), p. 20.
86. On the genesis of the Acheson Plan see Dean Acheson, *Present at the Creation: My Years in the State Department* (New York: W.

W. Norton, 1969), pp. 437–40. See also Marc Trachtenberg and Christopher Gehrz, 'America, Europe, and German Rearmament, August–September 1950', *Journal of European Integration History*, vol. 6, no. 2, December 2000, pp. 9–35 and the slightly revised versions Marc Trachtenberg and Christopher Gehrz, 'America, Europe, and German Rearmament, August–September 1950: A Critique of a Myth', in Marc Trachtenberg (ed.), *Between Empire and Alliance: America and Europe During the Cold War* (Lanham, MD: Rowman & Littlefield, 2003), pp. 1–31 and Marc Trachtenberg, *The Cold War and After: History, Theory, and the Logic of International Politics* (Princeton, NY: Princeton University Press, 2012), pp. 110–41.

87. For Bevin's concerns about German rearmament see 'Record of a Meeting Held in the Secretary of State's Room, August 21, 1950', calendar 3i; D.O. (50) 66, 'German Association with the Defence of the West', 29 August 1950, calendar 3i, both in *DBPO*, II, III. See also Bevin to Acheson, 4 September 1950, *FRUS*, 1950, vol. 3, pp. 264–6.

88. Minute by Mr Mallet, 12 September 1950, *DBPO*, II, III, pp. 32–4. See also Saki Dockrill, *Britain's Policy for West German Rearmament 1950–1955* (New York: Cambridge University Press, 1991), pp. 24–8.

89. Frank R. Douglas, *The United States, NATO, and a New Multilateral Relationship* (Westport, CT: Praeger, 2008), p. 130. See also Massimo de Leonardis, 'Defense or Liberation of Europe: The Strategies of the West against a Soviet Attack (1947–1950)', in Ennio di Nolfo (ed.), *The Atlantic Pact Forty Years Later: A Historical Reappraisal* (Berlin and New York: De Gruyter, 1991), pp. 176–206.

90. Memorandum by Air Marshall Sir W. Elliot, 19 October 1950, *DBPO*, II, III, p. 178. Quoted in McAllister, *No Exit*, p. 189.

91. For Schuman's arguments against German rearmament see *FRUS*, 1950, vol. 3, pp. 296, 299–300, 312, 342. See also *DBPO*, II, III, p. 69. British Record of Conversation in *DBPO*, II, III, p. 36. Quoted in McAllister, *No Exit*, p. 190. See also Creswell and Trachtenberg, 'France and the German Question', p. 18.

92. Harvey to Foreign Office, 1 October 1950, *DBPO*, II, III, calendar 54i.

93. Quoted in Hughes, *Britain, Germany and the Cold War*, p. 21.

94. Dockrill, *Britain's Policy*, p. 41.

95. Craig Parsons, *A Certain Idea of Europe* (Ithaca, NY: Cornell University Press, 2003), p. 70.

96. Both quoted in Trachtenberg, *A Constructed Peace*, p. 110.

97. Herbert Blankenhorn, *Verständnis und Verständigung: Blätter*

eines Politischen Tagebuchs 1949 bis 1979 (Frankfurt/Main: Propyläen, 1980), pp. 115–16.

98. Adenauer had asked McCloy whether he should endorse the French proposal before making the speech; the US High Commissioner's reply had been that the plan was not acceptable in its present form. See RG 59, 762A.5/11-850, NA. Quoted in McAllister, *No Exit*, p. 196.

99. These conditions were spelled out by Adenauer in an aide-memoire presented to the High Commissioners on 16 November. See *FRUS*, 1950, vol. 4, pp. 780–4. Quoted in McAllister, *No Exit*, p. 198.

100. Large, *Germans to the Front*, pp. 62–3.

101. McAllister, *No Exit*, p. 198.

102. *FRUS*, 1950, vol. 3, pp. 419, 518. See also Large, *Germans to the Front*, p. 96.

103. *FRUS*, 1950, vol. 3, pp. 457–64.

104. Memorandum by Bevin, 24 November 1950, *DBPO*, II, III, pp. 291–6 (quotation on p. 293).

105. *DBPO*, II, III, Calendar to doc. no. 107, p. 272.

106. For a comprehensive account of Britain's position on Germany's rearmament see Dockrill, *Britain's Policy*.

107. Kirkpatrick to Bevin, 12 December 1950, *DBPO*, II, III, pp. 354–5. See also CAB 129/43, CP (50) 311, 'German Participation in the Defence of Western Europe', 12 December 1950, *Cabinet Papers*. Both quoted in McAllister, *No Exit*, p. 199, fn. 91.

108. Large, *Germans to the Front*, pp. 137–8.

109. Memorandum of Conversation between René Massigli and Dixon, 30 October 1950, *DBPO*, II, III, calendar 84i. Quoted in McAllister, *No Exit*, p. 194; see also p. 244.

110. Quoted in Chris Gifford, *The Making of Eurosceptic Britain: Identity and Economy in a Post-imperial State* (Aldershot: Ashgate, 2008), pp. 32–3. See also Rohan, *The Western European Union*, pp. 29–34.

111. Quoted in Rohan, *The Western European Union*, p. 31.

112. Quoted in Gowland and Turner, *Reluctant Europeans*, p. 60.

113. Mastny, *The Cold War*, pp. 110–15.

114. Trachtenberg, *A Constructed Peace*, p. 119.

115. Quoted in Robert Beisner, *Dean Acheson: A Life in the Cold War* (New York: Oxford University Press, 2006), p. 461.

116. Joseph Smith and Simon Davis, *Historical Dictionary of the Cold War* (Lanham, MD: Scarecrow Press, 2000), p. 200. See also Bowie and Immerman, *Waging Peace*, p. 26.

117. On the origins of Stalin's note of 10 March 1952 see Wilfried Loth, 'The Origins of Stalin's Note of 10 March 1952', *Cold War History*, vol. 4, no. 2, January 2004, pp. 66–88. See also

Achilleas Megas, *Soviet Foreign Policy towards East Germany* (Berlin: Springer, 2015), pp. 42–4.

118. The Stalin note is published in *FRUS*, 1952–54, vol. 7, *Germany and Austria*, pp. 169–72.

119. When presidential advisor and psychological warfare specialist Charles Douglas Jackson, in response to the Soviet peace proposal, suggested that Eisenhower should make a speech, emphasising the White House's desire to 'negotiate all the major outstanding issues between the free world and the Soviet bloc, including the unification of Germany and disarmament', Dulles reacted that if such a speech were given, 'the governments of [Italian Prime Minister A.] de Gasperi, Adenauer and [French Premier R.] Mayer would fall in a week; and that EDC would be postponed, if not destroyed'. Quoted in Christian Ostermann, 'The United States, the East German Uprising of 1953, and the Limits of Rollback', *The Cold War International History Project Working Paper Series*, no. 11 (Washington, DC: Woodrow Wilson International Center for Scholars, 1994), p. 11 and Christian Ostermann, '"Keeping the Pot Simmering": The United States and the East German Uprising of 1953', *German Studies Review*, vol. 19, no. 1, February 1996, p. 65. See also Summary of Discussion, 12 March 1953, 136th Meeting of the NSC, quoted in James D. Marchio, *Rhetoric and Reality: The Eisenhower Administration and Unrest in Eastern Europe, 1953–1959*, PhD dissertation (American University Microfilms, 1990), pp. 98–100 (quotation on p. 98). Dulles is quoted in Walt W. Rostow, *Europe after Stalin* (Austin: University of Texas Press, 1982), Appendix C, p. 108.

120. 'The Secretary of State to the Office of the United States High Commissioner for Germany', *FRUS*, 1952–54, vol. 7, p. 190. Recently declassified documents from former Soviet archives have confirmed that Stalin's note was a mere ploy to facilitate the GDR's incorporation into the Eastern bloc and to blame the West for Germany's division. Peter Ruggenthaler, 'The 1952 Stalin Note on German Unification: The Ongoing Debate', *Journal of Cold War Studies*, vol. 13, no. 4, 2011, pp. 172–212.

121. Henning Hoff, *Großbritannien und die DDR 1955–1973: Diplomatie auf Umwegen* (Munich: Oldenbourg, 2003), pp. 40–1.

122. Gowland and Turner, *Reluctant Europeans*, p. 61.

123. McAllister, *No Exit*, p. 222.

124. Hitchcock, *France Restored*, p. 185.

125. On Italy's attitude towards the Brussels Treaty and the EDC see Antonio Varsori, *Il Patto di Bruxelles (1948): Tra integrazione europea e alleanza atlantica* (Rome: Bonacci, 1988); Alfredo Breccia, *L'Italia e la difesa dell'Europa. Alle origini del Piano*

Pleven (Rome: I. S. E., 1984). On the Benelux states' attitude to European military cooperation see Wichard Woyke, *Erfolg durch Integration: Die Europapolitik der Benelux Staaten von 1947 bis 1969* (Bochum: Brockmeyer, 1985).

126. Nicholas J. Crowson, *Britain and Europe: A Political History since 1918* (Abingdon and New York: Routledge, 2011), pp. 69–70.

127. Steven J. Brady, *Eisenhower and Adenauer: Alliance Maintenance under Pressure, 1953–1960* (Lanham, MD: Lexington Books, 2010), p. 25.

128. Rolf Steininger, 'John Foster Dulles, the European Defense Community, and the German Question', in Richard H. Immerman (ed.), *John Foster Dulles and the Diplomacy of the Cold War* (Princeton, NJ: Princeton University Press, 1990), p. 85.

129. Dockrill, *Britain's Policy*, pp. 130–1.

130. The text of Dulles's speech is published in *FRUS*, 1952–54, vol. 5, *Western European Security*, pp. 461–8.

131. The quotation is from Eden. See 'Top Secret Record of Conversation at the White House, June 27, 1954', NA, PREM 11/618; US Department of State memorandum of conversation, 27 June 1954, *FRUS*, 1952–54, vol. 5, p. 986. Quoted in Steininger, 'John Foster Dulles', p. 88.

132. Frank Roy Willis, *France, Germany, and the New Europe, 1945–1967* (Oxford: Oxford University Press, 1968), p. 185.

133. McAllister, *No Exit*, p. 243. For Eden's crucial role in September 1954 see Anne Deighton, 'The Last Piece of the Jigsaw: Britain and the Creation of the Western European Union, 1954', *Contemporary European History*, no. 7, 1998, pp. 181–96.

134. Kevin Ruane, 'Agonizing Reappraisals: Anthony Eden, John Foster Dulles and the Crisis of European Defence, 1953–54', *Diplomacy and Statecraft*, vol. 13, no. 4, 2002, pp. 151–85.

135. The text of the Paris protocols is printed in *Documents on Germany, 1944–1959: Background Documents on Germany, 1944–1959, and a Chronology of Political Developments Affecting Berlin, 1945–1956* (Washington, DC: Government Printing Office, 1959), pp. 124–41 and in *The American Journal of International Law*, vol. 49, no. 3, July 1955, pp. 126–8.

136. Large, *Germans to the Front*, pp. 213–20.

137. John Lewis Gaddis, *Strategies of Containment: A Critical Appraisal of Postwar American National Security Policy* (New York: Oxford University Press, 1982), p. 155. See also Ostermann, 'The United States', p. 40.

138. *FRUS*, 1952–54, vol. 2, *National Security Affairs*, pp. 1699–706. See also Rolf Steininger, *Austria, Germany, and the Cold War: From the Anschluss to the State Treaty* (New York: Berghahn

Books, 2008), p. 101. On Western perceptions of the prospect for negotiations with Moscow and the Soviet bloc in the early 1950s see Klaus Larres and Kenneth Alan Osgood (eds), *The Cold War after Stalin's Death: A Missed Opportunity for Peace?* (Lanham, MD: Rowman & Littlefield, 2006); Evanthis Hatzivassiliou, *NATO and Western Perceptions of the Soviet Bloc: Alliance Analysis and Reporting, 1951–69* (London and New York: Routledge 2014).

139. Minutes, NSC meeting of 28 April 1953, *FRUS, 1952–54*, vol. 5, p. 399. Quoted in Ostermann, 'The United States', p. 12, fn. 44. See also McAllister, *No Exit*, p. 220.

140. Trachtenberg, *A Constructed Peace*, p. 135.

141. The original Locarno agreement – the so-called Rhineland Pact – had been signed in 1925 by Germany, France, Belgium, the United Kingdom and Italy. Its aim was to overcome Franco-German divisions that had been left open by the Versailles Treaty and by the 1923 Ruhr crisis, by prompting German recognition of its Western borders, restoring a European Concert and devising a multilateral solution to Germany's post-War borders. On the genesis of the Locarno treaty see Stephanie C. Salzmann, *Great Britain, Germany and the Soviet Union: Rapallo and after, 1922–1934* (Rochester, NY: Boydell Press, 2003), pp. 55–68.

142. Martin Gilbert, 'From Yalta to Bermuda and Beyond: In Search of Peace with the Soviet Union', in James W. Muller (ed.), *Churchill as Peacemaker* (New York: Woodrow Wilson Center Press and Cambridge University Press, 1997), pp. 317–18.

143. On Churchill's summit initiative see Klaus W. Larres, *Politik der Illusionen. Churchill, Eisenhower und die deutsche Frage 1945–1955* (Göttingen: Vandenhoeck & Ruprecht, 1995), pp. 91–154; Michael Steven Fish, 'After Stalin's Death: The Anglo-American Debate Over a New Cold War', *Diplomatic History*, vol. 10, no. 4, 1986, p. 335.

144. Lord Salisbury, the Lord President of the Council, had been appointed acting foreign secretary on 29 June following Churchill's stroke, while Eden had been sidelined by gallstones in his bile duct. Salisbury was a staunch imperialist, who lacked international experience and had a poor reputation in Washington. Robert Barnes, *The US, the UN and the Korean War: Communism in the Far East and the American Struggle for Hegemony in America's Cold War* (London: I. B. Tauris, 2014), p. 183. As for Eden, having undergone two unsuccessful operations in Britain in the spring, he had travelled for surgery to the US and received a third operation at the New England Baptist Hospital in Boston. Churchill is quoted in Manfred Overesch, 'The Alternative Prospect: The Plan for a Neutralized United Germany', in Ennio di Nolfo (ed.),

Great Britain, France, Germany and Italy and the Origins of the EEC, 1952–1957 (Berlin and New York: Walter de Gruyter, 1992), pp. 93–4, fn. 30. On Eden's biliary misfortunes see John W. Braasch, 'Anthony Eden's (Lord Avon) Biliary Tract Saga', *Annals of Surgery*, vol. 238, no. 5, November 2003, pp. 772–5.

145. Megas, *Soviet Foreign Policy*, pp. 49–54.

146. Ostermann, 'The United States', p. 21.

147. On British policy during the uprising see Klaus Larres, 'Neutralisierung oder Westintegration. Churchill, Adenauer, die USA und der 17. Juni 1953', *Deutschland Archiv*, vol. 26, no. 6, 1993, pp. 568–83; Michael Gehler, 'Der 17. Juni 1953 aus der Sicht des Foreign Office', *Aus Politik und Zeitgeschichte*, 25 June 1993, pp. 22–31; John W. Young, 'Cold War and Détente with Moscow', in John W. Young (ed.), *The Foreign Policy of Churchill's Peacetime Government, 1951–55* (Leicester: Leicester University Press, 1988), pp. 55–80.

148. Memorandum of Selwyn Lloyd to Prime Minister Churchill, National Archives (hereafter NA), PREM 11/673, 22 June 1953. Quoted in Hughes, *Britain, Germany and the Cold War*, p. 16.

149. Hubertus Knabe, *17. Juni 1953: Ein deutscher Aufstand* (Berlin: Propyläen, 2003); see also Hubertus Knabe, *17. Juni 1953: Der Anfang vom langen Ende der DDR* (Munich: Olzog, 2003). On Churchill's lack of sympathy for the revolt see Hoff, *Großbritannien und die DDR*, p. 43. See also Lothar Kettenacker, *Germany 1989: In the Aftermath of the Cold War* (Harlow: Pearson Longman, 2009), p. 39; Daniel Gossel, *Briten, Deutsche und Europa: die Deutsche Frage in der britischen Außenpolitik, 1945–1962* (Stuttgart: Steiner, 1999).

150. High Commissioner for Germany (hereafter HICOG) Bonn to Department of State, 6 July 1953, NA, RG 59, 762B.00/7-653. See also James G. Hershberg, '"Explosion in the Offing": German Rearmament and American Diplomacy', *Diplomatic History*, vol. 16, no. 4, 1992, pp. 528–31. Both quoted in Ostermann, 'The United States', p. 22, fn. 108.

151. Brady, *Eisenhower and Adenauer*, pp. 60, 88, fn. 11. See also the memoirs of Adenauer's press aide, Felix von Eckardt, *Ein unordentliches Leben* (Düsseldorf: Econ, 1967), pp. 255–6.

152. Ostermann, 'The United States', p. 4. For the concept of 'dual' or 'double' containment see Schwartz, *America's Germany*, p. 299. See also Wolfram F. Hanrieder, *Germany, America, Europe: Forty Years of German Foreign Policy* (New Haven, CT: Yale University Press, 1989), pp. 6–11, 142–4.

153. Ostermann, 'The United States', pp. 28.

154. Michael S. Harris to Harold Stassen, 2 August 1953, Dwight D.

Eisenhower Library, C. D. Jackson Records, Box 1; also in *FRUS*, 1952–54, vol. 7, pp. 1633–6. Director of the Mutual Security Agency Harold Stassen later maintained, 'There is no doubt in my mind that the window of freedom those millions of East Germans glimpsed during this period, and their brutalization by the Soviet oppressors, laid the foundations for the political events of 1989.' See the memoirs that Stassen co-authored with Marshall Houts, *Eisenhower: Turning the World Towards Peace* (St. Paul, MN: Merrill/Magnus Publishing, 1990), p. 189. Quoted in Ostermann, 'The United States', p. 36, fn. 208 and Ostermann, '"Keeping the Pot Simmering"', p. 87, fn. 42.

155. Peter G. Boyle, *The Churchill–Eisenhower Correspondence, 1953–1955* (Chapel Hill, NC and London: University of North Carolina Press, 1990), p. 10.

156. See FO Minute, Roberts to Strang, 6 July 1953, NA, FO/371/103843, CS 1016/161; Kirkpatrick to FO, 6 July 1953, NA, FO/371/103843, CS 1016/158.

157. HICOG Berlin to Secretary of State, 24 July 1953, NA, RG 59, 862B.49/7-2453.

158. Dillon/Paris to Secretary of State, 24 June 1953, NA, RG 59, 762A.0221/6-2453; HICOG Berlin to Secretary of State, 23 July 1953, NA, RG 59, 862B.49/7-2353. Both quoted in Ostermann, 'The United States', pp. 21, 37.

159. HICOG Berlin to Secretary of State, 16 July 1953, NA, RG 59, 862B.49/7-1653; HICOG Berlin to Secretary of State, 22 July 1953, NA, RG 59, 862B.49/7-2253.

160. Conant to Eisenhower, 19 October 1953, Dwight D. Eisenhower Library, Dwight D. Eisenhower Papers, Administrative Series, Box 10. Quoted in Ostermann, 'The United States', p. 37, fn. 219.

161. Jebb to FO, 9 September 1953, NA, FO 371/103846, CS1016/237.

162. Conant to Eisenhower, 19 October 1953, Dwight D. Eisenhower Library, Dwight D. Eisenhower Papers, Administrative Series, Box 10. Quoted in Ostermann, 'The United States', p. 38, fn. 223.

163. The State Department had specifically recommended against 'detailed consultation' with the Federal government in the initial stages of the programme. See Riddleberger to General Smith, 6 July 1953, NA, RG 59, 862B.49/7-653. As late as 24 July the FRG's Secretary of State Walter Hallstein 'indicated that the chancellor had not been consulted'. HICOG Berlin to Secretary of State, 24 July 1953, NA, RG 59, 862B.49/7-2453.

164. Gaddis, *Strategies of Containment*, pp. 145ff.

165. For a documentary collection on the origins, significance and implications of the 1953 East German uprising see Christian F.

Ostermann, *Uprising in East Germany 1953: The Cold War, the German Question, and the First Major Upheaval behind the Iron Curtain* (Budapest and New York: Central European University Press, 2001).

166. Julian Lindley-French, *The North Atlantic Treaty Organization: The Enduring Alliance* (London and New York: Routledge, 2007), p. 28.

167. Fredrik Logevall, *Embers of War: The Fall of an Empire and the Making of America's Vietnam* (New York: Random House, 2012), pp. 433–5.

168. *FRUS, 1952–54*, vol. 7, Part 1, doc. no. 383, pp. 871–7. For the text of the Eden plan see doc. no. 510, pp. 1177–80; *Documents on Germany, 1944–1959*, pp. 115–17.

169. On Molotov's initiative see Geoffrey Roberts, *Molotov: Stalin's Cold Warrior* (Washington, DC: Potomac Books, 2012), pp. 141–53.

170. Deborah Welch Larson, *Anatomy of Mistrust: U.S.–Soviet Relations during the Cold War* (Ithaca, NY: Cornell University Press, 2000), p. 59; Steininger, *Austria*, p. 105.

171. Daniel C. Williamson, *Separate Agendas: Churchill, Eisenhower, and Anglo-American Relations, 1953–1955* (Lanham, MD: Lexington Books, 2006), pp. 26–7, 35.

172. *New York Times* 27 and 28 June 1954; the sentence was later paraphrased by Harold Macmillan in 1958 during a visit in Canberra. See Gilbert, 'From Yalta to Bermuda', p. 326, fn. 60. See also Martin Gilbert, *Churchill and America* (New York: Free Press, 2005), p. 430. Churchill is also quoted in David Carlton, *Churchill and the Soviet Union* (Manchester: Manchester University Press, 2000), p. 202.

173. Hermann-Josef Rupieper, 'American Policy toward German Unification, 1949–1955', in Jeffry M. Diefendorf, Axel Frohn and Hermann-Josef Rupieper (eds), *American Policy and the Reconstruction of West Germany, 1945–1955* (Washington, DC: German Historical Institute and Cambridge University Press, 1993), pp. 45–67. See also Steven J. Brady, 'The U.S. Congress and German–American Relations', in Detlef Junker, Philipp Gassert, Wilfried Mausbach and David B. Morris (eds), *The United States and Germany in the Era of the Cold War, 1945–1990: A Handbook. Vol. 1, 1945–1968* (Washington, DC: Cambridge University Press, 2004), p. 138.

174. Steven Z. Freiberger, *Dawn Over Suez: The Rise of American Power in the Middle East, 1953–1957* (Chicago: Ivan Dee, 1992), p. 188.

175. Peter Mangold, *Almost Impossible Ally: Harold Macmillan and*

Charles de Gaulle (London: I. B. Tauris, 2006), pp. 82–3.

176. John Simpson, 'The US–UK Special Relationship: The Nuclear Dimension', in Alan P. Dobson and Steve Marsh (eds), *Anglo-American Relations: Contemporary Perspectives* (London and New York: Routledge, 2013), p. 246. On the significance of the mutual defence agreement see also John Baylis, 'The 1958 Anglo-American Mutual Defence Agreement: The Search for Nuclear Interdependence', *Journal of Strategic Studies*, vol. 31, no. 3, 2008, pp. 425–66.

177. Frank Heinlein, *British Government Policy and Decolonisation, 1945–63: Scrutinising the Official Mind* (London: Frank Cass, 2002), pp. 166–70, 217–28.

178. Richard T. Griffiths, 'A Slow One Hundred and Eighty Degree Turn: British Policy towards the Common Market, 1955–61', in George Wilkes (ed.), *Britain's Failure to Enter the European Community 1961–63: The Enlargement Negotiations and Crises in European, Atlantic and Commonwealth Relations* (London: Frank Cass, 1997), pp. 45–8.

179. Geraint Hughes, *Harold Wilson's Cold War: The Labour Government and East–West Politics, 1964–1970* (Rochester, NY: Boydell Press, 2009), p. 25.

180. Anne Deighton, '"A Different 1956": British Responses to the Polish Events, June–November 1956', *Cold War History*, vol. 6, no. 4, 2006, pp. 455–75. See also Anne Deighton, 'British Responses to the Polish Events, June–November 1956', in Jan Rowiński and Tytus Jaskułowski (eds), *The Polish October 1956 in World Politics* (Warsaw: PISM, 2007), pp. 239–62.

181. Michael J. Turner, *British Power and International Relations during the 1950s: A Tenable Position?* (Lanham, MD: Lexington Books, 2009), p. 279.

182. Martin Thomas, 'From Dien Bien Phu to Evian, Anglo-French Imperial Relations, 1954–1962', in Alan Sharp and Glyn Stone (eds), *Anglo-French Relations in the Twentieth Century: Rivalry and Cooperation* (London: Routledge, 2000), p. 305. See also Logevall, *Embers of War*, pp. 342ff.; Alan P. Dobson and Steve Marsh, *US Foreign Policy since 1945* (London: Routledge, 2007), p. 102; Eugenie M. Blang, *Allies at Odds: America, Europe, and Vietnam, 1961–1968* (Lanham, MD: Rowman & Littlefield, 2011), p. 52.

183. Rupieper, 'American Policy', p. 66.

184. William Glenn Gray, *Germany's Cold War: The Global Campaign to Isolate East Germany, 1949–1969* (Chapel Hill, NC and London: University of North Carolina Press, 2003), p. 82.

185. Gottfried Niedhart, 'Ostpolitik: Phases, Short-term Objectives,

and Grand Design', *German Historical Institute Bulletin*, supp. no. 1, 2004, p. 137. See also Stefan Berger and Norman LaPorte, *Friendly Enemies: Britain and the GDR, 1949–1990* (Oxford: Berghahn Books, 2010), p. 301; Klaus Larres, 'Britain and the GDR: The Politics of Trade and Recognition by Stealth', in Jeremy Noakes, Peter Wende and Jonathan Wright (eds), *Britain and Germany in Europe, 1949–1990* (Oxford and New York: Oxford University Press, 2002), pp. 213–15. On East German efforts to win recognition in Africa and Asia see Gray, *Germany's Cold War*, pp. 87–95.

186. On Adenauer's *Ostpolitik* see Michael Kreile, 'Ostpolitik Reconsidered', in Ekkehart Krippendorf and Volker Rittberger (eds), *The Foreign Policy of West Germany: Formation and Contents* (London and Beverly Hills: Sage, 1980), pp. 125–6; Klaus Gotto, 'Adenauers Deutschland- und Ostpolitik 1954–1963', in Rudolf Morsey and Konrad Repgen (eds), *Adenauer-Studien Bd. III. Untersuchungen und Dokumente zur Ostpolitik und Biographie* (Mainz: Matthias-Grünewald, 1974), pp. 3–91.

187. Robert B. Rakove, *Kennedy, Johnson, and the Nonaligned World* (New York: Cambridge University Press, 2013), p. xxvi.

188. R. Gerald Hughes, '"Possession is Nine Tenths of the Law": Britain and the Boundaries of Eastern Europe Since 1945', *Diplomacy and Statecraft*, vol. 16, no. 4, 2005, pp. 723–47.

189. NA, FO 371/118455, Hoyer Millar to Kirkpatrick, 15 October 1955.

190. NA, FO 408/82, Williams to Selwyn Lloyd, 23 August 1957. See also Roger Morgan, 'The British View: West German Foreign and Security Interests', in Edwina Moreton (ed.), *Germany between East and West* (Cambridge: Cambridge University Press, 1987), pp. 85–6.

191. Quoted in Hughes, *Britain, Germany and the Cold War*, p. 106.

192. R. Gerald Hughes, 'Unfinished Business from Potsdam: Britain, West Germany, and the Oder–Neisse Line, 1945–1962', *The International History Review*, vol. 27, no. 2, June 2005, pp. 259–94; Hughes, '"Possession is Nine Tenths of the Law"', pp. 723–47. See also Hughes, *The Postwar Legacy*, pp. 61–73.

193. Helga Haftendorn, *Coming of Age: German Foreign Policy since 1945* (Lanham, MD: Rowman & Littlefield, 2006), p. 125. See also Wanda Jarzabek, 'Polish Reactions to the West German Ostpolitik', in Poul Villaume and Odd Arne Westad (eds), *Perforating the Iron Curtain: European Détente, Transatlantic Relations, and the Cold War, 1965–1985* (Copenhagen: Museum Tuscolanum Press, 2010), p. 52, fn. 12.

194. Debra J. Allen, *The Oder–Neisse Line: The United States, Poland,*

and Germany in the Cold War (Westport, CT and London: Praeger, 2003), p. 243.

195. In the same year the publication in Britain, under the auspices of the Royal Institute of International Affairs, of Elizabeth Wiskemann's book *Germany's Eastern Neighbours: Problems Relating to the Oder–Neisse Line and the Czech Frontier Regions* (London: Oxford University Press, 1956) triggered outrage in the Federal Republic as a result of the author's open criticism of West German claims on the Eastern territories. Allen to Selwyn Lloyd, 11 August 1956, NA, FO 408/81.

196. Matthew Elderfield, 'Rebuilding the Special Relationship: The 1957 Bermuda Talks', *Cambridge Review of International Affairs*, vol. 3, no. 1, 1989, pp. 14–24.

197. Sylvia Ellis, *Historical Dictionary of Anglo-American Relations* (Lanham, MD: Scarecrow Press, 2009), p. 59.

198. *FRUS, 1955–57*, vol. 27, *Western Europe and Canada*, doc. no. 271, p. 719.

199. *FRUS, 1955–57*, vol. 27, doc. no. 273, p. 729. See also Daniel Gossel, 'Zur Innenarchitektur der westlichen Allianz: Die sicherheitspolitische Integration der Bundesrepublik als Aufgabe und Problem der Special Relationship zwischen den USA und Großbritannien (1945–1965)', in Michael Wala (ed.), *Gesellschaft und Diplomatie im transatlantischen Kontext* (Stuttgart: Steiner, 1999), p. 282.

200. Hoff, *Großbritannien und die DDR*, p. 51.

201. Gearson, *Harold Macmillan*, p. 5. See also Rolf Steininger, *Der Mauerbau. Die Westmächte und Adenauer in der Berlinkrise 1958–1963* (Munich: Olzog, 2001), pp. 28–40.

202. Trachtenberg, *A Constructed Peace*, p. 221. See also Gossel, 'Zur Innenarchitektur der westlichen Allianz', p. 286; Alistair Horne, *Macmillan: The Official Biography* (New York: Pan Macmillan, 2008).

203. Kitty Newman, *Macmillan, Khrushchev and the Berlin Crisis, 1958–1960* (New York: Routledge, 2007), pp. 63–82.

204. Gearson, *Harold Macmillan*, p. 59.

205. Larres, 'The Politics of Trade', p. 192. See also Klaus Larres, 'Britain and the GDR: Political and Economic Relations, 1949–1989', in Klaus Larres and Elizabeth Meehan (eds), *Uneasy Allies: British–German Relations and European Integration since 1945* (Oxford: Oxford University Press, 2000), pp. 81–2.

206. Gossel, 'Zur Innenarchitektur der westlichen Allianz', p. 286.

207. As part of the preparations for Macmillan's Moscow trip, Jebb had written a paper in January 1959 in which he suggested making an offer to recognise the Oder–Neisse line. Sir G. Jebb,

'Berlin and Germany: A Memorandum', 21 January 1959, NA, FO 371/145818; Hughes, 'Unfinished Business from Potsdam', p. 280. See also Brian White, *Britain, Détente and Changing East–West Relations* (London and New York: Routledge, 1992), p. 79.

208. Timothy J. Botti, *Ace in the Hole: Why the United States Did Not Use Nuclear Weapons in the Cold War, 1945 to 1965* (Westport, CT: Greenwood, 1996), p. 118.

209. Both statements are reported in NA, CAB/128/33, 'Conclusions of a Meeting of the Cabinet held at 10 Downing Street, 28 May 1959'. See also Gearson, *Harold Macmillan*, p. 3.

210. Christian Nuenlist, 'Into the 1960s: NATO's Role in East–West Relations, 1958–1963', in Andreas Wenger, Christian Nuenlist and Anna Locher (eds), *Transforming NATO in the Cold War: Challenges Beyond Deterrence in the 1960s* (London and New York: Routledge, 2007), p. 69; Oliver Bange, *The EEC Crisis of 1963: Kennedy, Macmillan, de Gaulle and Adenauer in Conflict* (London: Macmillan, 2000).

211. David Gowland and Arthur Turner (eds), *Britain and European Integration, 1945–1998: A Documentary History* (London: Routledge, 2000), pp. 39–40. See also Wallace J. Thies, *Why NATO Endures* (New York: Cambridge University Press, 2009), p. 166.

212. Constantine A. Pagedas, *Anglo-American Strategic Relations and the French Problem, 1960–1963: A Troubled Partnership* (London: Frank Cass, 2000), pp. 97–8.

213. Mangold, *Almost Impossible Ally*, p. 120.

214. Press Conference, 25 March 1959, in Charles de Gaulle, *Discours et messages*, 5 vols (Paris: Plon, 1970), vol. 3, pp. 84–5. On de Gaulle's attitude to the German question see Renata Fritsch-Bournazel, 'The French View', in Edwina Moreton (ed.), *East Germany and the Warsaw Alliance: The Politics of Détente* (Boulder, CO: Westview Press, 1979), p. 74. See also Frédéric Bozo, *Two Strategies for Europe: De Gaulle, the United States, and the Atlantic Alliance* (Lanham, MD: Rowman & Littlefield, 2001), p. 32; Frédéric Bozo, *Mitterrand, the End of the Cold War, and German Unification* (New York: Berghahn Books, 2009), p. xxii.

215. 'Remarks of the Secretary, Opening Session, Western European Chiefs of Mission Meting', Paris, 9 May 1958; NA, RG 59, Lot 64, D 199. See also Box 137, John Foster Dulles Papers, Mudd Library, Princeton University, Princeton. Quoted in Gossel, *Briten, Deutsche und Europa*, p. 170 and Frank Costigliola, 'An "Arm around the Shoulder": The United States, NATO and German

Reunification, 1989–90', *Contemporary European History*, vol. 3, no. 1, March 1994, p. 93, fn. 20.

216. *FRUS, 1958–60*, vol. 8, *Berlin Crisis, 1958–1959*, doc. no. 133, pp. 266–9.
217. Report by President Eisenhower to the American People, on Security in the Free World, 16 March 1959. *Documents on Germany, 1944–1959*, p. 408.
218. Quoted in Newman, *Macmillan*, p. 177.
219. Mangold, *Almost Impossible Ally*, p. 135. See also Michael R. Beschloss, *Mayday: Eisenhower, Khrushchev, and the U-2 Affair* (New York: Harper & Row, 1986).
220. William R. Smyser, *From Yalta to Berlin: The Cold War Struggle over Germany* (New York: St. Martin's Press, 1999), p. 151.
221. Joost Kleuters, *Reunification in West German Party Politics from Westbindung to Ostpolitik* (Basingstoke: Palgrave Macmillan, 2012), pp. 89–106. See also Arne Hofmann, *The Emergence of Détente in Europe: Brandt, Kennedy and the Formation of Ostpolitik* (New York: Routledge, 2007).
222. John C. Ausland to Mr. Hillenbrand, 'Discontent in East Germany', 18 July 1961. Burr (ed.), *The Berlin Crisis 1958–1962*, National Security Archive Electronic Briefing Book No. 354, The National Security Archive, available at <http://nsarchive.gwu.edu/NSAEBB/NSAEBB354> (last accessed 28 September 2016).
223. State Department cable to Bonn Embassy, 22 July 1961. Burr, National Security Archive Electronic Briefing Book No. 354.
224. Caccia to Macmillan, 7 July 1961, NA, PREM 11/3616. See also William R. Smyser, *Kennedy and the Berlin Wall: 'A Hell of a Lot Better than a War'* (Lanham, MD: Rowman & Littlefield, 2009), pp. 60–1. See also Jack Cunningham, *Nuclear Sharing and Nuclear Crises: A Study in Anglo-American Relations, 1957–1963*, PhD dissertation (University of Toronto, 2010), p. 195.
225. Kori Schake, 'A Broader Range of Choice? U.S. Policy in the 1958 and 1961 Berlin Crises', in John Gearson and Kori Schake (eds), *The Berlin Wall Crisis: Perspectives on Cold War Alliances* (Houndmills: Palgrave Macmillan, 2002), pp. 22–42. See also Allen, *The Oder–Neisse Line*, p. 242.
226. *The Public Papers of the Presidents of the United States* (hereafter *Public Papers*): *John F. Kennedy, 1961* (Washington, DC: Government Printing Office, 1962), pp. 533–40. See also Nuenlist, 'Into the 1960s', p. 77.
227. Bonn Embassy Airgram A-135 to State Department, 3 August 1961, Limited Official Use. Burr, National Security Archive Electronic Briefing Book No. 354. See also Smyser, *From Yalta to Berlin*, p. 157.

228. Moscow Embassy Cable 258 to Department of State, 24 July 1961, Secret, Source: RG 59, Decimal Files 1960–1963, 762.00/7-2461 (from microfilm).
229. Fabian Rueger, *Kennedy, Adenauer and the Making of the Berlin Wall, 1958–1961*, PhD dissertation (Stanford University, 2011), pp. 199–200.
230. On the inter-German dynamics leading to the construction of the Wall see Patrick Major, *Behind the Berlin Wall: East Germany and the Frontiers of Power* (Oxford: Oxford University Press, 2009).
231. Memorandum of conversation, 'Secretary's Meeting with European Ambassadors', Paris, 9 August 1961. *FRUS, 1961–63*, vol. 14, *Berlin Crisis, 1961–1962*, doc. no. 102, p. 319.
232. State Department cable 340 to Embassy Bonn, 13 August 1961, unclassified, in Burr, National Security Archive Electronic Briefing Book No. 354. See also Minutes of the Berlin Steering Group, *FRUS, 1961–63*, vol. 14, 15 August 1961, p. 334. See also Schake, 'A Broader Range of Choice?', pp. 22–42.
233. Bonn Embassy cable 354 to State Department, 17 August 1961, in Burr, National Security Archive Electronic Briefing Book No. 354.
234. Central Intelligence Agency, Office of Current Intelligence, 'Current Intelligence Weekly Summary', 17 August 1961, secret, excised and incomplete copy, in Burr, National Security Archive Electronic Briefing Book No. 354.
235. Mary N. Hampton, *The Wilsonian Impulse: U.S. Foreign Policy, the Alliance, and German Unification* (New York: Praeger, 1996), p. 74; Hanrieder, *Germany, America, Europe*, pp. 161–2.
236. Douglas-Home memorandum, 'Berlin', 26 July 1961, C(61)116, NA, CAB 129/106. See also Cunningham, *Nuclear Sharing*, p. 195.
237. Quoted in Smyser, *From Yalta to Berlin*, p. 163.
238. Gearson, *Harold Macmillan*, pp. 2–3. See also John P. S. Gearson, 'Britain and the Berlin Wall Crisis 1959–1962', in John Gearson and Kori Schake (eds), *The Berlin Wall Crisis: Perspectives on Cold War Alliances* (Houndmills: Palgrave Macmillan, 2002), pp. 43–72.
239. Harold Macmillan, *Pointing the Way, 1959–1961* (London: Harper & Row, 1972), p. 408. See also Hoff, *Großbritannien und die DDR*, p. 237.
240. Allen, *The Oder–Neisse Line*, p. 241.
241. Allen, *The Oder–Neisse Line*, pp. 239–43 (quotations on pp. 239, 243).
242. Allen, *The Oder–Neisse Line*, p. 255.
243. Ronald J. Granieri, 'Political Parties and German–American Relations: Politics beyond the Water's Edge', in Detlef Junker,

Philipp Gassert, Wilfried Mausbach and David B. Morris (eds), *The United States and Germany in the Era of the Cold War, 1945–1990: A Handbook. Vol. 1, 1945–1968* (Washington, DC: Cambridge University Press, 2004), p. 146. See also Hofmann, *The Emergence of Détente*, p. 154.

244. William I. Hitchcock, 'The Marshall Plan and the Creation of the West', in Melvyn P. Leffler and Odd Arne Westad (eds), *The Cambridge History of the Cold War. Vol. 1: Origins* (Cambridge: Cambridge University Press, 2010), p. 163.

245. Hubert Zimmermann, *Money and Security: Troops, Monetary Policy and West Germany's Relations with the United States and Britain, 1950–1971* (Washington, DC: German Historical Institute and Cambridge: Cambridge University Press, 2002), p. 42.

246. Sabine Lee, *Victory in Europe? Britain and Germany since 1945* (Harlow: Longman, 2001), pp. 118–19; Hughes, *Harold Wilson's Cold War*, p. 100.

247. Quoted in Baylis, *Anglo-American Relations since 1939*, p. 129.

248. Quoted in Mangold, *Almost Impossible Ally*, p. 186.

249. Andrew Holt, *The Foreign Policy of the Douglas-Home Government: Britain, the United States and the End of Empire* (Basingstoke: Palgrave Macmillan, 2014), p. 3.

250. Quoted in Holt, *The Foreign Policy*, p. 23.

251. Stephan Kieninger, *Dynamic Détente: The United States and Europe, 1964–1975* (Lanham, MD: Lexington, 2016), p. 26.

252. The bloc of expellees and of those of deprived of rights (*Bund der Heimatvertriebenen und Entrechteten*) had been established in 1950 as a national political party, voicing the interests of the between thirteen and sixteen million ethnic Germans that fled or were expelled from Central and Eastern Europe at the end of the War. In 1957 the party's activity was superseded by the newly established Federation of the Expellees (*Bund der Vertriebenen*). Daniel Levy, 'Integrating Ethnic Germans in West Germany: The Early Postwar Period', in David Rock and Stefan Wolff (eds), *Coming Home to Germany? The Integration of Ethnic Germans from Central and Eastern Europe in the Federal Republic* (New York and Oxford: Berghahn Books, 2002), p. 22.

253. Both quoted in Allen, *The Oder–Neisse Line*, pp. 256, 239.

2 The US, the UK and the German Question from Détente to the Second Cold War (1961–1985)

The special relationship and the Federal Republic's *Ostpolitik* (1961–1973)

'Willy Brandt should be cooled off . . . to slow down the mad race to Moscow'
(Dean Acheson, 10 December 1970)

'What had happened up to now is not dangerous. What the long-term chance may be is another matter'
(Henry Kissinger, 17 December 1970)

The US, the UK and the origins of Bonn's Ostpolitik

This second chapter focuses on Anglo-American approaches to the German question during East–West détente. It first debates the evolution in Anglo-American policies in the context of East–West relations, their encouragement for an evolution in West Germany's attitude to détente, and their reactions to the FRG's *Ostpolitik* and *Deutschlandpolitik* in the late 1960s and early 1970s until the signing in August 1975 of the CSCE Final Act. The chapter argues that, while Washington and London formally maintained a commitment to German unity, during détente an Anglo-American consensus consolidated around the understanding that the country's division would be a long-term feature of East–West relations. It then debates how US and British views of the German question evolved in the second half of the 1970s, following the rapid deterioration in relations with Moscow which was brought about by the Euro-missiles crisis, conflicting approaches to the CSCE third basket and the Soviet invasion of

Afghanistan in December 1979. The chapter concludes that, after a period of tension in US–German relations, which coincided with the presidency of Jimmy Carter in the US and the chancellorship of Helmut Schmidt in the FRG, in the early 1980s Helmut Kohl's commitment to NATO proved a major factor in reassuring Washington.

In the early 1960s the cautious Anglo-American reactions to the Berlin Wall had made it evident that Washington and London saw no immediate urgency in ameliorating the situation in Germany and Berlin. Bonn interpreted allied conduct during the Berlin crisis as proof of a receding Western commitment to German unity. This perception was one of the key factors in prompting an evolution in the Federal government's policy towards the Soviet bloc and the GDR. With Anglo-American policy encouraging more flexibility, in the early 1960s the Federal Republic began a fundamental re-examination of its Eastern policy. While being partly prompted by US and British strategies, this introspection also reflected a growing distrust of Anglo-American motives, as wider sections of the West German political and cultural elite now contemplated alternative routes to unification. Both the White House and Whitehall were aware of this mounting discontent. The Christian Democrats were reluctant to come to terms with Germany's division and the loss of the Eastern territories.

However, West Germany's Social Democrats played a leading role in ushering in a more flexible policy towards the countries of Eastern Europe. Although by the end of the decade the party had embraced NATO membership, its leaders felt betrayed by the West's response to the Berlin Wall. They also remained critical of Adenauer's ostracism of the GDR. In the early 1960s influential members of the Evangelical Church and even officials within the Federal Republic's Foreign Ministry and the Ministry for Intra-German Relations (*Bundesminister für innerdeutsche Beziehungen*) also began voicing the view that the ruling Christian Democratic Party's reunification policy was too rigid.[1] In effect, they were echoing the views long taken by the SPD and now also embraced by sections of the FDP. So a wider consensus began to emerge that in order to break the deadlock, sooner or later Bonn would have to come to terms with the loss of the Eastern territories and the existence of the GDR. Willy Brandt, West Berlin mayor between 1957 and 1966, played a leading role as a Social Democratic leader, advocating alongside NATO membership a new policy towards Eastern Europe to ameliorate the situation of the German nation.[2] Nonetheless, while discontent towards Western inaction was a triggering factor behind Bonn's new Eastern strategy, Anglo-American pressures on the Federal government also contributed to the inception and early developments of a policy, which became known popularly as new Eastern policy or *Neue Ostpolitik*.[3]

Its first steps were taken in the early 1960s, as the CDU reluctantly opted to put the issue of unification on the back burner and seek dialogue with the Soviet bloc. Adenauer resigned in October 1963 and was succeeded by his minister for economics, Ludwig Erhard. The new chancellor and his foreign minister, Gerhard Schröder, initiated a gradual opening to the East, endeavouring to strengthen relations in all areas from trade to sport. However, this policy was not addressed to the GDR. In contrast, Erhard's strategy aimed at exploiting West German financial strength in order to win political concessions from Moscow and its satellites and isolate East Berlin from its allies.[4] Nonetheless, the new cabinet collapsed in November 1966. Its downfall followed a budgetary crisis, which was triggered by Washington's refusal to grant an extension on West German payments for US troops in the FRG.[5] Erhard's resignation paved the way to the creation of the Great Coalition between the Christian Democrats and the Social Democrats. The SPD had made a significant advance in the 1965 Federal elections but failed to obtain a majority in the *Bundestag*.[6] New Chancellor Kurt Georg Kiesinger and Foreign Minister Willy Brandt were now eager to pursue a more dynamic international strategy. They inaugurated a policy of 'building bridges' with the countries of Eastern Europe, which were interested in strengthening political and economic ties with the Federal Republic.[7] The new policy was cheered along by the US and Britain. While resisting Western pressures for recognising the status quo, Erhard had sought America's constant reassurance against Moscow's nuclear and conventional prowess. He and his successor Kiesinger also backtracked away from Adenauer's policy of strengthening ties with de Gaulle's France, which had culminated in the signing of the 1963 Franco-German treaty, to a policy of loyal alliance with the US. The importance of preserving the transatlantic link was now also accepted by the SPD's leadership.[8]

Meanwhile in the US, President Johnson and Secretary of State Rusk had further developed earlier ideas about challenging Soviet domination in Eastern Europe with increased communication and exchanges between East and West. Now convinced that the most appropriate tool in the struggle with the Kremlin would be human contacts of all sorts, culture and, above all, the exchange of information, the president and his secretary of state also proclaimed a policy of bridge-building. With American armed forces bogged down in Vietnam and faced with a growing Soviet nuclear arsenal, following Moscow's efforts to achieve strategic parity in the late 1960s, the White House and the State Department reversed the view that détente would not be possible without progress on the German question. Now progress on the former was seen in Washington as a prerequisite for progress on the latter. In 1964 Johnson, having defeated in the US presidential election Republican candidate Barry Goldwater, who advocated a much more bellicose approach to East–West relations, told Britain's new prime minister, Harold Wilson, that his 'overwhelming interest was to make sure that the Germans did not take us into World War III'.[9]

Washington was eager to search for a lasting détente with Moscow and encouraged Bonn to follow its lead. Between 1964 and 1968 Johnson's strategy of 'building bridges' replaced the static notion of peaceful coexistence with a broader vision of progressive engagement.[10] In 1966, at a time of growing crisis within NATO following de Gaulle's announcement on 7 March that Paris wished to withdraw from the organisation's integrated military command structure, the president made public views that had been discussed privately in Washington for some time. Johnson stated that unification could 'only be accomplished through a growing reconciliation. There is no shortcut.'[11] Evolving US views also affected NATO's strategy. In December the alliance embraced Belgian Foreign Minister Pierre Harmel's proposal of a wide-ranging study of NATO. This study became the centrepiece of Washington's response to de Gaulle's criticism and consolidated Western consensus for a policy of détente with the East. The concluding report, published in December of the following year, identified mutual defence and the promotion of East–West dialogue as the twin pillars of NATO's policy, laying the groundwork for further dialogue between the two blocs and paving the way for the eventual breakthrough of *Ostpolitik* a few years later.[12]

American demands for a multilateral policy of peaceful

engagement with the East and for change in the FRG's policy were expressed through a flexible mix of incentives and pressures. Washington encouraged Bonn to open up its own channels towards the Soviet bloc countries in the belief that Western Europeans, as a result of their geographical proximity and long-established cultural ties, had far more opportunities to expand East–West contact and perforate the Iron Curtain. The British did not oppose US views. If anything, as the next section will show, they facilitated them. As a result, West German *Ostpolitik*, rather than maturing as a mere reaction to Western inertia, became part of a complex process aimed at bringing Bonn's strategy on the German question in tune with Anglo-American calls for greater flexibility when dealing with the East. This was primarily a means of reducing overall tensions and the danger of war, when the West felt more vulnerable than in the past because of Vietnam and the rise in Soviet nuclear capabilities.[13] In the following years the West German government was able to undertake a process of transformation that, while promoting dialogue with Moscow and its satellites, did not call into question relations with the West. As Holger Klitzing puts it, Bonn was prodded to switch 'from trailing behind to driving in the fast lane when it came to seeking rapprochement with the East'.[14]

American reception of Ostpolitik

Kiesinger and even more so Brandt gradually impressed a dynamic turn on Germany's Eastern policy. Whereas during the 1950s and early 1960s the FRG had acted as a stumbling block when the allies tried to identify new avenues towards détente, Bonn now developed an overall strategy aimed at penetrating the Iron Curtain through a policy of peaceful engagement.[15] Nonetheless, such was the degree of transformation in Bonn's Eastern policy that between the late 1960s and early 1970s West German initiatives overcame allied expectations. *Ostpolitik* paralleled but also diverged from the course of East–West and US–Soviet détente. Generally, West Germany's Eastern endeavours elicited similar reactions in Washington and London. However, Anglo-American views were not always identical in the detail. More specifically, *Ostpolitik* triggered mixed feelings, including negative and sometimes differing reactions in the US and Britain.[16] One of the bluntest critics during his office, US National Security Advisor Henry

Kissinger thirty years later referred to the Federal Republic's new Eastern policy as a 'tremendous achievement of Brandt [who] dared to raise the question of German national interests, attempted to relate them and indeed succeeded in relating them to the common interests of the West'.[17]

While Britain slowly saw potential in Bonn's new Eastern policy, US decision-makers gradually grew uneasy at West German undertakings, fearing that the Federal government might endanger Western interests. In the late 1960s dynamics in Vietnam remained the main concern for the US government. Vietnam was also regarded in Washington as a test of Soviet goodwill for the prosecution of a policy of détente. In August 1964 both Houses of Congress had passed with near unanimity the Tonkin Gulf resolution, giving implicit authorisation to the administration for the use of force in South East Asia without a formal declaration of war. In March 1965 Johnson's decision to meet the North Vietnamese challenge with guns blazing prompted the beginning of a sustained aerial bombardment campaign under the code-name Operation Rolling Thunder.[18] However, its limited effectiveness against the North Vietnamese forces and impact on the civilian population rapidly fuelled opposition to the War. The chair of the Senate Foreign Relations Committee and Arkansas Senator Fulbright, and senators Wayne Morse of Oregon, Ernest Gruening of Alaska and Robert Kennedy of New York all raised question about US goals and the conduct of the War.[19] Vice President Humphrey had been an early opponent of protracted American participation to the War, and in 1965 had publicly pushed for a political solution to the conflict.[20] In the following years, although publicly supporting Johnson, the former senator from Minnesota continued to have lingering doubts about the effectiveness of the US war effort. In the spring of 1968, with the aerial campaign having neither forced North Vietnam to the negotiating table nor inflicted much strategic damage, he strongly advised a halt in the bombing. Following Johnson's announcement in March not to seek re-election and the assassination of Robert Kennedy in June 1968, Humphrey became the frontrunner Democratic candidate for the presidency. In his address at the Democratic National Convention in Chicago in August 1968 he stated a willingness to continue a policy of engagement with the East, remarking:

in Eastern Europe, as elsewhere, the old era will surely end and, there, as here, a new day will dawn. And to speed this day, we must go far beyond where we've been, beyond containment to communication, beyond differences to dialogue, beyond fear to hope.[21]

In the Republican camp too there was widespread support for the continuation of a policy of détente. In his presidential nomination acceptance speech on 8 August Richard Nixon had stated that after an era of confrontation, the time had come for an era of negotiation. The Republican candidate had suggested that there was no acceptable alternative to a diplomatic solution to the East–West stalemate.[22] Nonetheless, following his election in November Nixon embraced a more cautious approach to East–West relations. The new president and his national security advisor, Henry Kissinger, feared the erosion of America's strength and had a more static view of East–West détente than the previous administration. After Brandt became chancellor in October 1969 at the head of a coalition between the Social Democrats and the Free Democrats, Kissinger confirmed to the Social Democratic leader's spokesman and Foreign Policy Advisor Egon Bahr overall American support for *Ostpolitik*, stating that Washington would 'deal with Germany as a partner, not a client'.[23] However, Washington rapidly became worried about the prospect of an inversion of global arrangements. The US government now viewed *Ostpolitik* as a policy that was full of risks. As the FRG became the trigger and the political weight capable of tipping the balance of East–West relations from confrontation into an 'era of negotiation', the White House reacted to *Ostpolitik* with an ambiguous 'mix of encouragement, tolerance, suspicion, and jealousy'.[24] US reservations about Bonn's Eastern policy were the consequence of three main dynamics: first, a degree of incomprehension of the Federal government's long-term objectives; second, a structural difficulty in adjusting US–West German relations to the new realities of international politics that had been brought about by détente; and third, US uneasiness at dealing with the new Social Democratic leadership in Bonn.[25]

While Johnson had contemplated engagement as a strategy towards peaceful change, Nixon's efforts focused on stabilising East–West relations and mitigating the consequences of the conflict in Vietnam. The president and his national security advisor tended to see the search for a smoother cohabitation

between the two blocs in Europe as part of a broader redefinition of relations with Moscow, were unwilling to expand trade
with the East and endeavoured to restore US nuclear superiority.[26] In contrast, Bonn's strategy was aimed at undermining the
Iron Curtain through reconciliation with the East. Nixon and
Kissinger did not subscribe to the ideas at the heart of Brandt's
transformation policy; they merely tolerated them. Generally,
these initiatives elicited positive reactions in Washington. The US
government believed that the FRG's Eastern policy could help
stability in East–West relations, while contributing to containing
congressional pressure for unilateral reductions in the number of
American troops on the continent.[27] However, the White House
lacked confidence in some of the Federal government's members,
gradually grew uneasy at West German undertakings and became
worried about the prospect of an inversion of global arrangements. Nonetheless, the Nixon administration, as a result of
the State Department's benign views on West German conduct,
did not try to hinder *Ostpolitik*. A number of US officials, such
as Undersecretary of State and later Secretary of Defense Elliot
Richardson, the director of the State Department's European
Bureau Martin Hillebrand and the deputy chief of the US mission
to NATO and later head of the US delegation to the CSCE,
George S. Vest, saw potential in Bonn's transformation strategy. Together with the West Germans they continued to pursue
Johnson's transformation approach, endeavouring to reconcile
American interests with Bonn's strategy.

   However, US perspectives on *Ostpolitik* differed from those
of the Federal government and, to a certain extent, those of the
United Kingdom. American concerns focused on three main issues:
the impact of *Ostpolitik* on East–West relations, unification and
the question of Berlin. Unlike West German and British decision-
makers, the Nixon administration tended to see the search for
a smoother cohabitation between the two blocs in Europe as
part of a broader redefinition of relations with the Soviet Union,
which also embraced the Middle East, South East Asia and negotiations on strategic arms, following the opening of the Strategic
Arms Limitation Talks (SALT) in Helsinki in November 1969.
There was considerable concern in Washington about the possible
repercussions that developments in Germany and Europe might
have on these other areas. More specifically, the White House
was worried about the side effects of *Ostpolitik* that, although

not reflecting the Federal government's intentions, might have damaged American interests outside Europe. Furthermore, US negotiators did not want to be pushed by Bonn to make hasty and unreturned concessions to the Russians for the sake of Germany and Berlin.

Kissinger acknowledged the importance of maintaining an amicable working relationship with the Federal government. However, he also assumed that Moscow would not be forthcoming in its responses. In contrast, Brandt's strategy was aimed at transforming the Federal Republic into a magnet for the countries of Central and Eastern Europe; the problem for US decision-makers, as Kissinger put it, was to understand 'which side of the dividing line would in fact be the magnet'. Nixon's national security advisor regarded *Ostpolitik* and the attempts by other European allies to promote their own détente with Moscow as late manifestations of European nationalism and feared that Bonn's Eastern policy might develop into a new form of appeasement.[28] Ultimately, the US government was aware that Bonn's initiatives could not endanger American leadership. However, West German strategy would have to be constrained when it threatened Washington's bargaining position with Moscow. Kissinger's greater insight and general knowledge of German affairs and Nixon's thinking in relation to the German question ran more or less parallel. Kissinger reinforced the president's stereotypes about the SPD in Bonn. Nonetheless, he also tempered Nixon's concerns when it came to shaping the official American position towards *Ostpolitik*. Nixon believed that any Soviet gains should have been matched by 'something appropriate' in the wider field of bargaining with the Kremlin.[29] However, on occasion the White House took a much more diffident approach, disliked the independence and confidence displayed by Bonn, and feared that the Federal government's strategy of reconciliation with the East might undermine quadripartite rights and responsibilities and unwittingly precipitate a *Pax Sovietica* in the whole of Europe. Washington perceived an inherent contradiction, not to say a latent incompatibility, between Germany's intensifying Eastern focus and its commitment to the West, and worried about the prospect of a further erosion of Western unity. The US government's latent concern was that, in the search for breakthroughs towards unification, the Federal Republic might embrace the path that France had traced in 1966 and withdraw from NATO's military structure.

The White House found ways to make its misgivings heard without being publicly implicated. However, statements that the German question was for the Germans to decide were undermined by the frenzy of American demands for close consultation, which reflected the fear that Bonn's initiatives might be detrimental to US interests. These concerns also influenced the Nixon administration's views about Brandt's inter-German policy. The US administration wanted to restructure the global balance of power and did not desire any alteration to the status quo in Germany in the short term. Nixon did not expect an immediate breakthrough towards unification.[30] However, in 1970, after East German crowds had given a warm reception to Brandt, who was travelling through GDR territory for a meeting in the town of Erfurt with the SED leadership, Nixon emphatically stated that the chancellor had 'scare[d] hell out of the Soviets'.[31] Nevertheless, following the signing of the treaties of Moscow and Warsaw in August and December 1970 respectively, while welcoming West German recognition of the Oder–Neisse line and reconciliation with Poland, the White House felt that the prospects for unification were limited. Many in the Pentagon also had deep reservations towards the ultimate success of Bonn's Eastern policy. Defense Secretary Melvin Laird believed that sections of the West German Social Democrats might harbour 'illusions about the Soviet Union'.[32] Although the Federal Republic's main negotiator, Egon Bahr, had direct and unique back-channel access to Kissinger, the US government resented the fact that it was not Washington ushering in a serious détente initiative but rather a European ally.[33]

Nonetheless, US perceptions of West German strategy were not monolithic. The State Department's views continued to be more benign and less suspicious than those prevailing in the White House and the Pentagon. US diplomats generally speaking continued to see more benefits to *Ostpolitik*.[34] The State Department took a favourable stand toward Bonn's Eastern policy without ignoring, however, its potential pitfalls and dangers. Officials at the German desk viewed the prospect that *Ostpolitik* might weaken Bonn's ties with the West as extremely 'remote'.[35] The Intelligence and Research Unit called Bonn's Eastern policy 'a boon to NATO' and expected the alliance's cohesion to benefit from it.[36] Nonetheless, the US consul general in Munich remarked in Washington with bitterness that the Federal government had taken the initiative in European East–West relations, when Nixon and Kissinger had little to show for it in terms of Vietnam, China or superpower relations.[37] Ultimately, the White House was sceptical of Bonn's ability to bring about noticeable improvements in the Berlin situation and did not share the Federal government's positive assessment of the Berlin talks. Despite Brandt's efforts to coordinate *Ostpolitik* with Washington, the new cabinet in Bonn was perceived in the White House as overeager for a quick and superficial agreement on Berlin. US interests required that free access to Western sectors not be undercut, as the viability of West Berlin symbolised the credibility of the American commitment to Western Europe's defence.

There was also widespread scepticism in the US about Soviet demands for a European Security Conference (ESC). The Nixon administration feared that, despite the linkage established by the allies between a quadripartite agreement on Berlin and an ESC, the West would be able to extract only minimal concessions from the Kremlin. Furthermore, both Nixon and Kissinger were concerned that Moscow might use the increased European interest in dealing more independently with the USSR to split off the allies from each other.[38] Occasionally, West German reactions to American concerns further contributed to exacerbating tension. In December 1970 during a visit to Washington the head of the Chancellor's Office, Horst Ehmke, tried to convince the Nixon administration of the need to accelerate the rhythm of quadripartite negotiations in order to avoid 'a new Berlin crisis'. Ehmke stated that the Federal government was ready to undertake negotiations on Berlin with the GDR without receiving a formal authorisation from the quadripartite talks. These kinds of statement contributed to increasing US concerns that Bonn was not adequately coordinating policy with its allies; Kissinger's cool reply was that 'the Germans could not jeopardise our interests in Europe without jeopardising their own'.[39]

Ostpolitik elicited conflicting reactions in Congress also. In the Senate Foreign Relations Committee a number of senators, such as Hubert Humphrey, Mike Mansfield and Edmund Muskie, tended to perceive the FRG's Eastern policy favourably and hoped that its success would make possible a reduction in the number of American troops in Europe.[40] In contrast, Democratic congressman and chairman of the Internal Security Committee, Richard H. Ichord, as well as Republican senators Strom Thurmond and Jacob Javits, manifested significant concern about the impact of

Ostpolitik on US interests. They feared a sell-out of Western positions and resented the fact that Washington was being put under pressure by one of its more politically dependent allies.[41]

Britain, détente and Ostpolitik

In Britain, after the Labour Party's return to power in 1964 with a slim majority of four seats, there was strong support for continuing the policy of détente. New Prime Minister Harold Wilson continued the approach of his Conservative predecessors to East–West relations. London sought improved relations with the Soviet Union in the belief that Whitehall could act as a 'go-between' for Washington and Moscow.[42] Nonetheless, there was significant strain in Anglo-American relations, caused to a large extent by disagreements over the US war effort in Vietnam, Britain's economic crisis and Johnson's low esteem of Wilson. The Labour leader was a keen advocate of close Anglo-American ties. Wilson firmly supported the notion of a special relationship between London and Washington and hoped that a strong bond with the Americans would preserve Britain's seat at the 'top table' of world politics, while enhancing his own standing as a statesman. At the same time, he was an early supporter of a policy of 'building bridges' with the Soviet Union and wanted to use his relationship with the White House to strengthen his credentials as a middleman between the two superpowers. At the Commonwealth Prime Ministers' Conference in June 1965 Britain's prime minister endorsed a peace plan for Vietnam. While a number of former British possessions opposed US policy, both Australia and New Zealand had troops in Vietnam. As a member of SEATO, London was also partly responsible for South Vietnamese security. Nonetheless, the British feared the repercussions of the War on the unity of the Commonwealth at a time when London was embroiled in a struggle over the future of Rhodesia and in the middle of a new balance of payments crisis. Wilson's attempt was viewed with circumspection in Washington. What the Americans wanted was not a peace initiative but a contribution to the military effort in Vietnam. Furthermore, London's peace endeavours were disregarded by the USSR, China and North Vietnam, the governments of which believed that the British were too connected to US strategy.[43] Faced with the hesitancy of some Commonwealth members, American reluctance for a pause in military operations and opposition from the communist camp, Whitehall later shelved the initiative, insisting that there could be no meaningful negotiations until there was a ceasefire by the Vietcong guerrillas.[44] Ultimately, Wilson's efforts yielded no lasting results.

In the following years, London sought US support for the pound in return for Britain's commitment to preserving a meaningful international role. The Labour cabinet maintained military bases in Malaysia, Borneo and Singapore and increased the number of British troops in southern Asia in response to the confrontation between Indonesia and the federation of Malaysia. The same approach was followed for British forces that were stationed in Germany as part of the British Army of the Rhine (BAOR). The White Paper on defence, issued in February 1966, stated that Britain should 'maintain . . . forces in Germany at about their existing level until satisfactory arms control arrangements have been agreed in Europe'.[45] However, Wilson continued to keep Britain out of the Vietnam conflict, much to the disquiet of the Americans. Johnson was enraged that Whitehall could not even send 'a platoon of bagpipers', while Secretary of State Dean Rusk threatened that Britain should not expect any US assistance in the future. At some point he even stated, 'they can invade Sussex and we wouldn't do a damn thing about it'.[46] Secretary of Defense McNamara was also disappointed by London's conduct and at one time remarked that Whitehall should send troops to Vietnam as part of 'the unwritten terms of the special relationship'.[47]

Nonetheless, US remonstrations did not prompt Britain to reconsider its stance on Vietnam. After the prime minister's trip to the Soviet capital in February 1966, in June Whitehall publicly dissociated itself from the US bombing of Hanoi and Haiphong. In a further visit to Moscow in July Wilson impressed on the Soviet premier, Alexei Kosygin, the danger of further escalation of the War, endeavouring to resume the 1954 Geneva Conference.[48] In February 1967 Kosygin returned the visit to the United Kingdom. The Soviet premier's trip to Britain was a public relations success, prompting the beginning of negotiations for an Anglo-Soviet treaty of friendship.[49] Nonetheless, hopes that Whitehall and the Kremlin might broker a ceasefire in Vietnam were dashed by American lack of sympathy for London's initiatives and by an increasingly tense relationship between Johnson and Wilson.[50] Although the Labour government provided diplomatic support to the US, London's mediatory efforts met with limited consensus from the White House and were also disregarded by the Soviet leadership.

Wilson's peace initiatives in Vietnam proved to be a major incident in the history of Anglo-American relations.[51] While for Whitehall a historic opportunity to improve East–West relations had been missed, the Americans attributed questionable motives to the British, were reluctant to give London power of attorney in dealing with the Kremlin and viewed Wilson's zeal as embarrassing for Washington.[52] Although Wilson was a great personal admirer of Johnson and the White House did not try to hinder British mediatory efforts, the US president did not feel much enthusiasm for London's initiatives, viewed with circumspection the idea of a special Anglo-American relationship and at times could not conceal his disdain for the Labour leader.[53] Relations between the White House and Whitehall soured dramatically in the later years of Johnson's presidency, leading the US ambassador to London, David Bruce, to remark in 1967 that the 'so-called Anglo-American special relationship' had become 'little more than sentimental terminology'.[54]

Nonetheless, persistent economic difficulties prompted the British to continue a policy of détente. In January 1968 Wilson visited Moscow for his third visit in his first premiership. The visit was preceded by the announcement of a drastic reduction in defence expenditure. The cuts included the termination by December 1971 of the withdrawal of British forces from east of Suez, an operation that was initially planned for completion by the mid-1970s.[55] The new round of talks with the Soviet leadership focused on the Vietnamese and Middle Eastern crises but also included bilateral issues, such as trade and technology.[56] The Kremlin was aware of Britain's economic troubles, which had been exposed by the pound's devaluation in November 1967. Now, the Soviet leaders endeavoured to drive a wedge between Britain and its allies. They suggested that the USSR could increase its exports to the United Kingdom in order to free London from its excessive dependence on the United States. Soviet officials also warned Wilson of the threat of West German revanchism.[57]

Britain's attempt to bolster dialogue with Moscow was source of concern for the Americans and the West Germans. The Federal government was particularly suspicious of Whitehall's ambition to reach a friendship treaty with Moscow. Bonn feared that London might discount Washington's warnings about Soviet attempts to divide the alliance and prompt the British to change their position on the German question. The issues of West German adhesion to the nuclear Non-Proliferation Treaty (NPT) and the offset payments for the BAOR further strained Anglo-German relations.[58] In the late 1960s the British Labour government strenuously advocated West German adhesion to the NPT as a step to improve relations with the East.[59] This was a view also held by the Americans, who considered the FRG's adhesion to the NPT as a precondition for change in Germany's image in Eastern Europe. However, the West Germans reacted with caution to Britain's advice, fearing that London wanted to use the NPT as a lever to perpetuate control over the FRG.[60] A few months earlier, with the British armed forces facing conflict in Borneo and South Arabia, following the peak of the nationalist insurgency in Aden, Britain's only Crown Colony in the Middle East, Whitehall had threatened to reduce the number of forces deployed in the FRG in the event of an unsatisfactory solution to the offset question, causing alarm in Washington.[61] Nonetheless, Wilson's Moscow visit was perceived in the alliance as a sterile affair. The Soviet leaders failed to divide the alliance and produce a major breakthrough in British policy towards Germany. The draft friendship treaty prepared by the Kremlin demanded London's endorsement of Moscow's views on the German question and Foreign Office officials regarded it as completely unacceptable. Furthermore, dynamics in Vietnam rapidly deprived Britain's mediatory endeavours of any significance: for example, the beginning of the Tet offensive by the North Vietnamese at the end of January 1968. With Johnson announcing in March that he would not stand for re-election, negotiations for a peace deal were convened in Paris in May between the Americans and the North Vietnamese.[62]

The failure of the Labour cabinet's mediatory campaigns had a lasting impact on British perceptions of East–West relations. By the end of the 1960s, dissatisfied by the manner in which the two superpowers had responded to its initiatives, Whitehall became rather diffident about détente and its implications. London now viewed détente as a Soviet- and American-sponsored idea, which Britain had been forced to embrace as a result of growing popular support and in the hope of convincing Washington not to implement unilateral reductions of its forces in Europe. Since 1966 eminent Democratic senators led by their majority leader, Mike Mansfield, but eventually also Republican congressmen, had complained about the costs of European defence and had begun to introduce legislation calling for substantial reductions in US troop levels in order to redress a growing balance of payments deficit.[63] The White House, fearing that unilateral reductions in US forces might undermine Western defences, pressed its allies to work together and follow its lead in defence planning.

The Warsaw Pact's invasion of Czechoslovakia in August 1968 to crush the Prague Spring temporarily halted calls for bridge-building and quashed the debate about burden-sharing in the US Congress. At the same time, it increased concerns in the FRG and other West European countries, giving Washington much greater leverage over its allies.[64] It also cooled off enthusiasm in Britain for prosecuting a policy of détente with the Kremlin. Moscow's expansionist policy in the Mediterranean, the Middle East and the Indian Ocean fuelled doubts in London about Soviet negotiating will. Professional diplomats were diffident towards Moscow's European ambitions. Some were concerned that, while the immediate Soviet aim was to fix the status quo in Eastern Europe, in the longer term the Kremlin aimed to draw Germany away from the Atlantic Alliance, encouraging the forces of neutralism in Western Europe and weakening the cohesion of the West. A number of British diplomats were troubled by Soviet conduct. After the merger between the Commonwealth Office and the Foreign Office in October 1968 FCO officials opposed unilateral concessions to the Soviets, particularly on Germany.[65]

Nonetheless, London had little appetite for an aggressive stance towards the Russians. While Conservative and Labour leaders drew a comparison between Moscow's action and Germany's aggressive attitude to Czechoslovakia in the late 1930s, Defence Secretary Denis Healey stated privately, 'the Russians used force to maintain the status quo, not to challenge it'.[66] Ultimately, after the Soviet invasion of Czechoslovakia the British continued to support Brandt's initiatives. US concerns about the implications of Bonn's Eastern policy were only partially shared in Whitehall, where *Ostpolitik* was assessed from an inevitably narrower and more benign perspective. London's quest for EEC membership also contributed to a more positive British assessment of Bonn's strategy. West German support was deemed fundamental in Whitehall in order to overcome remaining French resistance after de Gaulle had vetoed Britain's second application in December 1967 on the grounds that the United Kingdom's admission would change the nature of the European Communities and result in the creation of an organisation more akin to a wide Atlantic grouping.[67] In 1967 Lord Chalfont, Minister of State at the Foreign Office, told journalists at the margins of an EFTA summit that London might reconsider its policy of non-recognition of the GDR, if Bonn proved unable to help Britain join the Common Market.[68] In those circumstances Whitehall could hardly afford to voice opposition to the Federal Republic's Eastern policy. Difficulties in the special relationship, particularly over Vietnam and Britain's economic policy, also increased London's interest in strengthening cooperation with the FRG. In September 1968 the FCO's American Department advised Foreign Secretary Michael Stewart that, while Anglo-American relations remained good, by mutual agreement:

> [their] special character is being played down. America continues to support the pound but mainly as the dollar's first line of defence. In view of our reduced world responsibilities and decision to enter the European Economic Community there is a tendency for Americans to write us off and to leave it to us to find a new role in the world.[69]

After the West German Federal elections in October 1969 Wilson sent a personal message to Brandt, asking him to use Bonn's strong position in the EEC to speed up the beginning of negotiations between the six and the United Kingdom.[70]

In the late 1960s the Nixon administration remained on guard against West German initiatives but attitudes in London were much less nervous.[71] By visiting Romania in 1969 and Yugoslavia in 1970 the US president proved that Washington had an interest in the fate of Eastern Europe.[72] However, the US government had not fully grasped the potential of Brandt's transformative strategy. This was the view of Britain's ambassador to Bonn, Roger Jackling. In his correspondence with the FCO Jackling complained that some influential members of the US Congress, and perhaps even some high-ranking figures within the Nixon administration, had not fully realised the significance of *Ostpolitik* and perceived Brandt's policy as clinching a static settlement of the German question, which could be interpreted as the signal for American troop withdrawal from Europe. In contrast, when in January 1970 Nixon asked Wilson whether *Ostpolitik* might erode the FRG's commitment to the Atlantic Alliance, the prime minister replied that he did not 'feel anxious' about Brandt's Eastern policy.[73]

Nonetheless, the British felt that Bonn should not become so committed to progress in negotiations with the Soviet bloc at the price of endangering Western interests. For them, as for the Americans, Berlin was the touchstone of Western policy. Like Washington, London was particularly concerned about the Federal government's eagerness to finalise an agreement with the Soviets on Berlin without having extracted significant concessions from Moscow.[74] More specifically, the British government feared that the Federal Republic might be tempted to discuss with the Soviet Union and the GDR questions affecting Berlin access and inner-Berlin improvements in anticipation of a quadripartite agreement. For Whitehall it was fundamental that the Federal government's conduct did not undercut Western rights on the capital of the former Reich. For this reason, the British expected that issues that were covered in the quadripartite talks should not be addressed by the two German sides until an agreement had been reached between the Four Powers. Ultimately, despite approaching *Ostpolitik* from different standpoints and, as a result, manifesting not always converging perceptions of it, both London and Washington viewed a satisfactory agreement on Berlin as a fundamental prerequisite for supporting Bonn's Eastern policy. They also regarded the conclusion of a quadripartite agreement on Berlin as a precondition for assenting to Moscow's calls for an ESC.[75]

Anglo-American fears of Germany's neutralisation

The signing of the treaties of Moscow and Warsaw in August and December 1970 reduced differences in Anglo-American perceptions of *Ostpolitik*. Bonn's Eastern initiatives now also triggered a degree of anxiety in Whitehall. In the early summer, as contact between Bonn and Moscow intensified, Britain gradually moved closer to US views. The Conservative Party's victory in the June 1970 elections was a first step in this direction. Unlike the previous Labour cabinet, Britain's new Conservative government conceived of détente as a static rather than a dynamic process. President Nixon 'did not conceal his pleasure in private conversation at the conservative victory', feeling that new Prime Minister Edward Heath would be a more natural ally of a Republican administration.[76] Although Heath was determined to secure EEC membership and gave priority to Britain's relationship with Europe over partnership with the US, the slow progress made in negotiations on Berlin and Heath's meeting with Nixon in December 1970 steered Britain's position closer to that of the White House.[77] The change in the British position also reflected the views of several other NATO members about *Ostpolitik*. In Paris, concerns about Germany's Eastern policy helped reduce the gulf opened by de Gaulle in US–French relations. The general's successor, Georges Pompidou, feared the long-term implications of Brandt's policy, including the prospect of a US military withdrawal from Europe.[78] Pompidou was also wary about the implications of *Ostpolitik* on inter-German dynamics and dreaded the emergence of violent reform movements, which might trigger bloodshed and border skirmishes in the GDR.[79]

After the signing of the Treaty of Moscow in August 1970 the British position became more cautious. By then, many of Bonn's Western allies had become concerned about the tempo and tactics of the Federal government in negotiations with the Soviets, particularly on the question of Berlin. In the Foreign Affairs debate of 9 December 1970 Douglas-Home clarified that Britain regarded a Berlin settlement as a basic precondition for participating in an ESC. The foreign secretary declared that it would not be

> much use setting up another body for reconciliation when the opportunity is right there before the Soviet Union, if it wants to take it, to demonstrate that it is willing to ease tension between the Warsaw Pact area and NATO, and particularly in the city of Berlin.[80]

A letter from Brandt to Heath on 15 December 1970 in which, while reassuring the British prime minister that Four Power rights on Germany would not be affected, the chancellor proposed to give the Berlin negotiations a conference character caused anxiety in Whitehall.[81] During his visit to the US from 16 to 18 December 1970, ten days following the signing of the Treaty of Warsaw between the FRG and Poland, Heath held talks with the president and other senior figures of the American political establishment. Britain's prime minister complained about the West German government's 'growing disposition' to overlook its original commitment to making ratification of the Treaty of Moscow conditional upon the conclusion of a satisfactory agreement on Berlin and asked whether Bonn was perhaps going 'too far and too fast' in its desire to normalise relations with the Soviet Union.[82] The British prime minister also suggested that the chancellor's proposal to give the Berlin negotiations 'a conference-like character' would simply provide the Kremlin with an opportunity to step up pressure on the West.[83] Heath's words reinforced Nixon's belief that the Soviets were getting more than they were giving on *Ostpolitik*.[84] The West German ambassador to Washington, Rolf Friedemann Pauls, feared that Britain, together with France, might influence US perceptions of *Ostpolitik* and drag the Americans towards a more sceptical reception of West German initiatives.[85] Although the British often exaggerated their actual influence on Washington, to a certain extent Whitehall was able to influence American views.[86]

Nonetheless, reactions in the US continued to outweigh Anglo-French concerns. In December 1970 a number of former American officials, including many who had played a central role in the FRG's establishment, such as former State Secretary Dean Acheson, US Military Governor in Germany Lucius D. Clay, former US High Commissioner John J. McCloy, former Governor of New York Thomas Dewey and former US Undersecretary of State and Ambassador to the UN George Ball, publicly expressed their concern about the implications of *Ostpolitik*.[87] Whereas Brandt urged the allies to accelerate the pace of negotiations on Berlin, in a press conference held on 9 December Acheson publicly invited the West German chancellor to 'cool down his irresponsible run to Moscow'. An article published in *The Washington Post* attributed to the former US secretary of state statements, such as, 'Willy Brandt should be cooled off . . . to slow down the mad race to Moscow.'[88] On 13 December in a conversation with the FRG's ambassador to Washington, Pauls, Acheson complained that 'both in the treaties of Moscow and Warsaw we only made concessions, without obtaining anything'.[89] Some of these assessments were shared by the administration. The White House was anxious that some of the people who were closest to Brandt were ready to strike a deal with the Soviets regardless of the cost. According to the US president, if Brandt 'sold out so cheaply' to Moscow, the Kremlin's interest in pursuing talks on strategic arms limitation or promoting an ESC would diminish considerably. In his talks with Heath, the US president also suggested that the Soviet Union's ultimate objective was 'the detachment of Germany from NATO'.[90] For this reason, the White House deemed it essential 'to tie Germany into Western Europe in both political and military terms'. According to the president's viewpoint, *Ostpolitik* remained a dangerous affair and the US 'would do nothing to encourage it'.[91] In an article published by *The New York Times* on 11 November 1970 Brandt had reiterated his government's opposition to unilateral reductions in US forces in Europe. However, one of the major sources of Washington's anxiety remained the possibility that Bonn might be tempted to trade improvements in the situation in Germany for the FRG's neutralisation.[92] Nixon was also concerned by the influence of West German domestic dynamics on *Ostpolitik* and believed that the West should be on guard 'against allowing the internal political situation in Germany to dominate the policy of the Atlantic Alliance'.[93] During the meeting with Heath in December National Security Advisor Kissinger summarised the American position in the following terms: 'What had happened up to now is not dangerous. What the long-term chance may be is another matter.'[94] Nonetheless, Kissinger's worry was not so much that Brandt would intentionally destroy the Western alliance; rather, his fears were about what Bonn might unintentionally do.[95]

Anglo-American concerns about *Ostpolitik* reached a peak in the first weeks of 1971. Heath was particularly fearful that the West German interest in accelerating negotiations with the Soviets might put the West under pressure.[96] His concerns were now shared by part of the British diplomatic establishment, which until then had nurtured a more benign view of Bonn's Eastern initiatives. John A. Thomson, minister at the British delegation to NATO, feared that the Federal government might seek 'quick successes in the foreign policy field, possibly without complete regard for the risks involved'.[97] His view was that the improvement in relations with the Soviet Union was being pushed ahead 'with greater urgency than in the past and a greater willingness to take the risk of making unrequited concessions'.[98] Nevertheless, others, particularly the ambassador to Bonn, Roger Jackling, remained supportive of Brandt's initiatives. The ambassador believed that Britain's attitude should have differed from the American stance for at least two main reasons. First, while for the White House the Berlin talks were one of many fronts of dialogue between the two superpowers, for Britain these talks in particular and *Ostpolitik* in general had a much more penetrating impact.

Second, Britain continued to have a general need to maintain the 'best possible relations' with the Federal Republic in order to pursue its European policy.[99] Assistant Undersecretary of State David Bendall also played down US fears about Bonn's policy. He argued that doubts about *Ostpolitik* were the consequence of the administration's lack of confidence in the SPD and some of its members, such as Bahr and the chairman of the parliamentary group, Herbert Wehner. Nonetheless, while appearing in personal commentaries, these doubts were 'in no sense the basis for American policy decisions'.[100]

However, some FCO officials feared that the long-term objectives of the Soviet Union were Germany's neutralisation, Western Europe's 'Finlandisation' and, finally, Western Europe's separation from the US.[101] Others worried that Moscow might secure West German acceptance of the status quo in Eastern Europe without having to give away much in return.[102] These concerns were now reflected by the negative comments in the British press about *Ostpolitik*.[103] In their correspondence with Bonn, the FRG's ambassadors to the US and Britain, Pauls and Karl Günther von Hase, repeatedly emphasised Anglo-American concerns. On 2 January 1971 von Hase remarked that, while London understood Bonn's interest in finding a 'modus vivendi' with the Soviet Union, Whitehall's support for *Ostpolitik* had a clear limit. More specifically, Britain would object to deals that affected the original British rights on Berlin and Germany as a whole.[104]

Political dynamics in the FRG also contributed to increasing British concerns. At the beginning of his chancellorship in October 1969 Brandt had relied on a majority of 254 seats against 242 from the Christian Democratic opposition in the *Bundestag*. However, after the signing of the Treaty of Moscow some of his allies from the Free Democrats had begun to express scepticism about *Ostpolitik*. In October 1970 three FDP members of parliament, Erich Mende, Heinz Starke and Siegfried Zoglmann, had left the party to join the Christian Democrats, reducing the ruling coalition to a slim majority of 251.[105] Discontent within the FDP had boosted the efforts of the CDU's leader Rainer Barzel to unseat Brandt. At the same time, it fuelled concern in London that the Federal government might for domestic political reasons become content with a fast, but in substance unsatisfactory, solution for Berlin with considerable damage to Western interests.[106]

The special relationship, the GDR and the CSCE

'An excess of "realism" about accepting the division of Germany will enable the Soviet Union to shift the responsibility for thwarting unification on us'
(Henry Kissinger, July 1959)

'The West may have to acquiesce in the division of Germany but it cannot condone it'
(Henry Kissinger, July 1959)

'In American eyes the German lift going up may . . . sooner or later pass the British lift coming down'
(Julian Bullard, 23 September 1976)

Anglo-American relations, the GDR and the Helsinki Conference

During the late 1960s and early 1970s Anglo-American relations were often fraught with divergences. However, opinions about Germany were not so far apart. Furthermore, elements of the special relationship, particularly those related to intelligence and nuclear cooperation, persisted outside wider political difficulties. Bilateral channels of communication were continually used by the US, particularly by Kissinger, as a means of convincing London to follow more amenable policies. While there were many similarities in Anglo-American views about *Ostpolitik*, these views were not identical, but by the end of January 1971 many of Washington's concerns were shared in London. However, these apprehensions did not provoke open opposition to *Ostpolitik*. To a certain extent Nixon resented the fact that Brandt had taken the lead in negotiations with the East, but the US government did not try to hinder West German initiatives. Rather, the Americans were anxious to oversee the overall evolution of East–West relations and to retain a final say on the German question.[107] The White House entertained no illusions about the chances of unification. Nevertheless, its position remained one of prudent support for the Federal government. As early as 1959 Kissinger had summarised the US's views in the following terms: 'The West may have to acquiesce in the division of Germany but it cannot condone it.'[108] The president's national security advisor stood firm against recognising the GDR before Bonn was ready to establish diplomatic relations with East Berlin, fearing that any hasty American move towards the East German leadership would elicit serious disillusionment in the FRG.

In early 1971 Bonn intensified efforts to reassure the Western allies about its Eastern policy. In January the FRG's foreign minister, Walter Scheel, remarked that the 'West must not be and must not seem to be in a hurry' in the Berlin talks. In a conversation with the US ambassador to Bonn, Kenneth Rush, on 20 January Scheel clearly stated that the Soviet Union 'should not be given the slightest encouragement to believe it possible to divide the allies'.[109] In his annual report on the state of the nation on 28 January Brandt underlined the complementary nature between the development of peaceful and constructive relations with the East and the FRG's loyalty to NATO. Nonetheless, the Christian Democrats remained critical of the FRG's Eastern policy. On the following day CDU member Kurt Birrenbach, the party's foreign policy expert and one of Barzel's closest advisors, accused the chancellor of having reached through the Treaty of Moscow the main decisions of a peace treaty, without involving the Western allies in the negotiations. These decisions entailed the ultimate acceptance of Germany's division and of the Brezhnev doctrine of limited sovereignty, which asserted Moscow's right to intervene militarily in the Eastern bloc's member states.[110] Furthermore, according to Birrenbach, *Ostpolitik* was loosening the link between Bonn and the West in favour of an imaginary Pan-European order. The CDU's *Bundestag* member explicitly referred to the concerns that this policy had caused in the US and to the discussions held in December between Acheson, Clay, McCloy, Dewey and Nixon.[111]

Washington and London continued to encourage Bonn to engage in full and timely consultation. The American attitude remained one of watchful waiting. In January 1972, when Brandt thanked Nixon for his support, the US president plainly replied that his policy was not to support but, merely, not to oppose *Ostpolitik*.[112] The administration was preoccupied with Vietnam and pursued a generalised policy of linkage as a precondition for progress in East–West relations.[113] The White House refused to go ahead with full-blown détente with Moscow until it had secured a satisfactory settlement for Vietnam and a quadripartite deal on Berlin.[114] Despite Whitehall's increasing concerns, FCO officials continued to play an important role in defusing tension between Bonn and Washington. London strongly encouraged the Federal government to make timely and full use of the inter-allied working group in Bonn, which served as a consultative forum between the three Western powers and the FRG. Whitehall also insisted that Four Power negotiations be given priority above discussions between the two German states.

Nonetheless, linkage was also in the interests of the West German government. Brandt had an eroding majority in the *Bundestag*. He needed a satisfactory Berlin settlement in order to obtain ratification of the treaties of Moscow and Warsaw. The links established in early 1971 by the FRG and its Western allies between ratification of the Eastern treaties, an agreement on Berlin and the beginning of preparatory talks for an ESC had contributed to allaying Anglo-American concerns that the Kremlin might take advantage of *Ostpolitik* in order to divide the alliance.[115] During Scheel's visit to London on 4 and 5 February 1971, Foreign Secretary Alec Douglas-Home praised the Federal government's linkage policy, emphasising that the Federal Republic's effort to bring about flexibility in the rigidity of East–West relations was of great value. [116]

On the issue of an ESC there was no fundamental Anglo-American friction. Both Washington and London were not in principle against an adequately prepared ESC.[117] However, the White House and Whitehall were more cautious about West German proposals to reduce military forces in Europe. The US government's priority was that American forces should not be reduced unilaterally. Nixon and Kissinger were much less enthusiastic than the West Germans about negotiations on conventional armaments and feared isolationist tendencies in the US. In May 1971 the administration faced the impending success of the Mansfield Amendment in Congress. The proposal of the Democratic majority leader from Montana foresaw a reduction in American forces in Europe by a half. Its implementation would have led to the withdrawal of 150,000 US soldiers, causing serious damage to NATO and raising fears of Europe's Vietnamisation.[118] Washington rejected unilateral troop cuts, discouraged West German enthusiasm and was determined to retain control of negotiations on Mutual and Balanced Force Reductions (MBFR) in order to contain congressional pressure. London shared this approach and insisted that on the issue of conventional forces clarification and coordination of Western objectives should take priority over negotiations with the Soviet bloc.[119]

The successful conclusion of a quadripartite agreement on Berlin in September 1971, confirming Four Power rights on Germany, further allayed Anglo-American concerns. At the same time, it postponed to an indefinite future any discussion about unification. Following the signing of the Basic Treaty between the two German states in December 1972 and the opening of the CSCE in Helsinki on 3 July 1973 German unity dropped further in Anglo-American priorities. While Whitehall became absorbed by the practical consequences of membership of the European Communities, American attention shifted towards strategic arms negotiations with the Kremlin and attempts to bring hostilities in Vietnam to an end. A new North Vietnamese offensive in the spring of 1972 and Nixon's visits to the People's Republic of China and to the Soviet Union, in February and May respectively, preceded the signing of the Paris agreements in January 1973, ending direct US military involvement in Vietnam. Nonetheless, if linkage had worked in Europe, it failed to produce the desired results in Asia. Coordination of West German and Anglo-American strategies had secured the success of *Ostpolitik* and of a transatlantic strategy of multilateral linkage in Europe. In contrast, in Asia Washington was unable to induce the Soviets to terminate their assistance to the North Vietnamese and continued to suffer severe setbacks in Vietnam, where the War raged on despite the departure of American troops.[120] The normalisation of relations between the two German states did not imply Bonn's final acceptance of Germany's division, however. In the Basic Treaty the FRG and the GDR did not establish embassies and agreed to exchange permanent representatives rather than ambassadors. For both sides this arrangement avoided the appearance of official, diplomatic recognition of the other German state.[121] Nonetheless, the treaty marked Bonn's abandonment of its claim to the exclusive representation of the German people. It also deprived the unification issue of any immediate significance. One of its direct consequences was to make it possible for the two German states to join the UN in September 1973.

The agreement between Bonn and East Berlin also prompted a reassessment of Anglo-American strategies towards the GDR. Inevitably, this reconsideration of policy occurred in Britain with much greater urgency than in the US. Since the late 1950s London had entertained mild trade links with East Germany, while British unions and members of Britain's peace movement had endeavoured to develop cultural relations with some sectors of East German society. Nonetheless, until the late 1960s Whitehall's temptation to establish closer links with East Berlin had been restrained by the fear of West German and American reactions. Whereas Britain had often been tempted to expand commercial relations with East Berlin, London had continued to prioritise ties with the FRG. Prevailing representations of East Germany in Britain remained overwhelmingly negative. Furthermore, the erection of the Berlin Wall in 1961 had undercut support for a normalisation of relations, delegitimising the arguments of British left-wing intellectuals and academics, such as Gordon Schaffer and Sir Eric Hobsbawm, that the East German state represented a truly peaceful alternative to any reconstituted militarism in the FRG.[122] Following the signing of the Basic Treaty in 1972, any ambition to expand trade links with the GDR was cooled by Britain's increasing commerce within the European Community.[123] Nonetheless, while political relations remained minimal, by the end of the decade Britain had become East Berlin's second largest trading partner in the West behind the Federal Republic. Ultimately, the British, together with the French, had moved quickly to formalise official ties with the GDR, establishing diplomatic relations in early February 1973.[124] Nonetheless, even after the return to power of the Labour Party in 1974 Whitehall avoided any step that could irritate West German susceptibility. In the same year Foreign Secretary James Callaghan turned down an invitation to visit East Berlin, pending the release of two British citizens who had been imprisoned in the GDR, accused of providing assistance to East German defectors trying to flee to the West.[125]

Relations between Washington and East Berlin followed an even more tortuous path. Until the early 1970s official interaction between the US and the GDR had been scarce. On all matters relating to Berlin, Washington dealt with the Soviet Union. In the American strategy East Germany was largely viewed, when considered at all, through the prism of the political discourse in the Federal Republic. Scant official interest was also a consequence of the lack of public debate: there was, of course, no East German ethnic constituency in the US, while the GDR's image as a very orthodox, almost dogmatic communist country with Prussian-style socialism evoked little enthusiasm across the

Atlantic.[126] In 1972 Washington was still against East Germany's admission to the UN; as Bahr had told SED's new general secretary, Erich Honecker, the Americans were 'more rigidly opposed' to East German membership of the UN than any other NATO state.[127] While Britain, together with France, had moved quickly to formalise official ties with the GDR, Washington avoided any appearance of haste with East Berlin so as not to provoke West German susceptibility. Nixon wanted the State Department to defer negotiations until the *Bundestag*'s ratification of the Basic Treaty.[128] After making initial contacts at the UN in New York in January 1973, followed up in East Berlin in August 1973 and March 1974, Washington delayed an agreement to exchange ambassadors until September 1974. East German obstruction of transit traffic to West Berlin and its refusal to acknowledge compensation requests by American citizens for confiscated properties and persecutions suffered under the Nazi dictatorship were also sources of tension.[129] On 20 December 1974 Republican Senator John Sherman Cooper presented his credentials as first American ambassador to the GDR, but relations between Washington and East Berlin continued to stagnate in the following years.

Only in the second half of the 1970s did a number of factors combine to bring about a partial reassessment of US–East German ties. First, Bonn no longer feared an enhancement of East Berlin's international prestige. Second, Washington now acknowledged the GDR's increasing political and economic influence within the Soviet bloc. Third, the US started believing that, as a consequence of its increasing economic influence and political stature, the GDR would be able to make its views and concerns heard in Moscow 'instead of simply parroting the Soviet line on all issues'.[130] After East German leaders were confronted by the FRG's endeavours for maintaining the unity of the German nation at Helsinki, they responded by trying to boost East Germany's international prestige. Following the end of the CSCE conference in August 1975 Washington started to consult directly with East Berlin about the implementation of the human rights provisions in the Helsinki Final Act's third basket. The intensification in US–East German dialogue was a consequence of the West's strategy of linkage, which had tied recognition of existing borders to a commitment to respecting basic human and civil rights, including the right to free movement, freedom of information, family reunification and visits. The SED leadership believed that it could handle expanding contacts between the two German states through an increase in the surveillance and policy activity of the Ministry for State Security: the infamous Stasi.[131] Nonetheless, the relative internal stability and international prestige that the regime had achieved in the mid-1970s began to dissipate by the end of the decade. The GDR's political decline was the consequence of a deepening economic and social crisis, which had been triggered by the rise in oil prices, economic recession and increasing East–West contacts.

Economic and political difficulties quickly affected East Germany's relations with the US. In the late 1970s East Berlin grew wary of American efforts to encourage a more liberal domestic climate, fearing that Western ideas and West German visitors could infiltrate the GDR with Western ideology and undermine the socialist system. The SED leadership now feared external political interference and responded by intensifying its policy of demarcation – *Abgrenzung* – to limit interaction with capitalist societies.[132] Furthermore, as the internal economic situation continued to deteriorate, East Berlin embraced a number of repressive measures, such as new restrictions for foreign journalists and a revision of the Penal Code. The new legislation was designed to crack down on political dissidents, root out Western influence and pre-empt the emergence of serious unrest.[133] In the following years sharp disagreements on the implementation of the CSCE conference's third basket and the GDR's declining capacity to trade with the West further burdened US–East German relations. By the end of the decade American distaste for East German leaders and East Berlin's diffidence towards US policies had brought the relationship between Washington and East Berlin to a near standstill.[134]

Washington, Bonn and Britain's economic crisis

In the first half of the 1970s, parallel to the development of *Ostpolitik*, economic and financial issues gained increasing prominence in Anglo-American relations with the Federal Republic. The collapse of the Bretton Woods monetary system in 1971 and the effects of the 1973 oil crisis, following the embargo declared by the Arab members of the Organization of Petroleum Exporting Countries (OPEC), were the cause of widespread uncertainty in the West. Subsequent economic stagnation and financial concerns rapidly took priority away from the issue of Germany's division. Political dynamics in the FRG and the US also contributed to slowing down the prospect of further progress on the German question. Brandt resigned in May 1974 over accusations that one of his personal assistants, Günther Guillaume, was a spy for the GDR. Nixon left the presidency over the Watergate scandal in August 1974 and was replaced by his deputy, Gerald R. Ford. Following the conclusion of the CSCE conference in August 1975 the German question continued to drop in Anglo-American priorities.[135] The Helsinki Final Act left open the prospect of a peaceful change in the European borders and, hence, of unification. Nonetheless, now the West somehow formally acknowledged that there would be no unification without the Kremlin's consent. Furthermore, after the CSCE's conclusion, Washington and London rapidly became distracted by other and more pressing issues, which had no immediate relation to the situation in Germany.

In Britain economic recession, which had been complicated by the dollar's devaluation in 1971 and had resulted in a significant contraction of the country's gross domestic product, rather than foreign policy took priority. Indeed, the US continued to focus on East–West relations and Asia at the expense of the special relationship. The deepening of bilateral diplomacy with Moscow, re-engagement with the People's Republic of China and the administration's Vietnam strategy had been largely decided without involving the British.[136] The special relationship was affected by these dynamics. For London it remained natural that wider security issues had to be dealt with in close association with Washington. Nonetheless, on a number of issues Anglo-American approaches clashed. The White House and Whitehall viewed the conflict in the Middle East through different prisms. During the 1973 Yom Kippur War there was Anglo-American tension over London's refusal to grant the Americans access to British airbases in Cyprus, ceasefire negotiations and the US airlift to Israel.[137] In addition, the conflict between India and Pakistan over East Bengal in 1971 triggered conflicting Anglo-American reactions. While the US viewed the War as an act of Indian aggression on Moscow's instigation, London initially tried to mediate between Islamabad and New Delhi. The British refuted any involvement, much to the displeasure of the Americans, who openly came out in support of Pakistan. In an interview twenty years later Heath asserted that Nixon and Kissinger had tried to get Britain involved in the War, just as in the 1960s Kennedy and Johnson had tried to involve London in Vietnam. Britain's former prime minister stated, 'there was the question of the Indo-Pakistan war and what Henry wanted was to land us in that and I was determined not to be landed'.[138]

These tensions reflected a temporary shift in Anglo-American priorities away from the special relationship. While the Nixon administration endeavoured to scale down US global commitments without impairing Western defences, in the early 1970s relations with the EEC took priority for London at the expense of those with Washington. Heath referred to Britain's ties with the US as a 'natural' rather than a 'special' relationship, implicitly denying that their character had anything special beyond historical and cultural similarities. The prime minister strengthened relations with Bonn, continuing to seek West German support for Britain's EEC application.[139] Relations with France also improved. Paris now looked at British membership as a counterweight to the prospect that the FRG might come to dominate the policy of the European Communities.[140]

Nonetheless, the election in 1974 of Valéry Giscard d'Estaing to the French presidency ushered in a period of cordiality in the FRG's relations with France, with positive repercussions for West Germany's European role. Bonn had responded more efficiently than its European partners to the economic crisis, playing an important role in the setting up of the European Monetary System (EMS) and in the process of stabilising former dictatorships in southern Europe.[141] In order to make its strong economic position more tolerable for its partners, the Federal government was willing to appear as the 'paymaster of Europe'. Bonn had become an attractive economic partner for the Soviet Union and also an economic force to be reckoned with for Washington: the West German share of world trade almost matched that of the US and would not be overtaken by that of Japan until the late 1970s. In 1975 German investments in the US exceeded for the first time American investments in the FRG. However, a number of areas of friction persisted in relations between West Germany and the US. They were a consequence of a deteriorating economic situation in Washington and of Bonn's endeavour to preserve amicable ties with Moscow, despite a gradual return of tension in East–West relations. Public opinion in the FRG was frustrated by the presence of American forces and their regular exercises; it was far less convinced that military strength was important for West

German security, and believed that Bonn might negotiate its way out of any crisis.[142] In contrast, the US was angered by the FRG's autonomous conduct and deepening ties with the East.

US irritation with Bonn was part of a wider feeling of frustration with Europe. Washington complained that its allies were reluctant to increase defence spending and promote a stronger European pillar within the alliance. This feeling had been exposed by the enunciation of the Nixon doctrine in 1969. During a press conference in Guam the US president had stated that, although respecting its security commitments, in future Washington would delegate to the allies the main responsibility for raising manpower.[143] A number of American congressmen also continued to demand a reduction in conventional commitments in Europe. In the early 1970s Democratic Senators Sam Nunn and Henry M. Jackson resurrected the Mansfield tradition, increasing pressure on the allies to provide offset payments for the maintenance of US troops.[144] In late September 1973 the US Congress passed overwhelmingly the Jackson–Nunn Amendment to the Defence Appropriation Acts, formalising a link between the maintenance of US forces at current levels and a resolution of Washington's balance of payments problems. The amendment established that American support troops should be reduced by the same percentage that Washington's allies failed to fully offset the US military balance of payments deficit in Europe. However, in order not to undermine Western defences, it also allowed for reductions in American forces to be filled by new combat units.[145]

Nonetheless, even at the height of *Ostpolitik*, neither Washington nor Bonn was willing to let economic disputes overshadow political relations. In order to assuage European fears, Secretary of Defense James R. Schlesinger promptly announced the deployment to Europe of two active brigades to enhance the fighting abilities of NATO forces.[146] Furthermore, a consolidated budgetary stability allowed the Federal government to comply with the Jackson–Nunn requirements and avoid the troop-cut provision invoked by Congress. Despite an overall economic downturn in Europe, which had been augmented by the effects of the 1973 Yom Kippur War and the resulting energy crisis, West Germany's international stature and prestige continued to increase. Having carved for itself the role of 'paymaster' of the European Communities, the Federal government now tried to break the impasse between the US and its European allies.[147]

Although there was widespread scepticism in Bonn about fundamental American intentions, Brandt had been the first European
head of government to discuss Kissinger's 'year of Europe'
proposal during a visit to Washington.[148] Furthermore, while
Heath had prioritised relations with the EEC to the detriment
of the special relationship, Brandt's successor Helmut Schmidt
was determined to reinforce cooperation with the US. The new
Federal chancellor belonged to the right wing of the SPD and was
perceived in Washington as a firm ally of the United States. Close
personal ties between Schmidt and Ford contributed to further
increasing Bonn's status in transatlantic power hierarchies.[149] In
August 1974 Schmidt was defined by White House officials as
'our strongest ally in Europe'.[150]

At a time when Britain's entry into the European Communities
decreased its strategic importance for the Federal Republic,
Bonn's increasing international stature produced contrasting feelings in the United Kingdom. Although Heath 'had showed no
desire to rock the Anglo-American boat', he had given priority to cementing Britain's ties with Europe, often against the
advice of his foreign secretary, Douglas-Home, who had been
reluctant to endanger relations with the Americans.[151] In 1973
Whitehall had been unable to coordinate a shared response with
the White House to the Arab oil boycott. Although the prime
minister had been willing to sacrifice European solidarity at the
1974 Washington Energy Conference, at the end of his cabinet
the special relationship appeared worn out.[152] As a means of
persuading London into taking a more amenable line, Kissinger
suspended nuclear and intelligence collaboration with the British.
Nonetheless, Washington's coercive diplomacy achieved mixed
results, particularly after the return of Labour to power at the
head of a minority government following the general elections
of February 1974 and Heath's failure to form a coalition cabinet
with the Liberals.[153] Having returned to lead the country after
a four-week miners' strike, which had seen coal production
come to a complete standstill and precipitated the elections in
February, Wilson's priority was to settle Britain's industrial problems, including a dramatic inflationary rise as a result of the
rising cost of oil. New elections in October resulted in a narrow
victory for his party. The Labour cabinet now endeavoured to
revive the special relationship and returned to a more comfortable
Anglo-American routine. Former Chancellor of the Exchequer

James Callaghan, who was appreciated in Washington for his pro-Atlantic and pro-NATO views, became foreign secretary.[154]

Nonetheless, Whitehall's attempt to resuscitate the special relationship occurred at a time of profound transformation for the American role in the world. Following the US exit from Vietnam, Washington was far more interested in superpower dialogue on strategic arms limitations than in reviving bilateral ties with Britain.[155] During the Ford administration the special relationship was superseded by a significantly less privileged state of complex interdependence within the Western alliance. West German interests and policies gradually took on greater relevance for Washington. Initially, closer US–West German ties were judged positively in London in the belief that they would strengthen the American commitment to Europe and contribute to reinforcing the FRG's Atlantic loyalty. British decision-makers dismissed the risk that the special relationship might suffer as a result of closer US–West German relations and that the United Kingdom might be marginalised by an emerging Bonn–Washington axis. Despite its growing international influence, the FRG remained loath to embrace a more assertive international profile. Furthermore, for a number of reasons Britain remained the most reliable ally of the US in Europe. First, the Federal Republic's outlook remained predominantly, if not exclusively, European; this contrasted with a global outlook, which Britain alone shared with Washington. Second, not being a nuclear power, Bonn lacked London's understanding of the strategic nuclear problems faced by the US. Third, the Federal Republic's military contribution outside of NATO was still fairly negligible; in contrast, despite recent defence cuts, Britain could offer the Americans unique assistance, particularly in the field of maritime warfare, on extra-European theatres.[156]

Nonetheless, Britain's persistent economic problems continued to harm London's standing within the alliance and limit its ability to influence US policy. The Labour government started one of the most encompassing reviews of defence ever undertaken by a British cabinet in time of peace. Defence spending over the next decade would be held steady. However, Whitehall made it clear that the drastic cuts in the British military presence east of Suez signalled in the defence White Papers of 1966 and 1971 would continue. Remaining troops in Singapore and Malaysia would also be withdrawn by April 1976 and the British presence in Hong Kong and Cyprus would be reduced. Furthermore, London would not commit forces to NATO in the Mediterranean, to the dismay of US military planners.[157] The cuts in the defence budget further increased the need for cooperation with the US. They also led to a reorientation of British policy towards France. While Heath had regarded nuclear cooperation with Paris as part of a strategy for dealing with wider issues of European defence and foreign policy, Wilson showed renewed interest in negotiations with France as a gateway to promoting trilateral cooperation with the US. Nonetheless, nuclear talks between London and Paris remained a sensitive subject. This was a consequence of Washington's concerns about unauthorised transfer of US nuclear secrets to the French and of West German fears that Anglo-French cooperation could become the precursor to a bilateral nuclear pact.[158]

As London retreated from an enduring military world role, following Wilson's resignation in March in 1976 Prime Minister James Callaghan was forced to call in the International Monetary Fund (IMF) to rescue Britain's ailing economy. Whitehall applied for a loan of nearly US$4 billion, which resulted in deep cuts in public expenditure, greatly affecting the country's economy and social policy.[159] Washington and Bonn used Britain's economic travails to force London to implement major domestic economic and fiscal changes.[160] The British were disappointed by America's disinclination to soften the terms of the IMF loan. The White House kept a distant attitude during the negotiations. The prevailing opinion in Washington was that the British should tackle their domestic inflation and reduce public expenditure, while during talks with the IMF Callaghan was strongly influenced by his close relationship with Schmidt and, to a degree, Giscard d'Estaing.[161] Nonetheless, the multiple levels of dialogue between Washington and London persisted even at the nadir of the United Kingdom's international strength and Britain continued to exert an influence on US policy which was out of proportion to its objective role in East–West relations, particularly when it came to political and security affairs rather than economics.[162] However, some FCO officials resented the FRG's growing status in the alliance and were aware that British assets in Washington might decline as German assets appreciated. A number of British diplomats questioned whether 'in American eyes the German lift going up may not sooner or later pass the British lift coming down'. Whitehall never endeavoured to sabotage West German–American relations. However, there was concern in the FCO that a situation in which the German voice carried more weight in the White House could in the long run also have negative implications for the way in which London carried out quadripartite responsibilities in Berlin.[163]

The US, the UK, the German question and the second Cold War

'For all that separates us, we have one planet, and Europe is our common home, not a theatre of operations'
(Mikhail Gorbachev, 18 December 1984)

The decline of East–West détente

In the second half of the 1970s important differences emerged between the White House and the Federal government, as East–West relations rapidly deteriorated. The crisis and decline of détente were the result of the interplay of a number of dynamics, which heightened tensions between the two superpowers. They included a discrepancy in expectations on both sides of the Iron Curtain about a continuation of détente, the moral turn that was pressed on US foreign policy by a new incumbent Democratic administration and the massive military build-up of Soviet forces.[164] Moscow applied a muscular turn to its foreign policy, which led to renewed confrontation between the two blocs in Europe and in the Third World. The crisis of East–West détente also affected transatlantic relations and the Anglo-American special relationship. With American distrust of Soviet intentions increasing, Britain gradually regained a degree of influence over US strategy towards Germany. After Jimmy Carter took office in 1977, the White House hardened its stance towards the Kremlin. At the same time, Washington manifested uneasiness at its European allies' endeavours to appease the Russians and preserve profitable relations with Moscow. Germany was a major source of concern for the new administration. While advocating a strong and more united Europe to share the defence burden, the US government resented the Federal Republic's increasing international assertiveness and was particularly wary of Bonn's deepening ties with the East. This tension reflected the fact that

Washington and Bonn entertained different expectations about a continuation of East–West détente and relations with the USSR.

US–West German relations were now burdened by conflicting approaches to a number of issues, including human rights, the neutron bomb and the Soviet invasion of Afghanistan. Poor personal relations between Carter and Schmidt augmented the deterioration in bilateral relations: the West German chancellor held an undisguised low personal opinion of the US president and was concerned about the new Democratic administration's global strategy.[165] The Federal government was particularly annoyed by the White House's attitude towards a number of issues that affected West German interests, such as human rights; non-proliferation, which affected Germany's nuclear exports to the Third World, particularly to India, Pakistan, Argentina and South Africa; and American pressures on Bonn to accept greater responsibility in the defence field than the FRG as a non-nuclear power felt able to bear, especially over tactical nuclear forces. Bonn's increasing displeasure with Washington's economic and monetary policy also posed a further strain on US–West German relations. Recurring attempts by the Federal Reserve, particularly throughout 1978, to persuade the *Bundesbank* to appreciate the German mark exacerbated tension. The prevailing tendency in Bonn became to see a number of American decisions as manifestations of erratic and unilateral US leadership and failure to consult with the European allies. Furthermore, the Federal government felt that there was no influential figure in the administration that understood West German concerns or their preoccupations, while there were some that intentionally misunderstood Bonn's intentions and conduct.[166]

The overall effect of these dynamics was to cause considerable tension in US–West German relations in the second half of the 1970s. Bilateral differences were particularly evident in contrasting approaches to a continuation of détente. The changing attitude towards East–West relations in the United States contributed to further complicating the relationship. American public opinion was growing increasingly critical of détente, particularly of arms control and disarmament policies that West German decision-makers associated with progress in relations between the two blocs and the two German states. Changing public expectations made the White House wary of a rising domestic backlash against détente. The administration now emphasised democratisation and human rights as important prerequisites for measuring progress in the Soviet bloc and as strategic tools to weaken Moscow. In contrast, the Federal government sought to promote intensified human, economic and political contacts across the East–West divide with the aim of bringing about closer relations in the divided German nation.[167] While not questioning Western solidarity, Bonn aimed to sustain East–West détente, as it had been codified by the NATO allies through the 1967 Harmel Report, and to keep it centred on European or German interests, regardless of developments outside Europe. In 1977 Schmidt even suggested to Carter that he should be appointed as the US president's secret intermediary between Washington and Moscow to make the West more responsive to Soviet détente initiatives.[168] Differences were particularly marked on the modalities of pressuring the Kremlin into implementing the CSCE's third basket, which had tied the West's recognition of the European status quo to Moscow's respect for human and civil rights, including the right to free movement, freedom of information, family reunification and visits. In May 1976 the US Congress, under pressure from different ethnic constituencies, passed legislation that established the Commission on Security and Cooperation in Europe. In the following years this body pursued an activist agenda, monitoring the compliance of signatory states with the third basket's provisions of the Helsinki Final Act.[169]

Bonn was particularly worried by the Carter administration's aggressive approach to human rights. The Federal government feared the implications of American policy on the continuation of the Helsinki process. At the 1977 CSCE follow-up conference in Belgrade the West Germans refused to criticise the Soviets too harshly on the implementation of third basket measures, fearing that an excessively critical approach might jeopardise recently achieved improvements.[170] The Federal government was also irritated by the activity of the US-backed Radio Free Europe and Radio Liberty, which operated from Munich. Although Bonn shelved a confrontation with the US government over the radio stations' presence in the FRG, Schmidt viewed the anti-communist broadcasters as a Cold War relic and feared that their endeavours might undermine détente.[171] By the end of the 1970s the Carter administration continued to regard West Germany as one of the most important American allies on the continent. Nonetheless, a good deal of disenchantment had emerged in Washington towards Bonn's Eastern policy. Some in the US had not overcome their long-term suspicion of the West German Social Democrats. Although following the elections of October 1976 Schmidt had removed Bahr from the post of minister of economic cooperation and development, the left wing of the party was critical of the chancellor's balanced foreign policy, emphasised disarmament and called for a reinvigoration of *Ostpolitik*.[172] These views were perceived in the US as dangerous and detrimental to the interests of the Western alliance in a phase of renewed East–West tension. Washington also feared that the Federal government was conducting secret negotiations with the Soviet Union with the objective of bringing about the melting away of the border between the two German states or the FRG's neutralisation. The US government was particularly alarmed by the prospect that the Social Democrats could gain an absolute majority in the 1980 Federal elections and that the leader of the Free Democrats, Hans-Dietrich Genscher, might be replaced by Bahr at the head of the West German Foreign Ministry.

US concerns that Bonn's endeavours to preserve an amicable relationship with Moscow might undermine the FRG's commitment to NATO had little resonance in Britain. The White House's increasing anxieties about Germany were only partially shared in Whitehall. London believed that the Federal Republic had limited room for manoeuvre and discounted the notion that Moscow would be prepared to relinquish any significant degree of control over the GDR. Britain consistently supported the Helsinki process and pressed East Berlin to make improvements in human rights issues. However, in 1975 Wilson resumed the practice of visiting Moscow. His much-publicised trip to the Soviet capital resulted in the signing of a protocol on regular political consultation and of a ten-year agreement on industrial and political cooperation. Callaghan, like his predecessor, also sought to play a constructive role in East–West relations.[173] Anglo-American differences were particularly evident in their conflicting approaches to the implementation of the third basket of the Helsinki agreements. On this issue, unlike the Americans, Whitehall opted to exercise a low-key, cautious approach.[174] At the 1977 CSCE follow-up conference in Belgrade British representatives eschewed criticism of Soviet policies, fearing that an excessive emphasis on human rights and change in Eastern Europe might obstruct progress at state level. Rather than embarking on a loud campaign of denunciation,

London entertained limited expectations about fast additional progress in East–West relations. Hence, the British endeavoured to maintain a balance between the elements of confrontation and cooperation with the Soviet bloc.[175] In May 1977, confronted by Washington's aggressive stance, Callaghan remarked that Whitehall distinguished 'between support for human rights and support for human beings who used human rights to change their regime'.[176]

Britain's professional diplomats, unlike their US counterparts, did not question the Federal government's commitment to the alliance and the European Community. According to their viewpoint, there would be no or little incentive for West German decision-makers to be more forthcoming towards the Russians apart from seeking important but modest benefits in inter-German relations, a peaceful and quiet situation in Berlin, profitable economic links and somewhat warmer political relations.[177] Until the late 1970s this also remained the prevailing opinion in Whitehall. Writing to Carter in June, a few months before the beginning of the Belgrade conference, Callaghan advised the US president to win back the West German chancellor, remarking, 'Helmut is a strong Atlanticist, moody and tempestuous, but basically on the side of the angels.' Nonetheless, this approach confirmed that Britain had not fully grasped the implications of Bonn's Eastern policy and its transformative impact on the Soviet bloc. London's reaction was particularly slow in the field of human and civil rights, at a time when the formulation of US policy on these issues was shifting away from the State Department to Carter's national security advisor, Zbigniew Brzezinski. The newly established Commission on Security and Cooperation in Europe and the confrontational posture embraced by the former American ambassador to the UN and head of the US delegation to Belgrade, Arthur Goldberg, often overlooked London's expectations. The end result of these dynamics was the failure of Callaghan's attempts to mediate between Bonn and Washington on human rights issues.[178]

The Euro-Missiles debate and US–West German tension

In the second half of the 1970s the deterioration in East–West relations accelerated rapidly. Disputes about the application of the Helsinki agreements' third basket, Soviet penetration in Angola and Ethiopia, and Moscow's deployment of the new intermediate range SS-20 missiles and of the medium-range Backfire bomber in Eastern Europe brought superpower détente to an end. Growing East–West tension also affected dynamics within the Western alliance. First, it rekindled anxieties about Soviet intentions on both sides of the Atlantic. Second, in Europe it fuelled fears of a decoupling in transatlantic policies. Relations between Washington and Bonn experienced deepening strains, which were a consequence of different strategic priorities and approaches to relations with Moscow. Faced with deteriorating East–West relations, the FRG now demanded adequate security guarantees from the US. However, Bonn was also determined to continue détente. As relations between the blocs speedily deteriorated, the Federal government pursued a 'realistic détente policy', making ongoing engagement with the Soviet bloc conditional upon a reinvigoration of Western deterrence and defences. Schmidt attempted to keep the Americans, the Soviets and the SPD's left wing happy. His main concern became to bolster Western defences, while safeguarding the benefits derived from détente, such as an increase in East–West trade, a calm situation in Berlin, further development of relations with the GDR and closer links with the countries of Eastern Europe. However, Bonn was disappointed by the US response.[179]

While ties between Bonn and Washington were strained by different strategic priorities, Anglo-German relations were not affected by the rise in East–West tension. Britain's Labour cabinet, although endeavouring to revive the special relationship, maintained a good working relationship with the Federal government.[180] Callaghan's pragmatism contributed to the good state of Anglo-German relations, playing an important role in prompting decision-makers in Washington and Bonn to a more realistic assessment of their relations with Moscow. London was the site chosen by the West German chancellor to express the FRG's concerns about Europe's deteriorating security environment and appeal for a renewal of Washington's commitment to the defence of its allies. In October 1977, after having raised the issue at the NATO meeting of heads of state and government that had been held in the British capital in May, Schmidt delivered a fervent speech at the International Institute for Strategic Studies. The speech was the climax of a campaign the chancellor had been conducting since 1975, following Moscow's obtainment of strategic parity with Washington, under pressure from his defence advisors and West German conservatives, to convince the US to include Soviet theatre nuclear forces in the negotiations for a second SALT agreement. Schmidt's appeal also reflected his government's growing concern at the Soviet Union's deployment of new Intermediate-Range Ballistic Missiles (IRBMs) in Eastern Europe in March 1976.

The SS-20s were deployed by Moscow in Europe and Asia as additional weaponry to an already extended Soviet IRBM force. Their presence fuelled a sense of vulnerability in Washington's NATO allies, which were not defended by a comparable system.[181] In London Schmidt lamented a lack of American responsiveness to the Soviet deployment of the SS-20s. He stressed that the administration's concern to reduce the strategic threat to American territory and reluctance to contemplate an adequate response in Europe had created a crisis of credibility for the alliance, which needed to be addressed promptly. Ultimately, the chancellor called for NATO to maintain 'the balance of full deterrence strategy' or a 'Euro-strategic parity'.[182] The speech revealed the tension in US and West German approaches to NATO's nuclear strategy. The White House's problematic handling of the neutron bomb issue also contributed to augmenting US–West German friction. Although excluding the use of German territory as a deployment site, between 1977 and 1978 Schmidt invested considerable political capital in raising domestic support for the weapon. By the spring of 1978 the chancellor had succeeded in obtaining the SPD's assent before the White House decided to backtrack. Bonn felt betrayed and aggrieved by the administration's failure to produce the bomb. *The New York Times*' announcement in April 1978 that the White House had abandoned the project, without even informing the Federal government, left the chancellor isolated within his own party, exposing the widening gulf between Washington and Bonn.[183]

The administration was initially reluctant to contemplate new nuclear weapons in Europe, given the presence of US bombers in Britain and the increased number of submarine-based warheads allotted to NATO.[184] However, Schmidt's speech, exposing concerns that were shared by other European allies, prodded the Americans to consider nuclear force modernisation and redress the imbalance in European security. Schmidt's appeal triggered the process that began at NATO's meeting in Washington at the end of May 1978 and led in January 1979 to the adoption of the 'dual-track' decision at the Guadalupe summit of the US, British, French and FRG heads of state.[185] The agreement reached on the Caribbean island committed the allies to deploying a new generation of American missiles in Western Europe, but also to exploring the prospects of an agreement with the Soviet Union. Bonn's stance during the ensuing debate confirmed that, while the Federal government worried about Moscow's intentions, the West Germans were also anxious not to endanger the improvements brought about by détente, particularly in the framework of the CSCE and its follow-up process. While the chancellor endeavoured to harmonise domestic tensions in the FRG, the debate reverberated powerfully within the alliance. Bonn now feared that the Federal Republic might become the only non-nuclear host country for the American missiles and demanded that other NATO members also clarify their readiness to deploy. In December 1979 at a special meeting of foreign and defence ministers in Brussels the alliance confirmed the decision to deploy a force of 572 missiles in Western Europe, but also to offer negotiations to Moscow.[186]

Schmidt's appeal to the Americans also confirmed the soundness of British assessments about Bonn's commitment to NATO. A few weeks before the speech Britain's Defence Secretary Fred Mulley had made a rearmament plea in a letter to his US counterpart, Harold Brown.[187] While maintaining close ties with Bonn, Whitehall continued to view the special relationship as overwhelmingly important. Callaghan privileged close cooperation with Washington, deepening nuclear cooperation with the Americans. He also endeavoured to mediate between the White House and Bonn, establishing himself as a favourite with President Carter and senior members of the administration.[188] Nonetheless, despite Callaghan's mediatory efforts and NATO's endorsement of the dual-track decision, the decline in US–German relations continued to accelerate in the second half of 1979. The sources of tension between Washington and Bonn were a sense of declining American power and Western military vulnerability, the FRG's growing assertion of its political interests and the deepening of Franco-German ties within the European Communities, particularly after the creation of the European Council (EC) in 1975, and the close friendship that developed between Giscard d'Estaing and Schmidt.[189] Whereas the Federal authorities feared a decoupling of the US from Europe, Washington was concerned that, after having regained economic prowess and political standing, the Germans might be once again set on a dangerous course of their own. In contrast, Bonn viewed things through a different prism and believed that East–West negotiations should ease the burden of Germany's division. American conduct in relations with Moscow was a persistent source of concern and irritation for the West German government. The Carter administration's preference for bilateral disarmament with the Kremlin in the field of strategic arms caused serious friction with Bonn. The Federal government felt that US initiatives were not matched by adequate attempts at improving political relations between the two blocs. Schmidt was particularly alarmed by the US tendency to overlook the views of its West European allies and Bonn's interest in keeping East–West relations focused on the German question. Angered by American disregard for West German views, the chancellor once told Giscard d'Estaing that the 'Americans need to stop believing that they just have to whistle for us to obey'.[190] Hence, the president's moves towards Moscow were constantly met with demands from Bonn that European and German interests should also be taken into account.[191]

The Soviet invasion of Afghanistan

The beginning of the Soviet invasion of Afghanistan on 24 December 1979 complicated matters even further and placed an additional strain on relations between the US and the FRG. The Carter administration was outraged. Its reaction to the Soviet action prompted the final episode in a long list of strategic divergences between Washington and Bonn. The US believed that Soviet conduct posed a threat to neighbouring states, such as Pakistan, but also to Turkey within NATO. Furthermore, the administration already faced deteriorating security in the Persian Gulf region as a result of the Iranian revolution and was under increasing criticism at home for its moderate stance towards the hostage crisis in Tehran. The White House was determined to convey to the world its moral outrage at the invasion and promptly took a series of steps designed to punish the Soviets and protect crucial American interests, sending aid to the Afghan resistance and drastically curtailing East–West cooperation.[192] Washington expected an equivalent determination by the European allies. This expectation was made even more compelling by the fact that the Americans had been disappointed by Europe's response to the Iranian crisis. West Germany had been reluctant to adopt political and economic sanctions against Tehran; the British, after some initial resistance, had bent under pressure.[193] Nonetheless, a poignant 14 November 1979 column by James Reston, *The New York Times'* political commentator, opened with the question 'Where are the allies?' and complained about the lack of support by Washington's European partners for the release of US hostages in Iran.[194]

In case of Afghanistan, the US now expected the allies to demonstrate collective solidarity against Moscow's action. However, positions within the administration and within the alliance were mixed. While the president initially rejected the adoption of tougher measures under the advice of Secretary of State Cyrus Vance, National Security Advisor Brzezinski advocated a firm response. He called for immediate counter-measures in other areas of East–West relations, particularly trade and strategic arms negotiations, as a useful tool for punishing the Soviets for their expansionism.[195] After some initial hesitation Washington implemented a punitive strategy of linkage against Moscow. The US expected that the Europeans would adopt analogous measures to deter additional Soviet moves. Nonetheless, initial responses to Washington's demands were lukewarm. Britain, where the Conservative Party had returned to power following Margaret Thatcher's victorious electoral campaign in May, supported American views. London dispatched three warships to the Eastern Mediterranean both to signal displeasure with Soviet conduct and to free US ships for the Indian Ocean, while reinforcing its naval and air facilities on the island of Diego Garcia.[196] Whitehall's decision marked a realignment of Anglo-American strategies in the Indian sub-continent, after Heath had refused to align with the US in the East Bengal crisis in the early 1970s.[197]

Decision-makers in Bonn were reluctant to embrace a confrontational posture and to take steps that could affect relations with the Kremlin. Bonn feared the prospect of negative repercussions on the situation in Germany. Preserving an amicable relationship with Moscow was regarded by the Federal government as a basic prerequisite for gaining a degree influence on the USSR's German policy and for improving the situation in Berlin. There were also pressing economic reasons for the West Germans to avoid the Soviet invasion of Afghanistan precipitating another major crisis in East–West relations. With its vast oil, gas and raw materials reserves and potential market for manufactured goods the Soviet Union remained an attractive commercial partner for Bonn. West German decision-makers benefited from Moscow's appetite for modern Western technology and did not share Washington's concerns about the increased technological exchange between East and West. By maintaining close commercial relations with Moscow, Bonn also managed to secure the immigration of roughly 10,000 ethnic Germans per year from the Soviet Union.[198]

The Federal government's resistance to demands for tougher sanctions and West Germany's economic and commercial ties with Moscow caused disappointment in Washington, raising the question of whether superpower and European détente might be decoupled.[199] A different perception of the long-term impact of closer economic relations between the two blocs contributed to deepening differences between the US and the FRG. While the Americans worried that the Soviets might acquire Western technology, from Schmidt's viewpoint, drawing the Soviet Union out of its economic insularism and meshing it inextricably into the Western economies was in NATO's long-term interest. Having become dependent upon Western knowhow, Moscow would not be willing to face a return to Cold War style confrontation between the two blocs.[200] Furthermore, the Federal government believed that increasing trade between the two halves of Europe might undercut the GDR's industrial strength and political influence within the Soviet bloc, weakening the East German regime. Moscow was aware of tension between the US and the FRG and conflicting Western strategies allowed Leonid Brezhnev to play the allies off against one another. Nonetheless, the liberalising effect of East–West trade and increasing communications between the two sides of Europe had undermined cohesion within the Warsaw Pact and led to the accumulation of large-scale debts by the East European countries.[201]

The Federal government was also frustrated by Washington's attempt to recapture control of East–West relations through strategic arms control talks and by Carter's decision to withdraw the SALT II treaty from Senate ratification in January 1980. Bonn endeavoured to find alternative solutions and advocated a milder response to the Soviet invasion of Afghanistan.[202] When the White House suspended the 1975 US–Soviet grain agreement, which allowed American grain sales to the USSR, Bonn was particularly alarmed. The FRG was also critical of Washington's decision not to consult with the European allies before announcing other punitive measures, including a boycott of the 1980 Olympic Games in Moscow.[203] This measure had been proposed initially by West Germany's ambassador to NATO, Pauls, on the grounds that a boycott of the 1936 Olympics might have changed the course of history. The initial European response to the boycott plea was overall positive with the only exception being France. The French Olympic Committee had in fact already accepted Moscow's invitation. Schmidt, under pressure from the left of his own party and from the West German Olympic Committee, was disappointed by the US failure to consult the European allies in advance. The American proposal also elicited conflicting reactions in Britain where, despite Whitehall's substantial efforts to support Carter's request, the British Olympic Association eventually decided to attend the games.[204] Ultimately, the Federal Republic was the only European ally to go along with the US decision. However, the FRG's initiatives to reinvigorate détente continued to be a source of concern for the Americans. Schmidt's statement in the *Bundestag* on 17 January 1980 that he was ready to meet Brezhnev, together with leaks in April of the Kremlin's invitation to the chancellor to visit Moscow in the summer, were met with obvious anxiety in Washington.[205] While the Federal government stressed that consultation with the allies would precede any decision to accept the Kremlin's invitation, the announcement revived American suspicions of the West German pursuit of its own interests at the expense of Western unity.

Washington remained suspicious that the chancellor was attempting to pursue his *Ostpolitik* outside the reach of the US and the other NATO allies. In a major address on 10 April Carter reiterated US demands for allied unity, stating that it was 'vital that the burden of sacrifice be shared among our allies and among other nations'.[206] In the following days American fears were increased by a surprise move from the chancellor. At the SPD convention in Hamburg, held between 11 and 13 April, Schmidt, under bitter criticism from Moscow and from the left wing of his own party for supporting the dual-track decision and the Olympic boycott, suggested that both East and West declare a moratorium on IRBM deployment in Europe. Schmidt's proposal produced a wave of reaction among his political opponents in the FRG and in the US. The CSU's leader and candidate chancellor, Strauss, called it 'an open affront to NATO and an unveiled rebuff to the USA'.[207] American officials manifested concern that the proposal might mean a freeze in current strategic levels in Europe, thus legitimising present Soviet superiority. They also worried that Schmidt's statement might be interpreted as a weakening of the commitment undertaken by NATO in the previous December to deploy US missiles in Europe within three years, if no progress was made in European arms control negotiations. Ultimately, Schmidt's appeal did not conceal an outright rejection of the dual-track decision. The chancellor was aware that American missiles would not be ready for deployment before 1983. Hence, his suggestion was addressed at Soviet installations and was only a slight refinement of the original Western decision.[208] Nonetheless, Bonn's unilateral move annoyed the Americans. Frustrated by the moratorium proposal, which Schmidt reiterated at an extraordinary party meeting in Essen on 9 June, and by his upcoming visit to the USSR at the end of the month, on 12 June the US president wrote a personal letter to the chancellor. In the letter Carter criticised the Federal government's 'flip-flop' attitude, remarking that it was his duty to bring West German foreign policy back in step with that of the other members of the alliance.[209]

The increasing friction between Washington and Bonn peaked at the Group of 7 (G7) summit in Venice on 22 and 23 June. On this occasion, the chancellor emphasised West Germany's need to honour its trade agreement with Moscow, citing the disastrous effects that had resulted from Hitler's failure to keep his word. Schmidt also complained that he had been insulted by Carter's last message and that the Federal Republic was not the fifty-first state of the United States.[210] Schmidt's firm stance now forced the Americans to reach a compromise with Bonn. Carter convinced the seven Western leaders to publish a joint communiqué at the end of the summit that condemned the USSR for endangering world peace. Nonetheless, the US president agreed to lay aside demands for further punitive measures and to consider the possibility of new negotiations with the Kremlin at some later date. Carter also consented to a public statement expressing confidence in the Federal government's policy and acknowledging West German concurrence on theatre nuclear forces.[211] After the meeting Schmidt announced that both sides had agreed that the letter the US president had sent him ten days earlier was no longer relevant. However, the chancellor's resistance to American

calls for sanctions and his Moscow visit in late June infuriated Washington. Whereas Bonn had formally condemned Soviet
intervention in Afghanistan, the chancellor's trip to Moscow
made it clear that the FRG was ready to continue negotiations
with the Soviet leadership, regardless of American views.[212] West
German endeavours to continue a policy of détente remained a
constant source of preoccupation for the Carter administration.
The development of a vociferous anti-American and anti-NATO
peace movement in the Federal Republic also constituted an additional source of irritation for Washington. The West German
peace movement, having gained steam in the late 1960s, was revi-
talised by the 1977 neutron bomb controversy. It now staunchly
opposed theatre nuclear forces deployment.[213] By the end of 1980
more than four million people had signed an appeal issued by the
pacifist forum held in Krefeld in November against the stationing of nuclear weapons in the Federal Republic. In October 1981
300,000 people protested at a large rally in Bonn.[214] Schmidt's
commitment to a continuation of détente with Moscow and
Carter's recurrent anxieties did not fundamentally undercut bilateral relations. Nonetheless, they reflected the deep transformations that had occurred in the relationship between Washington
and Bonn since the Cold War's inception. The impact of these
transformations was soon also to be felt on the Anglo-American
relationship.

The special relationship and Germany under Thatcher and Reagan

The late 1970s had been a period of fundamental harmony in
Anglo-German relations. The Callaghan–Schmidt relationship
had probably been one of the most amicable between British
and German leaders of any period. The Labour prime minister
enjoyed a strong personal relationship with the chancellor, which
lasted into later life, and never doubted Schmidt's genuine commitment to NATO.[215] Nonetheless, in Britain the return to power
of the Conservative Party with a safe working majority, following
the May 1979 elections, quickly rekindled the prospect of closer
alignment with Washington, particularly on security and defence
issues. Margaret Thatcher, Britain's new prime minister, had been
a staunch opponent of détente since becoming Tory leader in
1975. In the 1970s Thatcher was among those who believed that
the CSCE would play into the hands of the Kremlin; only later did

she acknowledge that 'by making human rights a matter of treaty obligations rather than domestic law', the Helsinki agreements gave the dissidents a leverage which they employed to undermine the Soviet bloc from its foundations.[216]

The new cabinet was committed to rebuilding Western defences, while forcefully asserting British interests in the European Communities. Within her first few months in office, Thatcher initiated the process to replace Britain's obsolete Polaris nuclear missiles with the purchase of Trident. Her first meeting with Carter went very well during her tightly scheduled one-day visit to Washington on 17 December 1979. In the same month Whitehall agreed to let the Americans station the IRBM Cruise missiles on British soil. This was, however, in agreement with NATO's December 1979 dual-track decision.[217] Ultimately, during the twenty months they were in office together Thatcher and Carter got on better than either of them had expected.[218] Nonetheless, the new cabinet's hopes for a prompt rekindling of the special relationship were disappointed by Carter: the US president never seriously contemplated a deepening in 'Anglo-Saxon' ties, consistently favouring instead a more harmonious relationship between Britain and continental Europe as a way of promoting American views in the European Communities and defusing inter-allied tension. Britain's cautious reaction to the Soviet invasion of Afghanistan and Whitehall's reservations about imposing sanctions on Iran also contributed to stalling prospects of a fast-resurging special relationship.

The new government had come to power against the backdrop of a growing industrial and social crisis. Initially it was absorbed by the pressing domestic concerns that overshadowed Britain's role in East–West relations. As White remarks, in the late 1970s London was neither an architect not an initiator of Western policy towards the Soviet bloc.[219] The Americans were aware of British economic difficulties and of their impact on London's role in the global Cold War. A CIA assessment of relations with the Western allies prepared in October 1979 asserted that 'the special relationship between the United States and the United Kingdom, finally, has lost much of its meaning. The United States is no longer significantly closer to Britain than to its other major allies.'[220] The cabinet change at No. 10 had a more discernible impact on Anglo-German relations. The FRG's chancellor was the first foreign leader to visit Thatcher in London, on 10 May

1979, only a week after her electoral victory. In her conversations with Schmidt Britain's prime minister, while not manifesting any of the anti-German feelings that would appear in later years, told him to expect some differences in the new cabinet's approach to foreign policy, which would be 'more positive in its attitude to defence'.[221] Thatcher reiterated this view in her dinner speech. She remarked that the strongest link between the United Kingdom and the FRG was not the European Communities, but first and foremost their common membership of the Atlantic Alliance, emphasising how 'that membership is a cornerstone of our foreign policy, as it is of yours'.[222]

Nonetheless, Washington and London had different perceptions of dynamics in Germany. Unlike the Americans, the British disregarded the risk of ill-considered West German initiatives towards Moscow. Furthermore, the lack of any immediate breakthrough on the German question allowed the new cabinet to renew without hesitation its commitment to unification. On the twenty-fifth anniversary of the Bonn Relations Convention coming into force, in a letter to Genscher, Foreign Secretary Lord Carrington remarked that Britain supported 'the efforts of the Federal Republic of Germany to work for a state of peace in Europe in which the German people can recover their unity in free-determination'.[223] However, Germany was not a priority for Thatcher. Her policy now focused on the long-term restructuring of the British economy and on the re-establishment of 'the right balance between . . . resource constraints and our necessary defence requirements'.[224]

Ronald Reagan's assumption of presidential duties in Washington in January 1981 breathed additional life into the Anglo-American special relationship. It also coincided with a reassertion of American leadership within the Western alliance and a further deterioration in Washington's relations with the Soviet Union.[225] Like Thatcher, the former governor of California had been an early opponent of détente. As a presidential candidate in 1976 and 1980 Reagan viewed détente as a dangerous slide that, based on the flawed acceptance of moral equivalence between the two blocs, had led the West to make one-sided and self-defeating concessions to Moscow. While Reagan and Thatcher had met first in July 1972, when the then governor of California had made a visit to Europe as Nixon's emissary, their first one-to-one meeting did not occur until April 1975 at the House of Commons. Writing to Thatcher at the end of the month, Reagan had referred to fresh news of the fall of Saigon, stating that 'the shadows seem to have lengthened'.[226] Reagan's distrust of Soviet aims was confirmed from the early days of his administration. In his first conference upon assuming the presidency Reagan dismissed détente as 'a one-way street that the Soviet Union has used to pursue its own aims'.[227] The new administration was committed to restoring American strength, reversing strategic imbalances and challenging Moscow's domination over Eastern Europe.

Washington was now eager to set a new tone with the Kremlin. Under Reagan the White House pursued a comprehensive modernisation of US nuclear and conventional forces and endeavoured to roll back communism in South America, Africa and South Asia. The president held particularly bold ideas about challenging the Soviet sway over Eastern Europe. Throughout his political career he had expressed repeated criticism of American acquiescence to Moscow's control of the East European nations. Reagan viewed the countries of this region as Soviet captives, believed that the Helsinki agreements had given the Kremlin a legal recognition the Russians had been craving since the end of the War and was determined to help Eastern Europeans break out of the Soviet straitjacket. During a private visit to the Berlin Wall in November 1978 he had told his advisor, Richard Allen, 'we have got to find a way to knock this thing down'.[228] A few days after his victory over Carter the president's national security team had produced a report in which it was stated that the US 'does not accept as a permanent historical fact the occupation or control by a power hostile to the United States of any territory beyond the borders of that power'.[229] The White House's new energetic approach to East–West relations was summed up by the president's statement in March 1983 at an evangelical conference in Orlando that the Soviet Union was driven by 'the aggressive impulses of an evil empire'.[230]

Reagan's determination to roll back communism prompted a massive increase in the American defence budget. Nonetheless, the president's aggressive rhetoric was the cause of additional tension in US–West German relations. In the FRG Reagan was the least popular of American presidents since 1945. The Federal government was intent on a meticulous, at times frenzied, continuation of its détente policy and viewed with concern Reagan's ideological hostility to détente.[231] West German public opinion feared the implications of his bold rhetoric on East–West relations.[232]

Bonn's distrust of American motives was reciprocated somewhat across the Atlantic. Washington had been reassured by the results of the October 1980 Federal elections, which had increased the Free Democrats' share of the vote at the expenses of the SPD. Nonetheless, expanding ties between Bonn and Moscow remained a source of anxiety for the new administration. In November 1981, the White House expressed concern at the signing of a deal between the FRG and the Soviet Union, which arranged for the construction of a 3,300-mile pipeline to deliver Siberian natural gas to West Germany, France and other West European countries. According to Washington, the agreement, which had been finalised on the eve of Brezhnev's visit to Bonn at the end of the month, would make the European allies excessively reliant on Soviet energy at a time when many in the West feared Soviet military intervention in Poland. US Secretary of Defense Caspar Weinberger was among the pipeline's staunchest opponents. The CIA supported Weinberger's position but officials in the Pentagon took a more cautious approach.[233] Nonetheless, despite persistent differences in US and West German approaches to East–West relations, Reagan's election brought about no ruinous fractures between Washington and Bonn. The overall achievements of Brezhnev's Western policy and visit to the FRG in November were limited. Discussions on economic cooperation triggered, alongside the pipeline deal, the signing of a twenty-five-year economic and industrial agreement. However, the visit did not meet Moscow's expectations. While there was some limited progress in the Berlin talks, the Germans rejected the Kremlin's proposal to include the words 'friendship' and 'rapprochement' in the final communiqué.[234] Furthermore, while advocating a firm Western response to Soviet initiatives, Reagan also took steps to alleviate Cold War tensions, lifting in April 1981 the grain embargo as a show of good faith towards Moscow.[235]

Nonetheless, Washington and Bonn continued to evaluate dynamics in Eastern Europe differently. In December 1981 the crackdown on Solidarity and the imposition of martial law in Poland by a Committee of National Salvation, headed by General Wojciech W. Jaruzelski, rekindled US–West German divergences, becoming the subject of heated debate across the Atlantic. The White House declared further economic sanctions against Moscow and Warsaw and curtailed US–Soviet academic exchanges. Washington announced the measures against Poland on 23 December and further steps against the Soviets followed a week later.[236] The Federal government's reaction was more cautious. Bonn expressed regret at the imposition of martial law in Poland but Schmidt refused to blame either Moscow or East Berlin and did not cut short a visit to East Germany.[237] The FRG endeavoured to convince the Republican administration in Washington to maintain dialogue with the East, systematically invoking the mantra of the Harmel Report. The chancellor also attempted to reassure Reagan that, while Germany remained a loyal member of the alliance, it was Bonn's duty to 'strive for the U.S. and the USSR to talk with one another'.[238]

British reactions to the Polish crisis were also much more cautious than those prevailing in Washington. Facing its worst recession since the 1930s and in the middle of tough austerity policies, Whitehall was absorbed by the social travails of labour and economic reform. London was reluctant to forego economic cooperation with the Soviet Union and engage in a protracted policy of sanctions: US attempts to persuade the allies to halt the pipeline deal elicited strong British hostility. While Thatcher had been in touch with Reagan, she was surprised by the toughness of US measures and feared their repercussions on British firms with contracts to help build the gas pipeline. Whitehall viewed US arguments that the pipeline would make Europe dependent on Soviet energy supplies and amenable to the Kremlin's wishes a little far-fetched. Furthermore, in light of the loans granted by British banks to Poland, the cabinet was anxious about American threats to precipitate a Polish default. Although at the extraordinary meeting of the alliance's foreign ministers in Madrid in January 1982 Britain consented with the European allies to a tougher stance, London refused to endorse a policy of sanctions against Moscow.[239] The White House judged the Polish events of December 1981 as the 'chance of a lifetime', berating the West European allies as 'chicken littles'.[240] However, the British together with the other EEC members resisted US pressures for sanctions. Disappointed by allied reluctance to follow his lead on Poland, Reagan later recalled in his memoirs that the reaction of some allies suggested that 'money spoke louder than principle'.[241]

After NATO's dual-track decision, the pipeline deal and the Polish crisis marked additional episodes in a gradual reorientation of US policy towards Europe. However, they also confirmed important differences in US and West German approaches to relations with Moscow. While respecting its commitments on theatre missile deployment, Bonn endeavoured to maintain dialogue with the Kremlin, create the circumstances that would make deployment unnecessary and gain more independence in dealing with the USSR. This conduct remained a source of concern in the US. Nonetheless, the FRG avoided unilateral initiatives, eventually allowing the Reagan administration to come to terms with the strategy of 'zero option' that had been championed by Schmidt in 1979 and consistently backed by the SPD.[242] The proposal that NATO would forgo deployment of American missiles if Moscow was willing to dismantle its IRBMs was formalised by Reagan in a televised address on 18 November 1981, three days before Brezhnev's arrival in Bonn.[243]

While dynamics in Germany remained a constant concern for the Americans, the British slowly lost their central place in US policy towards Eastern Europe. Thatcher saw Eastern Europe in terms of captive nations under Soviet oppression and herself as the champion of self-liberation. However, Whitehall nurtured the illusion that transformation would be slow and that the Kremlin would be able to retain some form of control over its satellites.[244] An overall belief that East German domestic stability and international prestige had consolidated following the SED's implementation of a policy of strict demarcation – *Abgrenzung* – from the FRG contributed to assuaging latent fears of German resurgence in the United Kingdom. Nonetheless, Britain's hopes of a gradual transition in the East, which would not undermine the European status quo, were soon proved misplaced. In the early 1980s Reagan's bold stance to East–West relations, the political and economic costs of an extenuating Afghan campaign and simmering discontent across Eastern Europe began exerting mounting pressure on an ailing Soviet leadership. Their ultimate effect was to pave the way for the rise of a generation of young reformers in the USSR and East Germany's increasing isolation within the bloc.

The special relationship and the FRG in the early 1980s

'Not one of my generation can forget that America has been the principal architect of a peace in Europe which has lasted forty years . . . The

debt the free peoples of Europe owe to this nation . . . is incalculable'
(Margaret Thatcher, 20 February 1985)

'The Berlin Wall, that dreadful gray gash across the city, is in its third
decade. It is the fitting signature of the regime that built it'
(Ronald Reagan, 8 June 1982)

'The United States and the Federal Republic have established an historic relationship, not of superpower to satellite but of sister republics
bounded together by common ideals and alliance and partnership'
(Ronald Reagan, 16 April 1985)

'If we can't reconcile after forty years, we are never going to be able
to do it'
(Ronald Reagan, 3 May 1985)

'We who were enemies are now friends; we who were bitter adversaries are now the strongest of allies'
(Ronald Reagan, 5 May 1985)

The US, the UK and the return to power of the Christian Democrats

Schmidt's chancellorship ended in the autumn of 1982 following
an intense dispute between his party and the FDP over economic
policy. The second oil shock of 1979–80, which had been triggered by the Iranian revolution and by the eruption of the Iran–
Iraq War, had forced the government into a round of unpopular
austerity measures to tackle unemployment and a growing budget
deficit. In September the Free Democrats shifted their support
to the right, allowing in October the return to power of the
CDU and of the Bavarian CSU in a coalition government with
the FDP. Helmut Kohl led the cabinet. Kohl was a Catholic
Rhinelander from Ludwigshafen, who lacked previous ministerial experience. The new arrangement was ratified by a national
election in March 1983.[245] However, the change of leadership in
Bonn initially marked no significant breakthrough on the German
question. Although willing to maintain dialogue with the GDR
and the Soviet Union at a time of deepening East–West tension,
the new government prioritised Western unity over a deepening
of *Ostpolitik*.[246] Kohl and his defence minister, Manfred Wörner,
determinedly stood in favour of deployment of ninety-six Cruise

and 108 Pershing II missiles on West German territory in order to restore tactical parity with Moscow.[247] The cabinet's firmness, in the face of persistent popular opposition to deployment, allayed residual American fears about Bonn's commitment to the West. Kohl's personal support for deployment, in the absence of progress in arms control negotiations in Geneva, also reassured other NATO allies.[248] Faced with Western resoluteness, in November 1983 the Soviets walked out of the talks, as the first Pershing II deployments began in West Germany.

The new government's loyalty to the Western alliance did not imply, however, a renunciation of the policy of engagement with Moscow and the GDR. Although in the aftermath of deployment the Kremlin downgraded bilateral ties in order to punish Bonn, Kohl made it clear from the outset that he favoured continuity in the FGR's Eastern policy. The FDP's leader, Hans-Dietrich Genscher, who had been confirmed as foreign minister, was a firm supporter of *Ostpolitik*.[249] The cabinet's readiness to preserve dialogue with Moscow, address issues of national identity and protect all-German interests, together with the growth in the FRG of a peace movement that at its peak was several million strong, remained sources of concern in Washington. Kohl visited the new CPSU leader, Yuri Andropov, in Moscow in July 1983, and was warned by the Kremlin about the consequences of missile deployment. However, Bonn continued to deepen ties with the GDR on a number of levels. The CSU's leader and Minister President of Bavaria Strauss was the FRG's finance minister. During the 1960s Strauss had been a staunch opponent of Brandt's policy towards the GDR. Now he engineered a series of new financial credits to East Germany. These initiatives confirmed the degree of consensus in the FRG about the policy of engagement with East Berlin and Bonn's attempt to balance its strong pro-Western orientation with the preservation of dialogue with the East.[250] However, the pursuit of an active policy of engagement towards the GDR continued to fuel concerns in Washington about the compatibility of an active *Deutschlandpolitik* with the Federal government's long-term commitment to the Atlantic Alliance.[251]

In the early 1980s Bonn's inter-German policy also caused concern for some of Washington's European allies. A number of European NATO members were worried by the FRG's growing interest in expanding ties with the GDR. These concerns were particularly marked in Paris. They were one of the main reasons behind new French President François Mitterrand's strong support of NATO's dual-track decision and closer Franco-West German security cooperation. In Italy also there was increasing anxiety about the Federal government's objectives. On 13 September 1984, speaking at a festival in Rome of the Italian Communist Party's newspaper *Unità*, Foreign Minister Giulio Andreotti was asked a question about relations between the two German states and the peril of Pangermanism. In his reply the Christian Democratic leader remarked:

> we all agree that both German states are on good terms with each other . . . But it should be clear that one should not exaggerate in that direction, meaning that one must recognize: The Pangermanism has to be overcome. Two German states exist, and two German states should remain.[252]

His statement caused outrage among West German representatives in Italy and triggered a protest from the Federal government, prompting Rome to present an official apology to Bonn.[253] Nonetheless, in the following year Italian concerns about greater assertiveness in the FRG's foreign policy were confirmed in discussions at an EEC summit in Milan.[254]

In London there was also concern about the evolving dynamics in Germany. Britain's position was complex. In the early 1980s British public opinion manifested growing discomfort about prospects of a new nuclear standoff. A cable sent in March 1982 from the US embassy in London had stressed that six out of ten Britons believed that American policy had increased the risk of nuclear confrontation, while more than half supported the removal of American nuclear bases from British soil.[255] Nonetheless, Whitehall also feared that the FRG might outflank Britain as the main interlocutor of the US in Europe.[256] These fears had resurfaced in 1982 when Reagan failed to reply in a timely way to a personal invitation from the Queen. However, they were played down by FCO officials. A telegram from Britain's ambassador to the US, Nicholas Henderson, had remarked 'how much the President himself wanted to go to London' and ruled out the possibility that the Germans could be considered America's favourite allies.[257] The British also worried about Reagan's aggressive stance towards the Soviet bloc and its implications for the German question. In addressing the House of Commons on 8 June 1982 the US president had made no mystery of his determination to challenge Soviet rule in Eastern Europe. While paying tribute to Churchill's determination in the War as an example of freedom, Reagan referred to the Berlin Wall as the 'grey gash across the city' and 'the fitting signature of the regime that built it'. The US president also offered trenchant insights into the Soviet Union as a dysfunctional, doomed experiment, a vast land that could not even feed itself.[258] The speech, which was boycotted by 195 of the 225 Labour Party MPs, met with applause just once, when Reagan paid tribute to British troops who were fighting in the Falklands.[259] The cool reception to which the US president had been treated in the House of Commons confirmed the persistence of important divergences in Anglo-American views about Germany and policy towards the Soviet bloc.

Anglo-American relations, the Strategic Defense Initiative and Kohl's inter-German policy

Differences in Anglo-American approaches to relations with Moscow were confirmed by British reactions to Reagan's announcement on 23 March 1983 of plans for a project that would allow Washington to counter the Soviet strategic threat. The US president was laying the foundations for the Strategic Defense Initiative (SDI). However, this speech came as a big surprise to the British. Although the US had invited the European allies to take part in the project, Whitehall, like all other West European governments, was not consulted in advance. The reaction of British ministers and officials, caught off balance, was a mix of concern and hostility. London raised serious questions about the implications of American plans and similar reservations were expressed by Washington's other European allies. Among them the French, although having exited NATO's military structure in 1967, were particularly alarmed. Paris was concerned that the SDI might accelerate the arms race and pose a threat to the French nuclear arsenal. The French also worried that the administration's initiative might lead to a decoupling of the US from European defence arrangements, as a prelude to an imminent American disengagement from Europe.

In the early 1980s Paris had in fact embraced a more conciliatory policy towards the Anglo-Saxon powers and the European Communities, endeavouring to resume cooperation with the

Alliance and deepen relations with Bonn. This shift in French security policy reflected a concern to retain control of dynamics in Germany. Mitterrand's *Bundestag* speech in January 1983 had been emblematic of France's turn towards the Atlantic. On this occasion, which coincided with the twentieth anniversary of the 1963 Franco-German treaty, the French president had overtly called for the FRG to reaffirm its commitment to the West, taking a powerful line on the question of IRBM deployment and warning of the dangers of nuclear decoupling between the US and Europe.[260] The SDI also prompted French efforts towards a revitalisation of the WEU, the formation of a Franco-German brigade and the creation of intergovernmental army units, which became known as the Eurocorps. Like the French, the West Germans also expressed reservations about the SDI. The Federal government wanted to make sure that the programme would not impede arms control negotiations, alter the strategic balance and lead to transatlantic decoupling. Only after two years of intensive negotiations did Washington and Bonn complete a memorandum of understanding in April 1985. However, during a visit to Chequers in May Kohl continued to manifest Bonn's concerns about 'decoupling'.[261] In the same month former Chancellor Willy Brandt travelled to Moscow at the head of a delegation, meeting Soviet leaders and condemning the SDI.[262]

Whitehall's reaction was hesitant and, to a certain extent, disjointed. London's favourite option was a continuation of the work in progress on ballistic missile defence technologies. The British sought participation in SDI research and tried to deal on a bilateral basis with the White House. However, the cabinet gave no hasty response and provided only limited support to Reagan's initiative.[263] Furthermore, although Thatcher was a sincere admirer of the US president, the White House's approach to East–West relations clashed with Britain's resurfacing interest in an arrangement with Moscow. During the first half of 1982 Whitehall had endeavoured to work out a compromise among the allies on the Polish question and over the pipeline issue. Then, after the Conservative Party's unexpected victory in the general elections of June 1983, the cabinet initiated a review of British policy towards the Soviet bloc. This occurred at a time when, with arms control negotiations in Geneva continuing to stall, Anglo-American rearmament programmes were moving quickly. At the same time, the alliance was moving forward with IRBM deployment, which was due to be completed by the end of the year. Calls for a more active policy towards Eastern Europe led to the appointment as foreign secretary of Thatcher's former chancellor, Geoffrey Howe. His appointment demonstrated Thatcher's intention to closely supervise the evolution of relations with the Soviet bloc and the prospects of change in the East.

The shift in Britain's Eastern policy dramatically accelerated after a two-day seminar on the future of the Soviet Union, which was held at the prime minister's country residence Chequers on 8 and 9 September 1983. The seminar represented a turning point in Whitehall's attitude towards the Soviet bloc. It convinced Thatcher of an impending Soviet decline, while reinforcing her expectation that Western economic aid could stimulate internal political reforms in the East. In a memorandum sent on 12 September to Howe's private secretary, Brian Fall, Thatcher's private secretary, John Coles, noted that at Chequers it had been agreed that 'the aim should be to build up contacts slowly over the next few years'. However, 'there would be no public announcement of this change of policy'.[264] Thatcher's objective was to favour the development of economic pluralism in the East in the hope that increasing interdependence with the West could bring about growing political liberalisation. Her ambition was to promote a gradual transition in Eastern Europe, while asserting London's role as middleman in relations between Washington and Moscow. Britain would thus encourage a progressive transformation in the Soviet bloc, which could be embraced gradually and managed by the local elites without uncontrolled repercussions on East–West relations.[265]

Nonetheless, Whitehall's perceptions of relations between the two blocs differed from those prevailing in Washington. Whereas in his speech at the National Association of Evangelicals in Orlando in March 1983 Reagan had framed East–West relations as a struggle between 'good and evil', a Defence Ministry memorandum prepared for the prime minister in September stressed that one of the main reasons for concern in the current strategic scenario was 'the absence of dialogue with the Soviet Union'.[266] At the end of the month, having travelled to Washington for an official working visit and to receive the Winston Churchill Award, Thatcher delivered a speech at the British embassy. Her audience included, alongside the US president, many senior members of the administration, such as new Secretary of State George Pratt Shultz,

US Ambassador to the United Nations Jeane Duane Kirkpatrick, Deputy Chief of Staff Michael Keith Deaver, Undersecretary of State for Political Affairs Lawrence Eagleburger and Assistant Secretary of State for European and Canadian Affairs Richard R. Burt. Thatcher cogently made the case for negotiations with the Soviet Union, stressing that 'we live on the same planet and we have to go on sharing it'. She also argued that the West should 'stand ready therefore, if and when the circumstances are right, to talk to the Soviet leadership'.[267] Her words reflected a desire to work out an arrangement with the Kremlin on transformation in the East, while keeping dynamics in Germany under close scrutiny.

These fears were only partially shared in Washington. The Federal government's conduct on the Intermediate-Range Nuclear Forces (INF) issue had been an important motive of reassurance for the United States. Kohl's firmness to implement deployment had cleared a number of doubts about Bonn's commitment to NATO and prompted a more forthcoming American attitude to the German question. From then on, the rugged and open concerns that had first surfaced during the heyday of Brandt's *Ostpolitik* in the early 1970s and persisted throughout the Nixon, Ford and Carter administrations slowly began to evaporate. Those concerns were gradually replaced by a perception that the West German government was committed to preserving alliance unity and a trustworthy relationship with the United States.[268] Having been reassured that Bonn's active policy towards the GDR would not undermine its commitment to NATO, the Reagan administration became less suspicious of Bonn's Eastern initiatives and began to provide low-key but consistent support to the Federal government. A concern that opposition to closer relations between the two German states could prove counterproductive further reinforced the White House's positive disposition towards Kohl. In 1983 the finance minister and CSU leader, Strauss, engineered a loan of three billion Deutschmarks to the GDR, convincing the SED leadership to relax travelling and visiting regulations and to embrace a more generous approach to emigration and family reunification requests.

Bonn's Eastern policy was now also cheered on by the US. In a speech in Vienna on 21 September, after a tour that included stops in Yugoslavia, Hungary and Romania, Vice President George H. W. Bush praised the two countries for their independent policies. Bush also denied that the Yalta Conference had divided the continent into 'spheres of influence' and emphasised that the US accepted 'no lawful division of Europe'.[269] In November, in his address before the Korean National Assembly in Seoul during a trip to East Asia, Reagan reiterated American support for Bonn, stressing how some of the pain of Germany's division had been eased by the Basic Treaty of ten years earlier. Furthermore, the president portrayed the promising evolution in Germany as a potential model for the Korean situation.[270] In July 1984 State Department officials publicly supported the signing of two additional credit agreements between Bonn and East Berlin. The deal allowed the Deutsche Bank to offer the GDR a new loan through its subsidiary in Luxembourg, with a West German government guarantee. This was granted in exchange for additional East German measures towards the improvement and facilitation of travel in both directions.[271] In the same year East German authorities issued more than 40,000 foreign travel permits compared with slightly more than 13,000 and 11,000 in 1982 and 1983 respectively.[272]

The White House also endorsed West German views within NATO. At the end of the Washington foreign ministers' meeting in late May 1984 the alliance welcomed a continuation of the Federal government's dialogue with the GDR. In point 12 of the final communiqué the allies affirmed that 'the maintenance of a calm situation in and around Berlin, including unimpeded traffic on all the access routes to the city, remains of fundamental importance for East–West relations'. They also expressed 'the hope that the continuation of the Federal Government's dialogue with the GDR . . . will directly benefit Berlin and the Germans in both states'. [273] However, in August the Soviet leaders summoned Honecker to Moscow, warning him that he should refrain from visiting West Germany, as a rapprochement with the FRG, premised on a weakening of socialist positions, would cause great damage to the entire bloc. When on 4 September Honecker cancelled his planned visit, the State Department reconfirmed American support for increasing contact between the two German states, blaming pressures on East Berlin by the Soviet leadership for cancelling the visit.[274] In the same month, in his address to the thirty-ninth session of the UN General Assembly, Reagan reiterated his support for closer relations between the two halves of Germany, praising Bonn's efforts 'to reduce barriers between the two German states'.[275]

Nonetheless, positions in Washington were varied and not everybody shared Reagan's optimism. The State Department feared that an excessively positive perception of the FRG posed a risk for the alliance. Kohl's strong Atlantic credentials and the support he enjoyed in the administration provided the Federal government with a much greater freedom of action than in the past. US officials worried that this might lead the chancellor to take initiatives that might damage Western interests. These concerns were shared in the Pentagon. More specifically, US defence planners were anxious about the implications of West German commercial and technological exchanges with the East. Although not questioning Bonn's loyalty to the West, some American officials continued to fear that increased inter-German trade might indirectly allow the USSR to obtain high-tech Western military technology with negative implications for the balance of forces in Europe.[276]

The US, Britain and the German question during and after the Falklands conflict

Reagan's overall support for Kohl and for his cabinet's inter-German policy was treated with circumspection in London. Nonetheless, in the early 1980s the special relationship was reinvigorated by political dynamics in the South Atlantic that were triggered by Argentina's attempt to gain control of the Falkland Islands. The effect was to increase Britain's international standing and prestige. This occurred nowhere more so than in the United States. Victory in the Falklands in 1982 against an unpopular Argentinian military junta, that had occupied the Islands and South Georgia on the eve of the 150th anniversary of the British permanent settlement and had received arms sales from the FRG, emboldened Whitehall. It also convinced Thatcher that the Americans would continue to privilege their relationship with Britain over closer ties with the FRG. However, the US government's initial reaction to the conflict had been hesitant. Some in the administration, particularly US Ambassador to the United Nations Kirkpatrick, believed that Washington needed to retain Buenos Aires' support in order to confront the Soviet–Cuban build-up in Central and Latin America. These views influenced the administration's response in the first phases of the War. Secretary of State Alexander Haig initially attempted to mediate between

America's hemispheric and Atlantic commitments in order not to alienate Argentina and offend other Latin American nations. Nonetheless, others in the administration, particularly Defense Secretary Caspar Weinberger, held much more robust pro-British views.[277]

Weinberger was a former state legislator and chairman of the Republican Party in California, where he had worked under Reagan's governorship. He was also a close admirer of Winston Churchill. The secretary of defence allowed Britain use of the Wideawake airbase on Ascension Island, which Washington held on a long-term lease from London, and even offered to make a US carrier available to the Royal Navy in the South Atlantic.[278] He also played a key role in shifting the president's initial scepticism into outright support for Britain.[279] Those in the administration who feared a backlash in US policy towards Latin America criticised Weinberger and Haig for their support for London. Kirkpatrick defined them as 'Brits in American clothes'. At one point she even suggested that Washington could simply allow 'the British Foreign Office to make our policy'. The secretary of state's response to Kirkpatrick was that she was 'mentally and emotionally incapable of thinking clearly about the Falklands' because of her close links to Latins.[280] US support for Britain revived London's enthusiasm for the special relationship. In 1988 Weinberger was awarded an honorary knighthood from Queen Elizabeth II for his endeavours in favour of the United Kingdom.[281] Thatcher remarked in her memoirs that, 'America never had a wiser patriot, nor Britain a truer friend.' Speaking to the US Congress in February 1985 she expressed her gratitude to the administration, declaring, 'not one of my generation can forget that America has been the principal architect of a peace in Europe which has lasted forty years . . . The debt the free peoples of Europe owe to this nation . . . is incalculable.'[282]

Victory in the Falklands stood as a spectacular foreign policy achievement for London. After a seventy-four-day occupation by Argentina, the Islands were liberated, albeit with the loss of 255 British lives. The War also reinforced Thatcher's position at home, contributing to the Conservative Party's electoral success of June 1983. The prime minister now felt able to boast that the 'Great' had been restored to 'Great Britain'.[283] Emboldened by this success, Whitehall endeavoured to exploit victory in the southern hemisphere in order to position Britain as middleman between the two superpowers in Europe and initiate a major policy reassessment towards the Soviet bloc countries. As the first signs of transition in Moscow had become noticeable, following Leonid Brezhnev's death on 12 November 1982, the prime minister attempted to establish a dialogue with his successor, Yuri Andropov, and the new generation of Soviet leaders. In June 1983 Francis L. Pym, who had stepped in as foreign secretary after Carrington's resignation over the Argentinian occupation of the Falklands in April 1982, was replaced by former Chancellor of the Exchequer Geoffrey Howe.[284]

Nonetheless, Whitehall's efforts were treated with circumspection in Washington. During bilateral discussions in the summer Britain's new foreign secretary found the Americans full of objections. Officially, Washington contemplated the possibility of resuming arms negotiations with the Soviets. However, new US Secretary of State George P. Schultz, who had replaced Haig at the State Department in the aftermath of the Falklands conflict in July 1982, had made it clear to the British that the American view was that Moscow's position in Eastern Europe held no legitimacy whatsoever.[285] On 1 September 1983 Moscow's shooting down, off the island of Sakhalin in the Soviet airspace, of Korean Air Lines Flight 007, on an overnight flight from New York to Seoul and with sixty-one Americans on board, hardened the US stance. The president deplored the Kremlin's 'act of barbarism', while the White House suspended negotiations on several bilateral arrangements.[286] In November the beginning of NATO's military exercise Able Archer, simulating a full-scale attack on the Soviet Union, threw the Kremlin into panic, sparking one of the most dangerous episodes in East–West relations since the 1962 Cuban missile crisis. Moscow feared that the operation was the disguise for a preventive nuclear strike and reacted by ordering its forces to prepare for a counter-strike on the West.[287] However, the US's lack of enthusiasm for British initiatives did not deter Thatcher. Rather, the episode played a significant role in reinforcing her determination to resume dialogue with Russia. In an interview with *The New York Times* in January 1984 Britain's prime minister announced her intention to pursue a new course in relations with the East, stating that 'the thing is not whether you agree with the other powerful bloc's political views. The important thing is that you simply must make an effort the more to understand one another.'[288]

The sequence of internal dynamics in the Soviet Union appeared to vindicate her efforts: Andropov fell ill almost immediately after taking power, suffering a relapse of kidney problems, and died in February 1984 after only fifteen months in office. The already ailing Konstantin Chernenko replaced him as the CPSU's general secretary, while Mikhail Gorbachev was appointed to the position of chairman of the Union Council's Foreign Affairs Commission. This made him second in command and logical successor to Chernenko.[289] However, as events unfolded in Moscow, Whitehall was not alone in seeking re-engagement with the Soviet leadership. In June Mitterrand travelled to the Soviet capital in an attempt to explore prospects for change in East–West relations and reaffirm France's international prestige. The French president avoided the pitfall of appearing too conciliatory with the Russians, telling Chernenko that the Kremlin had only itself to blame for the arrival of US missiles in Western Europe. He also denounced Soviet human rights abuses and the treatment of dissenter Andrei Sakharov.[290] While Paris also endeavoured to mediate between the West and the USSR in light of evolving dynamics in Germany, Thatcher searched for a middle way between acceptance of a political freeze and rejection of Soviet domination in the East.[291] Her efforts made a threefold contribution towards change in East–West relations. First, Britain's prime minister acted as a pathfinder in developing dialogue with the Kremlin. Second, she worked as an interpreter, explaining Western thinking to the new generation of Soviet leaders. Finally, she contributed to building higher levels of understanding and confidence between the two blocs.[292] After meeting Gorbachev in London in December 1984, in the first official visit by a notable Soviet politician to the British capital in twenty-eight years, in an interview with the BBC the British prime minister famously pronounced the words, 'I like Mr Gorbachev. We can do business together.'[293]

One of the main reasons behind Anglo-French attempts to rebuild bridges with the Kremlin was the concern caused in London and Paris by Kohl's increasing weight within the alliance and policy towards the GDR. Thatcher also worried about the growing complicity between Mitterrand and Kohl within the European Communities. For this reason, she also endeavoured to revive Anglo-French relations after a period of stagnation. The French were particularly concerned by dynamics in Germany. Mitterrand feared that West Germany's growing influence and prestige might marginalise France's role in East–West relations. In 1984 France endorsed an upgrade in bilateral relations with Britain as a counterweight to Germany, agreeing at a bilateral summit in November that neither country would embark on a rearmament programme without consulting the other.[294] Closer ties between Paris and London also benefited French efforts to revitalise the dormant WEU and breathe new life into the Western European mechanism. Although for Whitehall defence remained a matter for NATO and of close association with the US, London did not object to French plans for greater European policy cooperation.[295] Ultimately, Britain's efforts to revive bilateral cooperation and French attempts to revitalise the WEU were driven by overlapping concerns: to devise a counter-strategy to the FRG's growing influence in East–West relations and to supervise political dynamics in Germany.[296] Nonetheless, Moscow's opposition to a deepening of inter-German ties continued to allow Thatcher to renew Britain's official commitment to unification. At a meeting in Oxford in May 1984 she acknowledged with Kohl that 'real and permanent stability in Europe will be difficult to achieve so long as the German nation is divided against its will'.[297] However, while publicly reiterating a verbal commitment to Germany's self-determination, the British regarded unification as a remote prospect that could only come about 'in circumstances which cannot at present be foreseen'.[298]

Thatcher, Reagan and the Bitburg visit

The rapprochement between London and Paris, including the reactivation of bilateral defence cooperation, did not go unnoticed in Bonn. The West Germans supported efforts to revive the WEU.[299] Nonetheless, the Federal government was wary of persistent Anglo-French diffidence. Bonn feared the prospect of a new Anglo-French entente, which might influence US views and prompt Washington to adopt a less favourable stance towards closer ties between the two German states. In 1984 this concern elicited the FRG's request to the White House for a formal gesture of rehabilitation for the entire German nation. The need for an American public endorsement was perceived as particularly important by Kohl for both international and domestic reasons. First, it would serve as a reminder to the European allies of the FRG's contribution to Western defence, particularly in light of the ongoing IRBM debate. Second, it would prove to an increasingly pacifist public opinion at home that West German interests and voice received adequate consideration in the US.

The chancellor's request was made even more compelling by the extensive visibility that in early June had been given to celebrations in Normandy for the fortieth D-Day anniversary. On this occasion, the allies had endeavoured to take into account West German sensitivities. However, the unusual magnitude of the celebrations had been perceived in the FRG as a snub and affront. In his speech at the Ranger Monument at Pointe du Hoc, while paying tribute to the American veterans and to the US allies, Reagan had spoken of reconciliation with the former enemies, 'all of whom had suffered so greatly'.[300] In his later address on Omaha beach the US president had underlined the importance of the transatlantic alliance, which had succeeded in containing the threat and keeping the peace in Europe. At a later celebration at Utah Beach on the same day as Reagan's speech, Mitterrand had emphasised reconciliation with the Federal Republic, stating that 'the adversaries of yesterday are reconciled and are building the Europe of freedom'.[301] The French president had also invited Kohl to a joint commemoration of the World War I battle of Verdun.[302]

Nonetheless, many in the FRG perceived the grandeur of the celebrations as proof of persistent hostility towards Germany. The Federal government felt that the celebrations, which set a new standard for D-Day commemorations that would remain in place for the next twenty-five years, failed to take into account the German people's pain and overshadowed West Germany's commitment to NATO. Bonn's displeasure was exposed by the words of the chancellor and of other cabinet members. Kohl's poignant remark was that there was no reason 'for a German chancellor to celebrate when others where marking their victory in a battle in which tens of thousands of Germans met miserable deaths'. The minister of state at the German Foreign Office, Alois Mertes, noted that D-Day commemorations could turn into 'a day of alienation between Germany and its allies', if they generated the feeling that the 'Germans were a vanquished people or a nation of guilty men between East and West'. Mertes also warned that the beneficiaries of such a syndrome would be pacifists and neutralists, who favoured a 'special German role between East and West and an equidistance between the two superpowers'.[303]

Kohl formalised a demand for a symbolic gesture of American

support during his visit to the White House on 29 and 30
November. In Washington he invited the US president to celebrate
the reconciliation of their two countries at a German military cemetery in the following year.[304] Initially, the chancellor's request
met with resistance both in Congress and from US public opinion.
Many believed that the president's visit to a German military
cemetery would be a moral and political mistake. Nonetheless,
Reagan held a different view. He was willing to reward the chancellor for his supportive attitude. The administration endorsed
the prospect of a public and symbolic event of the type held by
Adenauer and de Gaulle in July 1962, when the leaders of the
FRG and France attended together a mass of reconciliation in the
cathedral city of Reims before de Gaulle returned the visit to the
Federal Republic in September. The opportunity came in May
1985 during Reagan's official visit to West Germany after a G7
economic summit in Bonn and on the fortieth anniversary of the
end of the War in Europe.

In February Deputy Chief of Staff Michael Deaver, a public
relations expert who had selected sites for many of Reagan's most
successful speeches, was sent by the White House to search for a
suitable site for the ceremony. This was identified in the military
cemetery of Kolmeshöhe, which was located less than one mile
from the US airbase at Bitburg. There 11,000 Americans lived with
the same number of Germans in one of the most Americanised
areas in the Federal Republic. Deaver was given assurances from
the German chief of protocol, Werner von der Schulenberg, that
no war criminals were buried in the cemetery. However, this was
not the case. In a follow-up trip in March both his successor,
William Henkel, and US diplomats in West Germany failed to
spot the graves of forty-nine Waffen-SS troops on the site. Reagan
and his staff approved the itinerary in the same month and public
announcement of the trip on 11 April caused unrest among World
War II veterans, who thought that only German soldiers would
be honoured. Coming at the height of the festivity of Passover, it
also provoked the furious reaction of the Jewish community in the
US. Anger turned into open disdain, when news of the graves of
the SS soldiers broke out during the weekend of 13 and 14 April:
fifty-three senators, including eleven Republicans, signed a letter
asking the president to cancel the trip, while 257 members of
the House of Representatives, including eighty-four Republicans,
wrote a letter to Kohl asking him to withdraw the invitation.[305]

Nonetheless, Reagan was determined to show support for the Federal government and 'to usher in an era of newly strengthened ties with West Germany'.[306] On 16 April, at a State Department sponsored conference on religious liberty, the president firmly defended his choice, stressing how since the close of World War II 'the United States and the Federal Republic have established an historic relationship, not of superpower to satellite but of sister republics bounded together by common ideals and alliance and partnership'.[307] Before sending Deaver back to West Germany for the third time, just two days before the scheduled visit, Reagan told his deputy chief of staff, 'I know you and Nancy don't want me to go through with this, but I don't want you to change anything when you get over there, because history will prove I'm right. If we can't reconcile after forty years, we are never going to be able to do it.'[308]

The White House linked the president's journey to Bitburg with a visit to a former concentration camp in order to defuse the controversy. While Dachau was the site initially chosen, the itinerary was modified after discussions with Kohl's staff. Preference was now given to the former concentration camp of Bergen-Belsen. On 5 May Reagan first drove to the hills overlooking the Rhine to place a wreath at the grave of Adenauer. He then stood before an obelisk at the site of the Bergen-Belsen camp, before presiding over, at a nearby military cemetery, a wreath-laying ceremony at the base of a brick tower looming over the graves of nearly 2,000 German soldiers. While Reagan's visit at the cemetery lasted less than ten minutes, speaking later to about 5,000 American military personnel and their families, and some 2,000 German residents at the Bitburg airbase, the president praised the friendship between the FRG and the US, stating that 'we who were enemies are now friends; we who were bitter adversaries are now the strongest of allies'.[309] Having been conceived as an attempt to buttress the alliance and bolster support for Kohl, the visit produced a stir of negative comments in the US and among Washington's European allies. Reactions were particularly negative in the Netherlands, where all major parties signed a letter to the president, demanding Reagan cancel the visit. In Britain the trip was harshly criticised by the Labour Party. Its leader, Neil Kinnock, remarked that, by visiting the cemetery, the US president was committing a 'dreadful mistake'. Another Labour MP, David Winnick, described Reagan's visit as 'deeply insulting and offensive' to the memory of those who had lost their lives in concentration camps. The prime minister's reaction was also cautious. Thatcher said that she was 'not responsible for the activities of the United States' and expressed 'considerable sympathy' with the critics.[310] Nonetheless, the British were sympathetic with Bonn's efforts to rehabilitate those Germans who had not committed heinous crimes during the War. Ultimately, a number of British professional diplomats shared the US president's view that the time was ripe to end Germany's forty-year-long discrimination.[311]

Anglo-American relations and Germany on the eve of perestroika

The Bitburg episode carried no lasting impact on Anglo-American relations. Lack of progress in East–West relations and uncertainty about the future direction of Soviet politics allowed London not to oppose US endeavours at consolidating relations with Bonn. Nonetheless, the British position remained complex. Whitehall had not opposed Germany's moral rehabilitation. However, Thatcher's support for the FRG was conditional upon her belief that transformation in the Soviet bloc would be gradual and would take place without direct repercussions on East–West relations. In other words, it rested on the assumption that 'communism's defeat could live inside the Cold War geo-political architecture'.[312] Britain's prime minister was convinced that it would take time to bring about change and that transformation should happen progressively and in a controlled fashion, rather than in a radical manner and at a swift pace.[313] Ultimately, Whitehall's preference for gradual transition in the East reflected a widespread lack of enthusiasm in Britain for ending Germany's division. Echoing Churchill's calls in the 1950s for a new Locarno and Macmillan's endeavours to mediate between the blocs in the second Berlin crisis, at the end of 1984 Defence Secretary Michael Heseltine called for greater mutual understanding between East and West, arguing that the recent increase in Soviet military strength had not been aimed solely at threatening Western interests. In contrast, Britain's defence secretary stressed how the Russians had been concerned for centuries about their security and concluded that the West should realise that the Soviet Union also had legitimate interests to defend.[314]

The desire to build bridges with Moscow and oversee transition in the East was confirmed by the string of practical initiatives taken by the British in 1984 and 1985. They included support for a Western financial package aimed at rescuing an ailing Hungarian economy and Thatcher's trip to Budapest in February 1984 for her first prime ministerial visit to an Eastern bloc country.[315] Her visit was preceded in September 1983 by that of Foreign Secretary Howe and US Vice President Bush, who both met Hungarian communist leader János Kádár. While dynamics in Germany figured prominently in the formulation of Britain's diplomatic strategy, opinions in the FCO and the government were not identical. Before the prime minister's departure for the Hungarian capital FCO officials suggested that she raise the topic of German unification with Kádár. However, Thatcher opted not to, deleting from a FCO paper the following sentence: 'the rest of the world would be no more able to prevent German reunification, if the Russians decided to permit it, than we can bring it about now, when the Russians are implacably opposed'.[316] In March 1985 the prime minister travelled to Moscow to attend Chernenko's funeral, making a new contact with Gorbachev.[317] Then, in April, before celebrations for the thirtieth anniversary of the Austrian state treaty in May, Howe undertook an extensive journey across Eastern Europe, which took Britain's foreign secretary to East Germany, Czechoslovakia, Poland, Romania and Bulgaria.[318]

The trip was aimed at expanding trade, building cultural relations and strengthening East–West confidence, while fostering the conditions for closer cooperation in future years. Nonetheless, it also reflected a concern to retain an influence on developments in Germany. As the first foreign secretary to visit the GDR, Howe held meetings with leading SED officials, including Foreign Minister Oskar Fischer, the SED's General Secretary Erich Honecker and Prime Minister Willi Stoph, and met representatives from East German Protestant churches. The foreign secretary emphasised the importance that Britain attached to human rights. However, he avoided the appeals of Western journalists to call for the Berlin Wall to be torn down and described the SDI as the main obstacle to progress in arms control negotiations. Howe made a strong impression on the SED leadership, which interpreted his firm but more forthcoming stance towards East Germany as a potential counterweight to Reagan's hardline approach.[319] Nonetheless, the foreign secretary avoided appearing too conciliatory with East Berlin, remarking that the ten-year-old Final Act 'was meant to sound a trumpet call which would bring down all the walls and barriers which still divide our peoples'.[320]

While exposing different Anglo-American expectations about transformation in Eastern Europe, the early 1980s also experienced a partial resurgence of the special relationship in other areas. First, despite conflicting viewpoints within the administration, the US had provided Britain with vital support during the Falklands conflict in intelligence and military equipment. Second, after its initial diffidence, Whitehall had been the first European government to sign a memorandum of understanding on the SDI in December 1985. Nonetheless, Britain's change of heart on missile defence occurred only following a meeting in December 1984, in which the US president assured Thatcher that the SDI's aim was to 'enhance deterrence', not to erode it.[321] Furthermore, in return for Whitehall's support, the Reagan administration had promised a number of extremely lucrative contracts to the British defence industry. Finally, in 1986 Whitehall allowed the US use of its airbases to bomb Libya.[322] On a number of issues there were serious Anglo-American fissures. These included Washington's ambivalence during the Falklands conflict's early stages, the peace process in the Middle East, where Britain had to coordinate its policy with the pro-Arab stance of other EEC members, and the effects of US monetary and fiscal policy on the British economy. Washington's economic policy aggravated Britain's economic problems. In the 1980s, in order to counteract the expanding federal budget and current account deficits, the Federal Reserve kept interest rates high, attracting foreign capital. High interest rates in the US placed a huge strain on the British pound, prompting Thatcher to appeal personally to Reagan. In 1985 Secretary of the Treasury James A. Baker III displayed understanding for British demands, but the US was far more concerned to secure consensus from Germany and Japan over concerted interventions in the exchange markets and coordination of macroeconomic policies.[323]

Nonetheless, the main disruptive event for Anglo-American relations had occurred in October 1983, when a US fleet destined for Lebanon was diverted to the small Caribbean island of Grenada, which had been a British colony until 1974. Washington's aim was to help neighbouring Commonwealth states unseat the Revolutionary Military Council that had been established following the murder of Prime Minister Maurice Bishop. Thatcher was strongly against the invasion and after consultation with Howe and Heseltine on the morning of 25 October she wrote to Reagan, 'this action will be seen as intervention by a Western country in the internal affairs of a small independent nation. . . . I ask you to consider this in the context of our wider East–West relations.'[324] Although the intervention was initiated ostensibly at the request of the Organisation of Eastern Caribbean States and of the Queen's representative in Grenada, Governor General Sir Paul Scoon, his written request to intervene was not actually received in Washington until two days after US and Caribbean forces had successfully overthrown the regime.[325]

However, although there were fissures in a number of areas, overall Anglo-American relations remained positive. In a briefing prepared for Secretary of State Schultz on the occasion of Thatcher's visit to the US in December 1984, Assistant Secretary of State Richard Burt noted that the White House's extensive consultation with the British on a wide variety of political and military topics seemed to be working, although economic issues remained a 'chronic irritant' and 'the source of our most bitter differences' in the relationship.[326] Latent differences, including those on relations with Moscow and developments in Germany, did not undercut the sense of a newly vibrant Anglo-American partnership. A secret memo prepared in February 1985 for Reagan's meeting with Thatcher, on the occasion of the 200th anniversary of the establishment of diplomatic relations between Britain and the US, emphasised that bilateral relations remained 'close and special' and that Washington and London pursued 'similar foreign policy goals'.[327]

In May 1985 the British followed the US lead and downplayed celebrations for the fortieth anniversary of Victory in Europe Day (VE Day).[328] As Deputy Foreign Secretary Baroness Janet Young explained in a letter to the foreign affairs spokesman of Britain's Social Democratic Party, John Cartwright, in January, Whitehall feared that 'any official British international celebration confined to wartime allies could appear at best nostalgic, and at worst anti-German, unbalanced and open to historical distortion by the Soviet Union'.[329] The British boycott of VE Day celebrations, in the aftermath of the visit to Chequers by Gorbachev in December 1984 and of Thatcher to the USSR in March 1985, caused outrage in Moscow. The Kremlin perceived it as an ill-concealed attempt 'to write the Soviet Union out of the victory', particularly in light of the massive celebrations of D-Day in the previous year. Moscow complained that celebrating D-Day was in itself a historical distortion, as it commemorated the landing of five allied divisions in occupied Europe, when the Red Army had kept over 200 divisions engaged in the War against Germany for more than three years. Furthermore, according to the Soviet viewpoint, Western accounts failed to mention the significance of a gigantic Red Army offensive against the German central front from the Baltic states to Belarus and across Eastern Poland that had begun on the night of 21–2 June 1944, three years after Germany's invasion of the USSR. The Soviet offensive had taken enormous pressure off the Americans, who had struggled to break out of the Normandy pocket.[330] However, this incident did not distract Thatcher from her concern to establish cooperation with the new Soviet leadership. It would not be long before a sudden acceleration in the process of transformation in Eastern Europe would place US and British strategies towards Germany on a collision course, prompting Whitehall to look at Russia as a counterweight to German influence in Europe.

Notes

1. The Federal Ministry of All-German Affairs had been created in 1949 with the purpose of dealing with the East German government and with former German territories east of the Oder–Neisse line. In 1969 it was renamed the Ministry for Inter-German Relations before being abolished in 1991 after unification. Stefan Creuzberger, *Kampf für die Einheit: Das gesamtdeutsche Ministerium und die politische Kultur des Kalten Krieges 1949–1969* (Düsseldorf: Droste, 2008).
2. In April 1982 Willy Brandt bitterly recalled that, during his tenure as governing mayor of West Berlin, Dulles once had told him that although there were many divisive elements in American and Soviet policies, the two countries had one objective in common: the 'wish to perpetuate the division of Germany'. Dulles's statement is quoted in Margarita Mathiopoulos, 'The U.S. Presidency and the German Question during the Adenauer to Kohl Chancellorships', *Aussenpolitik*, vol. 39, no. 4, 1988, p. 353.
3. On the role played by the US in fostering a more active West German policy towards the Soviet bloc and the GDR see Stephan Kieninger, *Dynamic Détente: The United States and Europe, 1964–1975* (Lanham, MD: Lexington, 2016).

4. Avril Pittman, *From Ostpolitik to Reunification: West German–Soviet Political Relations since 1974* (New York: Cambridge University Press, 1992), p. 8.
5. Suzanne Brown-Fleming, 'Personalities and Politics: The American Ambassadors to the Federal Republic', in Detlef Junker, Philipp Gassert, Wilfried Mausbach and David B. Morris (eds), *The United States and Germany in the Era of the Cold War, 1945–1990: A Handbook. Vol. 1, 1945–1968* (Washington, DC: Cambridge University Press, 2004), p. 154. See also George C. McGhee, *On the Frontline in the Cold War: An Ambassador Reports* (Westport, CT: Praeger, 1997), pp. 175–6; Lyndon Baines Johnson, *The Vantage Point: Perspectives of the Presidency, 1963–1969* (New York: Holt, Rinehart and Winston, 1971), p. 306.
6. Joost Kleuters, *Reunification in West German Party Politics from Westbindung to Ostpolitik* (Basingstoke: Palgrave Macmillan, 2012), p. 130.
7. Clay Clemens, *Reluctant Realists: The Christian Democrats and West German Ostpolitik* (Durham, NC: Duke University Press, 1989), pp. 47–8.
8. Kleuters, *Reunification*, pp. 123–30.
9. McGeorge Bundy, Memorandum for the Record, 7 December 1964, Box 18–19, Files of McGeorge Bundy, Lyndon Baines Johnson Library, Austin, Texas. Quoted in Frank Costigliola, 'An "Arm around the Shoulder": The United States, NATO and German Reunification, 1989–90', *Contemporary European History*, vol. 3, no. 1, March 1994, p. 94, fn. 23.
10. Raymond L. Garthoff, *A Journey through the Cold War: A Memoir of Containment and Coexistence* (Washington, DC: Brookings Institution Press, 2001), p. 226.
11. *The Public Papers of the Presidents of the United States* (hereafter *Public Papers*): *Lyndon B. Johnson, 1966, Book II* (Washington, DC: Government Printing Office, 1967), doc. no. 1503, pp. 1125–30. Quoted in James Ellison, 'Stabilising the West and Looking to the East: Anglo-American Relations, Europe and Détente, 1965–1967', in N. Piers Ludlow (ed.), *European Integration and the Cold War: Ostpolitik-Westpolitik, 1965–1973* (Abingdon: Routledge, 2007), p. 118. See also Frank A. Ninkovich, 'The United States and the German Question, 1949–1968', in Detlef Junker, Philipp Gassert, Wilfried Mausbach and David B. Morris (eds), *The United States and Germany in the Era of the Cold War, 1945–1990: A Handbook. Vol. 1, 1945–1968* (Washington, DC: Cambridge University Press, 2004), p. 123.
12. The 'Report of the Council on the Future Tasks of the Alliance' is published in US Arms Control and Disarmament Agency

(ACDA), *Documents on Disarmament, 1967* (Washington, DC: Government Printing Office, 1968), pp. 679–81.

13. Werner Link, 'Détente auf deutsch und Anpassung an Amerika: Die Bonner Ostpolitik', in Detlef Junker (ed.), *Die USA und Deutschland im Zeitalter des Kalten Krieges. Ein Handbuch*, vol. 2 (Stuttgart: DVA, 2001), pp. 56–65.

14. Holger Klitzing, 'To Grin and Bear It: The Nixon Administration and Ostpolitik', in Carole Fink and Bernd Schaefer (eds), *Ostpolitik 1969–1974: European and Global Responses* (Washington, DC: German Historical Institute, 2009), p. 83.

15. Kieninger, *Dynamic Détente*, pp. 51–2.

16. Gottfried Niedhart, 'Anglo-American Relations in the Era of Détente and the Challenge of Ostpolitik', in Ursula Lehmkuhl and Gustav Schmidt (eds), *From Enmity to Friendship: Anglo-American Relations in the 19th and 20th Century* (Augsburg: Wißner, 2005), pp. 115–30.

17. Henry Kissinger, 'Statement on the Occasion of the Unveiling of a Willy Brandt Portrait by Johannes Heisig', German Historical Institute, Washington, DC, 18 March 2003. Quoted in Carole Fink and Bernd Schaefer, 'Ostpolitik and the World 1969–1974: Introduction', in Carole Fink and Bernd Schaefer (eds), *Ostpolitik and the World: European and Global Responses* (New York: Cambridge University Press, 2009), p. 1.

18. Logevall, *Embers of War*, p. 712.

19. Maurice Isserman, *Vietnam War* (New York: Facts on File, 2003), pp. 108–9.

20. Carl Solberg, *Hubert Humphrey: A Biography* (New York: Norton, 1984), pp. 285–300. See also Michael A. Cohen, *American Maelstrom: The 1968 Election and the Politics of Division* (Oxford and New York: Oxford University Press, 2016), pp. 65–72.

21. Hubert H. Humphrey, '"A New Day for America": Address Accepting the Presidential Nomination at the Democratic National Convention in Chicago', 29 August 1968, in Gerhard Peters and John T. Woolley, *The American Presidency Project*, available at <http://www.presidency.ucsb.edu/ws/?pid=25964> (last accessed 29 September 2016).

22. Richard Nixon, 'Address Accepting the Presidential Nomination at the Republican National Convention in Miami Beach, Florida', 8 August 1968, in Gerhard Peters and John T. Woolley, *The American Presidency Project*, available at <http://www.presidency.ucsb.edu/ws/?pid=25968> (last accessed 29 September 2016). The full text of the speech was published by *The New York Times* on 9 August. See also *Foreign Relations of the United States* (Washington, DC: Government Printing Office) (hereafter *FRUS*),

1969–76, vol. 1, *Foundations of Foreign Policy, 1969–1972*, doc. no. 6, pp. 49–50.

23. Quoted in Jussi M. Hanhimäki, *The Rise and Fall of Détente: American Foreign Policy and the Transformation of the Cold War* (Washington, DC: Potomac Books, 2013), p. 66.

24. Klitzing, 'To Grin and Bear It', p. 80.

25. Gottfried Niedhart, 'Zustimmung und Irritationen: Die Westmächte und die deutsche *Ostpolitik*, 1969–1970', in Ursula Lehmkuhl, Clemens A. Wurm and Hubert Zimmermann (eds), *Deutschland, Großbritannien, Amerika. Politik, Gesellschaft und Internationale Geschichte im 20. Jahrhundert. Festschrift für Gustav Schmidt zum 65. Geburtstag* (Stuttgart: Steiner, 2003), pp. 227–45. See also Gottfried Niedhart, 'The Federal Republic's *Ostpolitik* and the United States: Initiatives and Constraints', in Kathleen Burk and Melvyn Stokes (eds), *The United States and the European Alliance since 1945* (Oxford: Berg, 1999), pp. 289–311.

26. Kieninger, *Dynamic Détente*, pp. 104–5, 117, 121. See also Francis J. Gavin, 'Nuclear Nixon: Ironies, Puzzles, and the Triumph of Realpolitik', in Fredrik Logevall and Andrew Preston (eds), *Nixon in the World: American Foreign Relations, 1969–1977* (Oxford and New York: Oxford University Press, 2008), pp. 126–45.

27. Hubert Zimmermann, 'The Improbable Permanence of a Commitment: America's Troop Presence in Europe during the Cold War', *Journal of Cold War Studies*, vol. 11, no. 1, 2009, p. 20.

28. Mario del Pero, *The Eccentric Realist: Henry Kissinger and the Shaping of American Foreign Policy* (Ithaca, NY: Cornell University Press, 2006), pp. 95–6 (quotation on p. 96).

29. Klitzing, 'To Grin and Bear It', p. 92.

30. Mary E. Sarotte, 'The Frailties of Grand Strategy: A Comparison of Détente and Ostpolitik', in Fredrik Logevall and Andrew Preston (eds), *Nixon in the World: American Foreign Relations, 1969–1977* (Oxford and New York: Oxford University Press, 2008), pp. 150–1.

31. Quoted in Mary E. Sarotte, *Dealing with the Devil: East Germany, Détente, and Ostpolitik, 1969–1973* (Chapel Hill, NC: University of North Carolina Press, 2001), p. 54. See also Stephen E. Ambrose, *Nixon: The Triumph of a Politician, 1962–1972* (New York: Simon and Schuster, 1989), pp. 385–6; Julia Von Dannenberg, *The Foundations of Ostpolitik: The Making of the Moscow Treaty between West Germany and the USSR* (Oxford: Oxford University Press, 2008).

32. Niedhart, 'The Federal Republic's Ostpolitik', p. 298.

33. Henry Kissinger, *White House Years* (Boston, MA: Little, Brown,

1979), p. 825. See also Jussi M. Hanhimäki, *The Flawed Architect: Henry Kissinger and American Foreign Policy* (London and New York: Oxford University Press, 2004), pp. 87–8.

34. On the diverging views between the White House and the State Department see Stephan Kieninger, 'Transformation or Status Quo – The Conflict of Stratagems in Washington over the Meaning and Purpose of the CSCE and MBFR, 1969–1973', in Oliver Bange and Gottfried Niedhart (eds), *Helsinki 1975 and the Transformation of Europe* (London: Berghahn Books, 2008), pp. 67–82.

35. Klitzing, 'To Grin and Bear It', p. 90.

36. INR Research Memo (Cline), 7 April 1970, Re: West Germany/ USSR: The Bahr–Gromyko Talks. Quoted in Klitzing, 'To Grin and Bear It', p. 90, fn. 28.

37. Letter Doherty to Camps, 2 April 1970, National Archives and Records Administration (hereafter NARA), RG59, S/PC 1969–73, Box 403, Germany 1970. Quoted in Klitzing, 'To Grin and Bear It', p. 93.

38. *FRUS, 1969–76*, vol. 40, *Germany and Berlin, 1969–1972*, doc. no. 113, Memorandum from the President's Assistant for National Security Affairs (Kissinger) to President Nixon, p. 121. See also Werner Lippert, *The Economic Diplomacy of Ostpolitik: Origins of NATO's Energy Dilemma* (New York: Berghahn Books, 2011), p. 83.

39. The comment is reported in the conversation between British Prime Minister Edward Heath and US Secretary of State William Pierce Rogers that took place on 17 December 1970. *Akten zur Auswärtigen Politik der Bundesrepublik Deutschland* (hereafter *AAPD*), 1970, doc. no. 610, pp. 2305–9 (quotation on p. 2309). See also *Frankfurter Allgemeine Zeitung*, 23 December 1970.

40. See for example Muskie's senate intervention of 23 November 1971. *Congressional Record Index*, Government Printing Office, 1971, p. 42909.

41. Congressional Record, Senate, 28 November 1971–17 February 1972, available at <http://www.kas.de/wf/doc/kas_25267-544-1-30.pdf?110826092319> (last accessed 29 September 2016).

42. Geraint Hughes, *Harold Wilson's Cold War: The Labour Government and East–West Politics, 1964–1970* (Rochester, NY: Boydell Press, 2009), pp. 62–9.

43. Michael J. Turner, *Britain and the World in the Twentieth Century: Ever Decreasing Circles* (London: Continuum, 2010), p. 152.

44. Sylvia Ellis, *Britain, America, and the Vietnam War* (Westport, CT: Praeger, 2004), pp. 101ff. See also Will Podmore, *British Foreign Policy since 1870* (Bloomington, IN: Xlibris, 2008), p. 162.

45. *Statement on Defence Estimates, 1966*, Command Paper 2901

(1966), 'The Defence Review', p. 6. Quoted in Terry Macintyre, *Anglo-German Relations during the Labour Governments, 1964–70: NATO Strategy, Détente and European Integration* (Manchester: Manchester University Press, 2007), p. 81.

46. Both quoted in Peter Jones, *America and the British Labour Party: The Special Relationship at Work* (London: I. B. Tauris, 1997), p. 150.

47. Quoted in Gerald Prenderghast, *Britain and the Wars in Vietnam: The Supply of Troops, Arms and Intelligence, 1945–1975* (Jefferson, NC: McFarland, 2015), pp. 104–5 (quotation on p. 105).

48. Brian White, *Britain, Détente and Changing East–West Relations* (London and New York: Routledge, 1992), p. 110. See also John Van Oudenaren, *Détente in Europe: The Soviet Union and the West since 1953* (Durham, NC: Duke University Press, 1991), p. 74.

49. Hughes, *Harold Wilson's Cold War*, p. 112.

50. Simon C. Smith (ed.), *The Wilson–Johnson Correspondence, 1964–69* (Farnham: Ashgate, 2015), doc. no. 192, pp. 210–11.

51. John Dumbrell and Sylvia Ellis, 'British Involvement in Vietnam Peace Initiatives, 1966–1967: Marigolds, Sunflowers and "Kosygin Week"', *Diplomatic History*, vol. 27, no. 1, 2003, pp. 113–49.

52. Jonathan Colman, *'A Special Relationship'? Harold Wilson, Lyndon B. Johnson and Anglo-American Relations 'At the Summit', 1964–68* (Manchester: Manchester University Press, 2004), p. 131. See also Harold Wilson, *The Labour Government 1964–1970: A Personal Record* (London: Weidenfeld & Nicolson and Michael Joseph, 1971), p. 365.

53. Colman, *'A Special Relationship'?*, pp. 92, 177. See also Jonathan Colman, *The Foreign Policy of Lyndon B. Johnson: The United States and the World, 1963–1969* (Edinburgh: Edinburgh University Press, 2010), pp. 72, 203.

54. National Security File UK, Boxes 211/212, Bruce to Rusk, 8 May 1967, Lyndon B. Johnson Presidential Library. Quoted in John Dumbrell, 'Personal Diplomacy: Relations between Prime Ministers and Presidents', in Alan P. Dobson and Steve Marsh (eds), *Anglo-American Relations: Contemporary Perspectives* (Routledge: London, 2013), p. 85.

55. Prenderghast, *Britain and the Wars*, p. 105. See also P. L. Pham, *Ending 'East of Suez': The British Decision to Withdraw from Malaysia and Singapore (1964–1968)* (Oxford and New York: Oxford University Press, 2010).

56. *Documents on British Policy Overseas* (hereafter *DBPO*), Series III, vol. I, *Britain and the Soviet Union, 1968–1972*, doc. no.

2, pp. 8–13 and doc. no. 3, pp. 14–22. See also Luca Ratti, *Britain, Ost- and Deutschlandpolitik, and the CSCE (1955–1975)* (Bern: Peter Lang, 2008), p. 58, fn. 70; White, *Britain, Détente,* pp. 108–13.

57. Hughes, *Harold Wilson's Cold War,* pp. 132–3.

58. Susanna Schrafstetter and Stephen Twigge, *Avoiding Armageddon: Europe, the United States, and the Struggle for Nuclear Nonproliferation, 1945–1970* (Westport, CT and London: Praeger, 2004), pp. 176–7.

59. The Federal government adhered to the treaty on 28 November 1969 but the process of ratification was completed by the *Bundestag* only in 1974. See Ratti, *Britain,* pp. 62–8, 82.

60. Kieninger, *Dynamic Détente,* p. 56.

61. Smith, *The Wilson–Johnson Correspondence,* p. 19. See also Helen Parr, *Britain's Policy towards the European Community: Harold Wilson and Britain's World Role, 1964–1967* (Abingdon: Routledge, 2005), p. 77.

62. 'The President's Address to the Nation Announcing Steps to Limit the War in Vietnam and Reporting His Decision Not to Seek Reelection', 31 March 1968, in *Public Papers: Lyndon B. Johnson, 1968–69, Book I* (Washington, DC: Government Printing Office, 1970), pp. 469–76. See also Hughes, *Harold Wilson's Cold War,* p. 79; Prenderghast, *Britain and the Wars,* p. 77.

63. Hubert Zimmermann, *Money and Security: Troops, Monetary Policy and West Germany's Relations with the United States and Britain, 1950–1971* (Washington, DC: German Historical Institute and Cambridge: Cambridge University Press, 2002), p. 235. See also Don Oberdorfer, *Senator Mansfield: The Extraordinary Life of a Great Statesman and Diplomat* (Washington, DC: Smithsonian Books, 2003).

64. John Dumbrell, *President Lyndon Johnson and Soviet Communism* (Manchester and New York: Manchester University Press, 2004), p. 169. On Western reactions to the Soviet repression of the Prague Spring see also Günter Bischof, '"No Action": The Johnson Administration and the Warsaw Pact Invasion of Czechoslovakia in August 1968', in Günter Bischof, Stefan Karner and Peter Ruggenthaler, *The Prague Spring and the Warsaw Pact Invasion of Czechoslovakia in 1968* (New York: Lexington, 2010), pp. 215–36; Evanthis Hatzivassiliou, *NATO and Western Perceptions of the Soviet Bloc: Alliance Analysis and Reporting, 1951–69* (London and New York: Routledge 2014), pp. 172–80.

65. *DBPO,* III, I, doc. no. 104, John Killick to Crispin Tickell, p. 497.

66. Quoted in Hughes, *The Postwar Legacy,* p. 78.

67. Garret Joseph Martin, *General de Gaulle's Cold War: Challenging*

American Hegemony, 1963–68 (New York: Berghahn Books, 2013), pp. 151–2, 161–6. See also James Ellison, 'Dealing with de Gaulle: Anglo-American Relations, NATO and the Second Application', in Oliver J. Daddow (ed.), *Harold Wilson and European Integration: Britain's Second Application to Join the EEC* (London: Frank Cass, 2002), pp. 172–87.

68. National Archives (hereafter NA), PREM 13/1468, 1498. See Klaus Larres, 'Britain and the GDR: Political and Economic Relations, 1949–1989', in Klaus Larres and Elizabeth Meehan (eds), *Uneasy Allies: British–German Relations and European Integration since 1945* (Oxford: Oxford University Press, 2000), p. 92.

69. Briefing paper by the American Department for Foreign Secretary Michael Stewart before his trip to New York, 30 September 1968, NA, FCO 7/803. Quoted in Niedhart, 'Anglo-American Relations', p. 116.

70. Melissa Pine, *Harold Wilson and Europe: Pursuing Britain's Membership of the European Community* (London and New York: I. B. Tauris, 2007), pp. 138–9.

71. NA, FCO 33/1547, Jackling to Alec Douglas-Home, 25 June 1970.

72. Kieninger, *Dynamic Détente*, p. 87.

73. Conversation between Wilson and Nixon, 27 January 1970, NA, FCO 7/1823. The White House was taken aback by Wilson's views. Klitzing, 'To Grin and Bear It', p. 87. See also Dumbrell, 'Personal Diplomacy', p. 91.

74. Macintyre, *Anglo-German Relations*, pp. 174–98.

75. Jean-François Juneau, 'The Limits of Linkage: The Nixon Administration and Willy Brandt's *Ostpolitik*, 1969–72', *The International History Review*, vol. 33, no. 2, 2011, p. 290. See also State Secretary Paul Frank's talks with Falin: memcon, Frank with Falin, 27 May 1971, *AAPD*, 1971, pp. 861–6.

76. Anglo/United States Relations. Brief by FCO, 23 September 1970, NA, FCO 7/1839. See also Kieninger, *Dynamic Détente*, pp. 86–8.

77. Dobson, *Anglo-American Relations in the Twentieth Century*, p. 141.

78. Geir Lundestad, 'The European Role at the Beginning and Particularly at the End of the Cold War', in Olav Njølstad (ed.), *The Last Decade of the Cold War: From Conflict Escalation to Conflict Transformation* (London: Frank Cass, 2004), p. 55.

79. Oliver Bange, 'The German Problem and Security in Europe: Hindrance or Catalyst on the Path to 1989/90?', in Mark Kramer and Vit Smetana (eds), *Imposing, Maintaining, and Tearing Open the Iron Curtain: The Cold War and East-Central Europe, 1945–1989* (Lanham, MD: Lexington Books, 2014), pp. 200–1.

80. House of Commons Debate, 9 December 1970, vol. 808, cols 435–638. See also NA, FCO 33/1416, Bendall to Cradock, 27 January 1971.

81. *AAPD*, 1970, doc. no. 600, pp. 2273–5.

82. Peter W. Unwin to Jackling, 1 January 1971, NA, FCO 33/1547.

83. Extract from record of the meeting between Prime Minister Heath and President Nixon at the White House on 17 December 1970, NA, FCO 33/1547.

84. Moon to Burke Trend, NA, FCO 7/1842.

85. *AAPD*, 1970, doc. no. 269, pp. 987–8.

86. Anne Deighton, 'Ostpolitik or Westpolitik? British Foreign Policy, 1968–75', *International Affairs*, vol. 74, no. 4, 1998, p. 894.

87. Bayne to Gladstone, 7 February 1972, NA, FO 1042/434. See also *The Washington Post*, 5 December 1971.

88. Chalmers M. Roberts, 'Acheson Urges Brandt's "Race" to Moscow Be "Cooled Off"', *The Washington Post*, 10 December 1970. See also *FRUS*, 1969–76, vol. 40, p. 412.

89. See the report sent on 10 December to Bonn by Pauls in *AAPD*, 1970, doc. 607, p. 2294, fn. 4. On the strain in US–West German relations that had been caused by Brandt's policy see also the article by David Binder, *The New York Times*, 20 December 1970; Irwin M. Wall, 'The United States and Two Ostpolitiks: De Gaulle and Brandt', in Wilfried Loth and Georges-Henri Soutou (eds), *The Making of Détente: Eastern Europe and Western Europe in the Cold War, 1965–75* (London: Routledge, 2008), p. 145.

90. Extract from record of the meeting between the Prime Minister and President Nixon at the White House on 17 December 1970. See also Peter W. Unwin to Jackling, 1 January 1971, NA, FCO 33/1547.

91. Quoted in Gottfried Niedhart, 'The British Reaction towards Ostpolitik: Anglo-West German Relations in the Era of Détente 1967–1971', in Christian Haase (ed.), *Debating Foreign Affairs – The Public and British Foreign Policy since 1867* (Berlin: Philo Fine Arts, 2003), p. 145. See also the conversation between Nixon and Heath held in Washington, 17 December 1970, NA, FCO 7/1842.

92. Willy Brandt, 'What Is Germany's 'Ostpolitik'?', *The New York Times*, 11 November 1970.

93. Unwin to Jackling, 1 January 1971, NA, FCO 33/1547.

94. Memorandum of Conversation, Nixon, Kissinger, Heath, Burke, 17 December 1970, NARA, Nixon Presidential Material Project, National Security Council, Box 1024, Memorandum of Conversation – The President, PM Heath. Quoted in Klitzing,

'To Grin and Bear It', p. 98 and Niedhart, 'The British Reaction', p. 131.

95. Mary E. Sarotte, '"Take No Risks (Chinese)"': The Basic Treaty in the Context of International Relations', *German Historical Institute Bulletin*, supp. no. 1, 2004, p. 113. See also Gottfried Niedhart, 'Deutsch-amerikanische Beziehungen in der Anfangsphase der sozial-liberalen Ostpolitik und Differenzen in der Perzeption der Sowjetunion 1969/70', in Manfred Berg and Philipp Gassert (eds), *Deutschland und die USA in der Internationalen Geschichte des 20. Jahrhunderts: Festschrift für Detlef Junker* (Stuttgart: Steiner, 2004), pp. 505–20.

96. Von Hase, London, to Auswärtiges Amt, 29 January 1971, PA AA: B 150/222.

97. Thomson to Burke Trend, 22 December 1970, NA, PREM 15/1579.

98. As stressed by Percy Cradock, then at the FCO planning staff, this was particularly worrying for Britain, which had always regarded itself as 'bound by alliance solidarity to a far greater extent than, for instance, the French'. Cradock to Gladstone, 15 January 1971, NA, FCO 33/1416.

99. Jackling to Brimelow, 8 January 1971, NA, FCO 33/1547.

100. Bendall to Cradock, 27 January 1971, NA, FCO 33/1416.

101. Draft steering brief prepared by the FCO on the occasion of Brandt's visit to London from 20 to 22 April 1972, no date, NA, FCO 14/1069.

102. Cradock to Gladstone, 15 January 1971, NA, FCO 33/1416.

103. While the conservative Daily Telegraph had long been critical of Bonn's Eastern policy, criticism of *Ostpolitik* was now also expressed by other national newspapers, such as *The Times* and *The Guardian*. See AAPD, 1971, doc. no. 1, p. 4. See also *The Times*, 2 June 1970 and 24 June 1970.

104. Von Hase to Bonn on 2 January 1971, AAPD, 1971, doc. no. 1, p. 4.

105. Udo Leuschner, *Die Geschichte der FDP: Metamorphosen einer Partei zwischen rechts, sozialliberal und neokonservativ* (Münster: Edition Octopus, 2005), p. 88. Already in October 1969 Mende, Starke and Zoglmann had voted against their party's decision to ally with the Social Democrats. Janusz Józef Wec, *Sozialliberale Ostpolitik: Die FDP und der Warschauer Vetrag, Die Haltung der FDP gegenüber den Verhandlungen mit Polen über den Warschauer Vertrag vom 7. Dezember 1970* (Potsdam: Friedrich-Naumann-Stiftung für die Freiheit, 2011), p. 9, fn. 11.

106. On the CDU's attempts to block Brandt's Eastern policy see *FRUS*, 1969–76, vol. 40, doc. no. 86, pp. 238–40.

107. Mary N. Hampton, *The Wilsonian Impulse: U.S. Foreign Policy, the Alliance, and German Unification* (New York: Praeger, 1996), p. 140. See also Richard Barnet, *The Alliance: America, Europe, Japan, Makers of the Postwar World* (New York: Simon & Schuster, 1983), p. 292.

108. Henry A. Kissinger, 'The Search for Stability', *Foreign Affairs*, vol. 37, no. 4, July 1959, p. 542; see also Stephen R. Graubard, *Kissinger; Portrait of a Mind* (New York: W. W. Norton, 1973), pp. 142–3; Hampton, *The Wilsonian Impulse*, pp. 140–1.

109. Both quoted in the paper prepared by the FCO on *Ostpolitik* before Scheel's visit to London in February 1971. Nonetheless, the paper excluded the possibility that *Ostpolitik* might undercut Western security. NA, PREM 15/1579.

110. On the origin and development of the Brezhnev doctrine see Matthew J. Ouimet, *The Rise and Fall of the Brezhnev Doctrine in Soviet Foreign Policy* (Chapel Hill, NC: University of North Carolina Press, 2003).

111. Bundesministerium für gesamtdeutsche Fragen (ed.), *Texte zur Deutschlandpolitik*, Band 7, 28. Januar 1971–29. Januar 1971 (Bonn: Bundesministerium für innerdeutsche Beziehungen, 1971), pp. 5–23, 605–17.

112. Lundestad, 'The European Role', p. 55.

113. Kissinger, *White House Years*, pp. 129–30.

114. Kieninger, *Dynamic Détente*, p. 175; Wall, 'The United States', p. 143; Sarotte, 'The Frailties of Grand Strategy', p. 154.

115. Willy Brandt, 'Germany's "Westpolitik"', *Foreign Affairs*, vol. 50, no. 3, April 1972, pp. 416–26.

116. Paper prepared by the FCO on *Ostpolitik*, NA, PREM 15/1579.

117. See Jackling to Douglas-Home, 5 May 1971, NA, FCO 33/1416.

118. Kieninger, *Dynamic Détente*, p. 131–41.

119. *AAPD*, 1971, doc. no. 47, pp. 242–4.

120. John Dumbrell, *Rethinking the Vietnam War* (London and New York: Palgrave Macmillan, 2012), p. 118. See also Hanhimäki, *The Flawed Architect*, pp. 228–57.

121. Clemens, *Reluctant Realists*, p. 137.

122. Stefan Berger and Norman LaPorte, *Friendly Enemies: Britain and the GDR, 1949–1990* (Oxford: Berghahn Books, 2010), pp. 50–2.

123. Klaus Larres, 'Introduction: Uneasy Allies or Genuine Partners? Britain, Germany, and European Integration', in Klaus Larres and Elizabeth Meehan (eds), *Uneasy Allies: British–German Relations and European Integration since 1945* (Oxford: Oxford University Press, 2000), p. 17; Larres, 'Political and Economic Relations', p. 65 and ff.

124. Martin D. Brown, 'A Very British Vision of Détente: The United

Kingdom's Foreign Policy during the Helsinki Process', in Frédéric Bozo, Marie-Pierre Rey, N. Piers Ludlow and Bernd Rother (eds), *Visions of the End of the Cold War in Europe, 1945–1990* (New York and Oxford: Berghahn Books, 2012), p. 126. On the early stages of British–East German diplomatic relations see Marianne Howarth, 'Vom Kalten Krieg zum "Kalten Frieden". Diplomatische Beziehungen zwischen Grossbritannien und der DDR 1972/73–1975', in Peter Barker, Marc-Dietrich Ohse and Dennis Tate (eds), *Views from Abroad: Die DDR aus britischer Perspektive* (Bielefeld: WBV, W. Bertelsmann, 2007), pp. 149–62.

125. Berger and LaPorte, *Friendly Enemies*, pp. 176–7.

126. Radio Free Europe Research, vol. 9, 1984, p. 53. See also Gerard R. Kleinfeld, 'The Genesis of American Policy toward the GDR: Some Working Hypotheses', in Reiner Pommerin (ed.), *The American Impact on Postwar Germany* (Oxford: Berghahn Books, 1995), pp. 53–64.

127. See the text of the discussion between Honecker and Bahr on 7 September 1972 in East Berlin in Heinrich Potthoff, *Bonn und Ost-Berlin 1969–1982: Dialog auf höchster Ebene und vertrauliche Kanäle, Darstellung und Dokumente* (Bonn: Dietz, 1997), p. 239.

128. 'Memorandum for the President, Initiation of Negotiations with the GDR on Establishment of Diplomatic Relations'. *FRUS*, 1969–76, vol. E-15, Part 1, *Documents on Eastern Europe, 1973–1976*, doc. no. 85, pp. 1–3.

129. Christian F. Ostermann, 'The Role of East Germany in American Policy', in Detlef Junker, Philipp Gassert, Wilfried Mausbach and David B. Morris (eds), *The United States and Germany in the Era of the Cold War, 1945–1990: A Handbook. Vol. 2, 1968–1990* (Washington and Cambridge: Cambridge University Press, 2004), pp. 96–7.

130. Ronald D. Asmus, 'Bonn and East Berlin: The View from Washington', Radio Free Europe Research, RAD Background Report/190, 17 October 1984.

131. Kieninger, *Dynamic Détente*, pp. 222, 288–9, 300.

132. Sigrid Meuschel, 'Auf der Suche nach Madame L'Identité? Zur Konzeption der Nation und Nationalgeschichte', in Gert-Joachim Glaessner (ed.), *Die DDR in der Ära Honecker: Politik – Kultur – Gesellschaft* (Opladen: Westdeutscher, 1988), pp. 80–4.

133. *FRUS*, 1977–80, vol. 20, *Eastern Europe*, doc. no. 133, pp. 411–18.

134. On Anglo-American views of the CSCE see Kieninger, 'Transformation or Status Quo'; Luca Ratti, 'Britain, the German Question and the Transformation of Europe: From Ostpolitik to the Helsinki Conference (1963–1975)', in Oliver Bange and

Gottfried Niedhart (eds), *Helsinki 1975 and the Transformation of Europe* (New York and Oxford: Berghahn Books, 2008), pp. 83–97. See also Kieninger, *Dynamic Détente*, pp. 189–209, 221–38, 247–68; Stephan Kieninger, 'Den Status quo aufrechterhalten oder ihn langfristig überwinden? Der Wettkampf westlicher Entspannungsstrategien in den Siebzigerjahren', in Oliver Bange and Bernd Lemke (eds), *Wege zur Wiedervereinigung. Die beiden deutschen Staaten in ihren Bündnissen 1970 bis 1990* (Munich: Oldenbourg 2013), pp. 67–86.

135. On the Guillaume affair see Jefferson Adams, *Strategic Intelligence in the Cold War and Beyond* (Abingdon and New York: Routledge, 2015), pp. 63–9.

136. Thomas Robb, *A Strained Partnership? US–UK Relations in the Era of Détente, 1969–77* (Manchester: Manchester University Press, 2013), pp. 39–40.

137. Dobson, *Anglo-American Relations in the Twentieth Century*, p. 142; Dumbrell, 'Personal Diplomacy', p. 85. See also John Sakkas, 'Conflict and Détente in the Eastern Mediterranean: From the Yom Kippur War to the Cyprus Crisis, October 1973–August 1974', in Elena Calandri, Antonio Varsori and Daniele Caviglia (eds), *Détente in Cold War Europe: Politics and Diplomacy in the Mediterranean and the Middle East* (London: I. B. Tauris, 2012), p. 145.

138. Quoted in John Baylis (ed.), *Anglo-American Relations since 1939: The Enduring Alliance* (Manchester and New York: Manchester University Press, 1997), p. 172. See also Michael J. Turner, *Britain's International Role, 1970–1991* (New York: Palgrave Macmillan, 2010), pp. 52–4.

139. Kristan Stoddart, *The Sword and the Shield: Britain, America, NATO and Nuclear Weapons, 1970–1976* (Basingstoke: Palgrave Macmillan, 2014), p. 13; Baylis, *Anglo-American Relations since 1939*, p. 169–71; Dobson, *Anglo-American Relations in the Twentieth Century*, p. 140–2. See also Christopher Hill and Christopher Lord, 'The Foreign Policy of the Heath Government', in Stuart Ball and Anthony Seldon (eds), *The Heath Government 1970–74: A Reappraisal* (London and New York: Routledge, 1996), pp. 285–314; Andrew Scott, *Allies Apart: Heath, Nixon and the Anglo-American Relationship* (Basingstoke and New York: Palgrave Macmillan, 2011).

140. Daniel Mockli, *European Foreign Policy during the Cold War: Heath, Brandt, Pompidou and the Dream of Political Unity* (London and New York: I. B. Tauris, 2009), pp. 298–9.

141. Antonio Varsori, 'Crisis and Stabilization in Southern Europe during the 1970s: Western Strategy, European Instruments', *Journal of European Integration History*, vol. 15, no. 1, 2009, pp. 5–14.

142. Peter H. Merkl, *German Unification in the European Context* (University Park: Pennsylvania State University Press, 1993), p. 62.

143. Sarotte, *Dealing with the Devil*, p. 24.

144. Sean Kay, *NATO and the Future of European Security* (Lanham, MD: Rowman & Littlefield, 1998), p. 168, fn. 44.

145. John S. Duffield, *Power Rules: The Evolution of NATO's Conventional Force Posture* (Stanford, CA: Stanford University Press, 1995), pp. 203–4.

146. Geoffrey Lee Williams, *The Permanent Alliance: The European–American Partnership, 1945–1984* (Leyden: A.W. Sijthoff, 1977), p. 324; David Walsh, *The Military Balance in the Cold War: US Perceptions and Policy, 1976–85* (London and New York: Routledge, 2008), p. 111. See also *FRUS, 1969–76*, vol. E-15, Part 2, *Documents on Western Europe, 1973–1976*, doc. no. 276, p. 857.

147. Luke A. Nichter, *Richard Nixon and Europe: The Reshaping of the Postwar Atlantic World* (Cambridge: Cambridge University Press, 2015), p. 142. See also *AAPD*, 1973, Gespräch des Bundeskanzlers Brandt mit Präsident Nixon in Washington, 29 September 1973, doc. no. 298, pp. 1448–9.

148. Mockli, *European Foreign Policy*, p. 151. Kissinger's 'Year of Europe' speech of 23 April 1973 is printed in *The Department of State Bulletin*, 14 May 1973, vol. LXVIII, pp. 593–8.

149. Schmidt dedicated a relevant section of his memoirs to his friendship with Gerald Ford, while the US president also had positive feelings for the FRG chancellor. Helmut Schmidt, *Menschen und Mächte* (Berlin: Siedler, 1987), pp. 202–21; Gerald R. Ford, *A Time to Heal: The Autobiography of Gerald R. Ford* (New York: Harper & Row, 1979), pp. 220–1.

150. Cabinet meeting, 26 August 1974, in Gerald R. Ford Presidential Library, National Security Advisor, MemCons, Box 5. Quoted in N. Piers Ludlow, 'The Real Years of Europe?: US–West European Relations during the Ford Administration', *Journal of Cold War Studies*, vol. 15, no. 3, 2013, p. 144.

151. Hill and Lord, 'The Foreign Policy', p. 311. For a less critical evaluation of Heath's attitude to relations with the Nixon administration see Alex Spelling, 'Edward Heath and Anglo-American Relations 1970–1974: A Reappraisal', *Diplomacy & Statecraft*, vol. 20, no. 4, 2009, pp. 638–58.

152. Thomas Robb, 'The Power of Oil: Edward Heath, the "Year of Europe" and the Anglo-American "Special Relationship"', *Contemporary British History*, vol. 26, no. 1, 2012, pp. 73–96. See also Robb, *A Strained Partnership?*, pp. 73–127.

153. R. Gerald Hughes and Thomas Robb, 'Kissinger and the Diplomacy

of Coercive Linkage in the "Special Relationship" between the United States and Great Britain, 1969–1977', *Diplomatic History*, vol. 37, no. 4, 2013, pp. 861–905.

154. Nichter, *Richard Nixon*, p. 169.

155. Robert Self, *British Foreign and Defence Policy since 1945: Challenges and Dilemmas in a Changing World* (London: Palgrave Macmillan, 2010), p. 87.

156. Steve Marsh, 'The Anglo-American Defence Relationship', in Alan Dobson and Steve Marsh (eds), *Anglo-American Relations: Contemporary Perspectives* (London and New York: Routledge, 2013), pp. 180–3.

157. Robert Boyce, 'In Search of the Anglo-American Special Relationship in the Economic and Financial Spheres', in Antoine Capet and Aïssatou Sy-Wonyu (eds), *The 'Special Relationship': La «relation spéciale» entre le Royaume-Uni et les Etats-Unis* (Rouen: Université de Rouen, 2003), p. 84.

158. Stoddart, *The Sword and the Shield*, pp. 138–46.

159. Kathleen Burk, 'The Americans, the Germans, and the British: The 1976 IMF Crisis', *Twentieth Century British History*, vol. 5, no. 3, 1994, pp. 351–69. See also James E. Cronin, *Global Rules: America, Britain and a Disordered World* (New Haven, CT: Yale University Press, 2014), pp. 23–5, 55–61; Kathleen Burk and Alec Cairncross, *Good-bye Great Britain: The 1976 IMF Crisis* (New Haven, CT: Yale University Press, 1992).

160. Burk and Cairncross, *Good-bye Great Britain*. See also Douglas Wass, *Decline to Fall: The Making of British Macro-economic Policy and the 1976 IMF Crisis* (Oxford and New York: Oxford University Press, 2008), pp. 241ff.

161. Kenneth O. Morgan, 'Labour and the Anglo-American Alliance', in Antoine Capet and Aïssatou Sy-Wonyu (eds), *The 'Special Relationship': La «relation spéciale» entre le Royaume-Uni et les Etats-Unis* (Rouen: Université de Rouen, 2003), pp. 181–2.

162. Ludlow, 'The Real Years of Europe?', p. 151. See also Gillian Staerck, 'The Role of the British Embassy in Washington', *Contemporary British History*, vol. 12, no. 3, 1998, pp. 115–38.

163. Julian Bullard to Sykes, 23 September 1976, NA, FCO 33/296.

164. Odd Arne Westad, 'The Fall of Détente and the Turning Sides of History', in Odd Arne Westad (ed.), *The Fall of Détente: Soviet–American Relations during the Carter Years* (Oslo: Scandinavian University Press, 1997), pp. 3–33. See also Hanhimäki, *The Rise and Fall of Détente*.

165. Kristina Spohr, *The Global Chancellor: Helmut Schmidt and the Reshaping of the International Order* (Oxford and New York: Oxford University Press, 2016), pp. 7, 56. See also Fritz Stern, *Five*

Germanys I Have Known (New York: Farrar, Straus and Giroux, 2006), pp. 294–5; Lawrence S. Kaplan, *NATO and the UN: A Peculiar Relationship* (Columbia, MO: University of Missouri Press, 2010), pp. 107–8.

166. Klaus Wiegrefe, *Das Zerwürfnis: Helmut Schmidt, Jimmy Carter und die Krise der deutsch-amerikanische Beziehungen* (Berlin: Propyläen, 2005); Oliver Bange '"Keeping Détente Alive": Inner-German Relations under Helmut Schmidt and Erich Honecker, 1974–1982', in Leopoldo Nuti (ed.), *The Crisis of Détente in Europe: From Helsinki to Gorbachev 1975–1985* (London: Routledge, 2009), pp. 234–5. See also Marion Gräfin Dönhoff, 'Bonn and Washington: The Strained Relationship', *Foreign Affairs*, vol. 57, no. 5, Summer 1979, pp. 1052–64.

167. Charles William Carter, 'The Evolution of US Policy toward West German–Soviet Trade Relations 1969–89', *The International History Review*, vol. 34, no. 2, 2012, pp. 221–44.

168. Zbigniew Brzezinski, *Power and Principle: Memoirs of the National Security Adviser 1977–1981* (New York: Farrar, Straus and Giroux, 1985), p. 307. See also Hampton, *The Wilsonian Impulse*, p. 142.

169. Breck Walker, '"Neither Shy nor Demagogic" – The Carter Administration Goes to Belgrade', in Vladimir Bilandžic, Dittmar Dahlmann and Milan Kosanovic (eds), *From Helsinki to Belgrade: The First CSCE Follow-up Meeting and the Crisis of Détente* (Göttingen: Vandenhoeck & Ruprecht and Bonn: Bonn University Press, 2012), pp. 187–8.

170. Angela Stent, *From Embargo to Ostpolitik: The Political Economy of West German–Soviet Relations, 1955–1980* (Cambridge: Cambridge University Press, 1982), p. 236.

171. Arch Puddington, *Broadcasting Freedom: The Cold War Triumph of Radio Free Europe and Radio Liberty* (Lexington: University Press of Kentucky, 2000), pp. 185–7. See also Brzezinski, *Power and Principle*, p. 293, quoted in Hampton, *The Wilsonian Impulse*, p. 142; Geir Lundestad, *The United States and Western Europe since 1945: From 'Empire' by Invitation to Transatlantic Drift* (Oxford: Oxford University Press, 2003), p. 204.

172. Spohr, *The Global Chancellor*, pp. 54–6.

173. Kai Hebel, 'Die Brückenbauer? Großbritannien als transatlantischer Vermittler in der KSZE 1972–1978', in Matthias Peter and Hermann Wentker (eds), *Die KSZE im Ost-West-Konflikt. Internationale Politik und gesellschaftliche Transformation 1975–1990* (Munich: Oldenbourg, 2012), pp. 112–20.

174. Margot Light, 'Anglo-Soviet Relations: Political and Diplomatic', in Alex Pravda and Peter Duncan (eds), *Soviet–British Relations*

since the 1970s (Cambridge: Cambridge University Press, 1990), p. 134.

175. White, *Britain, Détente*, p. 136.
176. Oliver Bange, '"The Greatest Happiness of the Greatest Number ...": The FRG and the GDR and the Belgrade CSCE Conference (1977–78)', in Vladimir Bilandžic, Dittmar Dahlmann and Milan Kosanovic (eds), *From Helsinki to Belgrade: The First CSCE Follow-up Meeting and the Crisis of Détente* (Göttingen: Vandenhoeck & Ruprecht and Bonn: Bonn University Press, 2012), pp. 233–4. See also Oliver Bange, 'Der KSZE-Prozess und die sicherheitspolitische Dynamik des Ost-West-Konflikts 1970–1990', in Oliver Bange and Bernd Lemke (eds), *Wege zur Wiedervereinigung. Die beiden deutschen Staaten in ihren Bündnissen 1970 bis 1990* (Munich: Oldenbourg, 2013), pp. 87–104.
177. Wright to Duff, 30 March 1979, NA, FCO 33/401.
178. Hebel, 'Die "Brückenbauer"?', pp. 117–18 (quotation on p. 118).
179. Spohr, *The Global Chancellor*, p. 138.
180. Sabine Lee, *Victory in Europe? Britain and Germany since 1945* (Harlow: Longman, 2001), pp. 167–8.
181. Steven J. Zaloga, *The Kremlin's Nuclear Sword: The Rise and Fall of Russia's Strategic Nuclear Forces, 1945–2000* (Washington, DC: Smithsonian Institution Press, 2002), p. 203.
182. Helmut Schmidt, 'The 1977 Alastair Buchan Memorial Lecture', *Survival*, vol. 20, no. 1, January–February 1978, pp. 2–10.
183. Kaplan, *NATO and the UN*, p. 107. See also Mark Gilbert, *Cold War Europe: The Politics of a Contested Continent* (Lanham, MD: Rowman & Littlefield, 2014), p. 225; Marilena Gala, 'From INF to SDI: How Helsinki Reshaped the Transatlantic Dimension of European Security', in Leopoldo Nuti (ed.), *The Crisis of Détente in Europe: From Helsinki to Gorbachev 1975–1985* (London: Routledge, 2009), p. 114.
184. Richard C. Eichenberg, 'Dual Track and Double Trouble: The Two-Level Politics of INF', in Peter B. Evans, Harold K. Jacobson and Robert D. Putnam (eds), *Double-Edged Diplomacy: International Bargaining and Domestic Politics* (Berkeley: University of California Press, 1993), p. 48.
185. Kristina Spohr-Readman, 'Conflict and Cooperation in Intra-Alliance Nuclear Politics: Western Europe, the United States, and the Genesis of NATO's Dual-Track Decision, 1977–1979', in *Journal of Cold War Studies*, vol. 13, no. 2, Spring 2011, pp. 39–89. See also Kristina Spohr, 'Helmut Schmidt and the Shaping of Western Security in the Late 1970s: The Guadeloupe

Summit of 1979', *The International History Review*, vol. 37, no. 1, 2015, pp. 167–92.

186. The final communiqué issued by the alliance on 12 December 1979 is available at <http://www.nato.int/cps/en/natolive/official_ texts_27040.htm> (last accessed 29 September 2016). See also Gala, 'From INF to SDI', p. 114.

187. Leopoldo Nuti, 'The Origins of the 1979 Dual Track Decision – A Survey', in Leopoldo Nuti (ed.), *The Crisis of Détente in Europe: From Helsinki to Gorbachev 1975–1985* (London: Routledge, 2009), p. 63.

188. Julie Smith and Joffrey Edwards, 'British–West German Relations, 1973–1989', in Klaus Larres and Elizabeth Meehan (eds), *Uneasy Allies: British–German Relations and European Integration since 1945* (Oxford: Oxford University Press, 2000), p. 59. See also Jeffrey S. Lantis, *Domestic Constraints and the Breakdown of International Agreements* (Westport, CT: Praeger, 1997), pp. 78–9; Jones, *America and the British Labour Party*, pp. 174–5.

189. Christopher Booker and Richard North, *Great Deception: The Secret History of the European Union* (London: Continuum, 2003), p. 162; Lily Gardner Feldman, *Germany's Foreign Policy of Reconciliation: From Enmity to Amity* (Lanham, MD: Rowman & Littlefield, 2012), p. 91. See also Michèle Weinachter, 'Franco-German Relations in the Giscard–Schmidt Era, 1974–1981', in Carine Germond and Henning Türk (eds), *A History of Franco-German Relations in Europe: From 'Hereditary Enemies' to Partners* (New York: Palgrave Macmillan, 2008), pp. 230–1.

190. Quoted in Emmanuel Mourlon-Druol, *A Europe Made of Money: The Emergence of the European Monetary System* (Ithaca, NY: Cornell University Press, 2012), p. 185 and Harold James, *Making the European Monetary Union: The Role of the Committee of Central Bank Governors and the Origins of the European Central Bank* (Cambridge, MA and London: Harvard University Press, 2012), p. 153.

191. Hampton, *The Wilsonian Impulse*, p. 142. See also Brzezinski, *Power and Principle*, p. 165.

192. David F. Schmitz, *Brent Scowcroft: Internationalism and Post-Vietnam War American Foreign Policy* (Lanham, MD: Rowman & Littlefield, 2011), p. 68.

193. Carter, 'The Evolution of US Policy', p. 231.

194. James Reston, 'Where Are the Allies?', *The New York Times*, 14 November 1979.

195. Ronald E. Powaski, *The Cold War: The United States and the Soviet Union, 1917–1991* (New York: Oxford University Press, 1998), pp. 203–5.

196. Wallace J. Thies, *Why NATO Endures* (New York: Cambridge University Press, 2009), p. 231, fn. 159; Kaplan, *NATO and the UN*, p. 109.

197. On the impact of the invasion of Afghanistan on British–Soviet relations see *DBPO*, Series III, Vol. VIII, *The Invasion of Afghanistan and UK–Soviet Relations, 1979–1982* (London and New York: Whitehall Publishing and Routledge, 2012).

198. Stent, *From Embargo to Ostpolitik*, pp. 236–9.

199. John P. D. Dunbabin, *The Cold War: The Great Powers and Their Allies* (London: Pearson Education, 2008), p. 332.

200. Bange, '"Keeping Détente Alive"', p. 232.

201. Lippert, *The Economic Diplomacy*, p. 180.

202. Hampton, *The Wilsonian Impulse*, p. 142. See also Angela Romano, 'The Main Task of the European Political Cooperation: Fostering Détente in Europe', in Poul Villaume and Odd Arne Westad (eds), *Perforating the Iron Curtain: European Détente, Transatlantic Relations, and the Cold War, 1965–1985* (Copenhagen: Museum Tuscolanum Press, 2010), p. 137.

203. Alan P. Dobson, *US Economic Statecraft for Survival, 1933–1991: Of Sanctions, Embargoes and Economic Warfare* (London and New York: Routledge, 2002), pp. 230–9.

204. Nicholas Evan Sarantakes, *Dropping the Torch: Jimmy Carter, the Olympic Boycott, and the Cold War* (New York: Cambridge University Press, 2010), pp. 75–94, 114–30, 196–213.

205. Deutscher Bundestag – 8. Wahlperiode – 196. Sitzung. Bonn, Donnerstag, den 17. Januar 1980, available at <http://dip21.bundestag.de/dip21/btp/08/08196.pdf> (last accessed 29 September 2016). See also 'Erklärung von Helmut Schmidt vor dem Bundestag (17. Januar 1980)', in Presse- und Informationsamt der Bundesregierung (ed.), *Bulletin des Presse- und Informationsamtes der Bundesregierung* (Bonn: Deutscher Bundesverlag), 18 January 1980, no. 8, pp. 61–5.

206. Quoted in Theodore Draper, 'The Western Misalliance', in Walter Laqueur and Robert Edwards Hunter (eds), *European Peace Movements and the Future of the Western Alliance* (New Brunswick, NJ: Transaction, 1985), p. 57.

207. Elizabeth Pond, 'US Keeps a Wary Eye on Soviet Overtures to W. Germany', *The Christian Science Monitor*, 18 April 1980.

208. Steve Breyman, *Why Movements Matter: The West German Peace Movement and U.S. Arms Control Policy* (Albany: State University of New York Press, 2001), p. 37.

209. See *AAPD*, 1980, doc. no. 170, p. 889, fn. 4. See also Jimmy Carter, *Keeping Faith: Memoirs of a President* (New York: Bantam Books, 1983), p. 536; Tim Geiger, 'Die Regierung Schmidt-

Genscher und der NATO-Doppelbeschluss', in Philipp Gassert, Tim Geiger and Hermann Wentker (eds), *Zweiter Kalter Krieg und Friedensbewegung. Der NATO-Doppelbeschluss in deutsch-deutscher und internationaler Perspektive* (Munich: Oldenbourg, 2011), p. 116; Brzezinski, *Power and Principle*, p. 309; Helga Haftendorn, *Coming of Age: German Foreign Policy since 1945* (Lanham, MD: Rowman & Littlefield, 2006), pp. 260–1; Schmidt, *Menschen und Mächte.*

210. The memorandum of the conversation between Carter and Schmidt is available at <http://www.margaretthatcher.org/speeches/displaydocument.asp?docid=110482> (last accessed 29 September 2016). See also Carter, 'The Evolution of US Policy', pp. 228–31.

211. Burton Ira Kaufman, *Presidential Profiles: The Carter Years* (New York: Facts on File, 2006), p. 440.

212. Haftendorn, *Coming of Age*, pp. 261–2.

213. Scott Erb, *German Foreign Policy: Navigating a New Era* (Boulder, CO and London: Lynne Rienner Publishers, 2003), p. 58.

214. Holger Nehring, 'A Transatlantic Security Crisis? Transnational Relations between the West German and the US Peace Movements, 1977–85', in Kiran Klaus Patel and Kenneth Weisbrode (eds), *European Integration and the Atlantic Community in the 1980s* (New York: Cambridge University Press, 2013), p. 178.

215. Kristan Stoddart, *Facing Down the Soviet Union: Britain, the USA, NATO and Nuclear Weapons* (Basingstoke: Palgrave Macmillan, 2014), p. 69; Kenneth O. Morgan, *Callaghan: A Life* (Oxford: Oxford University Press, 1997), p. 529.

216. Margaret Thatcher, *The Path to Power* (London: HarperCollins, 1995), pp. 349–53. See also Archie Brown, 'Margaret Thatcher and Perceptions of Change in the Soviet Union', *Journal of European Integration History*, vol. 16, no. 1, 2010, pp. 18–19.

217. Sean Greenwood, 'Helping to Open the Door? Britain in the Last Decade of the Cold War', in Olav Njølstad (ed.), *The Last Decade of the Cold War: From Conflict Escalation to Conflict Transformation* (London: Frank Cass, 2004), p. 269.

218. Jonathan Aitken, *Margaret Thatcher: Power and Personality* (London and New York: Bloomsbury, 2013), p. 297.

219. White, *Britain, Détente*, p. 143. See also Greenwood, 'Helping to Open the Door?', p. 269.

220. Carter Library: release 2005/01/28 NLC-7-16-10-14-1. The president took note of the observation, adding the comment, 'Partly accurate, partly fallacious.' Quoted in Aitken, *Margaret Thatcher*, p. 296.

221. Record of the Prime Minister's discussion with the Chancellor of

the Federal Republic of Germany, first session of discussion, 10 May 1979, PREM 19/58 f61. The record of the discussion is available at <http://www.margaretthatcher.org/document/117689> (last accessed 29 September 2016).

222. The text of the speech given by Thatcher at the dinner in Schmidt's honour is available at <http://www.margaretthatcher.org/document/104080> (last accessed 29 September 2016).

223. *DBPO*, Series III, vol. VII, *German Unification, 1989–1990* (London: Her Majesty's Stationery Office, 2009), p. x. See also doc. no. 9, Mallaby to Ratford, p. 27.

224. Quoted in Self, *British Foreign and Defence Policy*, p. 168.

225. For an assessment of the Reagan administration's impact on US–West European relations in the early 1980s see N. Piers Ludlow, 'The Unnoticed Apogee of Atlanticism? U.S.–Western European Relations during the Early Reagan Era', in Kiran Klaus Patel and Kenneth Weisbrode (eds), *European Integration and the Atlantic Community in the 1980s* (New York: Cambridge University Press, 2013), pp. 17–38.

226. The text of the letter is available at <http://www.margaretthatcher. org/archive/displaydocument.asp?docid=110357> (last accessed 29 September 2016).

227. Quoted in Ludlow, 'The Unnoticed Apogee of Atlanticism?', p. 21.

228. Quoted in Lawrence J. Haas, *Sound the Trumpet: The United States and Human Rights Promotion* (Lanham, MD and Plymouth: Rowman & Littlefield, 2012), p. 111.

229. Both quoted in Jeffrey L. Chidester, 'From Containment to Liberation: U.S. Strategy toward Eastern Europe', in Jeffrey L. Chidester and Paul Kengor (eds), *Reagan's Legacy in a World Transformed* (Cambridge, MA: Harvard University Press, 2015), p. 62. See also Christopher Hemmer, *American Pendulum: Recurring Debates in U.S. Grand Strategy* (Ithaca, NY: Cornell University Press, 2015).

230. *Public Papers: Ronald Reagan, 1983, Book I* (Washington, DC: Government Printing Office, 1984), p. 364.

231. John Prados, *How the Cold War Ended: Debating and Doing History* (Dulles, VA: Potomac Books, 2011), p. 31.

232. Harald Mueller and Thomas Risse-Kappen, 'Origins of Estrangement: The Peace Movement and the Changed Image of America in West Germany', *International Security*, vol. 12, no. 1, 1987, pp. 52–88. See also Nehring, 'A Transatlantic Security Crisis?', p. 177; Holger Nehring, 'Für eine andere Art von Sicherheit. Friedensbewegungen, deutsche Politik und transatlantische Beziehungen in den Achtziger Jahren', in Oliver Bange and Bernd Lemke (eds), *Wege zur Wiedervereinigung. Die beiden*

deutschen Staaten in ihren Bündnissen 1970 bis 1990 (Munich: Oldenbourg 2013), pp. 223–44.

233. Ksenia Demidova, 'The Deal of the Century: The Reagan Administration and the Soviet Pipeline', in Kiran Klaus Patel and Kenneth Weisbrode (eds), *European Integration and the Atlantic Community in the 1980s* (New York: Cambridge University Press, 2013), pp. 62–7, 73–4.

234. Stent, *From Embargo to Ostpolitik*, pp. 202–7; John Tagliabue, 'Soviet in Accord on Sending Gas to West Europe', *The New York Times*, 21 November 1981. See also Pittman, *From Ostpolitik to Reunification*, pp. 57–60; Martin Smith, *Russia and NATO since 1991: From Cold War through Cold Peace to Partnership?* (New York: Routledge, 2006), p. 3; Iver B. Neumann, *Russia and the Idea of Europe: A Study in Identity and International Relations* (London and New York: Routledge, 1996), p. 161.

235. Dobson, *US Economic Statecraft*, p. 252.

236. Carl-Ludwig Holtfrerich, *Economic and Strategic Issues in U. S. Foreign Policy* (Berlin and New York: de Gruyter, 1989), p. 283.

237. Pittman, *From Ostpolitik to Reunification*, p. 89. See also Clemens, *Reluctant Realists*, p. 222.

238. Schmidt's quotation is reported in the *Spartanburg Herald Journal*, 23 November 1981.

239. Turner, *Britain's International Role*, pp. 79–81; Demidova, 'The Deal of the Century', pp. 59–82; Prados, *How the Cold War Ended*, p. 24. On British policy towards Poland see also Sara Tavani, 'British Ostpolitik and Polish Westpolitik: "Push and Pull" Diplomacy', *Journal of European Integration History*, vol. 16, no. 1, 2010, pp. 79–93.

240. National Security Council Minutes, Reagan Library, 22 December 1981, NSC Country File Box 91283, available at <http://www.margaretthatcher.org/archive/displaydocument.asp?docid=110968> (last accessed 29 September 2016).

241. Quoted in Carter, 'The Evolution of US Policy', p. 231. See also Angela Romano, 'More Cohesive, Still Divergent: Western Europe, the US and the Madrid CSCE Follow-up Meeting', in Kiran Klaus Patel and Kenneth Weisbrode (eds), *European Integration and the Atlantic Community in the 1980s* (New York: Cambridge University Press, 2013), pp. 39–58.

242. Spohr, *The Global Chancellor*, p. 126.

243. Ronald Reagan, 'Remarks to Members of the National Press Club on Arms Reductions and Nuclear Weapons', 18 November 1981, *Public Papers: Ronald Reagan, 1981* (Washington, DC: Government Printing Office, 1982), pp. 1062–7. See also Richard C. Thornton, *The Reagan Revolution II: Rebuilding the Western*

Alliance (Victoria, BC: Trafford Publishing, 2005), pp. 123–4, 184–8.

244. Ilaria Poggiolini and Alex Pravda, 'Britain in Europe in the 1980s: East & West. Introduction', *Journal of European Integration History*, vol. 16, no. 1, 2010, p. 12.

245. John A. Reed, Jr., *Germany and NATO* (Washington, DC: National Defense University Press, 1987), p. 123.

246. Thomas F. Banchoff, *The German Problem Transformed: Institutions, Politics, and Foreign Policy, 1945–1995* (Ann Arbor, MI: University of Michigan Press, 1999), pp. 97–8. See also Wolfram F. Hanrieder, *Germany, America, Europe: Forty Years of German Foreign Policy* (New Haven, CT: Yale University Press, 1989), pp. 116, 360; Beatrice Heuser, 'Britain and the Federal Republic of Germany in NATO', in Jeremy Noakes, Peter Wende and Jonathan Wright (eds), *Britain and Germany in Europe, 1949–1990* (Oxford and New York: Oxford University Press, 2002), p. 153.

247. William Drozdiak, 'Bonn's Defense Minister Backs Deployment of Missiles in Europe', *The Washington Post*, 10 November 1982.

248. Lawrence S. Kaplan, *NATO Divided, NATO United: The Evolution of an Alliance* (Westport, CT: Praeger, 2004), pp. 92–3.

249. Angela Stent, *Russia and Germany Reborn: Unification, the Soviet Collapse, and the New Europe* (Princeton, NJ: Princeton University Press, 1999), p. 32.

250. Banchoff, *The German Problem Transformed*, p. 99.

251. Benedikt Dettling and Michael Geske, 'Helmut Kohl: Krise and Erneuerung', in Karl-Rudolf Korte (ed.), *Das Wort hat der Herr Bundeskanzler. Eine Analyse der großen Regierungserklärungen von Adenauer bis Schröder* (Wiesbaden: Westdeutscher, 2002), p. 232.

252. *L'Unità*, 18 September 1984.

253. Helmut Kohl, *Erinnerungen 1982–1990* (Munich: Droemer, 2005), p. 963.

254. Antonio Varsori, 'The Relaunching of Europe in the Mid-1980s', in Kiran Klaus Patel and Kenneth Weisbrode (eds), *European Integration and the Atlantic Community in the 1980s* (New York: Cambridge University Press, 2013), pp. 239–40.

255. Gala, 'From INF to SDI', pp. 117–18. On the views of the West German peace movement see Breyman, *Why Movements Matter*; David Gress, *Peace and Survival: West Germany, the Peace Movement, and European Security* (Stanford, CA: Hoover Institution Press, 1985). For the early development of peace movements in the Federal Republic and Britain during the Cold War see Holger Nehring, *Politics of Security: British and West German*

Protest Movements and the Early Cold War, 1945–1970 (Oxford: Oxford University Press, 2013). For a discussion of the roots, tactics and impact of the anti-nuclear movement in Europe in the early 1980s see Thomas R. Rochon, *Mobilizing for Peace: The Antinuclear Movements in Western Europe* (Princeton, NJ: Princeton University Press, 1988).

256. Turner, *Britain and the World*, p. 206. See also Lee, *Victory in Europe?*, pp. 184–6.

257. PREM 19/942 f217. The text of the telegram is available at <http://www.margaretthatcher.org/document/124318> (last accessed 29 September 2016).

258. The text of the speech is available at <http://www.heritage.org/research/reports/2002/06/reagans-westminster-speech> (last accessed 29 September 2016).

259. Romesh Ratnesar, *Tear Down This Wall: A City, a President, and the Speech That Ended the Cold War* (New York: Simon and Schuster, 2009), pp. 59–61. See also Robert C. Rowland and John M. Jones, *Reagan at Westminster: Foreshadowing the End of the Cold War* (College Station: Texas A&M University Press, 2010), p. 14; Nicholas Wapshott, *Ronald Reagan and Margaret Thatcher: A Political Marriage* (New York: Sentinel, 2007).

260. Phillip H. Gordon, *A Certain Idea of France: French Security Policy and Gaullist Legacy* (Princeton, NJ: Princeton University Press, 1993), pp. 118–20.

261. Sean N. Kalic, 'Reagan's SDI Announcement and the European Reaction: Diplomacy in the Last Decade of the Cold War', in Leopoldo Nuti (ed.), *The Crisis of Détente in Europe: From Helsinki to Gorbachev 1975–1985* (London: Routledge, 2009), pp. 104–5.

262. Stent, *Russia and Germany Reborn*, p. 66.

263. Trevor Taylor, 'Britain's Response to the Strategic Defense Initiative', *International Affairs*, vol. 62, no. 2, Spring 1986, pp. 217–30.

264. Quoted in Brown, 'Margaret Thatcher', p. 24.

265. Ilaria Poggiolini, 'Thatcher's Double-Track Road', in Frédéric Bozo, Marie-Pierre Rey, N. Piers Ludlow and Bernd Rother (eds), *Visions of the End of the Cold War in Europe, 1945–1990* (New York and Oxford: Berghahn Books, 2012), pp. 271–2.

266. Quoted in Gala, 'From INF to SDI', p. 120.

267. The transcript of the speech is available at <http://www.margaretthatcher.org/document/105450> (last accessed 29 September 2016).

268. Erb, *German Foreign Policy*, p. 61. See also Banchoff, *The German Problem Transformed*, pp. 97–101.

269. George H. W. Bush, 'Address at the Hofburg, Vienna, September

21, 1983', *The Department of State Bulletin*, November 1983, vol. LXXXIII, pp. 19–23. See also Raymond L. Garthoff, *The Great Transition: American–Soviet Relations and the End of the Cold War* (Washington, DC: Brookings Institution Press, 1994), p. 128; 'Bush Promises Aid for East Bloc States with Independence', *The New York Times*, 22 September 1983.

270. Ronald Reagan, 'Address before the Korean National Assembly in Seoul', *Public Papers: Ronald Reagan, 1983, Book II* (Washington, DC: Government Printing Office, 1984), p. 1589.

271. 'Erklärung zur Entwicklung der innerdeutschen Beziehungen von Staatsminister Dr. Philipp Jenninger, 25. Juli 1984', in Bundesministerium für innerdeutsche Beziehungen (ed.), *Innerdeutsche Beziehungen. Die Entwicklung der Beziehungen zwischen der Bundesrepublik Deutschland und der Deutschen Demokratischen Republik 1980–1986* (Bonn: Bundesministerium für innerdeutsche Beziehungen, 1986), pp. 178–80. See also Achilleas Megas, *Soviet Foreign Policy towards East Germany* (Berlin: Springer, 2015), p. 59.

272. Margit Roth, *Innerdeutsche Bestandsaufnahme der Bundesrepublik 1969–1989: Neue Deutung* (Berlin: Springer, 2014), p. 470.

273. The communiqué is available at <http://www.nato.int/docu/comm/49-95/c840531a.htm> (last accessed 29 September 2016).

274. The minutes of the meeting held in Moscow on 17 August between the East German delegation and Politburo officials, including interim General Secretary Konstantin Chernenko, Mikhail Gorbachev, who was then the CPSU's agriculture secretary, Defence Minister Dmitri Ustinov and the head of the Committee for State Security (KGB) Viktor Chebrikov, are reprinted in Detlef Nakath and Gerd-Rüdiger Stephan (eds), *Die Häber-Protokolle. Schlaglichter der SED-Westpolitik 1973–1985* (Berlin: Dietz, 1999), pp. 398–421. See also Megas, *Soviet Foreign Policy*, pp. 28, 195.

275. The text of the speech is printed in *Public Papers: Ronald Reagan, 1984, Book II* (Washington, DC: Government Printing Office, 1985), pp. 1355–61.

276. Bange, 'The German Problem', p. 203; Demidova, 'The Deal of the Century', pp. 59–60.

277. Dobson, *Anglo-American Relations in the Twentieth Century*, pp. 153–5.

278. Richard Aldous, *Reagan and Thatcher: The Difficult Relationship* (New York: W. W. Norton, 2012), pp. 92–3.

279. Margaret Thatcher, *Downing Street Years* (London: Harper Perennial, 1993), pp. 188, 212.

280. Both quoted in Mary McGrory, 'Not All Falklands Fighting Is

between British and Argentines', *The Washington Post*, 1 June 1982.

281. *The New York Times*, 2 February 1988.
282. John F. Lyons, *America in the British Imagination: 1945 to the Present* (London and New York: Palgrave Macmillan, 2013), p. 98. See also Richard Davis, 'The Falkland Islands and the Special Relationship', in Carine Berbéri and Monia O'Brien Castro (eds), *30 Years After: Issues and Representations of the Falklands War* (Farnham: Ashgate, 2015), p. 78, fn. 10.
283. Klaus Dodds, *Pink Ice: Britain and the South Atlantic Empire* (New York: I. B. Tauris, 2002), p. 6.
284. On the change of British policy towards Eastern Europe see p. 169.
285. Turner, *Britain and the World*, p. 203; Turner, *Britain's International Role*, pp. 102–3. See also the letter sent on 15 September 1983 by the US ambassador to London, John J. Louis, Jr., to the secretary of state. Reagan Library: European & Soviet Directorate NSC, Staff Memoranda File, NARA, Box 90902, available at <http://www.margaretthatcher.org/document/109408> (last accessed 29 September 2016).
286. Ronald Reagan, 'Radio Address to the Nation on the Soviet Attack on a Korean Civilian Airliner', *Public Papers: Ronald Reagan, 1983, Book II*, p. 1228.
287. John Lewis Gaddis, *The Cold War: A New History* (New York: Penguin Press, 2005), p. 228. See also Raymond Garthoff, *Détente and Confrontation: American Soviet Relations from Nixon to Reagan* (Washington, DC: Brookings Institution Press, 1994), pp. 138–9. For a discussion of scholarship on Able Archer see Michael V. Paulauskas, 'Reagan, the Soviet Union, and the Cold War, 1981–1985', in Andrew L. Johns (ed.), *A Companion to Ronald Reagan* (Oxford: John Wiley & Sons, 2015), pp. 284–6. See also Mark Kramer, 'Die Nicht-Krise um "Able Archer 1983": Fürchtete die sowjetische Führung tatsächlich einen atomaren Großangriff im Herbst 1983?', in Oliver Bange and Bernd Lemke (eds), *Wege zur Wiedervereinigung. Die beiden deutschen Staaten in ihren Bündnissen 1970 bis 1990* (Munich: Oldenbourg 2013), pp. 129–50. For a recently released collection of documents see Nate Jones, Tom Blanton and Lauren Harper (eds), National Security Archive Electronic Briefing Book No. 533, The National Security Archive, available at <http://nsarchive.gwu.edu/nukevault/ebb533-The-Able-Archer-War-Scare-Declassified-PFIAB-Report-Released/> (last accessed 28 September 2016).
288. *The New York Times*, 22 January 1984. Quoted in White, *Britain, Détente*, p. 144.

289. Richard F. Staar, *USSR Foreign Policies after Détente* (Stanford, CA: Hoover Institution Press, 1987), p. 38.

290. Frédéric Bozo, 'Before the Wall: French Diplomacy and the Last Decade of the Cold War, 1979–1989', in Olav Njølstad (ed.), *The Last Decade of the Cold War: From Conflict Escalation to Conflict Transformation* (London: Frank Cass, 2004), p. 295. See also Frédéric Bozo, *Mitterrand, the End of the Cold War, and German Unification* (New York: Berghahn Books, 2009), pp. 9–10; Alistair Cole, *François Mitterrand: A Study in Political Leadership* (Abingdon and New York: Routledge, 1997), p. 139.

291. Turner, *Britain's International Role*, p. 69.

292. Poggiolini and Pravda, 'Britain in Europe in the 1980s', p. 9.

293. The full text of Thatcher's interview with the BBC on 17 December 1984 is available at <http://www.margaretthatcher.org/document/105592> (last accessed 29 September 2016). For the record of Thatcher's conversation with Gorbachev see NA, PREM 19/1647.

294. Jean Chabaud, 'The Prospects for Franco-British Co-operation', in Yves Boyer and John Roper (eds), *Franco-British Defence Co-operation: A New Entente Cordiale?* (Abingdon: Routledge, 1989), p. 160.

295. Kalic, 'Reagan's SDI Announcement', pp. 104–5; Smith and Edwards, 'British–West German Relations', p. 59.

296. Henrik Larsen, *Foreign Policy and Discourse Analysis: France, Britain and Europe* (London and New York: Routledge, 1997), p. 145. See also Chabaud, 'The Prospects', p. 161.

297. FRG Embassy press release, 3 May 1984. Quoted in *DBPO*, III, VII, p. xi.

298. Sir G. Howe to Sir J. Bullard, 31 December 1984, *DBPO*, III, VII, p. xi.

299. Michael Sutton, *France and the Construction of Europe, 1944–2007: The Geopolitical Imperative* (New York: Berghahn Books, 2011), p. 203.

300. *Public Papers: Ronald Reagan, 1984, Book I* (Washington, DC: Government Printing Office, 1985), p. 819.

301. Mitterrand is quoted in Kate Delaney, 'The Many Meanings of D-Day', *European Journal of American Studies*, vol. 7, no. 2, 2012, p. 4, available at <http://ejas.revues.org/9544> (last accessed 29 September 2016) and John Vinocur, 'Mitterrand Stresses Conciliation', *New York Times*, 7 June 1984.

302. *AAPD*, 1984, vol. 1, doc. no. 155, pp. 749–57 and vol. 2, doc. no. 242, pp. 1115–16. See also Donald Abenheim, *Reforging the Iron Cross: The Search for Tradition in the West German Armed Forces* (Princeton, NJ: Princeton University Press, 1988), p. 287;

Ulrich Lappenküper, *Mitterrand und Deutschland: Die enträtselte Sphinx* (Munich: Oldenbourg, 2011), pp. 206–7.

303. James M. Markham, 'D-Day Ceremonies vex West Germans', *The New York Times*, 7 June 1984. See also James Heartfield, *An Unpatriotic History of the Second World War* (London: John Hunt Publishing, 2012), p. 440.

304. *AAPD*, 1984, vol. 2, doc. no. 322, pp. 1487–90; Christian Wicke, *Helmut Kohl's Quest for Normality: His Representation of the German Nation and Himself* (Oxford and New York: Berghahn Books, 2015), pp. 190–1.

305. Jack R. Fischel, *Historical Dictionary of the Holocaust* (Lanham, MD: Scarecrow Press, 1999), pp. 28–9. See also Deborah Lipstadt, 'The Bitburg Controversy', in *American Jewish Year Book*, vol. 87, 1987, pp. 21–37.

306. Richard J. Jenses, *Reagan at Bergen-Belsen and Bitburg* (College Station: Texas A&M University Press, 2007), p. 53–5 (quotation on p. 55).

307. Ronald Reagan, 'Remarks at a Conference on Religious Liberty', 16 April 1985, *Public Papers: Ronald Reagan, 1985, Book I* (Washington, DC: Government Printing Office, 1988), p. 440. Two days later the president defended his choice at a question and answer session with regional editors and broadcasters. Ronald Reagan, 'Remarks and a Question-and-Answer Session with Regional Editors and Broadcasters', 18 April 1985, *Public Papers: Ronald Reagan, 1985, Book I*, pp. 456–7.

308. Quoted in J. David Woodward, *The America That Reagan Built* (Westport, CT: Praeger, 2006), p. 88 and J. David Woodward, *Ronald Reagan: A Biography* (Santa Barbara, CA: ABC-Clio and Greenwood, 2012), p. 157.

309. Bernard Weinraub, 'Reagan Joins Kohl in Brief Memorial at Bitburg Graves', *The New York Times*, 6 May 1985. The text of Reagan's speech is available at <http://www.vlib.us/amdocs/texts/reagan051985.html> (last accessed 29 September 2016).

310. Alan Travis, 'Cemetery Visit Disowned: British Premier Thatcher Critical of US President Reagan's Visit to Bitburg, West Germany', *The Guardian*, 26 April 1985.

311. Jennifer M. Lind, *Sorry States: Apologies in International Politics* (Ithaca, NY: Cornell University Press, 2012), pp. 174–5.

312. Poggiolini, 'Thatcher's Double-Track Road', p. 266. See also Archie Brown, 'The Change to Engagement in Britain's Cold War Policy: The Origins of the Thatcher–Gorbachev Relationship', *Journal of Cold War Studies*, vol. 10, no. 3, 2008, pp. 4–12; Archie Brown, 'Preface: The Chequers Conference plus Ten', *Diplomacy and Statecraft*, vol. 5, no. 3, November 1994, pp. 421–510.

313. Thatcher, *Downing Street Years*, pp. 450–3.
314. White, *Britain, Détente*, pp. 154–5.
315. Preparations and reports of the visit are in NA, PREM 19/1271 and NA, PREM 19/1534.
316. FCO's Steering Brief, Annex A, 'Points for Use in Private Conversations in Budapest', available at <http://www.margaretthatcher.org/document/133919> (last accessed 29 September 2016).
317. The minutes of the meeting held on 13 March between Thatcher and Gorbachev in the Kremlin's St Catherine's Hall are in NA, PREM 19/1646.
318. The foreign secretary's report of the visit to the cabinet is in NA, CAB 128/81/13. See also Poggiolini, 'Thatcher's Double-Track Road', p. 271.
319. Stefan Berger and Norman LaPorte, 'Ein zweiter Kalter Krieg? Die Beziehungen zwischen der DDR und Großbritannien, 1979–1989', in Peter Barker, Marc-Dietrich Ohse and Dennis Tate (eds), *Views from Abroad: Die DDR aus britischer Perspektive* (Bielefeld: WBV, W. Bertelsmann, 2007), pp. 163–73.
320. Geoffrey Howe, *Europe Tomorrow: Five Speeches* (London: HMSO, 1985), p. 45. See also Timothy Garton Ash, 'Howe Attacks Berlin Wall', *The Times*, 9 April 1985; Berger and LaPorte, *Friendly Enemies*, p. 230.
321. The White House, 'Memorandum of Conversation', Subject: Meeting with British Prime Minister Margaret Thatcher, Camp David, Maryland, 28 December 1984, p. 6, available at <http://www.margaretthatcher.org/archive/displaydocument.asp?docid=109185> (last accessed 29 September 2016).
322. Marsh, 'The Anglo-American Defence Relationship', p. 183. See also Christopher John Bartlett, *'The Special Relationship': A Political History of Anglo-American Relations since 1945* (Harlow: Longman, 1992), p. 156.
323. Boyce, 'In Search of the Anglo-American Special Relationship', pp. 85–6. See also Nigel Lawson, *The View from No. 11: Memoirs of a Tory Radical* (London: Corgi, 1993), pp. 552–6.
324. Thatcher, *Downing Street Years*, p. 331. Quoted in Baylis, *Anglo-American Relations since 1939*, p. 211.
325. Robert J. Beck, *The Grenada Invasion: Politics, Law, and Foreign Policy Decisionmaking* (Boulder, CO: Westview Press, 1993); Bill Proctor, 'We'll Always Have Grenada', *Foreign Affairs*, vol. 85, no. 6, November/December 2006, available at <https://www.foreignaffairs.com/articles/united-states/2006-11-01/well-always-have-grenada> (last accessed 29 September 2016). See also Warren Kimball, 'The Anglo-American Relationship: Still Special after All

These Years', in Antoine Capet and Aïssatou Sy-Wonyu (eds), *The 'Special Relationship': La «relation spéciale» entre le Royaume-Uni et les Etats-Unis* (Rouen: Université de Rouen, 2003), p. 223.

326. Briefing Memorandum to the Secretary, United States Department of State, NARA, Box 90902. The memo, which is undated but assigned by editor to 19 December 1984, is available at <http://www.margaretthatcher.org/document/109393> (last accessed 29 September 2016).

327. The memo, which also stressed that Thatcher's political popularity was 'on the wane because of her uncompromising style and unresolved economic problems', is available at <http://www.thereaganfiles.com/19850219-mt.pdf> (last accessed 29 September 2016).

328. Heartfield, *An Unpatriotic History*, p. 439.

329. Martin Walker, 'British VE-Day Boycott Hits Raw Soviet Nerve', *The Guardian*, 12 January 1985.

330. Walker, 'British VE-Day Boycott'. See also David Reynolds, 'The Other D-Day and the Onset of Cold War', *The Guardian*, 21 June 2014; Ronald Smelser and Edward J. Davies II, *The Myth of the Eastern Front: The Nazi–Soviet War in American Popular Culture* (New York: Cambridge University Press, 2008), p. 1.

3 The US, the UK and the German Question at the Cold War's End (1985–1989)

'Mr. Gorbachev, open this gate. Mr. Gorbachev, tear down this wall'
(Ronald Reagan, 12 June 1987)

'The preamble of our Basic Law is not negotiable, as it corresponds to our conviction. It wants a united Europe and demands the entire German people to achieve in free self-determination the unity and freedom of Germany. This is our goal'
(Helmut Kohl, 7 September 1987)

'We are not in a Cold War now'
(Margaret Thatcher, 17 November 1988)

Anglo-American reactions to the prospect of change in Germany (1985–1988)

Gorbachev's election, the European security debate and the German question

Both the US and Britain greeted with enthusiasm Moscow's embrace of *glasnost* and *perestroika* following Gorbachev's election as the CPSU's first secretary in March 1985. Even before Gorbachev had come to power there had been signs of easing East–West tensions. Thatcher had already made clear her support for a thaw in relations with Moscow. The Reagan administration, now in its second term, also began to soften its stance. However, the new Soviet course rapidly rekindled latent Anglo-American differences over Germany. In the late 1980s as popular manifestations of dissent in the East forcefully brought the German question back on the international agenda, US and British strategies drifted apart. Washington cheered transformation, backing Bonn's quest for unification, on the condition that a united Germany remained firmly anchored into Western institutions. In contrast, the British reacted with caution mixed with concern at the prospect of change in Germany. Their first response was to reiterate a commitment to the principle of self-determination. However, London viewed with diffidence Bonn's initiatives, feared the implications of dynamics in Germany and attempted to strike an uncomfortable balance between change in the GDR, but not necessarily German unity, and its long-standing commitment to unification. In the following years Britain's preference for preserving the status quo caused irritation in Washington, weakening Anglo-American solidarity. How the special relationship between the US and the United Kingdom was affected by these dynamics is the detailed subject of this chapter.

Anglo-American decision-makers understood quickly that the wind of transformation in the Kremlin, which was brought about by Gorbachev's election to the CPSU's leadership and the reforms he swiftly implemented, might bring about dramatic breakthroughs in East–West relations. Gorbachev moved quickly to make a number of high-level changes in the party's leading cadres, particularly in the domain of foreign policy, replacing Brezhnev-era officials with younger and lesser-known figures. In July 1985 he terminated Andrei Gromyko's twenty-eight-year tenure as foreign minister. Gromyko had been appointed at the helm of Soviet diplomacy in 1957 by Khrushchev to replace Molotov. In the following years the experienced diplomat had been a protagonist of the process of détente, but by the late 1970s had adopted a harder line on East–West relations. By the early 1980s he was very much seen in the West as a figure of the old regime and a dour symbol of the Brezhnev period. Gorbachev appointed Gromyko to the largely ceremonial role of chairman of the Presidium of the Supreme Soviet and replaced him with the younger and more flexible Eduard Shevardnadze, who was the former party leader of the Soviet Republic of Georgia and had little foreign policy experience. Between 1985 and 1986 Gorbachev replaced almost two thirds of the USSR's ambassadors, including nine in the sixteen NATO countries. Yuli Kvitsinsky, a diplomat with extensive experience on Germany and arms control negotiations, became Moscow's ambassador to Bonn.[1] In May 1986 Anatoly Dobrynin was replaced as ambassador to the US by the USSR's former permanent representative to the UN, Yuri Dubinin. Dobrynin, who had been appreciated in Washington as an urbane and skilled diplomat, became the head of the International Department of the Central Committee; the party organisation responsible for relations with non-ruling socialist parties. In London the former director general of the Telegraph Agency of the Soviet Union (TASS), Leonid Mitrofanovich Zamyatin, replaced Viktor Ivanovich Popov, the former rector of the Diplomatic Academy of the Foreign Ministry, as ambassador to the United Kingdom. Gorbachev also quickly moved to regain the initiative in arms control negotiations. In August 1985 the Kremlin announced a temporary moratorium on Soviet underground nuclear testing, while in September the Soviet leader proposed that both Moscow and Washington reduce their strategic nuclear arsenals by a half.[2]

Nonetheless, the primary focus of Gorbachev's foreign policy and the most immediate target of his diplomatic initiatives was Western Europe.[3] The desire to influence political dynamics in Western Europe had been a recurrent feature of Soviet diplomacy and also a major concern for the Kremlin during the Brezhnev era. During two visits to Paris in October 1985 and February 1986 Gorbachev discussed with Mitterrand the prospects for transformation in Europe. A major component of his approach was the notion of a common European home. This concept had first been evoked by Gorbachev in his address to the House of Commons on 18 December 1984. Then, the then CPSU deputy secretary had remarked, 'for all that separates us, we have one planet, and Europe is our common home, not a theatre of operations'.[4] The notion of a common European home was not, however, Gorbachev's brainchild; it had first been raised by Brezhnev during a visit to Bonn and Hamburg in early May 1978. The ailing Soviet leader had refloated his Pan-European vision in a speech during his visit to the West German capital in November 1981.[5] Nonetheless, Gorbachev's understanding of it also entailed innovative elements. The new CPSU head not only envisioned a continent in which capitalist and communist countries could interact, trade and work together, despite different forms of government. He also believed that this growing interaction would gradually overcome the two rival blocs, leading to the replacement of NATO and the Warsaw Pact by a new Pan-European security system, of which the Soviet Union would be an integral and organic part.[6]

The new Soviet leadership's diplomatic offensive continued in the following months. From 14 to 16 July 1986 Foreign Minister Shevardnadze was dispatched to London, where he delivered Thatcher an invitation to visit Moscow. British reactions were positive but cautious. Thatcher was willing to deepen dialogue but not fully impressed by Gorbachev's ideas. She once remarked that homes are built with walls and the Berlin Wall was one too many.[7] Furthermore, although overtures to France and Britain were swift, the new thinking on foreign affairs did not result in an immediate breakthrough in the Kremlin's policy towards Germany. Like his predecessors, Gorbachev perpetuated the traditional Soviet approach to the German question. Somehow initially he even hardened it, continuing to view the persistence of two German states as a key pillar of the new security order.[8] At the eleventh SED Party convention in East Berlin in April 1986, while requesting Honecker cancel a visit to Bonn in July, the Soviet leader expressed a concern that the West German ruling class had not renounced its revanchist dreams and continued to speak of an 'open German question'.[9] Gorbachev also told Honecker that he considered Kohl 'only a lackey of the United States'.[10]

However, the new Soviet leader was well aware that he needed to draw upon Germany's technological and financial assistance in order to implement his modernisation plans and reform the Soviet economy. Later in the same month the Chernobyl nuclear disaster had exposed the Soviet Union's technological backwardness, economic rigidity and managerial ineptitude, reinforcing the need for cooperation with the West.[11] During Genscher's visit to the Soviet capital in July a number of bilateral agreements were initiated on the peaceful use of nuclear energy, agricultural research and health care.[12] The Federal government understood Moscow's desire for expanded commercial relations and endeavoured to exploit it in order to win concessions from the Kremlin on the German question. During the talks Genscher stressed that the FRG could not be excluded from the common European home, telling Gorbachev 'that there is no other door to Europe than Germany'.[13] However, the Kremlin remained adamant that unification was not on the agenda. In the following year Gorbachev told West German President Richard von Weizsäcker in Moscow that one had to proceed from the fact there were two German states with different political systems and that 'what there will be in 100 years is for history to decide'.[14] Nonetheless, despite

Moscow's apparent firmness and although remaining a remote prospect in the immediate future, unification was becoming the subject of a lively debate in the FRG. Whereas neither London nor Washington believed that transformation might be happening any time soon, Anglo-American decision-makers were aware of Bonn's desire to take advantage of dynamics in the USSR in order to improve the situation in Germany.

However, Britain and the US viewed differently the prospect of change in Germany. While Washington was more forthcoming towards Bonn's aspirations, Whitehall adopted a rigid, when not hostile, attitude towards the prospect of a sudden change in the European power balance. Unlike the Americans, the British viewed with increasing suspicion the Federal government's initiatives towards the GDR. At the end of March 1987, in the first official visit by a British prime minister to the USSR in twelve years, Thatcher, like her predecessors, endeavoured to assert Whitehall as an intermediary between the White House and the Kremlin; her discussions with Gorbachev ranged from economic reform to arms control and theatre nuclear forces.[15] Nonetheless, bilateral superpower diplomacy quickly superseded her ambition to play the role of middleman between East and West.[16] Britain's limited influence on the two superpowers was particularly evident on the issue of Berlin. After later in April Gorbachev reiterated his Pan-European vision in Prague, on 12 June during celebrations for the city of Berlin's 750th birthday Reagan publicly challenged the Soviet leader to tear down the Wall. The president portrayed the 109-mile concrete barrier as the ultimate symbol of 'creative imprisonment', inviting Gorbachev to the Brandenburg Gate as a proof of his commitment to liberalisation in the East.[17] Although Reagan's words had been suggested by a speechwriter rather than by the circle of foreign policy professionals, Thatcher's reaction was at best casual. The American memorandum of the conversation on 12 June reported that the prime minister had asked Reagan whether he 'was having a good day in Berlin'. As the president explained how he had 'called for the wall to come down', Thatcher's reply was that 'she had heard the crowd had roared its approval. She then moved on to ask after "Nancy" . . .'. Puzzled by Britain's lukewarm reaction to the speech, then Secretary of the Treasury James A. Baker III initially concluded, 'well damn, maybe it wasn't as important as I thought it was'.[18]

Reagan's words were welcomed in the FRG, although Brandt

later remarked that, while calling for the Wall to come down, the US president set other priorities in negotiations with Moscow and certainly did not try to question Germany's division.[19] In contrast, Thatcher's primary concern remained to build up dialogue with the Soviet Union in order to supervise transition in the East without altering the European status quo. On 17 November 1988 in a press conference with journalists from *The Washington Post* and *Newsweek* the British prime minister complained about the FRG's conduct, remarking, 'the Germans are in here doing this, that and the other!', and made reference to her determination to support Gorbachev in Moscow. She said that it was 'very good to have the kind of free, easy, discussion which we have. It is open. We have got the kind of relationship where we can say things.' Her conclusion was that East and West were no longer in a Cold War but in a new kind of relationship 'much wider than the Cold War ever was'.[20] Nonetheless, in the following months the impending crisis in the East and the acceleration of superpower diplomacy sharply diminished her ability to influence dynamics in Germany.

The INF Treaty and Anglo-American reactions to the prospect of change in Germany

British views about the prospect of a melting away of the two blocs were much more cautious than those prevailing in the US. Nonetheless, the accelerating pace of East–West relations and the successful course of arms control negotiations between Reagan and Gorbachev now also created a fertile ground for transformation in Germany. After their first meeting in Geneva in November 1985, Reagan and Gorbachev met in Reykjavik in October 1986 to revive stalled arms control negotiations. Although no agreement was reached in the Icelandic capital, the US president and the Soviet leader concurred in principle on the need to reduce their countries' nuclear arsenals.[21] In the following months the successful conclusion of the negotiations and the signing of the INF agreement in Washington in December 1987 brought about a dramatic improvement in relations between the White House and the Kremlin. It also reinforced Kohl's position at home and in East–West relations. The Federal government was now able to capitalise on its support for Reagan's 'zero-option' after the CDU, despite remaining the most numerous force in the *Bundestag*, had

seen its share of the vote decrease in the January 1987 elections to
the advantage of the anti-nuclear Green Party.[22] In his visit to the
US capital, shortly after the Reykjavik summit, Kohl expressed
support for the agreement but also argued that the alliance would
lose credibility if reductions in nuclear arsenals were not matched
by adequate measures in the field of conventional forces.[23]

The successful course of the INF negotiations also allowed
Bonn to intensify its inter-German policy. During Honecker's
state visit to Bonn from 7 to 11 September 1987 Kohl reaffirmed
the Federal government's commitment to striving for the self-
determination and unity of the German people in agreement with
the Basic Law of 1949.[24] On the surface, the trip had marked the
peak of East Germany's search for international acceptance and
equal treatment from Bonn. It also enhanced the prestige of the
GDR leader, who had made his delayed trip to West Germany
without a formal blessing from the Kremlin. Nonetheless, the
Federal government took pains to emphasise that the encounter
was not an official state visit. On 7 September at dinner Kohl
stated:

> the preamble of our Basic Law is not negotiable, as it corresponds
> to our conviction. It wants a united Europe and demands the entire
> German people to achieve in free self-determination the unity and
> freedom of Germany. This is our goal.[25]

The visit was also observed with curiosity by the West. However,
Bonn dampened expectations of closer cooperation between the
FRG and the GDR in order not to create anxiety among its
allies.[26]

Anglo-American reactions to dynamics in Germany were
mixed. The British were cautious. London discounted the prospect of immediate change in relations between the two German
states. However, there was growing awareness among British
diplomats of the evolving situation in Germany. A paper on 'the
German Question and Europe' prepared by FCO planning staff
and submitted to the foreign secretary categorically stated that,
on the question of German reunification, there was 'no prospect
of significant change in the medium term'. The paper also suggested that, as long as Soviet power in Eastern Europe remained
intact, the Federal Republic would not trade unity for neutrality.
Nonetheless, its authors called for a more active British policy

towards Eastern Europe. They also remarked that, in the longer term, change was 'inevitable'. Their conclusion was that the most likely outcome of this process would be the disintegration of both the Warsaw Pact and NATO, the withdrawal of the forces of the Four Powers from German territory and the emergence of a united, highly developed, neutral Germany of some seventy million people at the centre of 'a Europe of free states stretching from the Atlantic to the Black Sea and from the Arctic Circle to the Mediterranean'.[27] As the new situation was likely to have profound repercussions for British interests, their advice was that Britain should be seeking ways to strengthen relations with the Federal Republic and identify potential for change in the GDR. The paper impressed Foreign Secretary Howe, triggering an active debate within the FCO. Nonetheless, Whitehall continued to focus on its immediate recommendations rather than on explicit suggestions that change in Germany could begin much sooner than expected.

In the following months West Germany's growing international assertiveness contributed to increasing British anxieties. By early 1988, although ruling out the possibility that the Federal government would 'slide into neutralism in return for reunification', FCO officials began to detect worrying signs, particularly within the European Communities, of 'gradually increasing German self-confidence, and perhaps a desire to match their political weight to their economic power'. As John Fretwell, FCO political director, explained in a letter to Britain's new ambassador to Bonn, Christopher Mallaby, the Federal government was now likely to behave as 'the payer wanting to call more of the tune'.[28] His concerns were shared by the ambassador, who had taken up his new post in Bonn, where he had already served as minister between 1982 and 1985, after an absence of three years. According to Mallaby, while Bonn's Western orientation was not in question, an increasing insistence could be perceived in the FRG's debate that 'German interests must be given proper weight in the counsels of the West'.[29] For this reason, the deepening and development of West European integration would be fundamental in order to prevent any dangerous drift in the FRG's foreign policy. Five weeks later Mallaby reiterated his view. He stressed that while the post-War settlement remained at both the psychological and political levels profoundly unsatisfactory for the Germans, there was a danger that if the process of West European integration lost momentum, Bonn would be tempted to turn eastwards. The ambassador's conclusion was that, although there was no need for immediate concern, there were several things that they needed 'to keep a close eye on'.[30] The recurring concern of Britain's diplomats was that, faced with change in Eastern Europe, the United Kingdom lacked leverage on dynamics in Germany. While the Germans liked the British and got on well with them, they 'did not give full weight to British policies'.[31] Furthermore, unlike the French, Britain could not rely on anything comparable to the close institutional and personal bonds that united France and Germany in the framework of the European Community. Awareness of British weakness reignited an intense debate within the FCO on Britain's European policy. This also involved the meaning of the special relationship and its impact on the United Kingdom's role in the European Communities. Some officials were particularly critical of the Conservative cabinet's European strategy and believed that London's unpreparedness was largely a consequence of the government's denial of a policy of active engagement with Europe. Their view was that such a narrow approach had made it difficult for Britain 'to respond with sufficient vigour to the changes that were taking place in the east of the continent or to show sympathy for German aspirations'.[32] Nonetheless, while reflecting the cabinet's hostility towards the European Communities, Britain's lack of engagement with Europe or a long-term vision for Germany were also a consequence of an excessive belief in Moscow's ability to oversee transformation in the East. At least officially the CPSU leadership continued to firmly oppose any suggestion of closer relations between the two German states or unification. During Kohl's visit to Moscow in October 1988 Gorbachev had described attempts to raise the so-called German question, by pursuing 'unrealistic policies', as 'an unpredictable and even dangerous business'. Endeavours at eliminating the border between the two German states were condemned by the Soviet leader as 'disastrous'.[33]

US evaluations of these dynamics were much less pessimistic. The White House, unlike Whitehall, was more receptive to prospects for change in Eastern Europe. Nonetheless, as the Reagan administration's second term in office drew to a close, Washington also showed little awareness of the pace of transformation in Germany. The president was absorbed by arms control discussions with the Soviets, while some of the administration's members were not attracted by substantive proposi-tions to reshape Central and Eastern Europe. Assistant Secretary of State for European and Canadian Affairs Rozanne Ridgway believed that it would be premature and destabilising for the US to bring the German question onto the international agenda, as the present situation was stable and a source of peace between the two blocs.[34] It was only after George H. W. Bush's victory in the November 1988 presidential elections that the White House slowly turned its attention to developments in Germany. The president's national security staff and the State Department, under the vision-ary leadership of James A. Baker III, quickly began to address the prospect of the Soviet bloc's sudden collapse. National Security Adviser Brent Scowcroft's aides, particularly Harvard academic Robert Blackwill, who in March 1989 had been appointed special assistant to the president for national security affairs and senior director for European and Soviet affairs at the NSC, countered Ridgway's assumption that it would be premature and destabilis-ing for Washington to bring the German question back on the international agenda. Baker's counsellor, Robert Zoellick, and the director of the State Department's Policy Planning Staff, Dennis Ross, shared Blackwill's viewpoint. They suggested that, in order to counter Gorbachev's Pan-European appeal, the relationship between Washington and Bonn had to be redefined on a new basis.[35] In the following years their views significantly shaped Washington's policy on the German question.

In February 1989, shortly after the new administration's instal-lation, Baker left for an exhausting trip to the fifteen capitals of NATO's member states. The trip had been designed to familiarise the allies with the new administration and overcome intra-alliance fissures over the modernisation of NATO's Short-Range Nuclear Forces (SNF). On this matter a festering dispute had erupted over the wisdom of, and need for, a modern version of the Lance missile deployed in West Germany. The issue had assumed greater urgency following the signing of the INF Treaty in December 1987 and Gorbachev's announcement twelve months later at the UN of a dramatic unilateral reduction in Soviet conventional forces. The Lance missile, with a range of 125 km, would not be subject to control under the INF agreement. The Anglo-American allies pressed for modernisation in order to compensate for the loss of intermediate nuclear forces and to preserve the West's ability to stop a conventional military attack by the Warsaw

Pact.[36] Whitehall strongly favoured modernisation in order to prevent the risk of Germany's complete denuclearisation. In contrast, the German electorate, particularly the anti-nuclear left and the Green Party, opposed it. Genscher also excluded modernisation without negotiations with the East.[37] The divide between London and Bonn placed Washington in 'an extraordinarily difficult position'.[38] Baker's trip was aimed at devising a compromise and avoiding an open split between Germany and Britain on the eve of NATO's fortieth anniversary summit in Brussels.

The summit was held in the Belgian capital, despite Whitehall's proposals to hold it, symbolically, in London. On the issue of SNF Thatcher insisted in opposition to the West Germans that there should be no negotiations with Moscow. Worried by the implications of an Anglo-German fissure, Baker confessed to Bush in May 1989, 'you've got to lead the Alliance, and that means getting Margaret to compromise on SNF . . . if you don't, she won't pay the cost. You will.'[39] The secretary of state's journey through NATO capitals rapidly turned into a broader diplomatic exercise to preserve allied unity. This was also coming under increasing pressure as a result of conflicting reactions to demands for change and transformations in Eastern Europe. In August FCO officials noted Thatcher's 'gut feeling' that something had gone wrong in the Federal Republic. One of them remarked whether at some stage one might 'need surgery rather than syrup' in order to convince the prime minister about the inevitability of change in Germany.[40] Britain's reservations did not go unnoticed in Washington. As the US secretary of state later reflected, 'my European journey reinforced for me practically what I had known all along intellectually: the road to success with the Kremlin began not in Moscow, but in the capitals of Western Europe and Canada'.[41]

The GDR's crisis, the fall of the Wall and the Anglo-American schism

'If you can get reunification on a proper basis, fine'
(George H. W. Bush, 16 May 1989)

'Together, building on the values we share, we will be partners in leadership'
(George H. W. Bush, 31 May 1989)

'I think there is in some quarters a feeling – well, a reunified Germany would be detrimental to the peace of Europe . . . and I don't accept that at all, simply don't'
(George H. W. Bush, 18 September 1989)

'There will be one Germany, united and strong. This does not correspond to either yours or our interests'
(Zbigniew Brzezinski, 31 October 1989)

NATO's 1989 summit, Bush's Mainz speech and the opening of the Austro-Hungarian border

In the spring of 1989 Bonn's policies and demands for change in East Germany began to expose Anglo-American divisions. Although initially unhappy with Bonn's position, the US secretary of state proved open to West German arguments. Baker's mediation eventually produced a compromise at the NATO summit on 29–30 May 1989. Nonetheless, the solution eventually arrived at countered Britain's wishes and postponed modernisation. It established that the alliance would not begin negotiations with the East until a treaty on Conventional Forces in Europe (CFE) had been signed and reductions had begun. This formula met West German expectations, allowing the Federal government to postpone discussion until after the 1990 elections. Washington pressed on for a summit declaration that NATO could wait until 1992 or 1993 to accomplish conventional reductions and decide whether to go ahead with a new short-range missile to replace the eighty-eight Lance weapons in West Germany. The declaration also confirmed the alliance's support for a united Germany, brandishing the Berlin Wall as 'an unacceptable symbol of the division of Europe' and restating the West's commitment to 'seek a state of peace in Europe in which the German people regains its unity through free self-determination'.[42]

NATO's Brussels summit preceded a further a reorientation of US policy. In his first trip to Europe as president, Bush in a speech on 31 May in the Rheingoldhalle, in Johannes Gutenberg's home town of Mainz, used the kind of words that since the end of World War II most US presidents had reserved for British ears, describing the US and Germany as 'partners in leadership'. Bush also demanded free elections and pluralism in Eastern Europe, denounced the Berlin Wall as a 'monument to the failure of

communism' and explicitly countered Soviet calls for a common
European home, emphasising that 'there cannot be a common
European home until all within it are free to move from room
to room'.[43] Although on the following day in London he praised
'the judgment, the conviction and the principled stands' taken
by the British prime minister and promised that the intimate
association of London and Washington would continue in the
future, his Mainz statement reflected US acknowledgement of
Germany as a pivotal player in the process of East–West transition. It also confirmed the White House's intention to retain a
vital role in European politics.[44] Despite the president's reiterated
reassurances, the visit elicited concern in Britain that Whitehall's
influence on US policy, having rested for most of the 1980s on
the personal bond between Thatcher and Reagan, was now on
the wane.[45] These fears were confirmed by American officials in
private conversations with the British. In September 1989 the
Special Assistant to the President for National Security Affairs
Robert Blackwill told the United Kingdom's permanent representative to the NAC, Sir Michael Alexander, that, although Bush
greatly respected Britain's prime minister, the president's attitude
to Thatcher 'was not quite the same as that of Reagan'.[46]

With the US publicly praising Bonn's crucial role in East–West
relations, the United Kingdom's initial reaction to the intensification of the crisis in the GDR was a plain reiteration of its commitment to the principle of self-determination for the German
people. Foreign Secretary Howe had commissioned an FCO study
on the implications of the possible removal of the Berlin Wall as
early as January 1989. Nonetheless, Britain's professional diplomats underestimated the prospect of immediate change in the
East and continued to believe that the Soviet leadership possessed
the will and power to keep the situation under control. Until the
late spring Bonn also remained reluctant to admit publicly the
urgency of a debate on the German question, while ruling out the
prospect of unification in the short term. It was the rapid sequence
of events throughout the summer which, following Hungary's
decision in early May to begin dismantling its 240 km border
fence with Austria, forcefully put the 'German question' back
on the international agenda. Between 3 and 5 June the Chinese
leadership brutally repressed manifestations of dissent in Beijing's
Tiananmen Square. The fear of similar dynamics in East Germany
led Permanent FCO Undersecretary Sir Patrick Wright to ask the

Joint Intelligence Committee to examine the GDR's situation in light of developments in some detail. On 9 June, in talks with the US, British and French ambassadors, Kohl's chief national security advisor, Horst Teltschik, defined the situation in the GDR as 'potentially the most explosive'. Nonetheless, according to the British embassy in East Berlin, while East Germans were profoundly dissatisfied with their condition, the situation did not appear as potentially explosive as it did to Teltschik.[47]

Dynamics across Eastern Europe further deepened Anglo-American fissures. On 5 June Solidarity scored a major victory in Poland's first partially free elections, winning ninety-nine out of a hundred seats in the new Senate. The result of the Polish elections raised Anglo-American fears of civil war and of brutal Soviet intervention.[48] Nonetheless, reactions in London and Washington continued to diverge deeply. While both the White House and the State Department welcomed transformation in the East, London lacked a clear strategy for dealing with the rapidly accelerating speed of events. Whitehall reacted cautiously, displaying a preference for preserving the status quo. In the summer the massive outflow of East German 'holidaymakers' to Hungary and Czechoslovakia and their dramatic occupation of West German embassy buildings, calling into question the very existence of the East German state, caught Whitehall by surprise. On 19 August over 600 East Germans crossed the border from Hungary into Austria at a symbolic peace meeting named the 'Pan-European Picnic' organised by Hungarian dissidents and Austrian politicians at Sopron, where the wooden gate was symbolically opened for several hours. On 10 September 1989 the Hungarian government's decision to open its border allowed more than 13,000 East Germans, who had arrived in Hungary over the summer, to leave for Austria. The resulting public humiliation dramatically increased pressure on the SED leadership. FCO officials responded to the rapid pace of events, attempting to strike a balance between the demand for change in the GDR and Britain's long-standing commitment to, but little enthusiasm for, unification. This cautiousness also reflected the awareness that large Soviet forces were stationed in the GDR and that Germany's eastern neighbours, particularly Poland, were particularly sensitive to the crisis in East Germany.

In contrast, the US response was more enthusiastic. Bush's embrace of unification predated the dramatic events of November

1989. The administration's support for German aspirations was already forthcoming in the aftermath of Budapest's decision in May to begin dismembering the barbed wire fences and mines surrounding its border with Austria. Like his predecessor, Bush believed to his core that the Germans had suffered greatly in the War and that after a forty-year-long association with the West their identity had changed. The US president was also convinced of the importance of the transatlantic alliance for preserving peace in Europe and American prosperity. Furthermore, Washington saw in Germany a solution to many of the US and European problems and to the uncertainty of the post-Cold War period. For the administration Germany was the key to the alliance's ongoing viability in a time of growing insecurity about NATO's future role. While Washington remained the organisation's undisputed leader, Germany would serve as its European keystone and main base of operations.[49] Progress on arms control negotiations with Moscow also reinforced the US's positive perceptions of dynamics in Germany. Between 21 and 23 September the Baker–Shevardnadze meetings in Jackson Hole, Wyoming, increased US–Soviet trust, setting the stage for the Bush–Gorbachev Malta summit in December.[50] Nonetheless, the Americans closely followed the security implications of transformation in Eastern Europe and Germany, and initially sought London's cooperation to oversee them. Earlier in September, at the annual meeting of the International Institute for Strategic Studies in Oslo, Blackwill had told Britain's representative to NATO, Alexander, that Bush was increasingly concerned about 'how to manage the Germans', wished to see the development of a sound European framework with Germany's involvement in the security and defence field, and believed that Britain had a critical influence in this process.[51]

Nonetheless, the prospect of a collapse of communist authority in East Germany was viewed with utter anxiety in London. Furthermore, the US's words were interpreted in Whitehall as proof that German unification could still be delayed, if not avoided all together. By mid-September Permanent Undersecretary Patrick Wright had come to the conclusion that Britain's commitment to self-determination might no longer be sufficient and that 'some public redefinition may now be required'.[52] On 11 September new Foreign Secretary John Major held talks with Bush in Washington to discuss Thatcher's upcoming visit to the US and the situation in Poland and Hungary. Then he travelled to West Germany. In his conversations in Bonn Major stressed Britain's support for the self-determination of the German people, but he also added that there was likely 'to be some way to go before reunification can become a practical proposition'.[53]

Thatcher's evaluations were far less optimistic. Britain's prime minister was determined to put unification on hold. She also tried to use the special relationship to convince the Kremlin that US views were similar to those prevailing in London. On 23 September, a few weeks before Gorbachev's visit to East Berlin to celebrate the GDR's fortieth anniversary, during a stopover in Moscow on her way back from Japan, the prime minister told the Soviet leader that Britain and Western Europe had no interest in German unification. According to Thatcher, while the words written in the NATO Brussels communiqué may have sounded differently, Moscow should have disregarded them. She also added that Britain did not desire change in the post-War borders, as 'such a development would undermine the stability of the entire international situation'; neither was London interested in the destabilisation of Eastern Europe nor in the dissolution of the Warsaw Pact.[54] Thatcher also reassured Gorbachev that her views were those of the American president, too. However, her ideas were in stark contrast to those of Bush who, following the administration's approval of NSC directive 23 on the previous day regarding the changing nature of US relations with Moscow and the end of containment, had sent a note to the Soviet leader, stressing that Moscow should not fear change in Eastern Europe.[55] In contrast, the French shared Britain's concerns and were conveying much the same message to Moscow. Gorbachev's close advisor and personal assistant for international affairs, Anatoly Sergeevich Chernyaev, made the record of Thatcher's conversation. He noted in his diary entry on 9 October 1989 that Mitterrand's aide, Jacques Attali, in conversations with Vadim Zagladin, one of Gorbachev's top aides, had talked about a revival of a solid Franco-Soviet alliance, 'including military integration – camouflaged as the use of armies in the struggle against natural disasters'. In the same entry, commenting on Gorbachev's encounter with Thatcher, Chernyaev concluded, 'in brief, they want to prevent this with our hands'.[56]

The crisis in the GDR and the collapse of the Wall

Between September and October 1989 the crisis in East Germany accelerated dramatically. By the end of September over 3,500 East German citizens were crowded into the West German embassy in Prague, as they tried to avoid returning to the GDR. The SED leadership was caught by surprise by the number of people seeking a safe passage to the FRG. While the Federal government negotiated with the Czechoslovakian leadership to bring the refugees out, Honecker opted to avoid a diplomatic confrontation with Bonn. He now decided to allow the defectors to leave for the West on a special train that was required to travel through the GDR. This decision proved, however, an unwise move, resulting in a major public blow to the East German regime. On 30 September Genscher announced Honecker's decision to a cheering crowd from the balcony of the West German embassy. In the following days the enthusiastic reception given by crowds of bystanders to the train and its passengers during their journey through East Germany dramatically exposed the SED leadership's inability to silence internal dissent. It also betrayed the risk of a further deterioration of the situation. On 3 October the GDR closed the border to Czechoslovakia and Poland in order to halt the flood of refugees.[57] However, when one of the trains arrived in Dresden on the night of 4 October thousands of citizens flocked into the main railroad station attempting to board it. Only the energetic intervention of East German elite units and riot police succeeded in turning them back.[58] From then on the situation precipitated quickly.

Already in September there had been public protests in Leipzig. Over 5,000 people had gathered on 25 September. The demonstrations had continued to grow bigger at the beginning of October and in the days before the fortieth anniversary of the GDR's founding. Then they had spread to other cities, fuelling the prospect of a sudden collapse of authority in East Germany. It was only at this stage that a baffled Soviet leadership opted to react. Nonetheless, rather than resorting to the threat of military force to suppress the protests, the Kremlin now emphasised the need for reform. Moscow's pressure for rapid and drastic change climaxed during Gorbachev's visit to the GDR on 6 and 7 October 1989 on the occasion of the East German state's fortieth anniversary. In East Berlin the Soviet leader warned the SED leadership not to delay the necessary reforms, telling Honecker that 'life punishes those who come too late'.[59] Gorbachev's words made it clear that the East Germans would have to devise their own solution to the events. However, this is exactly what Honecker and his ministers, deprived of Soviet support, were unable to do. On this evening and the next, protests erupted in East Berlin and other towns. East Germany's *Volkspolizei* carried out attacks against demonstrators in front of the Palace of the Republic and made a number of arrests in the capital and other cities. By 8 and 9 October demonstrations in Dresden and Leipzig reached an unprecedented level. On the evening of 9 October 70,000 protesters marched in the centre of Leipzig with smaller protests also occurring in the towns of Halle and Magdeburg. While Honecker and East German Security Minister Erich Fritz Emil Mielke intended to subdue them using the GDR's security forces and troops, they never received the Kremlin's go-ahead for a crackdown. In contrast, the 380,000 Soviet troops that were stationed in East Germany were confined by Gorbachev to their garrisons. Under pressure for reform by Moscow and by then largely isolated within the Soviet bloc, the East German authorities did not attempt to resort to force, as they had done in several cities only two days earlier.[60] Nine days later, on 18 October, Honecker was outvoted and forced to stand down as head of state and SED general secretary in favour of his former protégé, Egon Krenz.[61]

Honecker's resignation also dramatically increased pressure on the West. Despite its growing reservations, well into October the British government was still perceived in Bonn, on the basis of official statements by both the foreign secretary and the prime minister, as 'being more sympathetic to German aspirations than the FRG's other European allies'.[62] In the same month the FCO's Western European Department circulated two papers that laid down contingency plans for the East German regime's sudden collapse and debated the potential implications of unification. The best strategy was identified in a reaffirmation of Britain's commitment to self-determination. Nonetheless, the FCO stance did not imply outright support for unification. In contrast, the British stressed a concern not to prejudice the wishes of the German people.[63] However, this attitude left London on a much slower track than the one that had been embraced in Washington. The rift in the Anglo-American camp widened in the early autumn. Among US officials there were different opinions about how best to proceed in Germany. Washington's ambassador to the FRG, Vernon Walters, was a convinced supporter of a rapid path towards unification. However, his view was only partially shared in the White House. The president's national security advisor, Brent Scowcroft, while not opposing unification in principle, believed that there was no reason for the US to be seen as instigating the process.[64] Scowcroft was a former US Air Force lieutenant general, military attaché in Yugoslavia, and deputy national security advisor during Nixon's second term in office and then national security advisor to President Ford. Unlike others in the administration and the president himself, the experienced diplomat wanted to move slowly and patiently to foster long-term change, fearing that precipitating action might endanger Gorbachev's position in Moscow and alarm the US's European allies.[65] Additionally, former President Richard Nixon and former National Security Advisor Zbigniew Brzezinski were doubtful about the US interests in fostering unification. For Nixon the recent loose talk about the inevitability of unification was 'irresponsible'.[66] During a visit to Moscow at the end of October 1989 Brzezinski had told Politburo member Alexander Yakovlev that 'there will be one Germany, united and strong. This does not correspond to either yours or our interests' and that 'the majority of Western leaders do not want to see the dissolution of NATO or the Warsaw Treaty Organization'.[67]

Nonetheless, the nuances in the American position were overcome by Bush's firm belief that Washington should support German aspirations. Bush's outright support for Bonn made the American position clear to the world, but also discouraged the opinions of those officials within the administration who had expressed reservations about Kohl's strategy.[68] The US president had backed unification in an interview with *The Washington Times* as early as 16 May, even before his Mainz speech.[69] On 18 September, speaking at a news conference in Helena, Montana, Bush said, 'I think there is in some quarters a feeling – well, a reunified Germany would be detrimental to the peace of Europe ... and I don't accept that at all, simply don't.'[70] While Whitehall and a number of US officials reacted with concern to the prospect of a united Germany, the US president did not share British anxieties. On the same day as Bush's interview in Montana, in Oslo Blackwill made Alexander aware of the president's concern that Thatcher's excessively negative statements could cut Britain 'out of the game'.[71] Between September and October the president and the secretary of state made it clear that a united Germany was no cause for alarm in Washington, explaining that the White House did not share the concerns that had been expressed by a number of European leaders. In a speech on 16 October Baker said that the reunification of their nation was a 'legitimate right' of the German people.[72] In an interview published by *The New York Times* on 25 October the US president acknowledged that unification would take time and require an 'understanding between the French and Germans and the Brits and the Germans'. Nonetheless, he also remarked that Washington did not 'share the concern that some European countries have about a reunified Germany' and that he did not see Germany 'going off onto . . . a neutralist path'. Furthermore, the president stressed that one could not 'turn the clock back' and that 'change would be inexorable', echoing the ominous warning that Gorbachev had given East German leaders a few weeks earlier.[73]

Public declarations of American support for Germany alarmed many of Washington's European allies. Nonetheless, they contributed to convincing the French that unification might not be delayed indefinitely. US statements were followed by a still cautious, but significantly more positive, stance by Mitterrand at the end of the regular German–French consultations in Bonn on 2 and 3 November 1989. On this occasion, the West Germans assured the French that the Federal government would respect the previously agreed schedule for deepening European integration.[74] The evolution in France's position marked an important change in West European responses. As late as May 1989 in discussions with Bush at Kennebunkport, Maine, Mitterrand had expressed the fear that German unification might lead to a return to pre-World War I conditions and ultimately war in Europe.[75] Nonetheless, neither US clarification nor evolving French ideas softened Britain's reservations. On the contrary, Whitehall's response to demands for unification remained unenthusiastic, if not obstructive. British reluctance to endorse change in Germany caused tension in the special relationship and elicited disappointment in the FRG. In a telephone conversation with Bush on 23 October Kohl complained that most of the media in the US and Western Europe accused the German government of being almost exclusively committed to unification and to have little interest in the health of the European Communities and the West. In contrast, the chancellor stressed that Bonn's firm belief remained that without a strong NATO and the necessary development of the European Communities, the process of transformation under way in the East would not have occurred. Kohl also made it clear that the FRG would continue to emphasise the importance of the transatlantic alliance and of further progress in European integration, and invited the American president to do the same. Renewing his support for Kohl, Bush further distanced his views from those of his European allies, stressing that NATO's strength had made changes in Eastern Europe possible and that Washington did not believe the 'spate of stories about German reunification resulting in a neutralist Germany and a threat to Western security'.[76]

Anglo-American divisions were exposed dramatically by contrasting reactions to the Berlin Wall's collapse on the night of 8–9 November. Both the US and Britain greeted with relief the SED's decision not to use force against the demonstrators. However, London and Washington reacted very differently to events in the GDR. Whitehall's response confirmed British misgivings about transformation in Germany. On the morning of 10 November, following the dramatic events of the previous night, the prime minister issued a statement that called for the creation of a genuinely democratic form of government and expressed Britain's support for free elections and a multiparty system in East Germany.[77] A similar cautiousness came from Foreign Secretary Douglas Hurd: in an interview with the BBC World Service Britain's former home secretary restated the message conveyed to Bonn by his predecessor John Major almost two months earlier, stating that the principle of German unity was not in doubt 'but the how and when . . . is not on the immediate agenda'. Hurd reiterated this viewpoint on at least three different occasions: at a press conference in The Hague on 9 November; in the BBC World Service interview the day after; and finally, in a BBC Radio interview in Bonn on 15 November.[78] In sharp contrast to British reactions, on the same day as Hurd's interview with the BBC World Service, in a telephone conversation with Kohl, Bush reiterated his support for the German people's aspiration to self-determination. The US president said that the White House was proud of the way in which the chancellor was 'handling an extremely difficult problem' and praised him for acknowledging the role of the US in the process.[79]

Nonetheless, some in Washington continued to worry about the prospect of unforeseen developments in the East. In the next

few days a number of American senators, including the chairman of the Senate Foreign Relations Subcommittee on European
Affairs, Joseph Biden, and Senator Carl Levin of Michigan, manifested apprehension about Bonn's conduct. Biden warned about
German 'emotions, which are running high, and may run amok';
even Kennan hinted at the possibility of a three-year moratorium
on German unification, while stressing the need for 'some great
European centre of coordination and guidance' to contain 'German
energies'.[80] These concerns led the president to adopt a more cautious attitude in his telephone conversation with Kohl a week later.
On this occasion, the US president reassured Kohl that, despite
ongoing congressional discussions, Washington would 'stay calm'
and support reforms. Nonetheless, he also added that there might
be a risk that the euphoric excitement in the US might lead to
unforeseen action in the USSR or the GDR with very negative consequences. For this reason, the US would not be making exhorta-
tions about unification or 'setting any timetables' and would not
exacerbate the problem by having its president posturing on the
Berlin Wall. Bush also remarked that there were 'nuances of difference' in the alliance about Germany and exhorted the chancellor
to consultation with Washington, ideally before his forthcoming
meeting with Gorbachev in Malta at the beginning of December.
Nonetheless, the conversation also proved that the US lacked
the ability to control fully dynamics in Germany. The chancellor
acknowledged the importance of coordination with the allies, but
he turned down Bush's request for a meeting with the justification
that he needed to concentrate on a rapidly evolving domestic political situation.[81] Kohl's resistance to Bush's demands anticipated a
dramatic acceleration in Bonn's efforts to overcome Germany's
division. In the following month, the chancellor's attempt to seize
the initiative triggered a further clarification of national positions,
exposing the widening rift between London and Washington.

US–West German convergence: Kohl's blueprint and Baker's response

Kohl's ten-point programme, Baker's four points and the Malta summit

Reactions to the Berlin Wall's collapse were emblematic of diverging Anglo-American priorities. London lacked a strategy for

dealing with a sudden collapse of East Germany. The British also feared Kohl's endeavours to gain the initiative ahead of the Four Powers. In contrast, Bush had confirmed US support for Bonn. In the following months Washington and London failed to coordinate their responses to the evolving situation in Germany. On 10 November Whitehall published a statement welcoming the lifting of travel restrictions from East to West Germany and supporting the installation of a democratic government in the GDR. Nonetheless, the British also stressed that one should proceed 'step by step'. Three days later, at the Lord Mayor's Banquet in London's Guildhall, Thatcher discussed free elections and a multiparty system in East Germany. However, on 18 November at a meeting of the EEC heads of government in Paris Britain's prime minister forcefully restated her reservations about unification. She argued that the European borders should not be altered and that both NATO and the Warsaw Pact should be kept intact.[82] Thatcher left the meeting with the impression that her arguments had won general acceptance by London's European partners. However, her views were in stark conflict with those prevailing in Washington.[83] At the Anglo-American meeting held in Camp David on 24 November Bush frustrated any expectation that Washington might be willing to delay unification, rejecting Thatcher's calls for a preservation of both European alliances. London's defence of the status quo and of Gorbachev's position in Moscow struck a chord with National Security Advisor Scowcroft, but failed to convince the president himself. Bush was particularly unimpressed by the prime minister pulling a map of Germany with its 1937 borders out of her handbag.[84] Nonetheless, at a House of Commons debate four days later, Thatcher insisted that first, it would be important to secure democracy in Eastern Europe and in the Soviet Union and that the question of borders should not be raised until this process was complete.[85]

US views were much less cautious. However, on the same day Kohl's attempt to give a decisive impulse to the process under way in Germany also rekindled latent anxieties in Washington. The chancellor's move was triggered by a back-channel communication between the former Soviet ambassador to Bonn and now head of the Central Committee's International Department, Valentin Falin, and one of his deputies, Nikolai Portugalov, who feared that the situation in the GDR might descend into chaos, and Kohl's inner circle of personal advisors. In the previous days, conversations with senior Soviet officials had convinced the chancellor's advisors that Moscow was ready to contemplate the prospect of a confederation between the two German states.[86] Being now confident that the Kremlin would not oppose unification, speaking to the *Bundestag* on 28 November in his first official response to the situation created by the Wall's collapse, Kohl presented a ten-point programme on relations between the two German states. The crucial passage of Kohl's proposal was contained in the fifth point. This point, while not establishing a specific timetable towards unification, made reference to the establishment of 'confederative structures ... with the aim of creating a federation, a federal order in Germany'.[87] Bonn had informed neither the Anglo-Americans nor the Federal Republic's other NATO allies of the speech, which had been drafted by the chancellor and his closest assistants following their discussions with Soviet officials. Its content mostly reflected thinking within Kohl's office. The chancellor only arranged for the US president to receive a letter containing a summary of the ten points when he was actually speaking in Bonn. The text of the speech also caught by surprise Kohl's foreign minister, who had not been consulted in advance.[88] Genscher's views did not always coincide with those of Kohl. The FRG's foreign minister and the chancellor belonged to different political parties, had diverging foreign policy views and operated under the pressure of the German elections of the following year. Genscher was less concerned than Kohl about Western unity and more about reassuring Moscow and Germany's Eastern neighbours. In his memoirs the foreign minister later explained that he refrained from publicly criticising some of the passages of Kohl's plan so as not to give the impression that the Federal government was divided about the pace and modalities of unification.[89] The task of reassuring the three allied ambassadors fell on Kohl's personal advisor, Teltschik. He endeavoured to present Bonn's initiative as aiming to bring about unification at the end of a lengthy process, while heading off calls for early unity.[90]

Nonetheless, US reactions were less pessimistic than those prevailing in Europe and in the Soviet Union. Once again the president supported Bonn's position. On the following day Bush eschewed a public confrontation with Kohl, opting instead to publicly defend his choice. The US president argued that the chancellor had probably been afraid of leaks or 'of being talked out of it'. He also added that, while being surprised by the speech, he was not 'too worried' about its implications, as the Federal government could not pursue reunification on its own.[91] However, despite Bush's conciliatory words, Kohl's initiative became a cause of concern for some in the White House. Scowcroft warned that American policy would lag behind, instead of leading, in the unification process: if the chancellor was prepared 'to go off on his own whenever he worried that we might object', then the US had 'very little influence' on the Federal government. In his joint memoirs with the president Scowcroft emphatically commented on how, in a telephone conversation on the next day, Kohl over and over pledged that there would be no going it alone, but that only one day after he had, in fact, 'gone it alone'.[92] A number of US officials feared that the ten-point programme might be followed by additional unilateral West German initiatives, precipitate a Soviet reaction and expose differences within the Western alliance. In the following days their concerns contributed to a further clarification of US views, which were expressed also in light of the upcoming Malta summit between Bush and Gorbachev at the beginning of December.

Whereas in his public reaction the president had employed amicable tones, the task of spelling out the American position was left to the secretary of state. On 29 November, at a White House press corps conference in Washington, Baker listed four principles that, according to the US viewpoint, should have governed unification. The four guidelines had been assembled together by the secretary of state's Policy Planning Staff director, Dennis Ross, and by the deputy director for European political and military affairs, Francis Fukuyama. While acknowledging the legitimate aspirations of the German people, Baker now unequivocally made US support for unification conditional upon Germany's ongoing participation in the Atlantic Alliance and a deepening of European integration.[93] The first point of his speech acknowledged Germany's right to self-determination without prejudice to the eventual form that unity might take. However, the second demanded compliance with its 'continued alignment with NATO and an increasingly integrated European Community'. The third further stressed that unification should be peaceful, gradual and implemented step by step. Finally, Baker made it clear that the US expected respect for the principle of the inviolability of the European frontiers, as enshrined in the Helsinki Final Act of 1975. However, this did not exclude the possibility that borders could be changed by peaceful means.[94] Baker's four principles confirmed the administration's support for Bonn. At the same time, they were a clear reminder, particularly the second and the fourth, that the US worried about the international and security aspects of unification, which to a significant extent Kohl had overlooked in his ten-point speech.

US demands for closer coordination of Bonn's initiatives with Germany's allies were not enough to allay British concerns. In London, where silence from Whitehall indicated a definite lack of enthusiasm, the ten points awaked a latent, yet deep-seated, prejudice about the FRG's conduct.[95] Henceforward, Britain's main objective became to prevent further West German initiatives that might limit the role of the Four Powers. Nonetheless, to this aim the special relationship proved of little help to the British. The White House was aware that Kohl's words had ignited allied misgivings and that Britain's concerns encountered significant consensus in Europe, particularly in Italy and the Netherlands. In addition, the French, although not manifesting outright opposition to the ten points, were disappointed not to have been forewarned. Paris lamented the lack of respect for Franco-German cooperation and was anxious about the weakness of the European dimension in Kohl's speech.[96]

However, most of the European concerns were not shared by the US administration. Washington saw no compelling reason for delaying unification. In contrast, faced with British and European resistance, at his meeting with Gorbachev in Malta at the beginning of December Bush now endeavoured to convince the Soviet leader of the inevitability of unification. On 2 December the US president told Gorbachev that some of the NATO allies, although paying lip service to unification, were actually 'quite upset'. Nonetheless, he stressed that the US would not take 'any rash steps' or try 'to accelerate the outcome of the debate'. Bush also attempted to convince Gorbachev of the inevitable outcome produced by the East German crisis, remarking that one had 'to think beyond the time when notions of the FRG and the GDR are history'. However, the US president was also concerned not to embarrass his interlocutor.[97] Hence, he reassured him that, although supporting Germany's aspirations, the US 'would tread cautiously' on the issue of unification and that he did not 'intend to jump up onto the Wall' or to take actions that, while looking attractive, 'could lead to dangerous consequences'. On the following day Bush told Gorbachev that Moscow could not expect the US not to approve of German unification. Nonetheless, the US president concluded that he was aware of the extent to which this was a 'delicate, sensitive issue' and, for this reason, was 'trying to act with a certain reserve'.[98]

The Malta summit made it clear to the Americans that Moscow lacked the resolve to block unification. Nonetheless, Bush's pledges were not enough to assuage anxieties in the Kremlin, where the specific content of the secret talks between Soviet and West German advisors had been unknown to Gorbachev himself.[99] Meeting Genscher in Moscow on 5 December Gorbachev accused the Federal government of having 'prepared a funeral for the European process', warning the FRG's foreign minister, 'you have to remember what mindless politics had led to in the past'.[100] On the following day, the Soviet leader told Mitterrand in Kiev that Kohl's plan was perfectly unacceptable, complaining that the third of the chancellor's ten points, calling for a fundamental transformation in the political and economic system of East Germany, constituted a 'diktat' and was unacceptable for Moscow.[101]

The US–West German Laeken and NATO's Brussels summits

After the Malta summit the priorities of US diplomatic efforts became to convince Moscow that a united Germany posed no threat to Soviet security and to press upon Kohl the need for a multilateral approach to unification. Bonn was aware of the concerns of its European partners and of the USSR and feared that they might also influence American views, leading Washington to adopt a less forthcoming stance on the issue of unification. On the evening of 3 December, on the eve of NATO's Brussels council, at a meeting held in the Belgian town of Laeken Kohl tried to reassure Bush, Scowcroft and White House Chief of Staff John H. Sununu of the convergence of his programme with Baker's four principles. The chancellor told the president and his advisors that the Federal government would not do 'anything reckless' and had not set up a timetable towards unification. While reiterating US support for Bonn, Bush reminded Kohl of the security implications of unification, particularly for the Soviet Union, emphasising that the US wanted to avoid developments that could make 'the situation impossible for Gorbachev'.

On this occasion, the president and the chancellor also discussed Britain's attitude towards unification. Kohl complained that Thatcher's views were simply 'pre-Churchill' and that in the mind of Britain's prime minister the post-War era had yet to come to an end. His description of London's standpoint as 'reticent' prompted an amused reply from Bush that the term chosen by the chancellor was probably the 'understatement' of the year. Kohl also assured Bush that Germany would continue to be part of the European Community, and that the ten points were not an alternative to Bonn's ongoing commitment to the West. In contrast, the Federal Republic's further integration in Europe was a precondition for the ten points and change in the East to become effective. Kohl's conclusion was that the CSCE's Final Act had made it clear that the European borders could be changed only by peaceful means and Bonn did not envisage unification to take place before two years.[102]

After the Bush–Gorbachev summit in Malta, the Laeken meeting was another important step in US endeavours to secure that unification would take place in a multilateral context and would not undermine Western cohesion. The conversations bridged the gap between US and West German approaches. While Bush had drawn Kohl's attention to the security implications of unification, which were crucial for assuaging the Soviets, the chancellor had reiterated the Federal government's commitment to NATO and the EEC. However, the meeting had also exposed Thatcher's limited influence on American views.

In the following days Washington endeavoured to reassure the allies that Bonn would not overlook the security implications of unification. Nonetheless, as coordination between the FRG and the US increased, the Anglo-American positions continued to drift apart. In the afternoon of 4 December, in his policy statement on 'the future shape of the new Europe and the new Atlanticism', Bush presented the administration's four points to the other allied leaders in Brussels, after having debriefed them in the morning on his Malta meetings. The US president reiterated the West's commitment to unification, stressing that the alliance had 'supported German reunification for four decades' and reassuring the allies that unification could take place only in agreement with the four principles that had been enunciated by Baker a few days earlier. Bush also pledged that the US would maintain significant military forces in Europe, praised the European Community's 'intensified' integration and said that Washington would seek closer ties with the EEC. Furthermore, building on the rhetoric of his May speech in Mainz, Bush proposed that the alliance should promote greater freedom in the East in this historic moment of transition.[103] As soon as the president finished his statement, Kohl stressed that no one could have done a better job of summarising the alliance's vision, commenting that the meeting should have simply adjourned. His national security advisor, Teltschik, later wrote, 'The signal stayed green – caution will be admonished, but the railway switches are all thrown the right way.'[104] Almost all allied leaders endorsed the American approach, although Mitterrand made French support conditional upon a precise timetable towards the establishment of an economic and monetary union.

Nonetheless, there was also resistance. More specifically, US reassurances were not sufficient to allay the concerns of London and some of Washington's other European partners. Thatcher perceived the four points as insufficient for safeguarding British interests. If anything, Bush's words conclusively convinced Britain's prime minister that she could not rely on the special relationship to block unification. The Italians were also very critical of the American vision. Italian Prime Minister Giulio Andreotti expressed deep reservations, warning that self-determination, if taken too far, might get out of hand and destabilise Europe.[105] Heartened by Andreotti's words, Thatcher commented that she wanted to study the US plan more carefully and that reunification should not take place for ten to fifteen years. Her words distanced Whitehall's position from that of the White House and stirred up emotions in the Federal Republic, where the British government's attitude now appeared to be both 'negative and mistrustful'.[106]

Nonetheless, Thatcher was reiterating views that were not isolated in Britain. In a telegram to Hurd of 6 December, Mallaby emphasised that the Federal Republic was not accustomed 'to acting on its own in pursuit of goals not shared by others', and that the way in which Kohl had handled the ten points showed 'lack of deftness and experience'. According to Britain's ambassador to Bonn, the chancellor was trying to pursue two objectives, which might not be 'entirely compatible': on the one hand, he aspired to be the one that would map the route to German unity; on the other, he was aiming to retain 'the support and comfort at all stages of his allies and partners'. His conclusion was that, whereas the Bush administration had been 'assiduous' in its public support, Germany's European neighbours, including France, were 'trickier for Kohl to handle'.[107] The French also continued to express concern about the FRG's conduct. On 6 December at a joint news conference with Gorbachev in Kiev Mitterrand argued that 'none of our countries, and especially one whose weight is so great and whose geographical position is such, can act without taking into account the balance of Europe'.[108] Nonetheless, the conversation did not result in any agreement to slow down unification.[109] Furthermore, it is likely that the accelerating dynamics in the GDR reinforced Mitterrand's belief that unification might not be blocked. On 3 December the SED's Politburo and Central Committee resigned, while on 6 December, after having reached an agreement with the Federal authorities that made Germany a single travel area, Egon Krenz, Erik Honecker's successor, stepped down as East German head of state.[110] By then Thatcher also acknowledged that 'with the United States – and soon the Soviets too – ceasing to regard this as anything more than a talking shop for discussion of the details of reunification', there was little Whitehall could do to influence the process.[111] However, she did not regard French acceptance of German unity as a foregone conclusion. On the contrary, she resolved that there was nothing Britain could expect from the Americans regarding the slowing down of unification and that 'if there was any hope it would only come from an Anglo-French initiative'.[112]

Notes

1. David H. Shumaker, *Gorbachev and the German Question: Soviet–West German Relations, 1985–1990* (Westport, CT: Praeger, 1995), pp. 16–17.
2. Geoffrey Roberts, *The Soviet Union in World Politics: Coexistence, Revolution and Cold War, 1945–1991* (London and New York: Routledge, 1999), p. 95. See also Coit D. Blacker, *Hostage to Revolution: Gorbachev and Soviet Security Policy, 1985–1991* (New York: Council on Foreign Relations, 1993), p. 97.
3. Robert F. Miller, *Soviet Foreign Policy Today: Gorbachev and the New Political Thinking* (London: Routledge, 1991), p. 72.
4. Excerpts from Gorbachev's speech to the House of Commons were published by *The New York Times* on 19 December 1984. See also *Documents on British Policy Overseas* (hereafter *DBPO*), Series III, vol. VII, *German Unification, 1989–1990* (London: Her Majesty's Stationery Office, 2009), doc. no. 1, Mallaby to Howe, p. 6, fn. 7.

5. On the origins of Moscow's common European vision see Neil Malcolm, 'The "Common European Home" and Soviet European Policy', *International Affairs*, vol. 65, no. 4, Autumn 1989, pp. 659–76. See also Norman Stone, *The Atlantic and Its Enemies: A Personal History of the Cold War* (London: Allen Lane, 2010), p. 350.

6. Philip Zelikow and Condoleezza Rice, *Germany Unified and Europe Transformed: A Study in Statecraft* (Cambridge, MA: Harvard University Press, 1995), p. 120.

7. Quoted in Stone, *The Atlantic and Its Enemies*, p. 350.

8. F. Stephen Larrabee, 'The New Soviet Approach to Europe', in Erik P. Hoffmann, Robbin Frederick Laird and Frederic J. Fleron (eds), *Classic Issues in Soviet Foreign Policy: From Lenin to Brezhnev* (New York: A. De Gruyter, 1991), p. 647; Shumaker, *Gorbachev and the German Question*, p. 23. See also Andrei Grachev, 'From the Common European Home to European Confederation: François Mitterrand and Mikhail Gorbachev in Search of the Road to Greater Europe', in Frédéric Bozo, Marie-Pierre Rey, N. Piers Ludlow and Leopoldo Nuti (eds), *Europe and the End of the Cold War: A Reappraisal* (Abingdon and New York: Routledge, 2008), pp. 208–12.

9. Jeffrey Gedmin, *The Hidden Hand: Gorbachev and the Collapse of East Germany* (Washington, DC: AEI Press, 1992), p. 41.

10. Quoted in Hans-Hermann Hertle, 'Germany in the Last Decade of the Cold War', in Olav Njølstad (ed.), *The Last Decade of the Cold War: From Conflict Escalation to Conflict Transformation* (London: Frank Cass, 2004), p. 271.

11. Sidney Monas, 'Perestroika in Reverse Perspective: The Reforms of the 1860s', in Thomas Lahusen and Gene Kuperman (eds), *Late Soviet Culture: From Perestroika to Novostroika* (Durham, NC and London: Duke University Press, 1993), p. 36.

12. F. Stephen Larrabee, 'The View from Moscow', in F. Stephen Larrabee, *The Two German States and European Security* (Basingstoke and London: Macmillan, 1989), p. 194.

13. Quoted in Randall Everest Newnham, *Deutsche Mark Diplomacy: Positive Economic Sanctions in German–Russian Relations* (University Park: Pennsylvania State University Press, 2002), p. 314. See also Angela Stent, *Russia and Germany Reborn: Unification, the Soviet Collapse, and the New Europe* (Princeton, NJ: Princeton University Press, 1999), p. 65.

14. Mikhail Sergeevich Gorbachev, *Perestroika: New Thinking in Our Country and the World* (New York: Harper & Row, 1987), pp. 199–200. See also Michael J. Sodaro, *Moscow, Germany and the West from Khrushchev to Gorbachev* (London: I. B. Tauris,

1991), p. 355; Gedmin, *The Hidden Hand*, p. 41; Shumaker, *Gorbachev and the German Question*, p. 54.

15. Martin McCauley, *Russia, America and the Cold War: 1949–1991* (London: Pearson, 2004), p. 94.

16. David Reynolds, *Britannia Overruled: British Policy and World Power in the Twentieth Century* (London: Longman, 2000), pp. 264–5.

17. On the eve of the visit East German youths had revolted near the Wall against attempts by the police to prevent them from listening to a rock concert in West Berlin. Romesh Ratnesar, *Tear Down This Wall: A City, a President, and the Speech That Ended the Cold War* (New York: Simon and Schuster, 2009), p. 3. See also *The Guardian*, 13 June 1987.

18. All quoted in Richard Aldous, *Reagan and Thatcher: The Difficult Relationship* (New York: W. W. Norton, 2012), p. 238.

19. Zelikow and Rice, *Germany Unified*, p. 20. For a broader account of the implications of Reagan's speech see James Mann, *The Rebellion of Ronald Reagan: A History of the End of the Cold War* (New York: Viking, 2009). On Gorbachev's Prague speech see also Shumaker, *Gorbachev and the German Question*, p. 82; Mark Galeotti, *The Age of Anxiety: Security and Politics in Soviet and Post-Soviet Russia* (Harlow: Longman Higher Academic, 1995), pp. 83, 197.

20. The text of Thatcher's press conference is available at <http://www.margaretthatcher.org/document/107390> (last accessed 30 September 2016).

21. Ronald E. Powaski, *The Cold War: The United States and the Soviet Union, 1917–1991* (New York: Oxford University Press, 1998), pp. 254–6. On the significance of the Reykjavik summit see also Sidney David Drell and George Pratt Shultz (eds), *Implications of the Reykjavik Summit on its Twentieth Anniversary: Conference Report* (Stanford, CA: Hoover Institution Press, 2007).

22. Walter Laqueur and Leon Sloss, *European Security in the 1990s: Deterrence and Defense after the INF Treaty* (New York and London: Plenum Press, 1990), pp. 13–14.

23. Herbert Dittgen, 'Strategy, Arms Control and Reassurance: Dilemmas in German–American Security Relations', in David Dewitt and Hans Rattinger (eds), *East–West Arms Control: Challenges for the Western Alliance* (London and New York: Routledge, 1992), p. 5.

24. 'Bericht über den offiziellen Besuch des Generalsekretärs [. . .] in der Bundesrepublik Deutschland vom 7. bis 11.9.1987 zur Sitzung des Politbüros am 15.9.1987' [Official Report on the visit of the general secretary [. . .] to the Federal Republic of Germany from

7 to 11 September 1987 to the session of the Politburo of 15 September 1987], in Hans-Hermann Hertle, Rainer Weinert and Manfred Wilke, *Der Staatsbesuch. Honecker in Bonn: Dokumente zur deutsch-deutschen Konstellation des Jahres 1987* (Berlin: Freien Universität Berlin, 1991), pp. XCIIIf.

25. Quoted in Axel Heck, *Macht als soziale Praxis. Die Herausbildung des transatlantischen Machtverhältnisses im Krisenjahr 1989* (Wiesbaden: Springer, 2015), p. 180.

26. Shumaker, *Gorbachev and the German Question*, p. 52. See also Stent, *Russia and Germany Reborn*, pp. 53–4; Hanns Jürgen Küsters and Daniel Hofmann (eds), *Dokumente zur Deutschlandpolitik, Deutsche Einheit. Sonderedition aus den Akten des Bundeskanzleramtes 1989/90* (Munich: Oldenbourg, 1998), p. 40; Helmut Kohl, *Erinnerungen 1982–1990* (Munich: Droemer, 2005), pp. 545–51.

27. Minute by D. A. Gore Booth (Head of Policy Planning Staff), 29 September 1987, covering planning paper 'The German Question and Europe' (RS 21/3/5), *DBPO*, III, VII, pp. xi–xii.

28. Sir John Fretwell to Sir Christopher Mallaby, 14 April 1988, *DBPO*, III, VII, p. xii.

29. Dispatch by Sir C. Mallaby, 3 June 1988, *DBPO*, III, VII, p. xii.

30. *DBPO*, III, VII, doc. no. 7, Mallaby to Fretwell, 8 July 1988, pp. 20–3; a new Planning Staff paper emphatically titled 'East/West Relations and the Future of Europe: Or, Genscher Looks for Opportunities and We Think We've Got Problems', which was circulated in July 1988, provided a less pessimistic outlook and called for a more forthcoming response to the changes in Germany and Eastern Europe. *DBPO*, III, VII, p. xii.

31. *DBPO*, III, VII, p. xii.

32. *DBPO*, III, VII, p. xii.

33. Sodaro, *Moscow, Germany and the West*, p. 355; Larrabee, 'The New Soviet Approach', pp. 648–9. See also *DBPO*, III, VII, doc. no. 159, p. 320.

34. Christopher Maynard, *Out of the Shadow: George H. W. Bush and the End of the Cold War* (College Station: Texas A&M University Press, 2008), p. 29.

35. Elizabeth Pond, *Beyond the Wall: Germany's Road to Unification* (Washington, DC: Brookings Institution Press, 1993), p. 162.

36. Richard A. Falkenrath, *Shaping Europe's Military Order: The Origins and Consequences of the CFE Treaty* (Cambridge, MA: MIT Press, 1995), p. 51.

37. Pond, *Beyond the Wall*, pp. 52, 162.

38. James A. Baker III, *The Politics of Diplomacy: Revolution, War and Peace* (New York: G. P. Putnam's Sons, 1995), p. 87.

39. Baker, *The Politics of Diplomacy*, pp. 87–94. Both Baker's statements are quoted in Michael M. Boll, 'Superpower Diplomacy and German Unification: The Insiders' Views', *Parameters*, Winter 1996–7, pp. 109–21. See also Mallaby to Howe, *DBPO*, III, VII, doc. no. 1, pp. 5–6.

40. *DBPO*, III, VII, doc. no. 7, Mallaby to Fretwell, p. 23, fn. 6.

41. Baker, *The Politics of Diplomacy*, p. 91. See also Boll, 'Superpower Diplomacy'.

42. The text of the declaration is available at <http://www.nato.int/docu/comm/49-95/c890530a.htm> (last accessed 30 September 2016). See also Falkenrath, *Shaping Europe's Military Order*, pp. 51–2; *The New York Times*, 17 February 1989; Brian White, *Britain, Détente and Changing East–West Relations* (London and New York: Routledge, 1992), p. 151; *DBPO*, III, VII, doc. no. 7, p. 21, fn. 2; Craig R. Whitney, 'Thatcher's Hopes for a Key Role as a Senior NATO Partner Fade', *The New York Times*, 1 June 1989.

43. 'A Europe Whole and Free', Remarks to citizens in Mainz, Federal Republic of Germany, 31 May 1989, *Public Papers: George Bush, 1989, Book I* (Washington, DC: Government Printing Office, 1990), pp. 650–4. See also *Frankfurter Allgemeine Zeitung*, 1 June 1989; Michael Cox and Steven Hurst, '"His Finest Hour"?: George Bush and the Diplomacy of German Unification', *Diplomacy and Statecraft*, vol. 13, no. 2, 2002, p. 132; Maynard, *Out of the Shadow*, pp. 33–4.

44. Raymond Walter Apple, Jr., 'Bush in Europe: Looking to Germans', *The New York Times*, 2 June 1989. See also Klaus Von Beyme, 'Redefining European Security: The Role of German Foreign Policy', in Carl Cavanagh Hodge (ed.), *Redefining European Security* (London and New York: Garland, 1999), p. 169.

45. White, *Britain, Détente*, p. 150. See also *The Guardian*, 2 June 1989; *DBPO*, III, VII, doc. no. 7, p. 20.

46. *DBPO*, III, VII, doc. no. 12, p. 32.

47. *DBPO*, III, VII, p. xiii and doc. no. 4, p. 17, fn. 3. See also Colin Munro, 'Britain, Berlin, German Unification, and the Fall of the Soviet Empire', *Bulletin of the German Historical Institute*, vol. 31, no. 2, November 2009, p. 61.

48. Stent, *Russia and Germany Reborn*, p. 83. See also Geir Lundestad, 'The European Role at the Beginning and Particularly at the End of the Cold War', in Olav Njølstad (ed.), *The Last Decade of the Cold War: From Conflict Escalation to Conflict Transformation* (London: Frank Cass, 2004), p. 59; *DBPO*, III, VII, p. 17, doc. no. 4, fn. 2.

49. Jeffrey A. Engel, 'Bush, Germany, and the Power of Time: How

History Makes History', *Diplomatic History*, vol. 37, no. 4, 2013, p. 660.

50. Derek H. Chollet and James M. Goldgeier, 'Once Burned, Twice Shy? The Pause of 1989', in William C. Wohlforth (ed.), *Cold War Endgame: Oral History, Analysis, Debates* (University Park: Pennsylvania State Press, 2003), pp. 162–3.

51. *DBPO*, III, VII, doc. no. 12, p. 31.

52. *DBPO*, III, VII, p. xiii.

53. Mallaby to Major, *DBPO*, III, VII, doc. no. 13, p. 33.

54. Before making her confidential remarks on Germany, Thatcher asked for this part of the conversation not to be recorded. See the record of Conversation between Mikhail Gorbachev and Margaret Thatcher, 23 September 1989, in Svetlana Savranskaya, Thomas Blanton and Vlad Zubok (eds), *Masterpieces of History: The Soviet Peaceful Withdrawal from Eastern Europe, 1989* (Budapest: Central European University Press, 2010), doc. no. 85, pp. 530–2. See also *DBPO*, III, VII, doc. no. 26, Wright to Wall, p. 79, fn. 4. For Thatcher's account of the discussion see Margaret Thatcher, *Downing Street Years* (London: Harper Perennial, 1993), p. 792. See also Rodric Braithwaite, *Across the Moscow River: The World Turned Upside Down* (New Haven, CT and London: Yale University Press, 2002), pp. 135–6. All quoted in *DBPO*, III, VII, pp. 79–80, fn. 4.

55. Zelikow and Rice, *Germany Unified*, p. 73; G. John Ikenberry, *After Victory: Institutions, Strategic Restraint, and the Rebuilding of Order after Major Wars* (Princeton, NJ: Princeton University Press, 2001), p. 224; G. John Ikenberry, 'German Unification, Western Order, and the Post-Cold War Restructuring of the International System', in Peter C. Caldwell and Robert R. Shandley (eds), *German Unification: Expectations and Outcomes* (Basingstoke and New York: Palgrave Macmillan, 2011), p. 24. The text of NSC 23 is available at <http://digitalarchive.wilson-center.org/document/116235> (last accessed 30 September 2016).

56. See Chernyaev's diary entry in Savranskaya et al., *Masterpieces of History*, doc. no. 89, p. 547. According to Chernyaev, the Soviet leader attempted to exploit Thatcher's resistance to unification to the Kremlin's advantage. Anatoly Sergeevich Chernyaev, Vadim Medvedev and Georgy Shakhnazarov, *V Politburo Tsk KPSS* (Moscow: Alfaprint, 2006). See also Rodric Braithwaite, 'Gorbachev and Thatcher', *Journal of European Integration History*, vol. 16, no. 1, 2010, p. 41.

57. Andreas Rödder, 'Germany: Revolution and Unification', in Elisabeth Bakke and Ingo Peters (eds), *20 Years since the Fall of the Berlin Wall: Transitions, State Break-up and Democratic*

Politics in Central Europe and Germany (Berlin: BWV, Berliner Wissenschafts and Cambridge: Intersentia, 2011), p. 126.

58. John O. Koehler, *Stasi: The Untold Story of the East German Secret Police* (Boulder, CO: Westview Press, 1999), p. 404. Koehler reports the wrong date of 4 September.

59. Quoted in David Childs, *The Fall of the GDR* (Harlow: Pearson Longman, 2001), p. 69. See also Konrad H. Jarausch and Volker Gransow (eds), *Uniting Germany: Documents and Debates, 1944–1993* (New York and Oxford: Berghahn Books, 1994), doc. no. 13, pp. 53–5. Other sources report this slightly different translation of Gorbachev's message: 'dangers await only those who do not react to life'. See, for example, *DBPO*, III, VII, p. xiii.

60. Mark Kramer, 'The Demise of the Soviet Bloc', in Terry Cox (ed.), *Reflections on 1989 in Eastern Europe* (London: Routledge, 2012), p. 50; Reinhold Andert and Wolfgang Herzberg, *Der Sturz: Honecker im Kreuzverhör* (Berlin: Aufbau, 1991), pp. 182–3.

61. Walter Süß, *Staatssicherheit am Ende: Warum es den Mächtigen nicht gelang, 1989 eine Revolution zu verhindern* (Berlin: Christoph Links, 1999), pp. 279–343.

62. *DBPO*, III, VII, p. xiii.

63. See Mallaby's statement in Gillian Staerck and Michael D. Kandiah (eds), *Anglo-German Relations and German Reunification* (London: Institute of Contemporary British History, 2003), p. 40. See also *DBPO*, III, VII, p. xiv.

64. Pond, *Beyond the Wall*, p. 163.

65. Zelikow and Rice, *Germany Unified*, p. 255.

66. In 1987 Scowcroft had referred to Reagan's invitation to Gorbachev to tear the Wall down as a 'lousy' statement, which was unlikely to 'advance anything' but rather to discourage a decision by Moscow to tear down the Wall. Bartholomew Sparrow, *The Strategist: Brent Scowcroft and the Call of National Security* (New York: PublicAffairs, 2015), p. 295; on Scowcroft's cautious views see also p. 305. Nixon is quoted on p. 368.

67. Brzezinski's quotation is reported in Svetlana Savranskaya, 'The Logic of 1989: The Soviet Peaceful Withdrawal from Eastern Europe', in Svetlana Savranskaya, Thomas Blanton and Vlad Zubok (eds), *Masterpieces of History: The Soviet Peaceful Withdrawal from Eastern Europe, 1989* (Budapest: Central European University Press, 2010), pp. 33–4 and doc. no. 96, pp. 553–68. Brzezinski's doubts about unification were also reported by Gorbachev in his conversation with Egon Krenz on 1 November 1989. John Prados, *How the Cold War Ended: Debating and Doing History* (Dulles, VA: Potomac Books, 2011), doc. no. 30, p. 234. See also *DBPO*, III, VII, doc. no. 40, Braithwaite to Hurd, p. 108.

68. Engel, 'Bush, Germany', p. 647, fn. 16. See also Paul Wolfowitz, 'Shaping the Future: Planning at the Pentagon, 1989–93', in Melvyn P. Leffler and Jeffrey W. Legro (eds), *Uncertain Times: American Foreign Policy after the Berlin Wall and 9/11* (Ithaca, NY: Cornell University Press, 2011), pp. 49–50.

69. In the interview the president stated that he 'would love' to see a united Germany, remarking to the German people, 'if you can get reunification on a proper basis, fine'. See 'Bush "Would Love" Reunited Germany', *The Washington Times*, 16 May 1989.

70. *Public Papers: George Bush, 1989, Book II* (Washington, DC: Government Printing Office, 1990), p. 1221. Quoted in Cox and Hurst, '"His Finest Hour"?', p. 133.

71. *DBPO*, III, VII, doc. no. 12, p. 32. See also Pond, *Beyond the Wall*, p. 163.

72. *Gazette Telegraph* (Colorado Springs), 17 October 1989. Quoted in Werner J. Feld, 'NATO and German Reunification', in Emil J. Kirchner and James Sperling (eds), *The Federal Republic of Germany and NATO: 40 Years After* (Basingstoke: Macmillan, 1992), p. 75.

73. *The New York Times*, 25 October 1989. See also Jarausch and Gransow, *Uniting Germany*, doc. no. 20, p. 63.

74. Helga Haftendorn, 'German Unification and European Integration are but Two Sides of One Coin: The FRG, Europe, and the Diplomacy of German Unification', in Frédéric Bozo, Marie-Pierre Rey, Piers N. Ludlow and Leopoldo Nuti (eds), *Europe and the End of the Cold War: A Reappraisal* (Abingdon and New York: Routledge, 2008), p. 136.

75. Scott Erb, *German Foreign Policy: Navigating a New Era* (Boulder, CO and London: Lynne Rienner Publishers, 2003), pp. 97–8. See also *DBPO*, III, VII, p. xv. In the early 1990s a number of French scholars argued that Mitterrand actively sought to block German unification. See, for example, Jacques Jessel, *La Double Défaite de Mitterrand. De Berlin à Moscou, les faillites d'une diplomatie* (Paris: A. Michel, 1992); Alain Genestar, *Les Péchés du prince* (Paris: Grasset, 1992). This view was reinforced by the publication in 1995 by the third volume of Jacques Attali's *Verbatim: Tome 3, Chronique des années 1988–1991* (Paris: Fayard, 1995). For a sharp critique of Attali's accounts see Frédéric Bozo, *Mitterrand, the End of the Cold War, and German Unification* (New York: Berghahn Books, 2009), p. xxviii, fn. 10. The view that the French posed certain conditions, particularly that a united Germany must be encased in Europe and devoted to European integration, including a single European currency, has been documented by the work of Tilo Schabert. Between 1992 and 1995 Schabert

was given privileged access to the French president's staff and documents. Nonetheless, Schabert's work also points to deep differences between Mitterrand and Thatcher on the issue of unification. See Tilo Schabert, *How World Politics Is Made: France and the Reunification of Germany* (Columbia, MO: University of Missouri Press, 2009). On the relevance for France of Bonn's ongoing engagement with European integration see also Frédéric Bozo, 'Mitterrand's France, the End of the Cold War, and German Unification: A Reappraisal', *Cold War History*, vol. 7, no. 4, 2007, pp. 455–78; Frédéric Bozo, 'France, German Unification and European Integration', in Frédéric Bozo, Marie-Pierre Rey, N. Piers Ludlow and Leopoldo Nuti (eds), *Europe and the End of the Cold War: A Reappraisal* (Abingdon and New York: Routledge, 2008), pp. 148–60. See also Frédéric Bozo, 'From "Yalta" to Maastricht: Mitterrand's France and German Unification', in Frédéric Bozo, Andreas Rödder and Mary Elise Sarotte (eds), *German Reunification: A Multinational History* (London and New York: Routledge, 2017), pp. 111–32.
76. Record of Telephone Conversation between George H. W. Bush and Helmut Kohl, 23 October 1989, in Savranskaya et al., *Masterpieces of History*, doc. no. 94, pp. 558–60.
77. *DBPO*, III, VII, p. 100, fn. 1.
78. *DBPO*, III, VII, p. xv and doc. no. 85, Mallaby to Hurd, p. 190, fn. 3. See also Yvonne Klein, 'Obstructive or Promoting? British Views on German Unification 1989/90', *German Politics*, vol. 5, no. 3, 1996, p. 406.
79. Record of telephone conversation between George H. W. Bush and Helmut Kohl, 10 November 1989, in Savranskaya et al., *Masterpieces of History*, doc. no. 102, pp. 587–9.
80. Foreign Relations Committee, *The Future of Europe*, 101st Cong., 2nd sess., 17 January 1990, pp. 79–80. Both quoted in Frank Costigliola, 'An "Arm around the Shoulder": The United States, NATO and German Reunification, 1989–90', *Contemporary European History*, vol. 3, no. 1, March 1994, p. 9, fnn. 30, 32.
81. Record of telephone conversation between George H. W. Bush and Helmut Kohl, 17 November 1989, in Savranskaya et al., *Masterpieces of History*, doc. no. 105, pp. 595–7.
82. Thatcher, *Downing Street Years*, pp. 793–4. See also François Mitterrand, *De l'Allemagne. De la France* (Paris: Odile Jacob, 1996), pp. 39–44; Maynard, *Out of the Shadow*, p. 57.
83. *The Times*, 25 November 1989.
84. Thatcher, *Downing Street Years*, pp. 794–5; Bush and Scowcroft, *A World Transformed*, pp. 192–3.
85. House of Commons Debate, 28 November 1989, vol. 162, cols

577–80, available at <http://www.margaretthatcher.org/document/107831> (last accessed 30 September 2016). See also <http://hansard.millbanksystems.com/commons/1989/nov/28/engagements-1> (last accessed 30 September 2016).

86. Savranskaya, 'The Logic of 1989', p. 36. See also Jacques Lévesque, 'In the Name of Europe's Future: Soviet, French, and British Qualms about Kohl's Rush to German Unification', in Frédéric Bozo, Marie-Pierre Rey, Piers N. Ludlow and Leopoldo Nuti (eds), *Europe and the End of the Cold War: A Reappraisal* (Abingdon and New York: Routledge, 2008), p. 103; Vorlage des Ministerialdirektors Teltschik an Bundeskanzler Kohl, 'Die Sowjetunion und die deutsche Frage', 6 December 1989, in Küsters and Hofmann, *Dokumente zur Deutschlandpolitik*, p. 616. See also James E. Cronin, *Global Rules: America, Britain and a Disordered World* (New Haven, CT: Yale University Press, 2014), p. 200.

87. Helmut Kohl, 'Zehn-Punkte-Programm zur Überwindung der Teilung Deutschlands und Europas', 28 November 1989, in *Bulletin des Presse und Informationsamtes der Bundesregierung*, 29 November 1989. See also Jarausch and Gransow, *Uniting Germany*, doc. no. 14, pp. 101–4. For excerpts of the speech see also *Survival*, vol. 32, no. 1, 1990, pp. 86–7. See *DBPO*, III, VII, p. xvi.

88. Thomas F. Banchoff, *The German Problem Transformed: Institutions, Politics, and Foreign Policy, 1945–1995* (Ann Arbor, MI: University of Michigan Press, 1999), p. 156. See also Henrik Bering, *Helmut Kohl: The Man Who Reunited Germany, Rebuilt Europe, and Thwarted the Soviet Empire* (Washington, DC: Regnery, 1999), pp. 72–3; Helga Haftendorn, 'The Unification of Germany, 1985–1991', in Melvyn P. Leffler and Odd Arne Westad (eds), *The Cambridge History of the Cold War. Vol. III* (Cambridge and New York: Cambridge University Press, 2010), pp. 341–4.

89. Hans-Dietrich Genscher, *Erinnerungen* (Berlin: Siedler, 1995), p. 1086.

90. *DBPO*, III, VII, doc. no. 59, Mallaby to Hurd, pp. 138–40.

91. Bush and Scowcroft, *A World Transformed*, p. 194.

92. Bush and Scowcroft, *A World Transformed*, pp. 194–6. See also Alexander Moens, 'American Diplomacy and German Unification', *Survival*, vol. 33, no. 6, November/December 1991, p. 542; Thomas Blanton, 'U.S. Policy and the Revolutions of 1989', in Svetlana Savranskaya, Thomas Blanton and Vlad Zubok (eds), *Masterpieces of History: The Soviet Peaceful Withdrawal from Eastern Europe, 1989* (Budapest: Central European University Press, 2010), p. 86.

93. Philip Zelikow and Condoleezza Rice, 'German Unification', in Kiron K. Skinner (ed.), *Turning Points in Ending the Cold War* (Stanford, CA: Hoover Institution Press, 2008), p. 236.

94. PA transcript, Press Conference by Secretary Baker on Bush–Gorbachev Malta Meeting, the White House, Washington, DC, 29 November 1989, pp. 7–8. See also *DBPO*, III, VII, doc. no. 76, p. 173, fn. 2.

95. Cronin, *Global Rules*, p. 189; Pyeongeok An, 'Obstructive All the Way? British Policy towards German Unification 1989–90', *German Politics*, vol. 15, no. 1, 2006, p. 113.

96. Bozo, *Mitterrand*, pp. 124–6.

97. Sparrow, *The Strategist*, pp. 306–7.

98. Excerpts of the Soviet transcript of Bush and Gorbachev's conversations on board the Soviet cruise ship *Maxim Gorky* off the coast of Malta are published in Savranskaya et al., *Masterpieces of History*, doc. no. 110, pp. 619–46. For US transcripts of the conversations see 'US Memorandums of Conversation, George H. W. Bush and Mikhail Gorbachev at Malta Summit, 2–3 December 1989', History and Public Policy Program Digital Archive, George Bush Presidential Library, National Security Council, Condoleezza Rice and Arnold Kanter files.

99. Savranskaya, 'The Logic of 1989', p. 36. See also Küsters and Hofmann, *Dokumente zur Deutschlandpolitik*, p. 616. For Gorbachev's own interpretation of Bush's words see Jacques Lévesque, *Fin d'un Empire, 1989* (Berkley and Los Angeles: University of California Press, 1997), p. 221.

100. The first quotation is in Savranskaya, 'The Logic of 1989', p. 37; the second quotation is in Savranskaya et al., *Masterpieces of History*, doc. no. 113, 'Record of Conversation between Gorbachev and Genscher', p. 656. See also Blanton, 'U.S. Policy', p. 90; William Taubman and Svetlana Savranskaya, 'If a Wall Fell in Berlin, and Moscow Hardly Noticed, Would it Still Make a Noise?', in Jeffrey A. Engel (ed.), *The Fall of the Berlin Wall: The Revolutionary Legacy of 1989* (New York: Oxford University Press, 2009), p. 89.

101. Bozo, *Mitterrand*, pp. 134–7.

102. Memorandum of Conversation of George H. W. Bush, John Sununu, Brent Scowcroft, and Helmut Kohl, 3 December 1989, in Savranskaya et al., *Masterpieces of History*, doc. no. 111, pp. 647–50. See also Julian Bullard, 'Great Britain and German Unification', in Jeremy Noakes, Peter Wende and Jonathan Wright (eds), *Britain and Germany in Europe, 1949–1990* (Oxford and New York: Oxford University Press, 2002), p. 221.

103. 'Outline of Remarks at the North Atlantic Treaty Organization Headquarters in Brussels', 4 December 1989, in *Public Papers:*

George Bush, 1989, Book II, pp. 1644–8.

104. Horst Teltschik, *329 Tage. Innenansichten der Einigung* (Berlin: Siedler, 1991), p. 67. Quoted in Zelikow and Rice, 'German Unification', p. 239. See also Bush and Scowcroft, *A World Transformed*, pp. 196–200.

105. Andreotti also demanded what might happen if the Baltic states, for example, attempted to assert their independence. Kohl bounced back that Italy's prime minister might not hold the same view if the Tiber divided his country. Zelikow and Rice, 'German Unification', p. 238. See also Andrei Grachev, *Gorbachev's Gamble: Soviet Foreign Policy and the End of the Cold War* (Cambridge: Polity Press, 2008), p. 154. For two broad accounts of Italian views see Antonio Varsori, *L'Italia e la fine della guerra fredda. La politica estera dei governi Andreotti (1989–1992)* (Bologna: Il Mulino, 2013), pp. 19–46; Leopoldo Nuti, 'Italy, German Unification and the End of the Cold War', in Frédéric Bozo, Marie-Pierre Rey, Piers N. Ludlow and Leopoldo Nuti (eds), *Europe and the End of the Cold War: A Reappraisal* (Abingdon and New York: Routledge, 2008), pp. 191–203.

106. *DBPO*, III, VII, doc. no. 85, Mallaby to Hurd, p. 190. See also Moens, 'American Diplomacy', pp. 532–3.

107. *DBPO*, III, VII, doc. no. 69, Braithwaite to Hurd, pp. 160–1, fn. 3.

108. Quoted in *DBPO*, III, VII, doc. no. 85, p. 190, fn. 2. See also Schabert, *How World Politics Is Made*, pp. 256–8.

109. Bozo, *Mitterrand*, pp. 134–7.

110. *DBPO*, III, VII, p. xvii. See also Bush and Scowcroft, *A World Transformed*, p. 201.

111. Thatcher, *Downing Street Years*, pp. 795–6.

112. Thatcher, *Downing Street Years*, pp. 795–6. See also Elisabeth Hellenbroich, 'Thatcher's Obsession to Block German Unity', *Executive Intelligence Review*, vol. 25, no. 32, August 1998, pp. 44–5.

Part 2 Anglo-American Relations and the Diplomacy of German Unification (1989–1990)

The second part of this book debates how the US and West Germany managed to build on the events of 1989 to harness the momentum of the East European revolutions, overcome widespread resistance to unification and enforce a major transformation in Europe and NATO. Nonetheless, as this process unfolded, division in the Anglo-American camp deepened and the special relationship was superseded by a growing convergence of US and West German strategies. As a result of diverging Anglo-American priorities, Britain's role became secondary, if not marginal, in hammering out the details of unification. London continued to affirm in public that stability in Europe would be difficult to achieve as long as Germany remained divided. However, Britain's prime minister maintained an openly critical attitude towards Bonn. Thatcher's difficult relationship with Kohl further augmented her determination to block or at least to slow down unification. At the beginning of 1990 Whitehall even contemplated the prospect of a continental bloc against German unity. Nonetheless, the British were unable to rally enough support from other European nations. London was also unwilling to support French efforts to deepen European integration. Ultimately, Thatcher attempted to work out a compromise with the Kremlin, supporting the preservation of a Russian presence in East Germany and backing Gorbachev's preferences for an expanded CSCE structure. Only when faced by US firmness and having failed to convince the French and the Russians to block unification did London reluctantly align with Washington, endorsing German unity within NATO and US plans for the alliance's reform.

4 The US, the UK and German Unification

The special relationship evaporates: Britain's search for a European bloc

'To strive for German unification is not a bargaining device but the condition for European stability'
(Henry Kissinger, July 1959)

'I don't want to see us decoupled from Europe; I don't want to see us pull out of Europe'
(George H. W. Bush, 16 December 1989)

'We find ourselves in the same situation as the leaders in France and Britain before the war, who didn't react to anything. We can't repeat Munich!'
(François Mitterrand, 8 December 1989)

'We do not want to wake up one morning and find that . . . German reunification is to all intents and purposes on us'
(Charles Powell, 8 December 1989)

'We beat you twice, and now you are here again'
(Margaret Thatcher, 8 December 1989)

'When the historic moment allows it, let us have unity in our country'
(Helmut Kohl, 19 December 1989)

Thatcher, Mitterrand and the EEC Strasbourg Council

This chapter explores Anglo-American views on the German question from late December 1989 until the spring of 1990. It shows how the Federal government's determination to press ahead with its version of German unity rapidly turned into a motive of Anglo-American controversy. While Whitehall denounced the risks of a hastened path towards unification, by mid-January 1990 the Bush administration backed Kohl's fast-track approach. Washington also endeavoured to reassure the Russians and its West European allies. Unable to influence American views, Thatcher initially turned to France, then she tried to delay unification with the Kremlin's help. Nonetheless, the British failed to work out an arrangement with either Paris or Moscow and London's initiatives to slow down unification were countered by the Bush administration. The US government pressed for a solution that would allow the two German states to play a role alongside the Four Powers in the unification process. In contrast, Whitehall tried to hold on to the remnants of Four Power sovereignty and only in the final stages of the negotiations supported US views.

In December 1989 Bonn's public calls for German unification had become a cause of serious concern in a number of European countries. These concerns had emerged first in early December at the NATO Brussels summit. On this occasion, the Italians and the British had expressed significant reservations about Kohl's ten points and Baker's four points. European apprehensions were then confirmed on 8 December at the Strasbourg meeting of the EC. At the summit, British and other European representatives had reiterated criticism of the FRG's conduct. Almost two decades later in a speech in Leipzig Kohl recalled how the British had been particularly obstructive and remarked that during the meeting Thatcher had come up to him and said, 'We beat you twice, and now you are here again.'[1] On the surface, the EEC summit cemented Anglo-French determination to prevent new unilateral West German initiatives after the concerns that had been caused by Kohl's enunciation of his ten points at the end of November. On the summit's margin, Thatcher had two private meetings with Mitterrand. The French president harshly criticised Kohl for the ten-point plan, drawing an analogy with the inter-war period. He had told Thatcher, 'we find ourselves in the same situation as the leaders in France and Britain before the war, who didn't react to anything. We can't repeat Munich!'[2] The French president and the British prime minister agreed that in times of great danger France and Britain had always established special relations and that such a time had come again. Other EEC members shared Whitehall's views: Italian Prime Minister Giulio Andreotti warned of a new Pangermanism; Dutch Prime Minister Ruud Lubbers also expressed major reservations; and only Spanish Prime Minister Felipe González and Ireland's premier, Charles Haughey, were unreservedly supportive of unification.[3] In his memoirs Belgian Prime Minister Wilfried Martens emphasised that unification was already a 'fait accompli in Kohl's mind' and that the chancellor was furious at Lubbers's strong reservations about German unity.[4]

Nonetheless, Thatcher and Mitterrand could not work out an arrangement to block unification. While the concerns manifested by Mitterrand reassured Thatcher, the French had grasped the logic of developments in Germany. Paris was reluctant to oppose unification outright and believed that if faced with European opposition, the Federal government might seek the approval of outside powers for its moves towards a united Germany. Hence, the French adopted a more accommodating attitude towards Bonn, choosing not to try to slow down unification but instead to strike a favourable deal with Kohl, by agreeing to it.[5] Mitterrand's foreign minister, Roland Dumas, believed that 'the remedy for any worries about a united Germany was to tie that country firmly into European integration'. This was also the view of European Commission President Jacques Delors who, with the support of West German Commissioner Martin Bangemann, endeavoured to dispel anxieties about the risk of German hegemony in Europe.[6] Furthermore, the French occupied the presidency of the EC in the second half of 1989 and so they were well placed to strike a favourable deal with the Germans.

After Kohl's enunciation of his ten-point plan in November Bonn's position in the EEC negotiations had become a key test of the FRG's commitment to European integration. Unwilling to embark on a divisive campaign against unification, Mitterrand made French assent to a united Germany conditional upon further integration in Europe. The French president had been disappointed by the lack of any significant reference to the European process in the ten points. He now demanded Kohl's support for the convening of an intergovernmental conference to amend the 1957 Treaties of Rome, which had established the EEC and the European Atomic Energy Community (EURATOM), and to prepare a new treaty towards European economic and monetary union. In return, Paris agreed to endorse Germany's unification along the guidelines proposed by Bush at NATO's Brussels summit a few days earlier. Bonn was initially reluctant to agree on a schedule for an intergovernmental conference on a European monetary union in the second half of 1990. However, it consented once this was postponed until after the Federal elections of December.[7] The Franco-German deal proved decisive in shaping the Strasbourg summit's conclusions. After a heated debate over Bonn's request for a formal declaration of support, the FRG's European partners reaffirmed the German people's right to regain unity through self-determination.[8] At the end of the summit a final communiqué was issued, which emphasised that this process should respect existing agreements and occur within the context of East–West cooperation and European integration. However, this document included no reference to the principle of the inviolability of the European frontiers, as Thatcher and other European leaders had insisted upon. Strasbourg had exposed the limits of London's attempt to strike a deal with Paris or influence opinion within the European Communities. Ultimately, however, the French view that the best way to contain a united Germany was to sublimate it in a reinforced European Community, held no attraction for Whitehall.[9]

Baker's 12 December speech and the rift between Thatcher and the FCO

NATO's Brussels summit and the EEC Strasbourg meeting confirmed the persistence of deep divisions on the issue of unification within both the alliance and the European Communities. In the aftermath of the Brussels summit the White House intensified efforts to reassure its European allies and Moscow. For the first time since the Berlin Wall's collapse, the US government now contemplated the prospect of a more cooperative and stable relationship between the alliance and the Soviet Union. In a speech to the Berlin Press Club on 12 December Baker hinted at the creation of a new European security architecture in order to overcome Germany's division and keep the US firmly linked to Europe.[10] On the following day the secretary of state paid the first visit by a senior American official to the GDR, encouraging the East German government to continue on the road towards free democratic elections and self-determination.[11] Two days later the NAC issued a declaration that Germany's unification would have to respect existing agreements and occur within the contexts of East–West cooperation and European integration.[12] On 16 December at a joint news conference with Mitterrand in the West Indies Bush also remarked that the Soviet bloc states wanted the US to remain involved in post-Cold War Europe, stating, 'I don't want to see us decoupled from Europe; I don't want to see us pull out of Europe.'[13]

Washington's initiatives took into account the concerns that the United Kingdom had been making publicly since September. However, they were of little reassurance to London. Furthermore, the rapidly evolving situation in Germany remained a persistent source of concern in Whitehall. After Kohl's enunciation of his ten-point programme at the end of November, Bonn's initial position had been that unification would come about only after a transition period of a few years. Nonetheless, the chancellor's visit to the GDR in December to conduct negotiations with the East German premier, Hans Modrow, impressed a dramatic acceleration on the Federal government's strategy. The ecstatic reception received by Kohl's speech before the ruined *Frauenkirche* in Dresden on the evening of 19 December, where the chancellor was cheered by a large crowd shouting, 'Wir sind ein Volk' ('We are one people'), convinced the Federal government that the date of the GDR's elections, initially scheduled for 6 May, should be brought forward.[14] While Kohl urged patience, in Dresden he also reiterated his ambition to achieve unification, by declaring to an enthusiastic crowd, 'when the historic moment allows it, let us have unity in our country'.[15]

Developments in Germany had an immediate echo within the alliance. French reactions to Kohl's GDR visit further undercut British hopes to work out an arrangement with Paris against unification. On 20 December Mitterrand embarked on a highly publicised three-day visit to East Germany in the first and only trip by one of the heads of state of the three Western powers to the GDR. On this occasion, the French president did not hide his hostility to an accelerated and uncontrolled path to German unity. However, he also made it clear that Paris was willing to accept a united Germany if the German people wanted to move in that direction.[16] At the turn of the year Thatcher urged the FCO and the Ministry of Defence to prepare possible diplomatic and contingency measures in the event of an eruption of violence, or of Soviet intervention, in East Germany. However, by early January US support for Bonn and French consent to unification on the condition of deeper integration in Europe undercut consensus for the prime minister among Britain's professional diplomats. Many in the FCO now believed that Thatcher was out of touch with dynamics in Germany and within the Western alliance. This perception created a disjuncture between Whitehall and the FCO that would continue to grow over time.[17] Britain's foreign secretary and an increasing number of professional diplomats, including London's ambassadors to Moscow and Bonn, feared that an openly hostile attitude might be detrimental to British interests. Lack of resistance from the Soviet side probably contributed to increasing these apprehensions. In his diary entry of 19 December Britain's ambassador to Moscow, Rodric Braithwaite, noted that Soviet officials had made it clear that 'the Russians were not going to snatch the chestnuts out of the fire for the French and the British'.[18] On 5 January Mallaby, who until then had shared some of the prime minister's concerns, warned that, as a result of the government's negative disposition, Britain was being perceived in Bonn 'as perhaps the least positive of the three Western allies, and the least important', with the risk of reducing British influence on the Federal Republic at a critical juncture.[19] However, FCO officials opted not to directly confront the prime minister. Rather, they tried to put up with a situation where, on the one hand, they could not openly criticise Whitehall and, on the other hand, they had to demonstrate a constructive British stance towards Germany in order to avoid international isolation.[20]

The US position was more optimistic but also nuanced. Although the Americans endeavoured to avoid a repetition of the embarrassment caused by Kohl's enunciation of his ten points in November, nobody in Washington questioned unification in principle. However, also among US officials there were different ideas about the best strategy to follow. By the middle of January opinions were becoming polarised around two views. These views reflected prevailing preferences in the White House and the State Department respectively. The administration's stance was apparently more forthcoming towards Bonn but less attentive to the concerns of Moscow and Washington's European allies. Most of the presidential staff members shared Bonn's belief that the GDR's crisis made a gradualist approach to unification impracticable. People in the NSC, such as Special Assistant to the President for National Security Affairs Robert Blackwill, Director of European Security Affairs Philip Zelikow and Director of Soviet and East European Affairs Condoleezza Rice, were all favouring a rapid path to German unity. This was now the viewpoint also of President Bush's national security advisor, Brent Scowcroft, who until then had maintained a more cautious approach. The unification of the two German states would be sanctioned by a Four Power blessing once it had been achieved. The main supporter of this fast-track approach was Robert Blackwill, who endorsed a hasty unification along lines negotiated between the US and the Federal Republic in order to present both Moscow and Washington's European allies, Britain included, with a fait accompli.[21]

In contrast, State Department officials privileged a more gradualist approach. They argued for unification to take place within an effective multilateral context and with the participation of the Soviet Union. Particularly, Baker's advisors, Dennis Ross and Robert Zoellick, advocated a cautious strategy, which would provide adequate reassurance to the US's NATO allies and to Moscow. Towards this aim they elaborated a 'Two plus Four' process. According to their viewpoint, while not subjecting the Germans to Four Power tutelage, this format would allow the United Kingdom, France and the Soviet Union to play a full part in the negotiations. Nonetheless, also within the State Department there were nuances about the best strategy to follow. Raymond Seitz, assistant secretary of state for European and Canadian affairs and de facto political director of the State Department's European Bureau, held much more pro-German views. On 1 February Seitz told Baker that a 'Four plus Two formula' would slow down unification, estrange the Germans and provide the Soviets with too much of a lever in the negotiations.[22] Ultimately, the overall American position was supportive of a united Germany and the split between the NSC and the State Department was not over unification as such, but over policy towards the European allies and the Soviet Union and, as a result, over 'the pacing and mechanisms' of German unity. While the State Department trusted the West Germans and, to a certain extent, also the Russians, people in the NSC fretted a good deal about both.[23] However, developments in Germany were also making their impact felt on the US position. By the end of January, they had elicited an overall belief in Washington that, in light of the GDR's desperate situation, the US needed to enforce its leadership now if it was to exert a decisive influence on events.[24]

Thatcher's illusion of a European bloc

Unlike the case for the White House, at the beginning of 1990 Whitehall refused to accept the inevitability of a fast track towards unification. The pace of transformation in Germany, US endeavours to mediate between the Federal government and the European allies, and the more conciliatory views of FCO officials did not discourage Thatcher from trying to sabotage Bonn's quest for a fast-track solution to German unity. Nonetheless, by then Britain's prime minister was aware that she would not receive any support from Washington. Hence, she now searched for consensus in Europe. However, rather than opposing unification outright, Whitehall endeavoured to create a European bloc of nations, which would delay it to an indefinite future. Although the EEC Strasbourg summit of December had already exposed the limits of French readiness to partner with Britain, Paris became the first port of call of her new strategy. On 10 January, in a conversation with Hurd, Thatcher argued that if the Americans could not be convinced to reverse the process, then it might be possible to slow it down with the support of the French and other Europeans. In a meeting with Mitterrand in Paris on 20 January, while Soviet troops intervened in Baku to crack down on widespread rioting and suppress independence demonstrations and anti-Armenian pogroms, Thatcher acknowledged that unification was likely to come about. However, she repeated that some ways should be found to slow it down.[25] According to the British prime minister, if London and Paris could hammer out a common position, it should be possible to bring other European countries, such as the Italians and the Dutch, on board and tie down the Germans on a substantial transitional period. Thatcher also hinted at the need for closer Anglo-French defence ties, in light of a likely increase in German opposition to the presence of foreign troops in the FRG after unification.

However, as in the previous December, when the two leaders had exchanged views at the margin of the EEC Strasbourg summit,

Britain's prime minister could not secure a firm commitment from Mitterrand. The French president concurred in principle with Thatcher's analysis. He said that if Kohl were to get his way, Germany might win more ground than Hitler ever did and Europe would have to live with the consequences.[26] Mitterrand also stressed that the Germans 'did not have the right to upset the political realities of Europe' and warned that if Germany were to expand territorially, Europe would be back to where it was before World War I. Nonetheless, he appeared to be at a loss as to what could be done and pointed out that it would be counterproductive to oppose unification. His bolder advice was a hint that the British and the French 'should perhaps try to persuade the Soviet Union to stiffen East German resistance'.[27] The conversation was emblematic of the illusory character of Thatcher's hopes. While confirming a degree of 'shared uneasiness' about Bonn's policy, the meeting also revealed a fundamental difference between the British and French approaches. Thatcher had unsheathed her 'anti-German register'. However, Mitterrand had remarked that France would not say 'no' to unification, stressing that an excessively obstructive attitude would be 'stupid and unrealistic' and that 'nothing would be worse than raising objections', as such conduct might arouse German 'anger' in reaction. Ultimately, the French president accepted Thatcher's proposals for consultations between the British and French foreign and defence ministers. In March London and Paris agreed to carry out the biggest Anglo-French military exercise in Germany since the end of the War.[28] However, no tangible agreement was reached to slow down unification.[29] In her memoirs Thatcher expressed bitterness about Mitterrand's reluctance to establish an Anglo-French counterweight to Germany.[30]

However, the disappointment of her conversations with Mitterrand did not deter Thatcher. Rather, she remained defiant that something could be done to slow down unification. A few days later *The Wall Street Journal* published a lengthy interview in which Britain's prime minister discussed the practical obstacles that would have to be overcome in order to make German unity possible. Her answers included such expressions as 'slowing down', emphasised that the process should not be rushed over the consolidation of democratic structures and stressed that any solution to the German question should not neglect its implications for European security. She concluded that her stance was to facilitate an agreement on unification, but in a way that would not deliberately harm the chances of Germany's neighbours to work towards greater freedom.[31] Thatcher also warned that unification would create imbalances, and complained that nationalism had not died in Germany and that the Federal government had not formally acknowledged the Oder–Neisse line. Furthermore, she made explicit references to examples of 'uncommunautaire' practices by Bonn on the question of East Germany's accession to the EEC as well as on the issues of free trade and capital movements.

Britain's prime minister was expressing concerns that were shared by other European nations, such as the Dutch and the Belgians.[32] Nonetheless, the transcript of the interview caused great irritation in the FRG. Kohl himself was significantly upset.[33] The prime minister's tone also increased the concern of the foreign secretary and of Britain's professional diplomats that her intransigence might harm London's interests, while damaging relations with Washington. Hurd's views were more cautious and pragmatic than those of the prime minister. The foreign secretary did not share Thatcher's anxieties and believed that transition, while being needed in 'its own right', should not be used as 'a delaying tactic'.[34] Hurd also understood the limits of Mitterrand's support for Thatcher and the impact of Franco-German reconciliation and European integration on French views, and attempted to convey them to the prime minister.[35] In their memoirs Genscher and his chief of staff, Frank Elbe, praised the constructive role of the FCO and Britain's foreign secretary. More specifically, the FRG's foreign minister felt 'that he could rely on Hurd', as they were 'in full agreement about the Oder–Neisse-Line, NATO and the EC'.[36]

Fearing that London might be perceived as the most reluctant of the Four Powers to endorse unification, at a Chequers seminar on 27 January the foreign secretary and a number of cabinet members endeavoured to convince the prime minister of the inevitability of unification.[37] The seminar occurred at a time of growing concern in Britain about the implications of Thatcher's attitude. Minister for Europe William Waldegrave, Defence Secretary Tom King, Minister of the Armed Forces Archie Hamilton, Minister for Defence Procurement Alan Clark, Chairman of the Joint Intelligence Committee Percy Cradock and Deputy Undersecretary of State for Defence and Political Director at the FCO John Weston all endeavoured to convince the prime minister.[38] Their advice for Thatcher was that obstructing

German unity was no longer an option given Washington's strong support for Bonn, the Franco-German axis and Moscow's resignation to accept unification. According to Hurd, the meeting had endured the 'usual diatribe against German selfishness'. However, Thatcher's determination to stop unification had appeared less frequent and intense. The foreign secretary ensured that the prime minister's suggestion of 'slowing things down' would not be enshrined in a message to be sent to Gorbachev. Talks were also made about reducing British troops in Germany and the seminar ended with a strong emphasis on the benign character of contemporary and future German identity.[39]

Nonetheless, while Hurd and senior FCO officials were trying to undercut Thatcher, they did so quietly.[40] Furthermore, not all the participants shared the impression that the prime minister was slowly resigning herself to the inevitability of unification. Alan Clark noticed that, although having argued cogently 'for accepting, and exploiting, German reunification while they still needed our support', Thatcher was determined not to do so.[41] It is plausible that the seminar contributed to reducing the prime minister's personal irritation with Bonn's 'impetuosity and high-handedness' and reinforced her belief in focusing on the practical aspects surrounding unification rather than conducting an isolated campaign against it. However, a number of officials were convinced that her intransigent attitude had already done much damage to Britain's interests. On 1 February the head of the FCO's Western European Department, Hilary Synnott, suggested that the prime minister send a personal message to Kohl or embark on a visit to Bonn, projecting 'the appearance of warm and sincere support for the prospect of reunification if that is what the German people decide upon'.[42]

Despite failing to work out an arrangement with the French, Thatcher continued to hope that at least the Russians might partner with the British in an attempt to slow down unification. Nonetheless, this too proved an illusory idea. In early January the Soviet leaders had emphasised the desirability of keeping negotiations about Germany within the 'Four Powers'. However, by the end of the month the Kremlin had accepted that unification should be negotiated in a 'group of six'.[43] Moscow's change in position was a consequence of an acceleration of the crisis both in the USSR and in the GDR. In early January Gorbachev had visited Vilnius, but failed to persuade the Lithuanian Communist

Party to remain in the CPSU. In the same month the Lithuanian and Latvian Supreme Soviets voted to end the Communist Party's monopoly on power.[44] In Germany the GDR's deteriorating internal situation undercut the prospect of any significant defence of the East German regime. On 28 January, just before his departure for Moscow for talks with Gorbachev, the East German premier, Modrow, was convinced by the roundtable between the GDR's government and the opposition into advancing the date for the parliamentary elections. The elections had been initially scheduled for May; they were now moved forward to 18 March. On the same day Kohl had constituted a 'unity committee' within his cabinet to avert the risk of a mass exodus from East Germany to the Federal Republic.[45] Two days later, on 30 January, Modrow presented to the Soviet leadership in Moscow a four-stage plan that attempted to prolong the GDR's existence but ultimately foresaw the creation of a united, neutral Germany. The Kremlin's reaction swept away any illusion that Moscow would stand in the way of German unity. Gorbachev assured Modrow that the Soviet Union would not tolerate a destabilisation of the GDR, but he also warned him that events in Germany were subject to the existence of dynamics which 'no one can any longer doubt', implicitly acknowledging that unification would take place.[46]

On the road to unification: Two plus Four rather than Two plus Zero

'The Americans would rather work with Britain than with anyone else in charting the way ahead . . . But they will feel able to do so only so long as we are seen to be central to the European debate'
(Anthony Acland, 23 February 1990)

'This *is it*: the Germans are going *full tilt* for reunification without waiting for *anyone*'
(Charles Powell, 5 February 1990)

The genesis of the Two plus Four

At the end of January 1990 Thatcher's hope that Moscow might slow down unification had been undermined by an accelerating sequence of events. First, a rapidly evolving situation in Germany;

second, Gorbachev's growing disposition, also as a result of the USSR's internal economic and political difficulties, to compromise with the West; and third, US determination to support Bonn and push ahead for a rapid transition to German unity. British influence on American policy was also declining rapidly. However, Washington did not completely ignore British views: when it came to discussing the practical modalities of unification, the US approached Britain ahead of France and the USSR. Unlike Thatcher, Hurd and a number of FCO officials now accepted the inevitability of unification. Nonetheless, Anglo-American views remained far apart. Furthermore, London's ideas were closer to those prevailing in Paris and Moscow than to those of Washington, which tended to mirror West German expectations. Hence, the Two plus Four formula, which set the guidelines for German unity, developed as a compromise between German–American preferences on the one side and the views of London, Paris and Moscow on the other. The negotiating format initially favoured by the Americans was based on a 'mechanism of six'. This foresaw a role for the two German states alongside the Four Powers. In contrast, Whitehall's favourite option was a 'Four plus Zero'. This formula would have allowed the Four Powers to discuss unification without any initial German involvement.[47] The French and the Russians, like the British, originally privileged a Four plus Zero approach, although Paris already acknowledged the possibility that the two German states might carry a role in mapping out unification without alienating Four Power rights.

Unlike Whitehall, the US government firmly opposed the view that unification should be dealt with exclusively among the Four Powers. Washington feared that a negotiating format that excluded the FRG and the GDR was likely to produce a majority of three against one, leaving the US as the only defender of unification. On the contrary, the White House endorsed a solution that would let the German states play a role in negotiating alongside the Four Powers. However, US views were still evolving when Hurd arrived in Washington on 28 January to discuss with Baker a framework for German unity and NATO. The conversations between the foreign secretary and the secretary of state went smoothly. On the following day, Hurd noted in his diary, '15 minutes alone and we agree on need for a framework for NATO and German unity'. Nonetheless, in their talks Hurd and Baker made no explicit reference to a Two plus Four formula.[48]

The specific modalities of the negotiating format were first discussed on the evening of 29 January during a meeting between US officials Zoellick and Blackwill and FCO representatives Wright and Wood at the British embassy.[49] When Zoellick told the British about the Two plus Four, they showed interest but refrained from making an explicit commitment.[50] Baker's advisors Ross and Zoellick then completed a memorandum on Two plus Four on 30 January. While endeavouring to convince the British of the need for German participation in the negotiations, the US also promoted the idea of Two plus Four with Bonn.[51] On the same day US Deputy Secretary of State Lawrence Eagleburger and Deputy National Security Advisor Robert Gates discussed with the FRG government in Bonn Kohl's extended talks with Bush at Camp David later in February and tested the ground on a Two plus Four approach.[52]

On 2 February Genscher arrived in Washington for talks with Baker, who laid out the Two plus Four formula to the West German foreign minister. Genscher did not reject the idea in principle. However, he also made clear Bonn's opposition to an arrangement that would not fully involve the two German states. The FRG's foreign minister stressed that for Bonn it was fundamental that the Germans play a key role in order to erase all memories of the humiliating negotiations in Geneva in 1959. Then, Moscow had supported the participation of the FRG and the GDR at the conference of the four foreign ministers. However, the British had insisted that their status be limited to that of 'advisors'. The humiliating result had been that the two German states were confined to a side table or, as Genscher put it, to the *Katzentisch*. Genscher also explained that neither a 'Council of Six' nor a Four plus Two would be acceptable. He also emphasised Bonn's opposition to an agreement between the two German states and the fifteen NATO members – that is, to a 'Two plus Fifteen' formula – or to an arrangement that foresaw the participation of the thirty-five CSCE members. The only option acceptable for Bonn was a negotiating mechanism with the format of Two plus Four.[53] When Kohl was briefed on Washington's proposal, he firmly objected to the 'four midwives'.[54] In the Federal government's view, it was fundamental that the two German states could determine the nature of the unification process on their own. Only at a second stage should the Germans deal with the Four Powers on external security issues. In other words, the victorious powers of the War would advise the Germans, but should not determine the modalities of unification. The Baker–Genscher talks further strengthened the personal bond between the secretary of state and the West German foreign minister, which had been forged during negotiations within the alliance over SNF in the previous spring. They also reinforced US determination to resist any attempts by the other three powers to marginalise the Germans.

In the following weeks there were conflicting accounts of the respective roles of Britain and the US in the drafting of a Two plus Four solution for German unity. A number of accounts described Britain's initial position as one of substantial hostility. On 1 February 1990 the *Bild Zeitung* published an article that stated that even at that stage Thatcher would have done everything possible to fight German unity. However, the British defended their role in the negotiations, arguing that the Two plus Four had emerged on a more collegiate basis. London also rejected interpretations of the deal as a US idea that was pressed upon a reluctant British government. A *New York Times* article on 16 February, which ascribed the paternity of the Two plus Four to the Americans and depicted the British as reluctant partners, drew substantial hostility from the FCO, although British diplomats acknowledged a predominating US role in the process.[55] Nonetheless, Hurd and a small number of FCO officials also played a role.[56] On 20 February Kevin Tebbit, counsellor at Britain's embassy in Washington, wrote to the head of the FCO's Western European Department, Hilary Synnott, that the formula had emerged on a more collegiate basis than reported in the *New York Times* article of 16 February. The FCO official complained that, 'in presenting the chronology of events in this way', the authors were likely to reinforce 'the old impression that America's policy towards Europe is one of "Germany first" and that Britain is a reluctant party in the process'.[57] Ultimately, despite Thatcher's hopes of delaying unification, the British contributed to the genesis of the Two plus Four approach, although their contribution was probably not decisive.[58]

Tension between London and Bonn

In early February British views were evolving considerably. FCO officials played an important role in assuaging Thatcher's fears and eliciting a more positive attitude towards Germany.

Nonetheless, Whitehall remained hostile to a fast-track approach to German unity. Still in early February the British advanced the proposal of discussions with the French and the Americans on the grounds that negotiations between the three Western allies would still be compatible with a meeting of the Four Powers and of the two German states at a later stage.[59] However, Washington continued to emphasise the need not to exclude the Germans at any stage of the negotiations and the French were also resigned to accepting an active German role in mapping out unification. Hence, Britain's proposal triggered a lukewarm response from both Washington and Paris. US cautiousness reflected the fear that tripartite discussions might marginalise Bonn and estrange the West Germans from their Western allies. The French reaction confirmed a reluctance to take any steps that would endanger the Franco-German relationship, as had been already evident during Mitterrand's meetings with Thatcher in Strasbourg in December 1989 and in Paris in January 1990. On 5 February in a telegram to Foreign Secretary Hurd, Britain's ambassador to Paris, Ewen Fergusson, remarked that the French, while feeling that their present bilateral contacts with the Germans were less than satisfactory, were unlikely to stand in the way of 'a determined German drive towards reunification' and were far more 'defeatist' than the British about the chances of controlling the process.[60]

The British continued to worry about the practical modalities of unification. Bilateral conversations with Bonn contributed to increasing their anxieties. On 5 February, during discussions in the FRG's capital with his opposite number, Dieter Kastrup, and other German officials, including Peter Hartmann of the Federal chancellery, the FCO's Political Director John Weston was flatly told that the Federal government would reserve the right to talk to the Russians bilaterally, did not feel that the Bonn group was an 'adequate mechanism for Western consultation' and that, 'while the Four Powers must be involved in a final resolution of the German question ... the current process of rapprochement between the two German states must take place solely on the basis of their right to self-determination'. Kastrup added that the Federal government would be 'very reluctant' to contemplate a formal role for the Four Powers in connection with the process of self-determination.[61] Upon reading the report of the conversation, the prime minister's private secretary, Charles Powell, laconically commented, 'this is it: the Germans are going full tilt for reunification without waiting for anyone'.[62] Whitehall was particularly upset by Bonn's attempt to limit the Four Powers' role. For Bonn, negotiations were a matter for the two German states alone. The Four Powers were to be consulted only on issues directly governed by the Bonn/Paris Relations Conventions of 1952–4 and in the 'final peace settlement'.[63] Furthermore, the Federal government rejected the prospect of a peace treaty and demanded the immediate restoration of full sovereignty for a united Germany.[64]

Faced with US disregard of British concerns and French reluctance to partner with London, by early February Thatcher concluded that her remaining hopes of influencing the modalities of unification rested with the Kremlin. In her view the British should persuade the Soviets that the modalities of unification should be established by the Four Powers rather than by the two German states. She also believed that the challenge posed by transformation in Germany created the need for a redefinition of Britain's relationship with Moscow. In other words, Whitehall should now be prepared to look at Russia as a counterbalance to a united Germany. In the House of Commons debate on 6 February Britain's prime minister reiterated that unification was a matter not only for the German people but also for other countries, concluding that a lengthy period of transition was needed so that 'the unification of Germany gives rise not to more worries but to greater security'.[65] On the same day, in a speech to the Konrad Adenauer foundation in Bonn, Britain's foreign secretary restated the need for 'reasonable periods of transition'.[66] Whereas in the aftermath of the Berlin Wall's collapse Hurd had emphasised that unification was not on the immediate agenda, the foreign secretary now called for transition and for the need to reconcile German membership of the Western Alliance with the security needs of the Soviet Union. Hurd's address was perceived at the Foreign Office as an attempt 'to repair the damage'.[67] Nonetheless, his discussions with Genscher and Kohl confirmed a substantial divergence of positions. Hurd argued that there were several issues to be discussed, such as Community membership, Four Power rights and the CSCE, as well as a NATO discussion about doctrine and posture. In contrast, Genscher stressed that, although there was no reason why the consequences of the reduced threat on the continent should not be discussed, the future political framework was subject to a dynamic process. Therefore, it would not be advisable to work on the basis of blueprints.[68] Hurd's conversation with Kohl confirmed Anglo-German differences. The chancellor stressed that he was unhappy at the state of Anglo-German relations, but he also made it clear that the Federal government had to respond to the deteriorating situation in East Germany.

By then, Bonn had decided not to prop up the ailing Modrow regime any longer and was evaluating the prospect of an economic and monetary union with the GDR. German officials were also discussing the possibility of absorbing the GDR into the FRG through article 23 of the Basic Law and of applying West German legislation, including EEC membership, on GDR territory. This formula had already been adopted in 1956 when the Saar had acceded to the FRG. It was favoured by Bonn over unification through article 146, which called for all-German elections before unification and for the entry into force of a new constitution.[69] London was particularly critical of East Germany's automatic entry into the EEC. Unlike European Commission President Jacques Delors, the British regarded East Germany's integration as an intolerable burden for the Community budget.[70] Hurd's reply to Kohl exposed Whitehall's irritation: the foreign secretary complained that Britain had been disconcertingly surprised by the ten-point plan and he concluded that the fewer such surprises remained in the future, the better it would be. Reactions in London reflected frustration at Bonn's conduct but also a concern that Whitehall was losing influence on dynamics in Germany. Commenting on the visit in a letter to the prime minister's private secretary, Charles Powell, Hurd's private secretary, Stephen Wall, remarked that the foreign secretary's visit had made it pretty clear that Genscher and Kohl were now 'not pushing but pulling' and that while the Americans believed that the British were being unduly alarmist, the French were more sympathetic to Britain's concerns. However, he concluded that Paris seemed to have no answer to these concerns, except one that Britain could not accept, namely more EEC institutional integration. On his copy of the letter, Powell minuted, 'Not at all satisfactory or reassuring. We are just told to leave it all to the Germans, even whether there should be a peace treaty.'[71] In the following days the accelerating pace of US and West German initiatives further exposed Britain's limited influence on Washington and Bonn and the illusory nature of Thatcher's hope of delaying unification with Russian help.

Baker's and Kohl's visits to Moscow

Baker's talks with Genscher in Washington at the end of January laid the foundation for a complex diplomatic arrangement. This was completed by the US government in the first weeks of February. After his meeting with the FRG's foreign minister, Baker embarked on a trip to the Soviet Union and Eastern Europe. The purpose of this journey was to make it clear to the Kremlin that an exclusive Four Power deal would not be acceptable to Bonn. Rather, the secretary of state now endeavoured to convince the Soviets of the need for a framework that would allow the active participation of the two German states.[72] On his way to Moscow, Baker added at the last minute a brief refuelling stopover at Shannon airport in Ireland. There, on 6 February he met France's foreign minister, Dumas, who was in Ireland for an EEC meeting, endeavouring to obtain his agreement to the Two plus Four concept. However, like his British counterpart a few days earlier, France's foreign minister also manifested an initial preference for a Four plus Zero. Then Dumas suggested reversing the negotiating format into a Four plus Two, which would allow the Four Powers to discuss unification before formal German involvement. Nonetheless, Baker was able to convince him of the need for an active German role in the process.[73]

On the same day, the secretary of state flew to Prague, where he met with President Václav Havel and delivered an address at Charles University, promising assistance to Czechoslovakia and endorsing a united Germany's membership of NATO. While Baker was negotiating with the Europeans, Bush further clarified the American position. On 7 February in a speech before the Commonwealth Club in San Francisco the president presented his vision for a 'Europe truly whole and free'. Bush said that he was encouraged by Kohl's commitment to keeping Germany tied into NATO in some way, although 'maybe not a NATO in exactly the same form'.[74] On the same and following day, Baker discussed West German views in Moscow with Shevardnadze. The USSR's initial response was cautious. The Soviet foreign minister, who was visibly struggling to keep up with the pace of events, attempted to defend the Modrow plan and requested a meeting of the Four Powers to discuss a peace treaty.[75] On 9 February the secretary of state presented the Two plus Four concept to Gorbachev in the

Kremlin's Catherine Hall. The Soviet leader shared the Anglo-French preference for Four plus Zero. He debated the Two plus Four approach, but remained noncommittal. Baker emphasised the dangers that an economic powerhouse like Germany might pose, if it remained neutral once united. Then, he stressed that German membership of NATO, together with a Western guarantee that the alliance would not expand its jurisdiction eastwards by even a centimetre, would provide better security for the Soviet Union than a united Germany outside of NATO, without US troops and potentially in possession of its own nuclear weapons.[76] Before departing from the Soviet capital, Baker left a three-page letter drafted by his advisor, Denis Ross, with the West German ambassador in Moscow, Klaus Blech, to prepare Kohl for his forthcoming talks with the Soviets. Then the secretary of state departed for Romania and Bulgaria, avoiding personal contact with the chancellor and Genscher when they arrived in Moscow on 10 February in order not to create the impression that the US and the Soviet Union were deciding Germany's fate without the British and the French.[77]

The US–Soviet meeting in Moscow ended without a definite deal, although Baker had made important progress in his talks with the Kremlin. Nonetheless, it produced conflicting expectations in the US and Russia. For Washington the encounter dealt exclusively with Germany and was only one in a number of conversations and negotiations. As such, it was subject to change until final documents were signed. However, the Russians believed that in the meeting Baker had given them an explicit guarantee that NATO would not expand eastwards.[78] The secretary of state's reassurances to the Soviets caused apprehension in Washington and were judged as excessive at the NSC. Staff members on the NSC viewed NATO's limited jurisdiction to the former FRG territory as neither desirable nor practical. NATO Secretary General Manfred Wörner was also sceptical of Baker's vision. Meeting Bush in Washington on 10 February, the former FRG defence minister emphasised that Germany should remain a full member of the alliance and of its military structure. Furthermore, any special military status for GDR territory should not imply its neutralisation or demilitarisation.[79]

Following Bush's meeting with Wörner, NSC staff drafted a letter to be signed by the president in advance of Kohl's visit to the Soviet Union on 10 and 11 February, which sounded a different note from Baker. The letter reached the chancellor on the night before his departure for Moscow. Bush's message reiterated US support for the Federal government. However, it also urged Kohl to insist on Germany's full NATO membership, although envisaging a 'special military status' for East Germany. In their talks in the Soviet capital Kohl and Genscher received Gorbachev's formal consent to go ahead with unification. They also assured the Soviets that, while a united Germany would remain a member of NATO, alliance forces would be restricted to former FRG territory. Furthermore, Soviet troops would be allowed to stay in East Germany for a transitory period. After the talks between Baker and Gorbachev, the West German–Soviet meeting further softened Moscow's position on the German question. Soviet news agency TASS reported that, 'the Germans themselves must resolve the question of the unity of the German nation and that they themselves decide in what time frame, at what speed, and under what conditions they wish to bring about unity'.[80] The positive outcomes of Baker's and Kohl's visits to Moscow reflected a growing coordination between the US and the FRG and allowed the West to secure the Kremlin's agreement to a united Germany's full membership of NATO. Nonetheless, their success hardly contributed to reassure Thatcher. Despite the more forthcoming attitude of Britain's professional diplomats, Whitehall was reluctant to relinquish Four Power rights and feared that, by engaging the Russians, the US and the West Germans were trying to minimise external influences on unification.

The not-so-special relationship: Ottawa and US rejection of a strengthened CSCE

'To put it bluntly, we have to bear in mind – although not to say – that we might one day need the Soviet Union as a counterbalance to a united Germany'
(Margaret Thatcher, 10 February 1990)

Thatcher's Russian track and the Ottawa Conference

Baker's and Kohl's trips to Moscow in February 1990 cleared the way for the USSR's acceptance that a united Germany would be a full member of NATO, but with a special military status for the GDR. Nonetheless, they did not divert Thatcher from her concern that Britain should look at Russia as a counterweight to a united Germany. Throughout February and March her search for an arrangement with Moscow resulted in a protracted campaign for a revitalisation of the CSCE. The British prime minister's argument was that, alongside NATO, the CSCE provided a multilateral forum in which the modalities of unification could be discussed with the participation of all of Germany's neighbours. On this issue there was a fundamental identity of views between Whitehall and the FCO. On 8 February in a conversation with Hurd, upon his return from the US, Thatcher emphasised the need to figure out a way 'of avoiding the unification becoming a fait accompli', before its overall implications had been worked out. While the foreign secretary reminded the prime minister of Washington's support for Kohl, they concurred that in the longer term the CSCE would provide 'a potential framework within which to dilute German influence in Europe'. Furthermore, they also agreed that, as no single European country was big enough to balance Germany, Britain might need to rely in the future on Russian support to keep the Federal Republic in check.[81]

The determination not to alienate Russia was confirmed by a paper prepared by the FCO on 9 February and which was later used by British negotiators as the basis for discussions with the French, the Americans and the Germans at the Ottawa 'Open Skies' conference. The idea of an Open Skies, or cooperative aerial monitoring, had first been proposed by Eisenhower at the Geneva summit of the Four Powers in July 1955. It was then rekindled by Bush in May 1989. In September an international Open Skies conference involving all NATO and Warsaw Pact countries opened in Ottawa. However, in February 1990 the conference ended up dealing mainly with Germany's unification.[82] The paper indicated as key British objectives: the retention of NATO, with an integrated military organisation; German membership of the alliance; a continued American military presence in Europe; and arrangements that would give an 'adequate sense' of security to Germany's neighbours and to the Soviet Union. This was also the firm opinion of the prime minister, provided that significant American forces and nuclear weapons remained in the FRG and that some consideration was shown for Gorbachev. Her conclusion was that one had to 'bear in mind' – although not to say this in public – that the Soviet Union might be needed one day in the future 'as a counterbalance to a united Germany'.[83]

On 10 February, at the Young Conservative Conference in Torquay, Thatcher restated her determination to engage the Russians, on the very same day that Kohl received, during his visit to Moscow, Gorbachev's consent to go ahead with unification. Answering questions at the end of her speech, Britain's prime minister explained that, according to the Helsinki Final Act of 1975, no European boundaries would be changed 'except by agreement' and that unification should be made conditional upon approval by all thirty-five CSCE signatory states.[84] Nonetheless, while giving satisfaction to Moscow, her words also exposed persistent nuances between the prime minister and her foreign secretary. On 19 February Wall wrote to Powell stressing that, as emphasised by Harold Wilson in July 1975, 'the Final Act was neither a treaty nor a peace settlement'. Hence, as Four Power rights and responsibilities had not been affected, there was no legal or political requirement for formal CSCE approval of unification. In his reply on the following day, Powell stressed that the prime minister had not referred to formal approval but only to 'massive consultation', questioning whether it would be right to connive in German endeavours to avoid a peace treaty.[85]

Nonetheless, Thatcher's hopes that Britain and the USSR might slow down unification, or at least influence its modalities, were once again undermined by Washington's endeavours and by the frenzied sequence of events. Upon their return from Moscow, Genscher and his aides immediately flew on to Ottawa; at the traditional 'Deutschland breakfast' that preceded NATO conferences, Genscher, Dumas, Baker and Hurd agreed on the framework for future negotiations on Germany. In a blow to Thatcher's plans, on 13 February Baker and Genscher individually met with Soviet Foreign Minister Shevardnadze. The secretary of state and his West German counterpart faced a hesitant Soviet colleague, who was lacking firm direction from Moscow.[86] The USSR's foreign minister interrupted his talks with Baker and Genscher several times for cross-checks with the Kremlin on the phone. At 3 p.m. in the Canadian capital, all six foreign ministers met for a photo session and presented their agreement to begin the Two plus Four talks on German unification after the GDR elections of 18 March.[87] The agreement highlighted once more Thatcher's inability to influence US preferences, constrain West German initiatives and drag the Russians towards a sterner opposition to unification. Washington also continued to reject Britain's demands for trilateral discussions with France: when Weston raised the issue with Zoellick and Seitz their reaction was that, while there was an objective case for such a meeting, the risk of ructions with the Germans was likely to outweigh the advantages.[88]

However, Whitehall was not isolated in manifesting dissent. Significant concerns were also expressed by other allied nations. A number of NATO's members, including Canada, the Netherlands, Italy, Luxembourg, Norway, Belgium and Spain, complained that their governments had not been consulted. As Frank Elbe, Genscher's chief of staff, who was present at the meeting, put it, 'most NATO partners felt steamrolled by the events'. Italy's foreign minister, Gianni De Michelis, and his Dutch colleague, Hans van den Broek, were extremely upset, while Genscher struggled to clarify that the number of participants had been restricted to those states that, as a result of the War, had responsibilities with regard to Germany as a whole. Blackwill quoted a Canadian who said, 'We felt like a piano player on the ground floor of a whorehouse, who has some sort of idea of what is going on in the upper floors.'[89] On 13 February De Michelis was flatly told by Genscher, 'You are not part of the game', although the German foreign minister later admitted that he was referring more to van den Broek than De Michelis.[90]

Feeling vindicated by the reaction of other European nations, Thatcher now blamed Bonn for not coordinating its policy with the other members of NATO, emphasised the concerns of Germany's Eastern neighbours and demanded that the FRG commit to an early recognition of the Oder–Neisse frontier. On 14 February during a meeting in London with Genscher, who was on his way back from the Ottawa Conference, Thatcher, who two days earlier had met Polish Prime Minister Tadeusz Mazowiecki, told the FRG's foreign minister how strong Polish feelings were about the need for a treaty that would confirm the border. She also stressed that it was very important that Germany did not threaten European stability and security and complained that the Federal government had not given sufficient attention to consultation with its allies. Genscher reassured Britain's prime minister that the FRG did not want anything to happen behind the backs of the Four Powers. Nonetheless, he firmly rejected the idea that unification might become the subject of a broader CSCE debate.

He also stressed that the Federal government would clarify its position on the border with Poland, but did not want to sign a peace treaty with anyone. Furthermore, Genscher emphasised that a divided Germany made no contribution to European stability and the allies should not give the impression that they had reservations about unification.[91] Thatcher's demands for reassurances also continued to worry FCO officials. Two days later, in a letter to Weston, Mallaby suggested the establishment of a formal linkage between the lifting of Four Power rights and an agreement on the security arrangements accompanying German unity as a way of appeasing the Russians. Nonetheless, he also stressed that the Americans were unlikely to support British demands and that London's influence on the Federal government was declining rapidly. According to the ambassador, the Americans were those with incomparably the most influence on the West Germans. The French, because of the Franco-German special relationship, also had a 'good bit'. In contrast, Britain was in a different position: it could exert influence effectively if it first convinced both or at least one of these two and, only at a subsequent stage put the matter to the Germans.[92]

The US rejection of a strengthened CSCE and emphasis on NATO

In the second half of February Thatcher continued to advocate a strengthening of the CSCE in order to appease the Russians. Nonetheless, her arguments met with firm opposition from the US and the FRG and with increasing scepticism from her foreign secretary. On 23 February Hurd told Thatcher that, having secured a proper forum for the discussion of the implications of unification, Britain should not appear 'to be a brake on everything' and should grasp the opportunity to 'come forward with some positive ideas'.[93] However, the prime minister remained convinced that Germany should not be allowed to unify without adequate guarantees to the Four Powers and all of its neighbours. The following day in a telephone conversation with Bush, Thatcher put forward a number of suggestions that reflected her firm belief that once unification had been achieved it would be wise to perpetuate a Russian role in Germany. First, Britain's prime minister informed Bush that in recent meetings with a number of European leaders she had detected recurring worries about the FRG's reluctance to consult its allies. Although the framework established at

Ottawa had allayed some of these concerns, some nations, such as the Poles, the Italians and the Dutch, feared that they were being left out. Thatcher stressed that it was desirable that the British and the Americans endeavour to reassure them and discussions about unification be carried out in NATO. She added that the best course to follow would be 'to strengthen and build on the CSCE', as this would not only prevent Soviet isolation but also 'help balance German dominance in Europe'. Second, Britain's prime minister suggested that Soviet troops should be allowed to stay in the GDR for a period of transition 'without any terminal date', as this was the only way of persuading Moscow that a united Germany should be in NATO. Finally, she added that the preservation of a Russian presence in East Germany would also require the stationing of Soviet troops in Poland for logistical reasons and advised the president to impress on the Germans the need for a treaty to guarantee Poland's border.[94]

Nonetheless, on this occasion, her arguments again failed to impress the White House.[95] Bush rejected the prospect that German sovereignty might be constrained in order to accommodate Soviet concerns. While stressing the importance of the continued integration of Germany into NATO, he emphasised that unification had to be taken 'as a fact'. The president also rejected the prospect of an ongoing Soviet presence in Poland and reminded Thatcher of the American interest in Kohl's success in the forthcoming West German elections, hinting at the risk that the Social Democratic leader, Oskar Lafontaine, 'might lead Germany off in the wrong direction'.[96] Bush also emphasised that the Two plus Four formula should satisfy Moscow's desire to be fully involved in the negotiations, but should not provide the Russians with a forum in which they could exploit the FRG's weaknesses in order to foster a looser association between Germany and NATO. However, the president's words failed to reassure Thatcher. Britain's prime minister urged Bush not to underestimate the prospect of German dominance in Europe. She explained that her concerns were also shared by Mitterrand, who had confessed in private that if the situation were not carefully dealt with there was a risk that 'Germany would win in peace what she had failed to achieve in war'. For this reason, Whitehall had endeavoured to bring about closer Anglo-French cooperation, particularly in the defence sphere, impressing on Mitterrand the need to retain American forces in Europe. Bush's reply was that the US was willing to work on the CSCE idea. The president also reassured Thatcher about the closeness of their positions and the prospect of future discussion between him, her and Mitterrand at some point. Nonetheless, he stressed that this ought to be presented in such a way that the Germans did not feel excluded and that 'NATO was fundamental, indeed more important than ever', particularly against the risk of 'apathy and unpredictability'.

Thatcher's conclusion was that Bush's stand 'was fully echoed by the United Kingdom'.[97] However, the conversation had further confirmed the differences in Anglo-American views and Whitehall's lack of leverage on US policy. More specifically, the prime minister's preference for a strengthened CSCE and building links with Eastern Europe, by providing the Helsinki agreements with some additional machinery, had failed to strike a chord with the president. In the following months the CSCE turned out to be of little significance for addressing the external implications of unification. Furthermore, Bush had firmly ruled out the prospect of preserving a Soviet presence in East Germany and Poland. In contrast, when Kohl arrived at Camp David later in the afternoon, Bush and Scowcroft insisted to him the need to anchor a united Germany firmly within NATO. On 25 February, at a joint press conference, the president and the chancellor declared that Germany should remain a full member of the alliance, including its military structure, although with a 'special military status' for the former GDR.[98]

By the end of February the powerless nature of Thatcher's endeavours to slow down German unity had become apparent to many in her cabinet and the FCO, undermining domestic support for her policy. On 28 February the FCO sent a guidance telegram to Britain's representatives overseas, which emphasised London's long-standing commitment to unification and welcomed the establishment of a framework in which its security implications would be properly considered.[99] On the same day the four allied political directors met in London under the chairmanship of John Weston. The French were represented by Bertrand Dufourcq, Dieter Kastrup represented the West Germans, while the American delegation was led by Robert Zoellick, alongside Raymond Seitz. The expectation of Britain's delegates was that, while there was now overall agreement on unification, negotiations on its practical aspects might last more than a year. However, US representatives, upon specific instructions from Baker, aimed at accelerating the process. In the following weeks Washington made it clear to the British that the Americans were in favour of a rapid conclusion of the negotiations and expected cooperation from Britain on this issue. In early March Deputy Secretary of State Eagleburger told Britain's ambassador to the US, Anthony Acland, that in some parts of the administration there was a perception that Whitehall 'remained unenthusiastic about German reunification and would like to slow it down'.[100] According to Eagleburger, while this perception certainly existed in the European Bureau of the State Department, it was not so strong with the secretary and his immediate staff. Eagleburger then continued that, while there were no major differences between Britain and the US on points of substance, there was some worry that the British and the French might form an alliance to the detriment of the Americans and the Germans. He added that there was equal anxiety in Washington that the French and the Russians might get together to the disadvantage of others. The deputy secretary of state explained that the German position was always central to American thinking and added that James Dobbins, as deputy assistant secretary at the European Bureau and also as a result of his time as minister at the US embassy in the Federal Republic, 'attached special importance to the German aspect'. While the president retained a very high regard for the prime minister and National Security Advisor Scowcroft had no problem at all with Thatcher, it was inevitable that the European Bureau, which had to deal with 'the immediate day to day problems', sometimes 'grew frustrated' if agreement was difficult to reach. Eagleburger also reminded Acland that one of the most important issues for the next few years would be the continued US military presence in Europe. Washington had absolutely no doubt that, on such an issue, the United Kingdom would be the US's 'most important and staunch ally'. In contrast, the French 'would not necessarily be supportive, nor perhaps would the Germans'. The deputy secretary of state also acknowledged that Kohl and, to some extent, Genscher, had 'failed to take account of the sensitivities of neighbouring and other countries'. However, his conclusion was that Whitehall should make an attempt to improve prevailing perceptions about Britain's role. The ambassador's reaction revealed significant irritation. Writing to Weston on 14 March, Acland noted that his talk with Eagleburger was unlikely to bring about 'any rapid change of attitude', particularly in the NSC, as a result of the US urge to help Kohl and distrust of Soviet motives. His conclusion was that those involved in German issues at the State Department and other parts of the administration should constantly be encouraged to concentrate on the substance of Britain's policy, 'rather than on some people's perceptions of it'.[101]

The Oder–Neisse question and Anglo-German acrimony

American pressures and the advice of FCO officials were not enough to convince Thatcher. Although unable to prompt the French and the Russians to slow down the pace of unification, Whitehall now received Mitterrand's support on the Oder–Neisse question. Kohl had failed to mention the Oder–Neisse in his ten-point plan, pointing out that neither the FRG nor the GDR had the legal authority to settle the border question and that only a united Germany could make the final decision.[102] The chancellor had also tried to link recognition of the border with a Polish renunciation of war reparations and a treaty securing the rights of the German minority in Poland.[103] However, the Polish government demanded the signing of a treaty recognising the border before unification took place. Bonn's commitment to respecting the border with Poland was viewed in France as a key test of Germany's reliability. On 8 March the *Bundestag* voted a resolution that reaffirmed Bonn's commitment to the inviolability of the Oder–Neisse frontier. However, Mitterrand did not think the resolution went far enough and on the following day formally demanded the conclusion of a Polish–German agreement. The US concurred with the need for a satisfactory solution to the border question. However, the White House's views were less exacting than those prevailing in Europe. While Scowcroft, Zelikow and Rice expressed disappointment at the way in which Kohl handled the Oder–Neisse question, Bush argued that the border was guaranteed by Germany's respect of the Helsinki Final Act.[104]

The British position was firmer. After the resolution was passed in the *Bundestag* Thatcher sent a message of congratulations to Kohl. It was followed by another message on the victory that the East German Democratic Union leader, Lothar de Maizière, and his allies in the Alliance for Germany had achieved in the GDR elections of 18 March.[105] Nonetheless, Whitehall continued to demand the inclusion of the Oder–Neisse line in a peace treaty and to express dissent for the way in which unification was being

dealt with by the US and the FRG.[106] Britain's anxieties were
confirmed by the proceedings of a seminar held at Chequers on
24 March. On this occasion, the participants, who included a
number of prominent academics, such as Gordon Craig, Fritz
Stern, Norman Stone and Timothy Garton-Ash, alongside the
prime minister and the foreign secretary, suggested that, while
a continuing American military presence in Europe was needed
as a balance to German power, limits should be imposed on the
size of Germany's armed forces together with a renewed self-
denying ordinance on the acquisition of nuclear and chemical
weapons. Furthermore, they restated the view that it would be in
Britain's interests to promote Moscow's institutional involvement
in Europe, particularly through the CSCE, 'because in the long
term the Soviet Union would be the only European power capable
of balancing Germany'.[107] The participants also expressed doubts
about the French argument that the best way to contain a united
Germany would be to dilute its power in the EEC. Some also
remarked that German behaviour in the European Community
was best explained by the mantra 'we pay so we must have our
way'. This attitude might become the harbinger of Germany's
economic dominance over Western Europe.[108] Two days later in
an interview with the German magazine *Der Spiegel* the British
prime minister accused Bonn of intransigence on the frontier
question. Thatcher recalled the conversation at the Strasbourg
European summit dinner of 8 December 1989, remarking, 'You
know what happened with previous assurances: they were over-
turned by the German courts, and I heard Helmut say: "No, I
guarantee nothing, I do not recognise the current frontier."'[109]
Her comments triggered a crisis in relations with Bonn only a few
days before the annual Königswinter Conference in Cambridge
and the British–German summit on 29 and 30 March. Although
Thatcher waited for Kohl at the airport, the chancellor was not
willing to talk to her when he arrived in London on 28 March.
The two leaders drove away from the airport to Saint Catharine's
College in separate cars, while during the reception the prime minister was at one end of the table and the chancellor at the other.
On 29 March Thatcher remarked in her conference speech that a
close Anglo-German relationship was at the heart of NATO and
Europe and was essential to the success of both, slightly improving the atmosphere.[110] Nonetheless, the climate between the two
leaders remained tense, frustrating the hope of those FCO officials

that had looked to these occasions as an opportunity to 'mend fences'.[111]

The issue of a peace settlement: Anglo-American differences of tone and substance

'The guiding principle for the Americans was to avoid a situation where the Germans appeared to be singled out by other powers for special, arguably, second-class, treatment'
(Robert Blackwill, 20 March 1990)

The peace settlement

The Two plus Four negotiations had confirmed fundamental divergences in Anglo-American views but in the following weeks US and British representatives worked closely to identify the legal questions to be solved before unification. However, on many occasions FCO delegates found themselves closer to the French and facing a united German–American front.[112] The Anglo-Americans were in accord only on the issues of the German state's legal character and of its relationship with NATO. In contrast, differences centred on three main issues: the starting date for negotiations; the unification's timeline; and the issue of a peace settlement. The first was also the least significant divergence. The US and the FRG expected the first ministerial meeting not to take place before the GDR's elections in the belief that their outcome would bolster Kohl's position. The timeline of unification was linked to the thorny question of a peace settlement and was the source of significant tension. Britain, like France, preferred unification and the creation of an all-German government before a settlement was signed. However, the Americans argued for a settlement to be concluded before unification.[113]

Nonetheless, the main divergence remained whether unification should constitute part of a wider peace settlement or be accompanied by the signing of a formal peace treaty. The issue of a peace settlement had been discussed at the end of the War. Already in the Berlin Declaration of 5 June 1945 the Four Powers had stated that they would determine the 'boundaries of Germany or any part thereof'. Then, the August 1945 Potsdam Protocol had instructed the CFM to draft a peace settlement. The Convention on relations between the three powers and the Federal Republic of May 1952 had also dealt with this issue. More specifically, in article 7.1 the contracting parties had stated that an essential aim of their common policy would be 'a peace settlement for the whole of Germany' and that 'the final determination of the boundaries of Germany must await such a settlement'.[114] The British and the French regarded a peace settlement as particularly important in order to protect Four Power rights. In contrast, the prospect of a peace settlement was regarded as humiliating by the Federal government.[115] While the US supported West German views, the British argued that an overall settlement of some kind was needed. Washington's resolve to terminate any remnants of Germany's defeated status also reflected the administration's concern to avoid a formal debate in Congress. However, it led to repeated concerns in Britain.[116]

Anglo-American divergences over this issue erupted in the first meeting of the Two plus Four that took place on 14 March in Bonn only four days ahead of the GDR's first democratic elections. On this occasion, the Germans, with American support, succeeded in dropping a general peace settlement from the agenda items, eliciting British frustration.[117] Hurd complained that US performance had been disappointing and that US delegates displayed an exaggerated attachment to protecting German interests.[118] The Bush administration endeavoured to reassure FCO officials. At a meeting with Andrew Wood, minister at the British embassy in Washington, on 20 March Blackwill asserted that 'the British and American approaches were very close'. However, he also stressed that the 'guiding principle' of the US was 'to avoid a situation where the Germans appeared to be singled out by other powers for special, arguably, second-class, treatment' and that 'it would be very desirable to achieve a common UK/US view'.[119] Britain's request for a legal settlement was reiterated during talks in April in London between State Department legal advisors and FCO officials.[120] Nonetheless, the Americans made it clear that they would prefer to avoid instruments which required the 'advice and consent' of the Senate. Furthermore, while in Britain's view unification should precede the final settlement, US representatives argued that a settlement should be concluded before unification, as this would prevent the other three powers from attempting to limit Germany's sovereignty. Ultimately, the American preference was that the Four Powers renounce their rights and responsibilities 'subject to specific agreements being ratified by the united Germany'.[121]

Only on the issue of Germany's legal identity were Anglo-American views not far apart. Both Whitehall and the White House aimed to make sure that there was continuity between the FRG and a united Germany. By contrast they envisaged a succession of states between the GDR and a united Germany. Such a solution ensured that FRG's treaties, mainly NATO membership, continued for a united Germany, while GDR treaties were terminated.[122] The Americans also supported Bonn's view that unification should take place under article 23 of the Basic Law, as this guaranteed legal continuity between the Federal Republic and a united Germany. In contrast, continuity would be less clear if unification were to take place under article 146 of the Basic Law, as insisted upon by the Soviet Union.[123] FCO officials concluded that the meeting had been a 'reassuring one' and that Anglo-American thinking seemed 'reasonably close'.[124]

Nonetheless, during the meeting of the 'One plus Three' held in Brussels on 11 April the British faced once again a united German–American front on the issue of a final settlement. This fuelled fears in London that the Americans were seeing things 'through the German prism', while the Germans were moving to the 'beat of their own drum' with the risk of drifting towards a 'minimalist interpretation' of the actual role of the Two plus Four.[125] Writing to Wood on the same day, Synnott defined Seitz's attitude as 'entirely misguided' and remarked that if German 'laissez-faire' attitudes were allowed to prevail, there was a risk that allied rights and responsibilities would be more directly at stake.[126] The American approach was based on the view that, rather than a 'bundle of interrelated rights' relating to Berlin and to Germany as a whole, there was 'an exhaustive list of distinct Four Power rights'.[127] However, according to FCO officials, to separate rights relating to unification from rights relating to a settlement might 'risk giving too much emphasis to the former', with Four Power rights being reduced to a mere non-interference stance. According to the British, the US interpretation also made it difficult to envisage how Berlin's occupation status could be preserved for the period in which Soviet troops remained in the territory of the former GDR once Four Power rights were terminated.[128] Only in late April did Whitehall reluctantly abandon demands for a peace settlement. However, the prevailing opinion in Britain remained that American conduct had shown worrying signs of weakening Western solidarity.

Notes

1. Quoted in Elisabeth Hellenbroich, 'Thatcher's Obsession to Block German Unity', *Executive Intelligence Review*, vol. 25, no. 32, August 1998, p. 45.
2. Quoted in Philip Zelikow and Condoleezza Rice, 'German Unification', in Kiron K. Skinner (ed.), *Turning Points in Ending the Cold War* (Stanford, CA: Hoover Institution Press, 2008), p. 246. See also Jacques Attali, *Verbatim: Tome 3, Chronique des années 1988–1991* (Paris: Fayard, 1995), pp. 337, 369.
3. Helmut Kohl, *Erinnerungen 1982–1990* (Munich: Droemer, 2005), pp. 1013–14.
4. Wilfried Martens, *Europe: I Struggle, I Overcome* (Dordrecht: Springer, 2009), p. 101.
5. James E. Cronin, *Global Rules: America, Britain and a Disordered World* (New Haven, CT: Yale University Press, 2014), pp. 188–9.
6. Gerhard A. Ritter, *The Price of German Unity: Reunification and the Crisis of the Welfare State* (Oxford and New York: Oxford University Press, 2011), p. 36. See also Richard McAllister, *From EC to EU: An Historical and Political Survey* (London and New York: Routledge, 1997), pp. 211–15.
7. Michael J. Baun, 'The Maastricht Treaty as High Politics: Germany, France and European Integration', *Political Science Quarterly*, vol. 110, no. 4, 1995, p. 613.
8. *Documents on British Policy Overseas* (hereafter *DBPO*), Series III, vol. VII, *German Unification, 1989–1990* (London: Her Majesty's Stationery Office, 2009), doc. no. 73, p. 168, fn. 3. See also Christopher Hill and Karen Elizabeth Smith (eds), *European Foreign Policy: Key Documents* (London: Routledge, 2000), p. 270.
9. Douglas Hurd, *Memoirs* (London: Abacus, 2004), p. 422.
10. James A. Baker, 'A New Europe, a New Atlanticism: Architecture for a New Era', *Berlin Press Club*, Berlin, 12 December 1989, State Department press release, reprinted in Vojtech Mastny, *The Helsinki Process and the Reintegration of Europe: Analysis and Documentation, 1986–1990* (New York: New York University Press, 2008), doc. no. 59, pp. 196–7. See also 'Speech by US Secretary of State James Baker to Berlin Press Club', in Lawrence Freedman, *Europe Transformed: Documents on the End of the*

Cold War – Key Treaties, Agreements, Statements, and Speeches (New York: St. Martin's Press, 1990), pp. 397–8; Mary E. Sarotte, *1989: The Struggle to Create Post-Cold War Europe* (Princeton, NJ: Princeton University Press, 2009), pp. 262–3, fn. 124; Cronin, *Global Rules*, p. 189.

11. Elizabeth Pond, *Beyond the Wall: Germany's Road to Unification* (Washington, DC: Brookings Institution Press, 1993), p. 169.
12. Final Communiqué of the North Atlantic Council, Brussels 14–15 December 1989, available at <http://www.nato.int/docu/comm/49-95/c891215a.htm> (last accessed 30 September 2016).
13. G. H. W. Bush, 'Joint News Conference Following Discussions with French President Mitterrand in St. Martin, French West Indies', 16 December 1989, in *Public Papers: George Bush, 1989, Book II* (Washington, DC: Government Printing Office, 1990), p. 1714.
14. Horst Teltschik, *329 Tage. Innenansichten der Einigung* (Berlin: Siedler, 1991), p. 110, entry for 17 January 1990. Quoted in *DBPO*, III, VII, p. xxi. See also Alexander von Plato, *The End of the Cold War? Bush, Kohl, Gorbachev, and the Reunification of Germany* (London and New York: Palgrave Macmillan, 2015), pp. 114–16.
15. Quoted in Henrik Bering, *Helmut Kohl: The Man Who Reunited Germany, Rebuilt Europe, and Thwarted the Soviet Empire* (Washington, DC: Regnery, 1999), p. 109. Helmut Kohl, 'Ziel bleibt die Einheit der Nation', in Presse- und Informationsamt der Bundesregierung (ed.), *Bundeskanzler Helmut Kohl: Reden und Erklärungen zur Deutschlandpolitik* (Bonn: Presse- und Informationsamt der Bundesregierung, 1990), pp. 138–42.
16. Frédéric Bozo, *Mitterrand, the End of the Cold War, and German Unification* (New York: Berghahn Books, 2009), pp. 142–3.
17. Jarrod Hayes and Patrick James, 'Theory as Thought: Britain and German Unification', *Security Studies*, vol. 23, no. 2, 2014, p. 413.
18. Rodric Braithwaite, *Diary* (unpublished), entry for 19 December 1989. Quoted in Rodric Braithwaite, 'Gorbachev and Thatcher', *Journal of European Integration History*, vol. 16, no. 1, 2010, p. 41.
19. *DBPO*, III, VII, p. xviii and doc. no. 85, Mallaby to Hurd, pp. 190–1.
20. Yvonne Klein, 'Obstructive or Promoting? British Views on German Unification 1989/90', *German Politics*, vol. 5, no. 3, 1996, p. 410.
21. Philip Zelikow and Condoleezza Rice, *Germany Unified and Europe Transformed: A Study in Statecraft* (Cambridge, MA:

Harvard University Press, 1995), p. 159. Quoted in *DBPO*, III, VII, p. xxii.

22. *DBPO*, III, VII, p. xxii.

23. Pond, *Beyond the Wall*, p. 165.

24. Von Plato, *The End of the Cold War?*, p. 115; *DBPO*, III, VII, p. xxiii and doc. no. 177, Acland to Hurd, p. 243.

25. Georgeta Pourchot, *Eurasia Rising: Democracy and Independence in the Post-Soviet Space* (London: Praeger, 2008), p. 66.

26. James Blitz, 'Mitterrand Feared Emergence of "Bad" Germans' and 'Why Britain and France Feared Fall of Berlin Wall', *Financial Times*, 9 and 10 September 2009. See also Margaret Thatcher, *Downing Street Years* (London: Harper Perennial, 1993), pp. 797–8.

27. *DBPO*, III, VII, doc. no. 103, Powell to Wall, pp. 215–19 (quotation on p. 218).

28. Klein, 'Obstructive or Promoting?', p. 413.

29. Bozo, *Mitterrand*, pp. 169, 196, fn. 8, 233–4.

30. Thatcher, *Downing Street Years*, pp. 796–9.

31. *The Wall Street Journal*, 24 January 1990. The text of the interview is available at <http://www.margaretthatcher.org/document/107876> (last accessed 26 September 2016).

32. Pond, *Beyond the Wall*, p. 157.

33. Teltschik, *329 Tage*, pp. 115–16. See also Hanns Jürgen Küsters and Daniel Hofmann (eds), *Dokumente zur Deutschlandpolitik, Deutsche Einheit. Sonderedition aus den Akten des Bundeskanzleramtes 1989/90* (Munich: Oldenbourg, 1998), doc. no. 148, pp. 719–20. Both quoted in *DBPO*, III, VII, p. xx, fn. 38.

34. *DBPO*, III, VII, pp. xix–xx and doc. no. 108, Minute by Hurd, pp. 229–30. On the diverging views between Thatcher and her foreign secretary see also James Blitz, 'Thatcher Clashed with Hurd on Germany', *Financial Times*, 10 September 2009.

35. Bozo, *Mitterrand*, p. 196, fn. 9. See also Thatcher, *Downing Street Years*, pp. 797–8; *DBPO*, III, VII, p. xxiv.

36. Klein, 'Obstructive or Promoting?', p. 411. See also Hans-Dietrich Genscher, *Erinnerungen* (Berlin: Siedler, 1995), pp. 676, 682, 722, 849, 1018.

37. Percy Cradock, *In Pursuit of British Interests: Reflections on British Foreign Policy under Margaret Thatcher and John Major* (London: John Murray, 1997), p. 112.

38. *DBPO*, III, VII, p. xix.

39. Ilaria Poggiolini, 'Thatcher's Double-Track Road', in Frédéric Bozo, Marie-Pierre Rey, N. Piers Ludlow and Bernd Rother (eds), *Visions of the End of the Cold War in Europe, 1945–1990* (New York and Oxford: Berghahn Books, 2012), p. 275. See also Hurd,

Memoirs; Douglas Hurd, *The Search for Peace: A Century of Peace Diplomacy* (London: Little, Brown, 1997).

40. Sarotte, *1989*, p. 252, fn. 55; Pyeongeok An, 'Obstructive All the Way? British Policy towards German Unification 1989–90', *German Politics*, vol. 15, no. 1, 2006, pp. 114–15.

41. Alan Clark, *Diaries* (London: Weidenfeld and Nicolson, 1993), pp. 276–7. Quoted in *DBPO*, III, VII, pp. xix–xx.

42. *DBPO*, III, VII, doc. no 116, Synnott to Weston, pp. 240–1.

43. Zelikow and Rice, *Germany Unified*, pp. 163–4. Anatoly Chernyaev (compiler), *Mikhail Gorbachev i Germansky Vopros. Sbornik dokumentov 1986–1991* [Mikhail Gorbachev and the German Question 1986–1991. Collected Documents 1986–1991] (Moscow: Ves' Mir, 1996), pp. 307–11. Both quoted in *DBPO*, III, VII, p. xviii. See also doc. no. 111, Powell to Wall, p. 233, fn. 2.

44. John Hiden and Patrick Salmon, *The Baltic Nations and Europe: Estonia, Latvia and Lithuania in the Twentieth Century* (London and New York: Longman, 1994), pp. 159–60.

45. Robert L. Hutchings, *American Diplomacy and the End of the Cold War: An Insider's Account of U.S. Policy in Europe, 1989–1992* (Baltimore, MD: Johns Hopkins University Press, 1997), p. 110. Between 1989 and 1992 Hutchings was director for European affairs at the NSC.

46. *DBPO*, III, VII, p. xxi. See also Bozo, *Mitterrand*, p. 172; Hannes Adomeit, *Imperial Overstretch: Germany in Soviet Policy from Stalin to Gorbachev* (Baden-Baden: Nomos, 1998), pp. 481–2; Hannes Adomeit, 'Gorbachev, German Unification and the Collapse of Empire', *Post-Soviet Affairs*, vol. 10, no. 3, 1994, pp. 197–230.

47. Cronin, *Global Rules*, p. 202.

48. See Baker's account, '"Two plus Four" was in the front of my mind, if not on the tip of my tongue.' In his memoirs the secretary of state praised Hurd's assistance in establishing the Two plus Four. James A. Baker III, *The Politics of Diplomacy: Revolution, War and Peace* (New York: G. P. Putnam's Sons, 1995), pp. 199, 210–11. See also *DBPO*, III, VII, p. xxii, fn. 47; Klein, 'Obstructive or Promoting?', p. 411; An, 'Obstructive All the Way?', pp. 115–16.

49. *DBPO*, III, VII, p. xxiii, fn. 48.

50. Zelikow and Rice, *Germany Unified*, p. 173.

51. *DBPO*, III, VII, doc. no. 117, Acland to Hurd, p. 243.

52. Küsters and Hofmann, *Dokumente zur Deutschlandpolitik*, pp. 739–43. See also Sarotte, *1989*, p. 271, fn. 89.

53. Genscher, *Erinnerungen*, pp. 717–19. See also Frank Elbe and Richard E. Kiessler, *Ein runder Tisch mit scharfen Ecken: Der*

diplomatische Weg zur deutschen Einheit (Baden-Baden: Nomos, 1993) (translated into English as *A Round Table with Sharp Corners: The Diplomatic Path to German Unity* and published in 1996), pp. 75, 108; Hans-Dieter Heumann, *Hans-Dietrich Genscher: Die Biographie* (Paderborn: Ferdinand Schöningh, 2012), p. 258; *DBPO*, III, VII, doc. no. 137, p. 280; Klein, 'Obstructive or Promoting?', p. 411.

54. Konrad H. Jarausch, *The Rush to German Unity* (New York: Oxford University Press, 1994), p. 111.

55. Thomas L. Friedman and Michael R. Gordon, 'Accord on Europe: Anatomy of a Decision', *New York Times*, 16 February 1990. See also Zelikow and Rice, *Germany Unified*, p. 420, fn. 38. Both quoted in *DBPO*, III, VII, p. xxii, fn. 46.

56. *DBPO*, III, VII, doc. no. 116, Synnott to Weston, p. 240.

57. *DBPO*, III, VII, p. xxiii, fn. 49. See also Pond, *Beyond the Wall*, p. 318, fn. 5.

58. An, 'Obstructive All the Way?', pp. 117–18.

59. *DBPO*, III, VII, doc. no. 130, Powell to Wall, p. 264.

60. *DBPO*, III, VII, doc. no. 125, Fergusson to Hurd, p. 256. In March Fergusson publicly suggested that France and Britain should form a counterweight to a united Germany. Philip Jacobsen, 'UK Call for New Entente Cordiale', *The Times*, 7 March 1990. Quoted in Klein, 'Obstructive or Promoting?', p. 413.

61. *DBPO*, III, VII, doc. no. 123, Mallaby to Hurd, p. 252, fn. 2.

62. *DBPO*, III, VII, doc. no. 123, Mallaby to Hurd, p. 254, fn. 8.

63. *DBPO*, III, VII, p. xxi.

64. Genscher, *Erinnerungen*, pp. 696–7, 717–19.

65. *Parliamentary Debates, 6th ser., House of Commons*, vol. 166, cols 757–8.

66. The text of Hurd's speech is printed in *DBPO*, III, VII, doc. no. 131, pp. 264–7.

67. *DBPO*, III, VII, doc. no. 135, Synnott to Ramsden, pp. 273–4, fn. 2.

68. *DBPO*, III, VII, doc. no. 129, Hurd to Mallaby, pp. 261–2. See also Mary E. Sarotte, 'A Broken Promise? What the West Really Told Moscow about NATO Expansion', *Foreign Affairs*, vol. 93, no. 5, September/October 2014, pp. 90–7.

69. *DBPO*, III, VII, p. xxi. See also Jean-Paul Jacqué, 'German Unification and the European Community', *European Journal of International Law*, vol. 2, no. 1, 1991, pp. 1–2.

70. Klein, 'Obstructive or Promoting?', p. 413.

71. *DBPO*, III, VII, doc. no. 133, Wall to Powell, pp. 270–2.

72. Baker, *The Politics of Diplomacy*, pp. 200–2; *DBPO*, III, VII, doc. no. 124, Acland to Hurd, pp. 254–555.

73. Bozo, *Mitterrand*, p. 176. See also Michael Beschloss and Strobe Talbott, *At the Highest Levels* (Boston, MA: Little, Brown, 1993), p. 185; Stephen F. Szabo, *The Diplomacy of German Unification* (New York: St. Martin's Press, 1992), p. 61; Richard A. Leiby, *The Unification of Germany 1989–90* (Westport, CT: Greenwood Press, 1999), p. 65, fn. 25; Friedman and Gordon (1990).

74. The text of Bush's speech is available at <http://www.presidency. ucsb.edu/ws/index.php?pid=18128> (last accessed 30 September 2016).

75. Bozo, *Mitterrand*, p. 177.

76. Mikhail Sergeevich Gorbachev, *Memoirs* (New York: Doubleday, 1995), p. 529. On Baker's report of the meeting see Baker, *The Politics of Diplomacy*, pp. 234–5. See also G. John Ikenberry, *After Victory: Institutions, Strategic Restraint, and the Rebuilding of Order after Major Wars* (Princeton, NJ: Princeton University Press, 2001), p. 229; Alexander Moens, 'American Diplomacy and German Unification', *Survival*, vol. 33, no. 6, November/ December 1991, p. 535.

77. Thomas Blanton, 'U.S. Policy and the Revolutions of 1989', in Svetlana Savranskaya, Thomas Blanton and Vlad Zubok (eds), *Masterpieces of History: The Soviet Peaceful Withdrawal from Eastern Europe, 1989* (Budapest: Central European University Press, 2010), p. 94; Baker' s letter is printed in doc. no. 120, Letter from Baker to Kohl, 10 February 1990, pp. 685–7. See also Frank Elbe, 'The Diplomatic Path to German Unity', *Bulletin of the German Historical Institute*, vol. 46, Spring 2010, pp. 37–8; Leiby, *The Unification*, pp. 61–2.

78. Sarotte, *1989*, pp. 107–111. See also Mary E. Sarotte, 'Not One Inch Eastward? Bush, Baker, Kohl, Genscher, Gorbachev, and the Origin of Russian Resentment toward NATO Enlargement in February 1990', *Diplomatic History*, vol. 34, no. 1, January 2010, pp. 119–40; Sarotte, 'A Broken Promise?', pp. 90–7; Mary E. Sarotte, 'Enlarging NATO, Expanding Confusion', *The New York Times*, 30 November 2009. Sarotte, 'Perpetuating U.S. Preeminence; The 1990 Deals to "Bribe the Soviets Out" and Move NATO In', *International Security*, Summer 2010, vol. 35, no. 1, pp. 110–37. For a similar account see James M. Goldgeier, *Not Whether but When: The U.S. Decision to Enlarge NATO* (Washington, DC: Brookings Institution Press, 1999), p. 15. See also Pekka Kalevi Hämäläinen, *Uniting Germany: Actions and Reactions* (Boulder, CO: Westview Press, 1994), pp. 114–16; Bush and Scowcroft, *A World Transformed*, pp. 240–2.

79. Bush and Scowcroft, *A World Transformed*, p. 241; Zelikow and

Rice, *Germany Unified*, p. 176–7, 180–4, 186–7, 195–6. See also Bozo, *Mitterrand*, p. 205, fn. 98.

80. Quoted in Teltschik, *329 Tage*, p. 143; Elbe, 'The Diplomatic Path', p. 38; Heumann, *Hans-Dietrich Genscher*, p. 256; Alexander von Plato, *Die Vereinigung Deutschlands. Ein weltpolitisches Machtspiel: Bush, Kohl, Gorbatschow und die geheimen Moskauer Protokolle* (Berlin: Christoph Links, 2002), p. 276. See also *DBPO*, III, VII, doc. no. 165, Weston to Wall, fn. 2; Teltschik, *329 Tage*, pp. 138–43; Sarotte, *1989*, p. 114; Bush and Scowcroft, *A World Transformed*, pp. 241–2; Marie Katherina Wagner, 'Das große Rätsel um Genschers angebliches Versprechen', *Frankfurter Allgemeine Zeitung*, 19 April 2014.

81. *DBPO*, III, VII, doc. no. 134, Powell to Wall, pp. 272–3.

82. Over the next three years, subsequent rounds of Open Skies negotiations were held in Budapest, Vienna and Helsinki. Peter Jones, *Open Skies: Transparency, Confidence-Building, and the End of the Cold War* (Stanford, CA: Stanford University Press, 2014).

83. *DBPO*, III, VII, doc. no. 140, Powell to Wall, pp. 285–6. See also *The Guardian* and *The Financial Times*, 2 February 1990.

84. The speech is available at <http://www.margaretthatcher.org/speeches/displaydocument.asp?docid=108011> (last accessed 30 September 2016). See also *DBPO*, III, VII, doc. no. 144, Synnott to Ratford, p. 289, fn. 1.

85. *DBPO*, III, VII, doc. no. 182, p. 355, fn. 1.

86. Genscher, *Erinnerungen*, pp. 728–30.

87. Elbe, 'The Diplomatic Path', pp. 38–9. See also Genscher, *Erinnerungen*, pp. 728–30, 788; Sarotte, *1989*, pp. 121–4; Jones, *Open Skies*, p. 66; *DBPO*, III, VII, p. xxv.

88. *DBPO*, III, VII, doc. no. 146, Hurd to Acland, pp. 293–4.

89. Elbe and Kiessler, *Ein runder Tisch*, p. 101. See also Elbe, 'The Diplomatic Path', p. 39; Zelikow and Rice, *Germany Unified*, pp. 191–5; Genscher, *Erinnerungen*, pp. 728–9; Bozo, *Mitterrand*, p. 180; Heumann, *Hans-Dietrich Genscher*, p. 259; Ursula Lehmkuhl, 'The "Ottawa Formula" and Transatlantic Relations: Politics and Diplomacy of the "Two-Plus-Four" Negotiations', *Eurostudia*, vol. 5, no. 2, 2009, p. 1.

90. Antonio Varsori, 'The Relaunching of Europe in the Mid-1980s', in Kiran Klaus Patel and Kenneth Weisbrode (eds), *European Integration and the Atlantic Community in the 1980s* (New York: Cambridge University Press, 2013), p. 34; Pond, *Beyond the Wall*, p. 181. See also Simon J. Nuttal, *European Foreign Policy* (Oxford: Oxford University Press, 2000), pp. 72–3. At the end of the 1980s De Michelis was promoting plans for quadripartite economic, industrial and cultural cooperation between Italy,

Austria, Hungary and Yugoslavia as a way of containing German influence in the Danube–Balkan area. See Leopoldo Nuti, 'Italy, German Unification and the End of the Cold War', in Frédéric Bozo, Marie-Pierre Rey, Piers N. Ludlow and Leopoldo Nuti (eds), *Europe and the End of the Cold War: A Reappraisal* (Abingdon and New York: Routledge, 2008), pp. 191–203; Leopoldo Nuti, 'De Michelis teme "la disentigrazione del blocco orientale"', *La Repubblica*, 9 November 1989.

91. *DBPO*, III, VII, doc. no. 147, Powell to Wall, pp. 294–7.
92. *DBPO*, III, VII, doc. no. 149, pp. 298–9. Jonathan Wright has argued that ever since 1945 'Germany had less need of Britain as its advocate with France and the United States, except when one or both of these relationships were in trouble'. Jonathan Wright, 'The Role of Britain in West German Foreign Policy since 1949', *German Politics*, vol. 5, no. 1, April 1996, pp. 26–42. Quoted in Klein, 'Obstructive or Promoting?', p. 407.
93. *DBPO*, III, VII, p. xxiv and doc. no. 153, Powell to Wall, p. 305.
94. *DBPO*, III, VII, doc no. 155, pp. 310–12. See also Jacques Lévesque, 'In the Name of Europe's Future: Soviet, French, and British Qualms about Kohl's Rush to German Unification', in Frédéric Bozo, Marie-Pierre Rey, Piers N. Ludlow and Leopoldo Nuti (eds), *Europe and the End of the Cold War: A Reappraisal* (Abingdon and New York: Routledge, 2008), pp. 99–100.
95. Bush and Scowcroft, *A World Transformed*, pp. 247–9. See also *DBPO*, III, VII, p. xxvi.
96. Thatcher concurred with the president and described Lafontaine as a 'buccaneer type'. *DBPO*, III, VII, p. 312.
97. *DBPO*, III, VII, pp. 312–13.
98. 'Joint News Conference Following Discussions with Chancellor Helmut Kohl of the Federal Republic of Germany', in *Public Papers: George Bush, 1990, Book I* (Washington, DC: Government Printing Office, 1991), pp. 264–74. See also *DBPO*, III, VII, p. xxvi and doc. no. 165, Weston to Wall, p. 328, fn. 2; Sarotte, *1989*, pp. 226–8; Adomeit, *Imperial Overstretch*, p. 502; Gerhard A. Ritter, *Hans-Dietrich Genscher, das Auswärtige Amt und die deutsche Vereinigung* (Munich: C. H. Beck, 2013).
99. *DBPO*, III, VII, p. xxiii.
100. *DBPO*, III, VII, doc. no. 171, Acland to Weston, pp. 339–41 (quotation on p. 340).
101. *DBPO*, III, VII, pp. 339–41.
102. Klein, 'Obstructive or Promoting?', p. 410.
103. Pond, *Beyond the Wall*, p. 195; Hämäläinen, *Uniting Germany*, p. 131; Bozo, *Mitterrand*, pp. 224–5.
104. 'Joint News Conference Following Discussions with Chancellor

Helmut Kohl of the Federal Republic of Germany'. See also Zelikow and Rice, *Germany Unified*, p. 216; Bush and Scowcroft, *A World Transformed*, pp. 249–55; Bozo, *Mitterrand*, pp. 222–33, 265, fn. 66; Debra J. Allen, *The Oder–Neisse Line: The United States, Poland, and Germany in the Cold War* (Westport, CT and London: Praeger, 2003), pp. 286–7.

105. Cronin, *Global Rules*, p. 203.
106. Klein, 'Obstructive or Promoting?', p. 411.
107. *DBPO*, III, VII, doc. no. 204, Burton to Hurd, pp. 397–9.
108. *DBPO*, III, VII, Appendix, The Prime Minister's Seminar on Germany, 24 March 1990, doc. no. 3, Powell to Wall, pp. 505–8. The leaked record of the seminar was published by the *Independent on Sunday* on 15 July and is available at <http://www.margaretthatcher.org/document/111047> (last accessed 1 October 2016). See also Klein, 'Obstructive or Promoting?', pp. 414–15.
109. Quoted in *DBPO*, III, VII, doc. no. 181, Mallaby to Hurd, p. 354, fn. 2.
110. The speeches given by the two leaders are available at <http://www.margaretthatcher.org/document/108049> (last accessed 1 October 2016). Excerpts of Kohl's speech are also printed in Daniel Rotfeld and Walther Stützle (eds), *Germany and Europe in Transition* (New York: Oxford University Press, 1991), pp. 123–6. See also *DBPO*, III, VII, doc. no. 220, Hurd to Neville-Jones, pp. 437–8.
111. Teltschik, *329 Tage*, p. 188. Quoted in *DBPO*, III, VII, p. xxv. See the remarks by then West Germany's ambassador to Britain, Hermann von Richthofen, at a Witness Seminar, Lancaster House, 16 October 2009, pp. 82–3. The seminar proceedings are available at <http://markus-meckel.de/wp-content/uploads/2009/01/Dokumentation-London.pdf> (last accessed 1 October 2016).
112. For a full picture of the French role in the negotiations see the account of the then head of the Political Affairs division at the French Foreign Ministry, Bertrand Dufourcq, '2+4 ou la négociation atypique', *Politique étrangère*, vol. 65, no. 2, Summer 2000, pp. 467–84. Quoted in *DBPO*, III, VII, p. xxvii. See also Bozo, *Mitterrand*, pp. 209–22; Leiby, *The Unification*, pp. 52–4.
113. *DBPO*, III, VII, doc. no. 202, Hurd to Mallaby, p. 393, fn. 2.
114. The texts of the Berlin Declaration of 5 June 1945, extracts of the Potsdam protocol of 1 August 1945 and the text of the 1952 Bonn Convention are in *Documents on Germany, 1944–1959: Background Documents on Germany, 1944–1959, and a Chronology of Political Developments Affecting Berlin, 1945–1956* (Washington, DC: Government Printing Office, 1959), pp. 13–18, 24–35, 102–3. For Western interpretation of those

commitments see *DBPO*, III, VII, doc. no. 25, Synnott to Ratford, p. 76 and doc. no. 174, Hurd to Acland, p. 345, fn. 8.

115. Jarausch, *The Rush*, p. 111. See also Genscher, *Erinnerungen*, p. 696; von Plato, *Die Vereinigung Deutschlands*, pp. 212–13; Ritter, *Hans-Dietrich Genscher*.

116. *DBPO*, III, VII, doc. no. 175, Mallaby to Hurd, p. 346.

117. Elbe, 'The Diplomatic Path', p. 40.

118. *DBPO*, III, VII, doc. no. 174, Hurd to Acland, pp. 344–5.

119. *DBPO*, III, VII, doc. no. 183, Acland to Hurd, p. 357, fn. 2.

120. *DBPO*, III, VII, doc. no. 189, Wood to Hill, p. 368.

121. *DBPO*, III, VII, doc. no. 189, Wood to Hill, p. 369.

122. *DBPO*, III, VII, p. 369.

123. *DBPO*, III, VII, p. 369; see also fn. 454.

124. *DBPO*, III, VII, pp. 370–1.

125. *DBPO*, III, VII, doc. no. 192, Weston to Wall, pp. 376–7.

126. *DBPO*, III, VII, doc. no. 194, Synnott to Weston, pp. 378–9.

127. Zelikow and Rice, *Germany Unified*, pp. 442, 456.

128. *DBPO*, III, VII, doc. no. 195, Draft Paper, German Unification and a Settlement: Legal Aspects, UK Comments, Annex, Comments on the US Draft Paper, pp. 383–4.

5 The US, the UK and German Unification within NATO

Germany's relationship with NATO and Britain's alignment with US positions

'We can't let the Soviets clutch victory from the jaws of defeat'
(George H. W. Bush, 24 February 1990)

'There are all kinds of events that we can't foresee that require a strong NATO, and there's all kind of potential instability that requires a strong U.S. presence'
(George H. W. Bush, 24 February 1990)

'A special friendship that is evident from the way we share a common vision for the future of humanity'
(George H. W. Bush, 13 April 1990)

Anglo-American views and West Germany's relationship with NATO

This chapter focuses on Anglo-American views of Germany's relationship with NATO. While the question of a peace settlement had caused tension, the issue of Germany's relationship with NATO was one of overall Anglo-American agreement. By April 1990 there was a strong consensus in Washington and London that a united Germany should remain a member of the Western alliance. Nonetheless, there were nuances in Anglo-American approaches. Britain's preference was to discuss unification in the CSCE in order to appease the Russians. Only after Washington's rejection of British proposals did London endorse US demands for a united Germany's membership of the alliance. The British also supported Washington's ambitious review of NATO's strategy, which made the organisation more political and less military and part of a security structure for the whole of Europe. Ultimately, Whitehall helped the White House overcome Soviet resistance and French uncertainties. The British also contributed to preventing Bonn from making excessive concessions to Moscow. However, although there was a closeness of positions, NATO's transformation was not the product of a joint Anglo-American initiative. In contrast, this process reflected the American vision for the alliance, rather than one that emerged through the usual channels of NATO bureaucracy or bilateral Anglo-American negotiations.

The Federal government's initial cautiousness on this issue had been a cause of apprehension for both the White House and Whitehall. As in the heyday of Brandt's Eastern policy – when Nixon and Heath had feared the Federal Republic's neutralisation – the perception that there might not be a firm consensus in Bonn over Germany's commitment to the alliance caused concern.[1] After Kohl's enunciation of his ten-point programme in November 1989 the Americans did not waste any time clarifying that Germany's ongoing membership of NATO would be a precondition for unification. Nonetheless, at the beginning of 1990 there was no firm consensus in the Federal Republic on this issue. In contrast, West German opinion was polarised around two distinct positions. The first of these views had been articulated by Genscher at a speech at the Evangelical Academy in the Bavarian village of Tutzing on 31 January. The FRG's foreign minister had reiterated it to the Soviet leadership in Moscow ten days later. Genscher's blueprint envisioned a minimalist solution for Germany's relationship with NATO. Formally, a united Germany would remain a NATO member, but there would be no alliance extension to the east. In other words, former GDR territory would remain outside of NATO's military structure and no alliance forces would be stationed there. This approach also involved a diminution in NATO's military role in order to appease Moscow. According to the FRG's foreign minister, after unification both NATO and the Warsaw Pact would 'have to define their role increasingly in political terms' and would eventually come together in a new security system under the CSCE.[2] The foreign minister's thesis was welcomed by Zoellick and Ross at the State Department, but met with the opposition of the NSC, who feared the creation of a demilitarised free zone in East Germany.

Defence Minister Gerhard Stoltenberg, the *Bundeswehr*'s Chief of Staff Klaus Naumann and West German defence planners envisioned a different solution. Two days after Genscher's speech, the FRG's defence minister stated publicly that all the territory of a united Germany would be an integral part of NATO. This scenario was more compatible with US expectations, which Baker had made clear in his four points speech in early December. However, the Federal government, also in light of Kohl's trip to Moscow in February, waited several weeks before clarifying its position.[3] As in the case of the Polish frontier, the chancellor preferred to wait for the GDR's elections in March before clarifying Germany's relationship with NATO.[4] Only on 19 February, almost ten days after his talks in the Kremlin, did Kohl intervene personally and he ordered the two ministers to issue a joint statement. This sounded less explicit than the Tutzing formula. However, it restated Genscher's view and the implicit promise made by Baker and Kohl in Moscow that no NATO forces, including those of the *Bundeswehr*, would be stationed on former GDR territory.[5]

The joint ministerial statement reflected Kohl's electoral calculations and need to appease the Soviets at a critical juncture. Nonetheless, by making the former GDR's military status dependent upon negotiations with Moscow, it appeared to London and Washington as an additional step in a pattern of ambiguity that had dotted Bonn's attitude since Kohl's enunciation of his ten-point programme in late November 1989. Its immediate effect was to raise Western fears of a security 'bifurcation' for a united Germany.[6] What especially worried the British was the possibility of damaging dynamics being set up during an electoral period, while the NSC staff feared the prospect of a 'French solution' for Germany. Although formally remaining an alliance member, a united Germany might withdraw from NATO's military structure, making it difficult for American troops to remain on German territory for too long. Such an outcome might be followed by the request that all foreign forces leave Germany, with the risk of spelling 'the effective end of NATO'.[7] For this reason, the White House believed that the reaffirmation of Bonn's commitment to the alliance should have taken priority over the course of the Two plus Four negotiations and over Thatcher's preference for a strengthened CSCE architecture.[8] In the Bush administration's view, while Germany should not be singled out, articles 5 and 6 of the Washington Treaty should be applicable to the whole of

German territory from the very moment of unification. FCO officials consistently supported American views. Nonetheless, while
sharing the US objective of preserving Germany's relationship
with NATO, they did not feel adequately reassured by US tactics.[9]

The Camp David, Bermuda and Key Largo meetings

Germany's relationship with the alliance was among the main
topics that were discussed at the Bush–Kohl meeting in Camp
David on 24 February. The meeting coincided with the first visit
to the US presidential retreat by a West German chancellor. On
this occasion, the Americans impressed on the Federal government the need to anchor a united Germany firmly within NATO
without giving in to Soviet demands. The president told the chancellor that, while former GDR *Länder* might be granted special
status, Moscow would not be allowed to dictate the conditions.
In other words, the Russians would not 'clutch victory from the
jaws of defeat'.[10] Bush's view reflected his strong belief about
the need to firmly anchor the US to post-Cold War Europe. A
few days later the president penned in his diary, 'There are all
kinds of events that we can't foresee that require a strong NATO,
and there's all kind of potential instability that requires a strong
U.S. presence.'[11] In the following months Washington continued
to worry about Kohl's ability to resist Soviet pressures. These
concerns also prompted the Americans to re-evaluate their relationship with Britain. The US now attempted to preserve Anglo-
American solidarity in order to prevent any hesitancy on the part
of the Federal government. The need for close Anglo-American
cooperation was also strengthened by persistent French hesitation. On 25 March in a television interview Mitterrand discussed
the prospect of a 'new-look' NATO after unification. In his view
Moscow would pull its troops out of East Germany in return for
the withdrawal of NATO forces from West Germany. The French
president also proposed the opening of talks in the EEC in order
to form a political union at the completion of the European Single
Market.[12] Two days later Zoellick told Wood that he 'heartily
endorsed' closer Western togetherness and hinted that Britain
might perhaps try to influence conflicting French views.[13]

Nonetheless, while the British were keen to have full bilateral
discussions, the Americans remained determined to avoid any
sense of German exclusion. For Washington not only bilateral

discussions with the British were important, but also those with the Germans. When Wood suggested that a first meeting be held on 9 April in the ambassador's residence in Washington, Zoellick replied that it would be important to 'ensure that the Germans were fully involved at every stage'. Furthermore, for the US government, it was vital that the other members of NATO be consulted.[14] In the meeting held on 2 April Zoellick stressed that the US wanted to make sure that all sixteen NATO members were kept 'properly in the picture' and that the Russians were eager for progress. After all, the Americans believed that treating Germany as a 'special case' could in the long term also harm Soviet interests, as a special military status for the GDR might have as its ultimate consequence the growth of German military forces outside of NATO. According to the US viewpoint, clarity would be particularly needed over the application of articles 5 and 6. Ultimately, once the transitional period was complete, Germany should be treated as a 'totally normal state', able to put its military forces where it liked, including the territory of the former GDR.[15]

In the following weeks developments in Germany further reinforced American convictions. After the success obtained by Kohl's allies in March 1990, Washington intensified its pressure in order to secure Germany's unrestricted membership of NATO. The British contributed to US efforts and endeavoured to reassure Moscow. On 11 April, during a visit to the Kremlin, Hurd stressed to Gorbachev that it would be better, even for the Soviet Union, to have Germany in NATO rather than 'loose, untied, and perhaps with U.S. troops having gone home'. The foreign secretary also reassured the Soviets that, while providing a good anchor and framework for a united Germany, the alliance would take on a more political role and safeguard Moscow's interests and dignity.[16] By then, even Thatcher was resigned to accepting American views. On 13 April in their meeting in the Bermudan capital Hamilton, Bush secured her agreement to the principle that the Two plus Four negotiations would bring all Four Power rights to an end. After the talks the president stressed that the US and Britain agreed with Kohl, the other members of the alliance and many of the countries of Eastern Europe that Germany should remain a full member of NATO, including its military structures. Bush also acknowledged the importance of the special relationship in making possible unification. The president remarked that Washington and London had 'worked together for peace and

freedom for many years', stating that the Anglo-American friendship was one of the kind 'that does not need the words to describe
it . . . a special friendship that is evident from the way we share
a common vision for the future of humanity'. Nonetheless, his
only concession to Thatcher was a statement that proposals for a
larger CSCE role held 'a lot of promise'.[17] On 20 April Britain's
prime minister sent a reassuring message to Kohl about her talks
with Bush in Bermuda.[18]

In Bermuda the Anglo-Americans also addressed French views
about unification. Bush emphasised that Paris could be difficult
as the US and France were not 'on the same wavelength' on some
issues. More specifically, the French were sceptical about the prospect of Washington acquiring an even greater say in European
security.[19] On 17 April the US president explained in detail the
American approach in a letter to Mitterrand. Two days later,
at Key Largo in Florida, Washington obtained France's formal
consent to terminate all Four Power rights. On this occasion,
there was hardly any discussion of the Two plus Four negotiations. Nonetheless, the French president manifested doubts about
the alliance's transformation and adaptation to a changing geopolitical environment. He also expressed French preferences for a
gradual Europeanisation of NATO. Although Bush felt that the
conversation had been a positive one, Mitterrand's ideas rekindled
the administration's concerns, particularly those of Scowcroft and
Baker, that French preferences might cause NATO to atrophy.[20]
Their immediate consequence was to increase Whitehall's importance for Washington on the issue of NATO's post-Cold War
transformation.

Bush's Oklahoma speech, Moscow's decoupling proposal and Baker's nine-point package

Britain was sceptical about Mitterrand's preferences for a
Europeanisation of NATO. London did not oppose closer collaboration with Paris, but this was not to be at the expense of the
special relationship and of the US role in Europe.[21] The Americans
also had doubts about French calls for a stronger European
element in post-Cold War NATO.[22] Washington was determined
to ensure that after the end of the East–West division the US
remained a European power, feared a loss of US control and
viewed NATO's endurance as the key institutional link between

North America and Europe.[23] Nonetheless, the administration acknowledged that keeping the alliance alive as a tool of US geopolitical influence and as an indispensable peace-keeper in Europe entailed radical reform.[24] After securing Anglo-French support for unification and with Soviet opposition rapidly eroding, on 4 May Bush outlined his plans for an encompassing review of NATO strategy in a speech at Oklahoma State University. At the commencement ceremony in Stillwater the president called for the preservation and revitalisation of the alliance. He stressed that Washington would remain politically, militarily and economically a European power and that NATO would continue to act as the foundation for the US's peaceful engagement with the continent.[25] The president also invited the allies to debate American plans at an early alliance summit, which was later scheduled for 5 July in London.

Nonetheless, on the following day the Kremlin made a last, desperate attempt to exploit Anglo-French fears about Germany and divide the allies. At the meeting of the Two plus Four in Bonn on 5 May Shevardnadze countered the principle that the negotiations would bring all Four Power rights to an end. The USSR's foreign minister now argued that the internal and external processes should be 'decoupled' and that external unification should occur at a later and unspecified date. According to the Soviet proposal, 'internal unification' would be followed by a transitional period during which 'a package of potential controversial issues', such as borders, military forces and Germany's military status, would be agreed in the final settlement.[26] The Two plus Four would act as a coordinating forum, while the resolution of all external aspects would proceed 'hand in hand' with progress on wider security issues, such as arms control, confidence- and security-building measures and the CSCE. Shevardnadze's proposal rekindled Anglo-American differences. Hurd noted that the Soviet Union's wish to lengthen the process of unification was aimed at minimising the extent to which German unity could be perceived as a diplomatic defeat for Moscow. The Kremlin's proposal also bolstered Whitehall's view that an expanded and intensified CSCE had an important role to play in the wider European context.[27]

Nonetheless, some FCO officials were less conciliatory and advocated a robust Western response to the Kremlin. Weston even contemplated the idea of a unilateral renunciation of Four Power rights.[28] Moscow's initiative also divided opinion in the

FRG. Genscher was willing to consider it. However, the inner circle of Kohl's advisors embraced a more critical line.[29] The American response was firm but also included conciliatory elements. It came in the form of a nine-point package that Baker presented to the Soviet leadership during a visit to Moscow from 16 to 19 May. The secretary of state's trip was preceded by an additional Western attempt to soften Soviet resistance. On 13 and 14 May Kohl's personal advisor, Teltschik, embarked on a secret mission to Moscow together with two West German bankers, Hilmar Kopper of the Deutsche Bank and Wolfgang Röller of the Dresdner Bank. In the Soviet capital West German emissaries confirmed the FRG's willingness to provide massive financial aid to the USSR.[30] Their mission aimed at making Washington's counterproposal more palatable to the Kremlin. This included a reduction in forces in the central region; an assurance that Germany would not try to acquire nuclear, biological or chemical weapons; the promise that, for a transitional period, no NATO forces would be stationed in the GDR, while Soviet forces would be allowed to remain in East Germany; a review of NATO strategy; the settlement of a united Germany's borders; concrete proposals for strengthening the CSCE and ensuring a significant role for the Soviet Union in Europe; and the satisfactory handling of economic ties between Germany and the USSR.[31]

However, Baker's long list of concessions received a lukewarm response from the Kremlin.[32] Gorbachev stressed that German membership of NATO would bring about a change in the existing balance and threaten European stability. Hence, it would force the Soviet Union to rethink its military doctrine. The Soviet leader also suggested that if Germany left NATO and became non-aligned like France, Moscow 'would ask to join NATO itself'. Gorbachev's reaction did not impress the US government. Washington remained convinced that a united Germany should be a full member of the alliance and that a Pan-European institution would be too ponderous to preserve the continent's security and to prevent the re-emergence of a security dilemma in Europe. The secretary of state's conclusion was that a Pan-European security institution was 'an excellent dream, but only a dream'.[33] However, once again Moscow's proposal rekindled Anglo-American differences. In two papers drafted for future multilateral negotiations FCO planners dropped their initially maximalist position, which envisaged full NATO membership for the whole of German territory, and embraced a more conciliatory solution, which contemplated NATO membership for Germany but excluded deployment of non-German forces on the territory of the former GDR. However, this occurred at precisely the same time that Baker was moving away from that view as he met with Gorbachev in Moscow.[34] During a meeting of the four Western political directors in Bonn on 22 May, while Zoellick emphasised that the West should make no concessions to Moscow and that the US had been considering whether it might be possible to go ahead without the Russians, the British appeared more conciliatory towards Soviet concerns. Even Weston emphasised that a solution that excluded Moscow would be very much 'a second best outcome'.[35] Nonetheless, with the French and the Russians having given up any ambition to block unification, at this stage British views carried limited importance for the Americans and the West Germans.

The US, Germany and the Camp David summit

'We will remain in Europe to deter any new dangers, to be a force for stability, and to reassure all of Europe, east and west – that the European balance will remain secure'
(George Bush, 2 August 1990)

The Bush–Gorbachev Camp David summit and Moscow's quest for NATO membership

In the following weeks a fast-worsening economic situation and the acceleration of the Lithuanian crisis, together with Bonn's agreement to provide the Soviet Union with much-needed credit, further weakened Soviet resistance. On 22 May Kohl offered Gorbachev a credit of five billion Deutschmarks to sustain the ailing Soviet economy. Although this offer fell short of an initial request of twenty billion Deutschmarks, the West German aid amounted to the largest sum ever granted to the USSR in its seventy-year history. Furthermore, it was coupled with a promise to cover the costs of maintaining Soviet troops in the GDR.[36] The FRG's offer contributed to creating a 'positive atmosphere' for the meeting between Genscher and Shevardnadze that took place in Geneva on 23 May. On that occasion, the Soviet foreign minister stated that the Kremlin was in favour of a speedy resolution of the German question, while Genscher explained that Moscow would benefit more from a united Germany than it had from two separate German states.[37] On 28 May the FRG's foreign minister flew to Britain to brief Hurd. He reported that the Russians accepted the idea of German membership of NATO, provided no alliance troops were deployed to East German territory.[38]

Nonetheless, by then the special relationship had been eclipsed by a tightening of the US–West German connection. Washington's support for Bonn was confirmed during a telephone conversation between the chancellor and the US president on 30 May 1990. The conversation preceded the Washington and Camp David summit between Bush and Gorbachev between 30 May and 2 June. On this occasion, Kohl reiterated that a united Germany would be a full member of NATO and encouraged the president to make it clear to Gorbachev that the FRG and the US stood 'side by side'. Bush reassured the chancellor that he would not endorse Moscow's decoupling proposal and that Washington was determined to bring to an end to Four Power rights at the time of unification without 'new constraints on German sovereignty'.[39]

Nonetheless, on the same day, in marked contrast to previous summits, Gorbachev arrived in the US capital under marching orders and severe constraints from his own Central Committee. Leading Soviet circles were dismayed over the loss of Eastern Europe and developments in the Baltic states and the Caucasus. They rejected Gorbachev's demilitarisation policy and opposed Germany's unification outright.[40] On this occasion, the Soviet leader presented the Americans with a proposal for Germany's associated membership of NATO and the Warsaw Pact. This was portrayed by Gorbachev as a first step towards the establishment of a new security structure in Europe. The Soviet leader argued that, by supporting a united Germany's membership of NATO, the US was making a 'methodological miscalculation', worrying that the FRG's withdrawal from the North Atlantic Treaty would spearhead 'the beginning of the alliance's end' and, therefore, of the US military presence on the continent. He acknowledged that the US had undertaken efforts to change the alliance's functions and role, trying to invite new members. Nonetheless, its transformation into a genuinely open, all-European organisation was a 'serious and completely different business'. In that case, the alliance's door could not be closed to any state whatsoever and the Soviet Union would then even consider becoming a member. According to Gorbachev, Germany's simultaneous membership of both NATO and the Warsaw Pact would act as a 'binding element, some sort of a forerunner of the new European structures'.[41]

Once again, the Soviet leader's vision was firmly rebuffed by Bush. The US president restated the case for not singling out Germany, explaining that the Western approach to the German question was more realistic, pragmatic and constructive, while mistrust 'oriented towards the past' could turn out to be an especially bad advisor. Bush acknowledged that some West European countries did not trust 'either Germany or the Germans as a whole'. Nonetheless, there was one common element which united the members of the Western alliance: the conviction that the main danger lay in separating Germany from the community of democratic states and in trying to impose some special status and humiliating conditions on it. According to Washington, such an attitude could lead to a revival of German militarism and nationalism, which was exactly the kind of concern held by the Soviet Union. Furthermore, the process of inserting a united Germany into the 'new Europe' would require the 'deep involvement' of the USSR and a 'fair consideration' of Moscow's interests. Bush added that the Soviet Union would benefit from the ongoing presence of the US in Europe. Rather than being a threat to the interests of the Soviet Union in any sense whatsoever, the American presence was right now a guarantee of peace and stability on the continent.[42] He emphasised that the public mood in Germany was completely supportive of the alliance, remarking that when the Berlin Wall fell the White House had taken into account Gorbachev's appeal 'to show caution'. Bearing in mind the fragility of the new processes under way in Europe, he had responded to those who accused him of 'cowardice' and of not being 'sufficiently energetic' that the US president did not intend 'to dance on the ruins of the Berlin Wall like a little boy'. Finally, Bush reassured Gorbachev that Washington had no remote intention 'to harm the Soviet Union in any fashion'. In contrast, the US approach also corresponded to Soviet interests: that was why Washington was speaking in favour of German unification in NATO, without ignoring the wider CSCE context.

Then, the secretary of state clarified the American viewpoint further: Baker added that the US had agreed to support Pan-European structures and endeavoured to adapt NATO to the new situation, strengthening its political component and trying to move in the direction of limiting its armed forces, including those of the *Bundeswehr*. In order to make such a step possible, however, a very 'close contact and trust' on the part of the Germans would be required. Baker continued that the US had assured the Soviet Union that during a defined period there would be no NATO troops in the GDR, was willing to allow Soviet troops to stay there for a short period of time, and had reached an understanding with the FRG regarding a united Germany's renunciation of nuclear, chemical and bacteriological weapons.[43] Furthermore, Washington was also trying to create favourable political conditions for further development of Soviet–German economic relations. While according to Baker all these efforts were clearly aimed at ensuring the Soviet Union's legitimate interests, the simultaneous obligations of a united Germany towards NATO and the Warsaw Pact smacked of schizophrenia. After Baker had spoken, Bush concluded that one had to take into account the exceptional pace of German unification: following the successful conclusion of the Two plus Four, a new Germany was right around the corner and at that moment one could only rely on NATO. Of course, it would also be wise to discuss expanding the CSCE's role, but according to US opinion, that institution was simply too ponderous to expect any fast and concrete result from it.[44]

Having come to the US under heavy pressure from his domestic opponents, in his reply Gorbachev stressed that it was possible that NATO and the Warsaw Pact would continue to exist in some form over a longer period of time. For this reason, it would be mutually advantageous to conclude an agreement towards their metamorphoses, while allowing Germany's associated and simultaneous membership of both institutions. According to the Soviet leader, the inclusion of a powerful, united Germany in one alliance would create an 'unbalanced situation', raising a number of issues 'to which nobody would be able to find an answer'. On the contrary, an associated membership would allow the two blocs to move closer together with Germany acting as a mediator in the process. Such a solution would not change the present obligations of either the FRG or the GDR and would be followed by a natural reform of the blocs themselves. Gorbachev's thesis was elaborated further by his advisor and former ambassador to the FRG, Valentin Falin. According to the Soviet diplomat, NATO and the Warsaw Pact were only 'temporary structures', even though they had existed for almost fifty years; their replacement with permanent structures, in which the Soviet Union and the US could unite for the foreseeable future, would also address American concerns that in the future the Federal Republic could raise the issue of withdrawing from NATO. Falin continued that only a Pan-European system, into which a united Germany would be integrated on equal conditions with everybody else, would give enough guarantees. His conclusion was that Germany's unification should become the end of the division of Europe rather than the event that solidified Europe's division for the future.[45]

By restating its preference for a gradual transformation of the two rival alliances and their subsequent dissolution into the CSCE, the Kremlin attempted to defend its preferred model of unification, which, in Moscow's view would have been synchronised with the 'European processes'. Nonetheless, Soviet arguments were disregarded by the US government.[46] Baker and Bush attempted to reassure Gorbachev that Washington was now in favour of building European structures and that at the next summit of NATO American representatives would support a 'wide-ranging' review of the alliance's strategy. However, they also made it clear that the US was unwilling to slow down unification, which in the words of Bush was now 'right around the corner'.[47] The Bush–Gorbachev Washington and Camp David summit was one of the most important US–Soviet meetings in the process leading to German unification and essentially unlike any summit that had taken place in the past. Together with the following London NATO summit, it paved the way for the dramatic encounter in the Caucasus between Kohl and Gorbachev in July 1990 that finalised the details of Germany's membership of NATO.[48] Nonetheless, Moscow had not yet accepted Washington's viewpoint. A cable sent by the State Department to US embassies in the alliance's member states on 15 June warned that Soviet thinking was still in flux. As such, it was likely to be affected by a number of internal contradictions, while Gorbachev had not clarified what 'freedom of choice' for Germany meant in practice.[49]

Anglo-German tension and Thatcher's growing isolation

'The deutschemark is always going to be the strongest currency, because of their habits'
(Nicholas Ridley, 12 July 1990)

Thatcher's Moscow visit and British recriminations

The Washington and Camp David summit confirmed US beliefs that a united Germany should be a full NATO member and that Moscow should not be able to delay unification or influence the post-Cold War European security framework. At the same time, it exposed Britain's decreasing importance in the American strategy and in establishing the modalities of unification. In the late spring London had dropped demands for a peace settlement and supported US efforts to secure Germany's full NATO membership. However, Anglo-American positions continued to diverge on a number of issues. Furthermore, Thatcher continued to believe that the United Kingdom had an interest in preserving good relations with Moscow. During a meeting with Gorbachev on 8 June, in her last official visit to the Soviet capital, Britain's prime minister emphasised the importance of keeping American forces in Europe. On the same day that NATO's foreign ministers concluded a meeting in Turnberry in Scotland to review the alliance's strategy and extend a hand of friendship to Warsaw Pact states, she told the Soviet leader that unification could no longer be stopped or slowed down. Nonetheless, she added, some way would have to be found 'to make sure that it did not threaten anyone's security'. For this reason, it was important that US troops remain in Europe. Germany was the only place, where American forces could be present in any significant numbers and 'their presence there represented security not just for Europe but also for the Soviet Union'. This required that a unified Germany remain a member of NATO, 'otherwise there would be no justification for the presence of U.S. forces'.

Nonetheless, Thatcher also reiterated her willingness to develop the CSCE and make it 'a forum for regular political consultation between East and West'. She also emphasised that the French shared her concerns about Germany: the only difference between her and the French president was that, while she expressed them publicly, Mitterrand did not.[50] Ultimately, Britain's prime minister told Gorbachev that it would be unwise to fight for causes which had already been lost, such as a longer transitional period before unification or a French model for German membership of NATO. While ways had to be found to give the Soviet Union confidence that its security would not be jeopardised, 'certain consequences flowed from German unification, and membership of NATO was one of them'. Her conclusion was that in previous months she had taken a lot of criticism for arguing that 'there should be a long transitional period before unification to enable all the details to be worked out', without receiving much support, even from Gorbachev himself.[51]

However, despite Whitehall's alignment with American positions, in Britain there was much resentment towards the Federal government. A deteriorating economic situation, following a rise in unemployment and inflation, and the fear that a unified Germany might experience a potential second post-War economic miracle fuelled a spate of anti-German animosity. These feelings became particularly vociferous in the wake of the English football team's defeat on penalties to West Germany in the World Cup semi-final in Milan on 4 July. On 8 July Dominic Lawson, son of former British Chancellor of the Exchequer Nigel Lawson, wrote a column in the *Sunday Correspondent*, complaining about the lack of news coverage of the 'German threat' to the finances and currencies of Europe.[52] Four days later further outcry was caused by an interview given by Minister of Trade and Industry Nicholas Ridley, the cabinet member who was closest in all respects to Thatcher, to the Conservative Party-linked *Spectator* magazine, edited by Nigel Lawson. In the interview Ridley criticised recent steps towards a joint European monetary policy as 'all a German racket designed to take over the whole of Europe' and accused the French of 'behaving like poodles to the Germans'. Asked how steps towards monetary integration in Europe could be perceived as a move by the FRG to take over the whole continent, Ridley answered that the German mark was 'always going to be the strongest currency, because of their habits', adding that for Britain to give up its sovereignty to a German-led European Community would be out of the question. He went on to define Britain's role and mission in Europe as one of always privileging the balance of power and of keeping other various powers balanced. This mission was never more necessary than now with Germany acting so uppity. Ridley emphatically concluded that, while he was not against giving up sovereignty in principle, he opposed relinquishing it to this lot, as one 'might just as well give it to Adolf Hitler, frankly'. Tellingly, the text of the interview was accompanied by cartoons that showed Kohl with a Hitler moustache painted on his face. The interview received extensive media coverage in Germany: the prevailing reaction in Bonn was that the crisis stemmed from Britain's loss of self-confidence and difficulty in adjusting to its current position in world politics. According to *Handelsblatt*, this situation had resulted in a loss of nerve, at a time when Britain could no longer rely on the special relationship 'to boost its ego'.[53]

However, some of the comments in the German press suggested that, while reflecting deep contradictions in Britain's European policy, the crisis might favour the more pro-European approach of Hurd and Chancellor of the Exchequer John Major.[54] On 14 July the West German newspaper *Bild Zeitung* remarked that the publisher of the *Spectator*, Conrad Black, was a close friend of Thatcher. On the same day the Social Democratic deputy speaker, Annemarie Renger, wrote in the daily *Die Welt* that Ridley's comments echoed the anti-German remarks made by British publishing magnate and former Labour Member of Parliament Robert Maxwell, when the latter had met Honecker in October 1989. Referring to Maxwell as a former British occupation officer, in light of his service after the War as head of the Foreign Office's press section in occupied Germany, Renger noted that on 3 October 1989 Maxwell had confessed to the BBC that a united Germany was 'a threat to Europe, to the Russians, the Poles, the Germans themselves, and to us'. Britain simply did not want it, as it was no good, 'neither for us nor for the Germans'.[55] A day earlier Lord Carrington had given the annual lecture at the elite Ditchley Park estate in Oxfordshire on the theme 'Towards a new Concert of Europe', an event attended by Hurd, in which he warned that history had not come to an end and that 'with history goes uncertainty and danger'.[56] On 12 July the prime minister remarked in the House of Commons that Ridley's comments did not represent the views of the government or her own views.[57] Two days later Ridley resigned, although Thatcher refused to fire him. The echoes of Ridley's interview and Carrington's lecture were not yet over on 15 July, when Britain's *Independent on Sunday* and Hamburg's *Der Spiegel* magazine leaked the minutes of the meeting that had occurred in March at Thatcher's Chequers country residence, involving the prime minister, members of her cabinet and six experts on Germany, four of whom were British. The minutes, which had been compiled by Thatcher's personal secretary, Charles Powell, contained dark premonitions about the potential re-emergence of a nationalist and expansionist German threat, including ostensible references to typical negative traits of the German people, such as 'angst, aggressiveness, bullying, egotism, inferiority complex, and sentimentality'.[58]

Anti-German displays in the United Kingdom elicited the cumulative effect of creating a widespread belief in the FRG that the British government, and particularly its prime minister, was essentially hostile to unification. The personal intransigence of senior Conservative Party figures and revelations about the Chequers seminar also caused outcry in the House of Commons. Labour leader Neil Kinnock, Liberal Democrat leader Paddy Ashdown and some Conservative backbench MPs heavily criticised the prime minister, leading to speculation that Thatcher would either face a new challenge to the Tory leadership in the autumn, or use the occasion of her sixty-fifth birthday in October to resign. Within the Conservative Party a 'damage-limitation' coalition began to shape up, which included Foreign Secretary Hurd, Deputy Prime Minister Geoffrey Howe, Chancellor of the Exchequer John Major and former Defence Secretary Michael Heseltine. Their common concern was that a too rigid and unsympathetic attitude to unification might not only harm Britain's interests in Europe but also cause friction in relations with Washington. The positive reception given by the Bush administration to Kinnock's trip to the US between 15 and 18 July further fuelled these concerns.[59] On 16 July Howe asserted that 'Europe is the most important game in town', while Heseltine remarked that 'Britain's interests lie in Europe. Anything that prejudices our ability to secure those interests is dangerous.'[60] Nonetheless, these statements could not assuage the prime minister's concerns about Germany. Many in Whitehall continued to express reservations about Bonn's conduct. On 16 July Hurd told BBC Television that the challenge the British now faced was 'the strength of the economy which the Germans have built for themselves'.[61] This was also the view of Thatcher. According to the prime minister, after Germany had undermined with Washington's connivance London's calls for a reinforced CSCE structure, only a continuing American presence in Europe and closer Franco-British ties could contain a reunified Germany.[62]

The special relationship and Germany's place in the Atlantic Alliance

'I will do what I can, but I fear that the train has already left'
(Michael Gorbachev, 15 July 1990)

'In times of great crisis, Britain and the United States stand as always together – and President Bush deserves our admiration and full support for the lead he has given'
(Margaret Thatcher, 12 October 1990)

The Turnberry, London and Houston summits

By late spring 1990 Britain thoroughly supported the American viewpoint that a unified Germany should be a full member of NATO. Whitehall's rejection of deeper European integration and Washington's disregard of British calls for a strengthened CSCE structure now made Germany's commitment to NATO a priority for London. Nonetheless, a number of differences persisted in Anglo-American positions. These divergences were not confined to the modalities of unification. They also extended to the issue of NATO's reform and role in post-Cold War Europe. The dynamics of NATO's transformation, which were set in motion by developments in Germany, were only in part the result of a joint Anglo-American vision. In contrast, as in the case of unification, they mainly reflected thinking within the White House and, to a lesser extent, the State Department. London had helped Washington overcome persistent French expectations that the US would play a diminished role in post-Cold War Europe. However, Britain's input in NATO's post-Cold War transformation was hardly decisive.

This issue was addressed on 7 and 8 June 1990 at the Turnberry meeting of NATO's foreign ministers. The summit endorsed the vision that President Bush had laid out in his Oklahoma State speech in May. As explicitly requested by the Americans, the allies agreed that articles 5 and 6 of the Washington Treaty would apply to the whole of Germany immediately after unification. The final communiqué that was issued at the end of the summit – the so-called 'Message from Turnberry' – celebrated the Berlin Wall's collapse, the end of the post-War era and Germany's unification, restating that German unity had been a primary goal of the alliance. The allies also expressed support for the efforts under way in the Two plus Four to achieve a final settlement that would terminate Four Power rights and responsibilities, without new constraints on German sovereignty. As such, a reunified Germany would have the right, as recognised in the Helsinki Final Act, 'to choose to be a party to a treaty of alliance'. The Turnberry declaration also reiterated that the stability of Europe required a unified Germany's full membership of NATO, 'including its integrated military structure, without prejudice to stated positions about nondeployment of NATO forces on the present GDR territory'. At the same time, the communiqué endeavoured to reassure the Soviet Union that the West sought no unilateral advantage from German unity, envisioned for the CSCE a function complementary to that of NATO and remarked that a 'free and democratic Germany would be an essential element of a peaceful order in Europe'.[63]

Nonetheless, Thatcher was unwilling to contemplate any weakening of NATO's nuclear deterrence policy.[64] She also played down the idea that the alliance could play a role in the former Soviet bloc and continued to emphasise the need for a reinforced CSCE structure. In her opening speech she stressed that it would be unrealistic 'to think of extending NATO's membership at present' to the countries of Eastern Europe and remarked that the West should build up the CSCE in order to 'provide a framework of growing trust and confidence which will make both East and West feel more secure – from the Atlantic right to the Urals'.[65] Furthermore, the British felt that on this occasion also, Washington had prioritised cooperation with Bonn to the detriment of the special relationship. A draft paper prepared by the Policy Planning Staff and dated 15 June 1990 expressed Britain's persistent misgivings, complaining that it was likely that NATO would be transformed according to German thinking. The paper also rejected French preferences, dismissing as 'political fantasy' the prospect of a fully federal Europe, with a single army and a single defence policy. Its conclusion was that Britain would do well, unlike Paris was doing, to avoid the language of binding Germany into Europe, as the perception of being treated as a 'dangerous breed' created a feeling of resentment among younger Germans, including the chancellor himself. The draft paper also reported that when asked in a private conversation how he felt about the notion of binding Germany into Europe, Kohl had replied that the people who adopted this language were enemies of Germany but 'he would take his revenge on them by doing precisely what they suggested'.[66]

Three weeks later, at the London summit of the alliance on 5 and 6 July, the US tabled a radical reshaping of NATO's strategy aimed at making the alliance 'more political, less military' and part of a security structure for the whole of Europe.[67] While not questioning US leadership, the British reception of the US blueprint was lukewarm. London felt that the allies had accepted the US draft of a resolution titled 'The NATO Summit: German Unification and the Soviet Audience', which reflected Washington's vision, 'rather than one that emerged through the usual channels of NATO bureaucracy'.[68] The French were also unhappy. The idea that an American-led organisation, with a full role for a united Germany, should acquire further clout in the sphere of European security was anathema to them.[69] Paris expected the US to play a diminished role in Europe after the end of the East–West division and perceived the collapse of the Soviet bloc as an opportunity to reshape the European political order along the lines of a stronger and more integrated Europe.[70] During his conversation with Bush at Key Largo in April Mitterrand had already advanced his ideas for a gradual Europeanisation of the alliance. Now, the French repeatedly expressed misgivings and disputed the wisdom of the renovation plans that were advanced by Washington.

In light of France's odd position within the alliance and preference for its gradual Europeanisation, Britain's support for US plans proved fundamental and contributed to a solution that also took into account Moscow's concerns. At the end of the summit the allies issued a declaration on a 'transformed North Atlantic Alliance'. This, although preserving the original US draft nearly intact, also made a number of concessions to the Kremlin, including an invitation to the Soviet Union and the countries of Eastern Europe to establish regular diplomatic liaisons with NATO.[71] Nonetheless, the United Kingdom's limited financial resources prevented Thatcher from establishing Britain as Moscow's main interlocutor in the West. In the following week, at the G7 major advanced economies summit in Houston between 9 and 11 July, the West Germans, honouring the commitment made by Teltschik in Moscow in May, pressed for immediate and unconditional aid to the USSR to help Gorbachev succeed in his reform policies. Nonetheless, the British supported the Americans and insisted on imposing the IMF's conditionality on aid to Moscow, fearing that Western credit would vanish in the sinkhole of the Soviet system.[72]

The Federal government was the USSR's main creditor, guaranteeing a short-term untied credit amounting to six billion Deutschmarks, provided by FRG's private banks. Germany was followed by Japan and Italy, which committed respectively 5.2 billion and 4.3 billion Deutschmarks. London's contribution came only in sixth place with a credit of 1.5 billion Deutschmarks, undermining Thatcher's reiterated attempts to position herself as Gorbachev's main interlocutor in the West.[73]

Wörner's and Kohl's Moscow visits and the Stavropol deal

The results of the London and Houston summits allowed Shevardnadze and Gorbachev to defend their policies against mounting critique in the USSR. However, the Kremlin refused to commit publicly to German membership of NATO until the CPSU's 28th Congress.[74] At what turned out to be the last congress in the CPSU's history Gorbachev scored an important victory against conservative critics, who blamed him for losing Eastern Europe and weakening his country strategically. The majority of party delegates backed the CPSU's secretary general and his foreign minister and voted his former second secretary, Yegor Ligachev, the loudest opponent of German NATO membership, and other hardliners out of the Central Committee.[75] A completely new Politburo was elected. Victory over conservative rivals freed Gorbachev to follow his own policy and paved the way for the last two major encounters, which sealed Soviet consent to a united Germany's membership of NATO: first, the visit on 14 July of the alliance's secretary general, Manfred Wörner, to Moscow – the first trip by a NATO secretary general to the Soviet capital – for a formal presentation of the London declaration; and second, on 15 and 16 July Gorbachev's meeting with Kohl first in Moscow and later in his hometown of Stavropol, in the Caucasus. Before the German delegation's arrival, which also included Foreign Minister Genscher and Finance Minister Theo Waigel, Falin presented Gorbachev with a memorandum. This restated the long-held Soviet view of a French scenario for a united Germany – that is, no German participation in the alliance's military structure, or, as a minimum concession, the stationing of no nuclear arms on the entire German territory. Gorbachev grimly replied to the advice, 'I will do what I can, but I fear that the train has already left.'[76] At the end of the two-day encounter with the West German delegation, the Soviet leader agreed to lift virtually all barriers to unification. Gorbachev surrendered all of the Soviet Union's remaining claims as an occupying power. He also renounced any restrictions on Germany's sovereignty, including its right to join NATO. In exchange, Kohl agreed to negotiate a bilateral treaty with Moscow, covering a number of military, political and economic issues and including detailed provisions for wide economic and technical cooperation.[77]

On 16 July, at a joint press conference in the tiny town of Zheleznovodsk, the Soviet leader publicly accepted that quadripartite rights and responsibilities would end at the time of unification, without any subsequent transitional period, and that a united Germany would be a full member of NATO. Kohl and Gorbachev also concurred that the agreement covering Soviet forces in Germany would be a withdrawal – and not a stationing – treaty, and that Soviet forces would leave after a period of three to four years.[78] The chancellor assured Gorbachev of the FRG's agreement to cover the costs of resettling in the USSR the 360,000 remaining Soviet troops in East Germany and that no non-German NATO troops and structures would be deployed there until the departure of Soviet troops. Furthermore, no nuclear weapons would be stationed in the GDR.[79] Kohl also pledged that *Bundeswehr* forces would be limited to 370,000. Kohl offered a compromise between a troop ceiling of 400,000 that had been proposed by his Defence Minister Stoltenberg, and of the 350,000, favoured by Genscher. However, his pledge did not meet an initial Soviet request of cutting the number of German troops to 200,000, which would have reduced a united Germany's army to about a third of the combined troops of the FRG and the GDR.[80] Ultimately, the agreement implied Gorbachev's explicit acceptance of fundamental Western views, particularly of the presence of *Bundeswehr* units, although not assigned to NATO, in East Germany and Berlin immediately after unification.[81] Moscow also agreed that US, British and French troops would be allowed to remain in Berlin until the Red Army had withdrawn. Finally, Kohl and Gorbachev promised that neither of their countries would initiate a military attack on the other, although this pledge ran counter to the FRG's obligation to come to the defence of a NATO ally if assaulted by the Soviet Union.[82]

The Stavropol arrangement, having been reached just before the third ministerial meeting of the Two plus Four in Paris on 17 July, strengthened the prospect that negotiations might be concluded at the Moscow ministerial meeting on 12 September.[83] Nonetheless, Stavropol also rekindled Anglo-American concerns that Bonn was not keeping its allies closely informed while it negotiated on issues that would affect the interests of the Western alliance.

Although the substance of the agreement had been finalised at the US–Soviet Camp David summit in early June, Kohl did not telephone Bush before announcing the deal. Both Washington and London eventually expected to relinquish their rights to garrison forces in West Berlin. However, Kohl's announcement that Western troops would leave Berlin when the Soviets withdrew from East Germany and that former GDR territory would remain denuclearised and off-limits for the stationing of non-German troops awoke fears that Bonn was undermining Western interests. In Washington the deal elicited bitter disappointment. The White House had wanted the chancellor to negotiate the Soviet withdrawal from East Germany bilaterally with Gorbachev in order to avoid the Kremlin establishing a link between US troop reductions in the FRG and in doing so take advantage of West Germany's anti-American left in order to put pressure on the Federal government.[84] Some in the administration felt, however, that the US had been bypassed by the FRG. Zoellick described the agreement as 'essentially bilateral'.[85] Baker was stunned, while one American diplomat laconically observed, 'we are getting more detailed reports from the Soviets on their meetings than we are getting from the Germans'.[86] Whereas the secretary of state was inclined to accept a perpetual and explicit provision that large-scale military manoeuvres by NATO should not take place in East Germany, the intimacy and consequences of the summit had gone far beyond what people in the State Department anticipated. Seitz complained that Washington found it discourteous to learn 'from the wire services' of West German concessions at Stavropol.[87] Nonetheless, rather than by the substance of the Stavropol deal, State Department officials were surprised by its sudden organisation and conclusion.

The NSC's evaluations were more nuanced. According to Blackwill, the 'basic policy' had been the administration's invention, as was the 'tactical game-plan for handling the Germans, Russians and neighbouring countries'. This policy had involved the 'most intensive' application of American diplomacy 'of all time'. In contrast, anyone who thought that the US had been 'upstaged' by the Stavropol meeting 'must have been living on the planet Zarkon'.[88] Publicly Bush praised the agreement as a right step towards strengthening 'efforts to build enduring relationships based on cooperation'. In his joint memoirs with Scowcroft, the president rejected interpretations of the deal as detrimental to Western interests.[89] Nonetheless, privately he expressed irritation at the fact that the West Germans and the Soviets 'had worked out the matter on their own'.[90] On 2 August, at the Aspen Institute Symposium in Colorado, Bush restated his view that the US should play a role in Europe after unification. The president explained once more that the American presence would also serve as a reassurance for Moscow and for the countries of Eastern Europe, stating, 'we will remain in Europe to deter any new dangers, to be a force for stability, and to reassure all of Europe – east and west – that the European balance will remain secure'.[91]

Nonetheless, it was the British who drew the most pessimistic conclusions about Bonn's conduct. In the United Kingdom the Stavropol deal was interpreted as confirmation of the wisdom of British concerns. Whitehall saw its fears vindicated and FCO officials felt that the Federal government had been reluctant to conduct timely and adequate consultations with its allies about its bilateral negotiations with Moscow. According to London, Bonn had gone 'a long way' towards meeting Soviet requirements with American acquiescence, while Kohl's promise that the alliance would not deploy non-German forces in the GDR was 'a long way down the slippery slope'. A week after the summit an article in *The Economist*, titled 'Encounter at Stavrapallo', drew a comparison with the secretly negotiated German–Soviet Rapallo Treaty of 1922, which had allowed Germany to evade restrictions imposed by the Treaty of Versailles through military cooperation with the USSR.[92] In contrast, reactions in France, as in the US, were less apprehensive. Although, according to Braithwaite, Britain's concerns were shared by the French, Paris had favoured a compromise that would preserve Western interests while allowing the Soviet government to 'save face'. Two days after the Stavropol meeting Mitterrand expressed his satisfaction, remarking that 'NATO should not profit from circumstances to advance its military arrangements'.[93]

Anglo-American views about the Status of Forces Agreement

'Germany will not simply be the Federal Republic plus, but a different entity'
(John Weston, 17 September 1990)

The Status of Forces Agreement and Anglo-American concerns

Stavropol had sealed the question of Germany's relationship with NATO and clarified the modalities of Soviet troop withdrawal. However, it had left unresolved the legal status of an allied military presence on East German territory. In the summer this issue became a last motive of Anglo-American concern. During the Cold War, the presence of foreign forces in the FRG had been initially regulated by the NATO Status of Forces Agreement (SOFA) of June 1951. Following the FRG's admission into NATO and the termination of the occupation regime, the SOFA had been supplemented by the Supplementary Agreement (SA) of August 1959.[94] Although the US had supported direct negotiations between Bonn and the Kremlin, the provisions agreed by Kohl and Gorbachev at Stavropol created uncertainty among the allies. Anglo-American concerns focused on whether the deal meant that NATO forces could not be stationed permanently in East Germany, while being allowed to conduct exercises there and overfly the territory, or whether it implied a thorough prohibition. Whereas the Soviets favoured the latter interpretation, there were dissonant positions in the Anglo-American camp.

Britain's views on this issue were much more 'robust' than those of Washington. In the following weeks the British entered into a serious dispute with the Germans on the interpretation of the arrangement. The real difficulties arose in how to deal with the Soviet proposal to preclude other NATO forces from 'ever crossing the line into East Germany', even just for exercise or manoeuvre purposes. Whitehall's favourite option was a provision precluding large-scale military manoeuvres during the transitional period to be followed by bilateral political assurances that 'the allies would exercise discretion and pay due regard to Soviet security interests in any activities east of the line'. London doubted, however, that such a provision would be attainable and lamented that the 'German heart' was not in it, while the Americans were in a 'fix-it' mood.[95] According to the British viewpoint, while the allies should hope never to have to deploy extra forces in the former GDR, they should not be precluded from doing so in times of tension.[96] British diplomats also highlighted the danger of a potential legal vacuum between unification and ratification of the final settlement, in which allied rights and responsibilities would be finally lifted. On 30 July, in a meeting with Genscher, Thatcher emphasised that, although things were now moving very fast and many of them were matters for Germany itself, one issue which would need to be resolved was the legal basis for the continuing presence of allied forces in Berlin.[97] A week later, in a telephone conversation with the FRG's foreign minister, Hurd stressed that the accelerating timetable towards unification required the allies to speed up work on the legal status of allied forces.[98]

Bonn's determination to put the final seal on unification further increased British anxieties. While Kohl and de Maizière had agreed in April that the two states would enter monetary, economic and social union on 1 July, a state treaty to that effect had been concluded on 18 May. Negotiations for a second state treaty, which would bring about political union, started on 6 July and were finally concluded on 31 August.[99] On 10 August, at the special meeting of NATO's foreign ministers that had been convened in Brussels to address the Iraqi invasion of Kuwait, Genscher told his Western colleagues that the date of unification would be moved forward to October. Although dynamics in the Middle East were shifting Anglo-American priorities away from the German question, West German conduct also caused apprehension in the US. On the same day the British and the Americans expressed serious reservations about points in the Federal government's draft declaration, to be annexed to the final settlement, which included some of the Stavropol provisions. In mid-August Bonn declined to arrange a One plus Three meeting on political and military aspects of unification.[100]

Despite their not always converging evaluations of West German conduct, Britain received strong US support during discussions on the legal basis for the stationing of allied forces in the FRG and Berlin. London favoured multilateral rather than bilateral agreements and an extension of SOFA and SA agreements to the whole of Germany.[101] The British viewpoint was that the West should not concede more than was agreed at Stavropol and that an extension of the legal arrangements for the presence of allied forces stationed in the FRG to Berlin and the former GDR would be 'by far the simplest solution'.[102] During the summer discussions of the legal basis for the stationing of allied forces restored a degree of Anglo-American solidarity. In bilateral and multilateral meetings, the Americans, alongside the British, argued powerfully against arrangements that would extend limitations on East Germany beyond non-stationing and thus constrain alliance options.[103]

However, at the meeting between Genscher and Shevardnadze in Moscow on 16 and 17 August the Federal government appeared to have come to accept the Kremlin's viewpoint that there should be a total prohibition of NATO's manoeuvres in East Germany.[104]

On 22 August the East German *Volkskammer* voted for German unity to be proclaimed on 3 October. However, British officials continued to worry that the Federal authorities might make additional concessions to Moscow. London now feared that the shortage of time before 3 October might increase the FRG's readiness 'to concede points' to the Soviets.[105] In the meeting of political directors that was held in the October Hotel in Moscow on 11 September, and which preceded the signing on the next day of the treaty on the final settlement, British and American delegates argued strongly against any arrangements which would extend limitations on East Germany beyond non-stationing and, as a result, constrain the alliance's options. Further private bilateral conversations between the Germans and the Russians were a source of additional irritation for Anglo-American officials. Writing to Mallaby on 17 September, Weston reported that, before the morning of 11 September, the German delegation had already held bilateral meetings with the Russians in an attempt to 'sew up a deal on the final points', misrepresenting US views into the bargain.[106]

The final solution bilaterally agreed by the West German and Soviet delegations was a simple 'no deployment' formula to be coupled with a four-point oral statement by Genscher at the plenary negotiating session. The four-point formula entailed: first, there would be no large-scale military manoeuvres on GDR territory; second, military activity below that threshold, although not explicitly ruled out, would not necessarily take place; third, the interpretation of the word 'deployment' would be left to the sovereign German state; and finally, Germany promised to exercise reason and responsibility and to respect the security interests of all. The terms of this deal caused 'sharp disagreement' between the FRG and the Anglo-Americans.[107] As one French diplomat remarked with some amusement, this last issue had opposed 'the Americans and especially the British to the Germans more than to the Soviet themselves'.[108] Western concerns were fuelled by the consideration that the alliance 'should not bind itself by treaty with the Soviet Union in a way which might foreclose options' that extended far beyond the foreseeable circumstances and 'would further limit German sovereignty beyond Stavropol'. In contrast, the formula preferred by Anglo-American delegations was that no military activity would be held for the transitional period, while thereafter there would be 'no deployment with the aim of holding large-scale military manoeuvres'. Baker also made it clear that, in order to obtain Congressional approval of the agreement, 'something in writing would be necessary about the provisions on military activity in the former GDR after Soviet troop departure'.[109] Firm Anglo-American objections required additional US–West German work to finalise the text of the agreed minutes, which were annexed to the treaty.

The special relationship after unification

On 31 August the signing of the treaty on German unity settled the domestic aspects of unification. Its preamble stated that a united Germany would 'contribute to the unification of Europe and to the building of a peaceful European order in which borders no longer divide'.[110] The agreement on internal unification was followed by the signing of the treaty on the final settlement at the Moscow ministerial meeting on 12 September, with suspension of the Four Power rights and responsibilities due to occur in New York on 1 October. On the same date, in an interview on US television, Britain's prime minister stated that the EC should incorporate and accept the unified Germany.[111] However, the final treaty precluded an automatic extension of the SOFA/SA to Berlin and East German territory. It also imposed strict limitations to the presence forces and a permanent prohibition to the deployment of nuclear weapons on GDR territory. More specifically, article 5.3 of the treaty prohibited the stationing of non-German armed forces and nuclear weapons in East Germany. As requested by the Americans, the final agreed minutes were annexed to the treaty and signed by all six ministers. The minutes clarified that troop deployment issues would be decided by a united Germany, taking into account the security interests of each contracting party.[112] Nonetheless, this solution confirmed a degree of Anglo-American disappointment.[113]

British reactions were particularly negative. Mallaby complained that Genscher had evidently judged that he could 'ride out the objections expressed repeatedly' by the US and Britain and present the allies with a 'fait accompli'.[114] According to Weston,

West German conduct had revealed that, with the achievement of unification, 'Germany will not simply be the Federal Republic plus but a different entity'. As he looked back on the entire process, the FCO political director saw 'something of a thread running through': Bonn's early reluctance to discuss political and military issues with the allies, the bilateral concessions that were made to the Russians at Stavropol, the following 'systematic ambiguity' about what kind of agreement had been reached there on the troop deployment issue and the 'fait accompli' over the exclusion of SOFA/SA from application on former GDR territory. While it would continue to be in Britain's interest to strengthen Western solidarity, he ominously concluded that from 3 October the Germans were unlikely to be 'the same people who left that station or who will arrive at any terminus'.[115] In a joint letter to Hurd on 2 October, Mallaby and the United Kingdom's ambassador to East Berlin, Patrick Eyers, emphasised the 'greater assertiveness in German foreign policy', complained that the Federal government had displayed 'insensitive high handedness' and suggested that once German sovereignty was fully restored the Germans were likely to pursue their interests without the 'rather deliberate restraint' that had been normal until a few years back. According to the ambassadors, East Germany's special military status – epitomised by the agreement that no nuclear weapons and no foreign forces would be stationed there after 1994 – now created the risk that, in the case of tranquillity in Europe for a number of years, more and more people in West Germany might call for its extension to the whole of the German territory. Furthermore, Germany's Western orientation might be supplemented by strong eastern links and by the wish to develop new accommodations with Russia. Their conclusion was that, while a reversion to the attitude which caused the two world wars should not be expected, Britain retained an interest in keeping Germany firmly 'embedded in a close Western framework'.[116]

Whitehall also hoped that the disappointment that West German conduct had provoked among American officials might now play into the hands of the British. Despite conflicting views with the US government about the modalities of unification, the special relationship remained fundamental for London. The Iraqi invasion of the former British protectorate of Kuwait in August further reinforced Whitehall's determination that the alliance was the only viable forum for protecting British interests and preserving European security. In British eyes, NATO would provide a framework through which to revive the special relationship and counterbalance any Franco-German axis in Europe.[117] At the Conservative Party conference in Bournemouth on 12 October Thatcher emphasised Britain's importance as a strong and reliable partner of the US and reiterated her support for NATO and for the United Kingdom's relationship with Washington. She also refrained from expressing criticism of US support for the FRG, stressing instead how, 'in times of great crisis, Britain and the United States stand as always together – and President Bush deserves our admiration and full support for the lead he has given'.[118]

Nonetheless, while Bonn's conduct in the latest phases of the negotiations had caused misgivings in the US too, American evaluations were less pessimistic.[119] Since late 1989 German unification had been the lynchpin of Washington's approach to the transformation of the European geopolitical architecture. The US's fundamental objective was the preservation of the transatlantic relationship, and Bonn's commitment to the alliance had ensured NATO's survival, securing the maintenance of the US political, economic and military presence in Europe after the end of the East–West division.[120] Hence, a constructive relationship with Germany was seen in Washington as the indispensable foundation for the preservation of a premier American role in post-Cold War Europe. The mutual trust and respect which Washington and Bonn were able to establish between 1989 and 1990 had laid the foundations for a durable, robust and stable relationship. Not for naught had President Bush offered a 'partnership in leadership' in 1989 to the FRG rather than to the United Kingdom. In contrast, Thatcher's fundamental distrust of West German motives and Britain's persistent fears about Germany and scepticism about deeper integration in Europe prevented London from claiming a leading role on the continent. While Whitehall strongly criticised Germany for its lack of determination and support for the US in the Gulf, its mistrust towards the European project and the Franco-German axis paved the way for a gradual deterioration in relations between the United Kingdom and the EU in the post-Cold War years.

Notes

1. Robert L. Hutchings, *American Diplomacy and the End of the Cold War: An Insider's Account of U.S. Policy in Europe, 1989–1992* (Baltimore, MD: Johns Hopkins University Press, 1997), pp. 120–2.
2. Hans-Dietrich Genscher, 'Zur deutschen Einheit im europaischen Rahmen', *Der Bundesminster des Auswärtigen informiert. Mitteilung für die Presse*, no. 1026/90 (31 January 1990). Copies of the Tutzing speech were distributed by the West German authorities in advance and translated into English, French and Russian to the Four Powers. Frank Elbe, 'The Diplomatic Path to German Unity', *Bulletin of the German Historical Institute*, vol. 46, Spring 2010, p. 37. See also Horst Teltschik, *329 Tage. Innenansichten der Einigung* (Berlin: Siedler, 1991), pp. 148–9; Gerhard A. Ritter, 'Deutschland und Europa. Grundzüge der Außenpolitik Genschers 1989 bis 1992', in Kerstin Brauckhoff and Irmgard Schwaetze (eds), *Hans-Dietrich Genschers Außenpolitik* (Wiesbaden: Springer Fachmedien, 2014), pp. 224–6; *Documents on British Policy Overseas* (hereafter *DBPO*), Series III, vol. VII, *German Unification, 1989–1990* (London: Her Majesty's Stationery Office, 2009), doc. no. 111, Powell to Wall, p. 233, fn. 3; Gerhard A. Ritter, *Hans-Dietrich Genscher, das Auswärtige Amt und die deutsche Vereinigung* (Munich: C. H. Beck, 2013).
3. Hanns Jürgen Küsters and Daniel Hofmann (eds), *Dokumente zur Deutschlandpolitik, Deutsche Einheit. Sonderedition aus den Akten des Bundeskanzleramtes 1989/90* (Munich: Oldenbourg, 1998), pp. 111–12.
4. *DBPO*, III, VII, p. xxv.
5. 'Erklärung des Bundesministers des Auswärtigen, Hans-Dietrich Genscher, und des Bundesministers der Verteidigung, Gerhard Stoltenberg, 19. Februar 1990', in Presse- und Informationsamt der Bundesregierung (ed.), *Bulletin des Presse- und Informationsamtes der Bundesregierung* (Bonn: Deutscher Bundesverlag), 21 February 1990, no. 28, p. 218.
6. *DBPO*, III, VII, doc. no. 154, Acland to FCO, p. 307. See also Hutchings, *American Diplomacy*, pp. 120–2; Küsters and Hofmann, *Dokumente zur Deutschlandpolitik*, p. 112.
7. *DBPO*, III, VII, doc. no. 154, Acland to FCO, p. 308.
8. Philip Zelikow and Condoleezza Rice, *Germany Unified and Europe Transformed: A Study in Statecraft* (Cambridge, MA: Harvard University Press, 1995), p. 187. Quoted in *DBPO*, III, VII, p. xxiii.

9. *DBPO*, III, VII, doc. no. 154, Acland to FCO, p. 310 and doc. no. 156, Braithwaite to FCO, p. 317.

10. Quoted in Mary E. Sarotte, 'Not One Inch Eastward? Bush, Baker, Kohl, Genscher, Gorbachev, and the Origin of Russian Resentment toward NATO Enlargement in February 1990', *Diplomatic History*, vol. 34, no. 1, January 2010, pp. 135–6. See also Bush and Scowcroft, *A World Transformed*, p. 253.

11. G. H. W. Bush, *All the Best, George Bush: My Life in Letters and Other Writings* (New York: Scribner, 1999), p. 461.

12. See Tilo Schabert, *How World Politics Is Made: France and the Reunification of Germany* (Columbia, MO: University of Missouri Press, 2009), p. 167.

13. *DBPO*, III, VII, doc. no. 183, Acland to Hurd, pp. 357–8.

14. *DBPO*, III, VII, pp. 357–8.

15. *DBPO*, III, VII, doc. no. 185, Hurd to Acland, pp. 363–5.

16. *DBPO*, III, VII, doc. no. 191, Braithwaite to FCO, p. 374.

17. 'News Conference of the President and Prime Minister Margaret Thatcher of the United Kingdom in Hamilton, Bermuda', 13 April 1990. See *Public Papers: George Bush, 1990, Book I* (Washington, DC: Government Printing Office, 1991), p. 495. The record of the Anglo-American conversation is available at <http://www.margaretthatcher.org/document/111020> (last accessed 1 October 2016).

18. Teltschik, *329 Tage*, p. 203. For a translation of the passage of Teltschik's diary see also <http://staging.margaretthatcher.org/document/111038> (last accessed 1 October 2016).

19. See the record of the Anglo-American conversation at Bermuda available at <http://www.margaretthatcher.org/document/111020> (last accessed 1 October 2016); Frédéric Bozo, *Mitterrand, the End of the Cold War, and German Unification* (New York: Berghahn Books, 2009), pp. 216, 248–50, 262, fn. 36.

20. Michael Sutton, *France and the Construction of Europe, 1944–2007: The Geopolitical Imperative* (New York: Berghahn Books, 2011), p. 259. See also Zelikow and Rice, *Germany Unified*, p. 442.

21. Len Scott, 'British Perspectives on the Future of European Security', in Colin McInnes (ed.), *Security and Strategy in the New Europe* (London: Routledge, 2002), p. 191.

22. Bozo, *Mitterrand*, pp. 255–6.

23. Robert L. Hutchings, 'The US, German Unification, and European Integration', in Frédéric Bozo, Marie-Pierre Rey, Piers N. Ludlow and Leopoldo Nuti (eds), *Europe and the End of the Cold War: A Reappraisal* (Abingdon and New York: Routledge, 2008), p. 128. See also Zelikow and Rice, *Germany Unified*, p. 169.

24. John L. Harper, 'American Visions of Europe after 1989', in Christina V. Balis and Simon Serfaty (eds), *Visions of America and Europe: September 11, Iraq, and Transatlantic Relations* (Washington, DC: CSIS Press, 2004), p. 29.
25. George Bush, 'Remarks at the Oklahoma State University Commencement Ceremony in Stillwater', 4 May 1990, *US Department of State Dispatch*, vol. 1, no. 1, September 1990, pp. 32–4, available at <https://bush41library.tamu.edu/archives/public-papers/1853> (last accessed 27 September 2016).
26. *DBPO*, III, VII, doc. no. 196, Hurd to Mallaby, p. 384. See also Bozo, *Mitterrand*, p. 217.
27. *DBPO*, III, VII, doc. no. 196, pp. 384–5.
28. *DBPO*, III, VII, p. xxviii.
29. *DBPO*, III, VII, doc. no. 197, Hurd to Acland, p. 387, fn. 7. For US views see Zelikow and Rice, *Germany Unified*, pp. 246–50. For French views see Bozo, *Mitterrand*, pp. 218, 264, fn. 45.
30. Alexander von Plato, *The End of the Cold War? Bush, Kohl, Gorbachev, and the Reunification of Germany* (London and New York: Palgrave Macmillan, 2015), pp. 258–9.
31. James A. Baker III, *The Politics of Diplomacy: Revolution, War and Peace* (New York: G. P. Putnam's Sons, 1995), pp. 250–1. The nine-point package was drafted by Zoellick and is reprinted in Zelikow and Rice, *Germany Unified*, pp. 263–4. See Zelikow and Rice, *Germany Unified*, pp. 262–6; G. John Ikenberry, *After Victory: Institutions, Strategic Restraint, and the Rebuilding of Order after Major Wars* (Princeton, NJ: Princeton University Press, 2001), p. 230; Bozo, *Mitterrand*, pp. 251–2.
32. Hannes Adomeit, 'Gorbachev's Consent to United Germany's Membership of NATO', in Frédéric Bozo, Marie-Pierre Rey, N. Piers Ludlow and Leopoldo Nuti (eds), *Europe and the End of the Cold War: A Reappraisal* (Abingdon and New York: Routledge, 2008), p. 112.
33. Quoted in Mary E. Sarotte, *1989: The Struggle to Create Post-Cold War Europe* (Princeton, NJ: Princeton University Press, 2009), p. 164.
34. *DBPO*, III, VII, p. xxiv.
35. *DBPO*, III, VII, doc. no. 202, Hurd to Mallaby, pp. 393–5.
36. Angela Stent, *Russia and Germany Reborn: Unification, the Soviet Collapse, and the New Europe* (Princeton, NJ: Princeton University Press, 1999), p. 126; Randall Everest Newnham, *Deutsche Mark Diplomacy: Positive Economic Sanctions in German–Russian Relations* (University Park: Pennsylvania State University Press, 2002), p. 235. See also Stephen F. Szabo, *The Diplomacy of German Unification* (New York: St. Martin's Press, 1992), p. 84.

37. Charles S. Maier, *Dissolution: The Crisis of Communism and the End of East Germany* (Princeton, NJ: Princeton University Press, 1997), p. 273.

38. *DBPO*, III, VII, doc. no. 205, Hurd to Mallaby, pp. 399–403.

39. Memorandum of Telephone Conversation [with President Bush], The White House, 30 May 1990, in Svetlana Savranskaya and Thomas Blanton (eds), National Security Archive Electronic Briefing Book No. 320, *The Washington/Camp David Summit 1990: From the Secret Soviet, American and German Files*, doc. no. 9, The National Security Archive, available at <http://nsarchive.gwu.edu/NSAEBB/NSAEBB320/> (last accessed 28 September 2016).

40. Andrei Grachev, *Gorbachev's Gamble: Soviet Foreign Policy and the End of the Cold War* (Cambridge: Polity Press, 2008), p. 202. See also Raymond Walter Apple, Jr., 'Summit in Washington; Besieged at Home, Gorbachev Arrives in U.S. for Summit', *The New York Times*, 31 May 1990.

41. Gorbachev had already made this suggestion to Secretary of State Baker and to the Czechoslovakian President Vaclav Havel during their visits to Moscow from 16 to 19 May and on 21 May respectively. See Record of Conversation, M. S. Gorbachev and G. Bush, Washington, DC, The White House, 31 May 1990, in Savranskaya and Blanton, National Security Archive Electronic Briefing Book No. 320, doc. no. 11, available at <http://nsarchive.gwu.edu/NSAEBB/NSAEBB320/11.pdf> (last accessed 28 September 2016). See also Hannes Adomeit, *Imperial Overstretch: Germany in Soviet Policy from Stalin to Gorbachev* (Baden-Baden: Nomos, 1998), pp. 112–13; Hannes Adomeit, 'East Germany: NATO's First Eastward Enlargement', in Anton Bebler (ed.), *NATO at 60: The Post-Cold War Enlargement and the Alliance's Future* (Fairfax, VA: IOS Press, 2010), p. 17; Richard T. Gray and Sabine Wilke (eds), *German Unification and Its Discontents: Documents from the Peaceful Revolution* (Seattle: University of Washington Press, 1996), p. xlvii; Stent, *Russia and Germany Reborn*, pp. 119–20.

42. Zelikow and Rice, *Germany Unified*, pp. 276–9. Quoted in *DBPO*, III, VII, p. xxviii.

43. Jürgen Weber, *Germany 1945–1990: A Parallel History* (Budapest: Central European University Press, 2004), p. 244.

44. All American officials that were involved in the process concur in describing this summit as a turning point. See Baker, *The Politics of Diplomacy*, pp. 253–4; Zelikow and Rice, *Germany Unified*, pp. 277–80; Hutchings, *American Diplomacy*, pp. 131–5. See also Ikenberry, *After Victory*, pp. 230–1; Joseph P. Harahan, 'The Post-Cold War Peace of Europe, 1989–1992', in Meenekshi Bose and Rosanna Perotti (eds), *From Cold War to New World Order: The*

Foreign Policy of George H. W. Bush (Westport, CT: Greenwood Press, 2002), p. 342. Genscher's memoirs emphasise the importance of his meetings with Shevardnadze in Geneva and Brest in May and June 1990 respectively as critical steps in obtaining Moscow's consent to Germany's full membership of NATO. See Hans-Dietrich Genscher, *Erinnerungen* (Berlin: Siedler, 1995), pp. 805–23.

45. News Conference of President Bush and President Mikhail Gorbachev of the Soviet Union, 3 June 1990, in *Public Papers: George Bush, 1990, Book I*, p. 758.

46. Taubman and Savranskaya have pointed out that, being based on misguided assumptions, Gorbachev's European vision produced a tragic outcome for Moscow: German unification within NATO and the deepening of a 'common European home' with no place for the Soviet Union or its successor. William Taubman and Svetlana Savranskaya, 'If a Wall Fell in Berlin, and Moscow Hardly Noticed, Would it Still Make a Noise?', in Jeffrey A. Engel (ed.), *The Fall of the Berlin Wall: The Revolutionary Legacy of 1989* (New York: Oxford University Press, 2009), pp. 69–95. For an extensive account of Gorbachev's Pan-European vision see also Svetlana Savranskaya, 'The Logic of 1989: The Soviet Peaceful Withdrawal from Eastern Europe', in Svetlana Savranskaya, Thomas Blanton and Vlad Zubok (eds), *Masterpieces of History: The Soviet Peaceful Withdrawal from Eastern Europe, 1989* (Budapest: Central European University Press, 2010), pp. 1–47. For a critique of Gorbachev's strategy see also Jacques Lévesque, 'In the Name of Europe's Future: Soviet, French, and British Qualms about Kohl's Rush to German Unification', in Frédéric Bozo, Marie-Pierre Rey, Piers N. Ludlow and Leopoldo Nuti (eds), *Europe and the End of the Cold War: A Reappraisal* (Abingdon and New York: Routledge, 2008), pp. 101–4. See also Vladislav Zubok, 'Gorbachev, German reunification, and Soviet demise', in Frédéric Bozo, Andreas Rödder and Mary Elise Sarotte (eds), *German Reunification: A Multinational History* (London and New York: Routledge, 2017), pp. 88–108.

47. Zelikow and Rice, quoting Hannes Adomeit's interview with Anatoly Chernyaev, argue that from this time on the Soviet leader never again voiced 'adamant opposition to Germany's presence in NATO'. Zelikow and Rice, *Germany Unified*, p. 283.

48. Hutchings, *American Diplomacy*, pp. 131–7. On the Washington summit's significance see also Sarotte, *1989*, pp. 167–9; Elizabeth Pond, *Beyond the Wall: Germany's Road to Unification* (Washington, DC: Brookings Institution Press, 1993), p. 215. For US evaluations of the summit see also 'Washington Summit Briefing Points', US Department of State to Deputy Secretary [Lawrence] Eagleburger, 4 June 1990, in Savranskaya and Blanton, National

Security Archive Electronic Briefing Book No. 320, doc. no. 14, available at <http://nsarchive.gwu.edu/NSAEBB/NSAEBB320/14.pdf> (last accessed 28 September 2016).

49. 'Briefing Allies on Washington Summit', US Department of State to US Embassies in NATO Capitals, Tokyo, Seoul, Canberra [and info. to Moscow], 15 June 1990, in Savranskaya and Blanton, National Security Archive Electronic Briefing Book No. 320, doc. no. 16, available at <http://nsarchive.gwu.edu/NSAEBB/NSAEBB320/16.pdf> (last accessed 28 September 2016).

50. *DBPO*, III, VII, doc. no. 209, Powell to Wall, pp. 414–15.

51. *DBPO*, III, VII, doc. no. 209, Powell to Wall, pp. 414–15.

52. Elisabeth Hellenbroich, 'Thatcher's Obsession to Block German Unity', *Executive Intelligence Review*, vol. 25, no. 32, August 1998, p. 46.

53. Mark Burdman, '"Ridley Affair" Is Fiasco for British Establishment', *Executive Intelligence Review*, vol. 17, no. 30, July 1990, pp. 38–9. See also Frank Costigliola, 'An "Arm around the Shoulder": The United States, NATO and German Reunification, 1989–90', *Contemporary European History*, vol. 3, no. 1, March 1994, p. 106.

54. *DBPO*, III, VII, doc. no. 217, Neville-Jones to FCO, pp. 432–4.

55. Burdman, '"Ridley Affair"', p. 39.

56. The text of Carrington's lecture is available at <http://www.ditchley.co.uk/conferences/past-programme/1990-1999/1990/lecture-xxvii> (last accessed 27 September 2016).

57. *Parliamentary Debates, 6th ser., House of Commons*, vol. 176, col. 449. See also Klein, 'Obstructive or Promoting?', p. 414. See also Patrick Salmon, 'The United Kingdom: divided counsels, global concerns', in Bozo, Rödder and Sarotte (eds), *German Reunification: A Multinational History* (London and New York: Routledge, 2017), pp. 153–76.

58. One Briton quipped on hearing this, 'they must have been talking about Margaret Thatcher'. Burdman, '"Ridley Affair"', p. 40.

59. *Public Papers: George Bush, 1990, Book II* (Washington, DC: Government Printing Office, 1991), p. 1021.

60. Both quoted in Burdman, '"Ridley Affair"', p. 38. See also Klein, 'Obstructive or Promoting?', pp. 415–17; Michael Heseltine, *The Challenge of Europe: Can Britain Win?* (London: Weidenfeld and Nicolson, 1989); see also the speech delivered by Lord Plumb at Chatham House, London, 11 December 1990, 'The European Community and Britain's Rightful Place', available at <http://gale.cengage.co.uk/images/upload/ChathamHouse/casestudies/britain-eu/plumb-franklin-the-ec-britains-rightful-place-1990.pdf> (last accessed 1 October 2016).

61. Burdman, '"Ridley Affair"', p. 38.
62. Margaret Thatcher, *Downing Street Years* (London: Harper Perennial, 1993), p. 791. Quoted in *DBPO*, III, VII, p. xv.
63. North Atlantic Council, Final Communiqué, Turnberry, 7–8 June 1990, available at <http://www.nato.int/docu/comm/49-95/c900608a.htm> (last accessed 27 September 2016).
64. Hutchings, *American Diplomacy*, p. 134.
65. The text of Thatcher's speech to the North Atlantic Council is available at <http://www.margaretthatcher.org/document/108106> (last accessed 1 October 2016).
66. *DBPO*, III, VII, doc. no. 210, p. 421.
67. Zelikow and Rice, *Germany Unified*, p. 303. Quoted in *DBPO*, III, VII, p. xxix.
68. *DBPO*, III, VII, p. xxix. See also Zelikow and Rice, *Germany Unified*, p. 321. See also Pyeongeok An, 'Obstructive All the Way? British Policy towards German Unification 1989–90', *German Politics*, vol. 15, no. 1, 2006, pp. 116–17.
69. Sutton, *France*, p. 260. See also Bozo, *Mitterrand*, pp. 256–8, 278–82.
70. Stephanie C. Hofmann, *European Security in NATO's Shadow: Party Ideologies and Institution Building* (Cambridge: Cambridge University Press, 2013), pp. 77, 90.
71. *DBPO*, III, VII, p. xxix. See also doc. no. 215, Mallaby to Hurd, p. 429, fn. 3. The full text of the London declaration is available at <http://www.nato.int/docu/comm/49-95/c900706a.htm> (last accessed 1 October 2016).
72. Marc Fisher and David Hoffman, 'Behind German Unity Pact: Personal Diplomacy from Maine to Moscow', *The Washington Post*, 22 July 1990. See also Costigliola, 'An "Arm around the Shoulder"', p. 106.
73. Lothar Kettenacker, *Germany 1989: In the Aftermath of the Cold War* (Harlow: Pearson Longman, 2009), p. 151.
74. David H. Shumaker, *Gorbachev and the German Question: Soviet–West German Relations, 1985–1990* (Westport, CT: Praeger, 1995), pp. 135–6.
75. Michael J. Sodaro, *Moscow, Germany and the West from Khrushchev to Gorbachev* (London: I. B. Tauris, 1991), p. 318.
76. Valentin Falin, *Politische Erinnerungen* (Munich: Droemer Knaur, 1993), pp. 393–4. Quoted in Bozo, *Mitterrand*, p. 303.
77. Adomeit, *Imperial Overstretch*, p. 523; Adomeit, 'Gorbachev's Consent', p. 114. See also Serge Schmemann, 'Evolution in Europe; Gorbachev Clears Way for German Unity, Dropping Objection to NATO Membership', *The New York Times*, 17 July 1990.
78. Pond, *Beyond the Wall*, p. 222.

79. Sarotte, *1989* p. 184; von Plato, *The End of the Cold War?*, p. 300.
80. Costigliola, 'An "Arm around the Shoulder"', p. 107; Sarotte, *1989*, pp. 184–5. See also Fisher and Hoffman, 'Behind German Unity Pact'.
81. *DBPO*, III, VII, doc. no. 218, Budd to Hurd, pp. 434–5.
82. Costigliola, 'An "Arm around the Shoulder"', pp. 107–8. See also von Plato, *The End of the Cold War?*, pp. 286–304.
83. *DBPO*, III, VII, pp. xxx; see also doc. no. 219, Hurd to Alexander, pp. 435–6.
84. Teltschik, *329 Tage*, p. 307. See also Costigliola, 'An "Arm around the Shoulder"', p. 106.
85. *DBPO*, III, VII, doc. no. 238, Weston to Mallaby, p. 470.
86. Quoted in Costigliola, 'An "Arm around the Shoulder"', p. 96.
87. *DBPO*, III, VII, doc. no. 221, Weston to Wall, pp. 438–9.
88. *DBPO*, III, VII, doc. no. 238, Weston to Mallaby, p. 470, fn. 9.
89. Bush and Scowcroft, *A World Transformed*, p. 298.
90. Gary Lee, 'Gorbachev Drops Objection to New Germany in NATO: Concession Removes Last Major Hurdle from Path to Unification', *The Washington Post*, 17 July 1990. See also Costigliola, 'An "Arm around the Shoulder"', p. 108.
91. *Public Papers: George Bush, 1990, Book II*, p. 1091.
92. *The Economist*, 21–7 July 1990; Costigliola, 'An "Arm around the Shoulder"', p. 107. See also Lonnie R. Johnson, *Central Europe: Enemies, Neighbors, Friends* (New York and Oxford: Oxford University Press, 1996), p. 204.
93. Bozo, *Mitterrand*, pp. 285–93 (quotation on p. 286). See also *DBPO*, III, VII, doc. no. 235, Braithwaite to FCO, pp. 463–4.
94. Simon Duke, *United States Military Forces and Installations in Europe* (Oxford and New York: Oxford University Press, 1989), pp. 71–7; Miriam Aziz, 'Sovereignty Über Alles: (Re)Configuring the German Legal Order', in Neil Walker (ed.), *Sovereignty in Transition* (Oxford: Hart Publishing, 2003), pp. 279–304.
95. *DBPO*, III, VII, doc. no. 235, Braithwaite to FCO, pp. 463–4.
96. *DBPO*, III, VII, doc. no. 236, FCO to Braithwaite, pp. 464–5.
97. *DBPO*, III, VII, doc. no. 222, Powell to Wall, p. 439.
98. *DBPO*, III, VII, doc. no. 226, Hurd to Neville-Jones, pp. 447–8.
99. *DBPO*, III, VII, p. xxx. See also Küsters and Hoffman, *Dokumente zur Deutschlandpolitik*, p. 1449, fn. 4.
100. *DBPO*, III, VII, doc. no. 228, Cox to Synnott, p. 450.
101. *DBPO*, III, VII, pp. 450–1.
102. *DBPO*, III, VII, doc. no. 230, Hurd to Mallaby, pp. 453–4.
103. *DBPO*, III, VII, doc. no. 237, Braithwaite to FCO, pp. 465–6.

104. Zelikow and Rice, *Germany Unified*, p. 356. See also *DBPO*, III, VII, p. xxxi.

105. *DBPO*, III, VII, doc. no. 229, Mallaby to Hurd, pp. 451–3 (quotation on p. 453).

106. *DBPO*, III, VII, doc. no. 238, Weston to Mallaby, pp. 467–8.

107. *DBPO*, III, VII, doc. no. 238, Weston to Mallaby, p. 468.

108. Bozo, *Mitterrand*, p. 293. See also An, 'Obstructive All the Way?', p. 117.

109. *DBPO*, III, VII, doc. no. 238, Weston to Mallaby, pp. 469–70 (quotation on p. 469).

110. Press and Information Office of the Federal Government (ed.), *The Unification of Germany in 1990* (Bonn: Press and Information Office of the Federal Government, 1991), p. 184.

111. The text of Thatcher's interview with NBC is available at <http://www.margaretthatcher.org/document/107972> (last accessed 1 October 2016).

112. The Treaty on the Final Settlement with Respect to Germany of 12 September 1990 is published in Presse- und Informationsamt der Bundesregierung (ed.), *Bulletin des Presse- und Informationsamtes der Bundesregierung* (Bonn: Deutscher Bundesverlag), 14 September 1990, no. 109, pp. 1153–6, available at <http://www.chronik-der-mauer.de/system/files/dokument_pdf/58707_cdm-900912-bulletin-vertrag.pdf> (last accessed 18 October 2016); Harold James and Marla Stone (eds), *When the Wall Came Down: Reactions to German Unification* (New York: Routledge, 1992), pp. 108–14; Sherill Brown Wells (ed.), *American Foreign Policy Current Documents 1990* (Washington, DC: US Department of State, 1991), doc. no. 191, pp. 354–7. For the significance of the agreed minute see also James M. Goldgeier, *Not Whether but When: The U.S. Decision to Enlarge NATO* (Washington, DC: Brookings Institution Press, 1999), p. 16.

113. Peter E. Quint, *The Imperfect Union: Constitutional Structures of German Unification* (Princeton, NJ: Princeton University Press, 1997), pp. 271–4. See also Eckart Klein, 'Deutchlands Rechtslage', in Werner Weidenfeld and Karl-Rudolf Korte (eds), *Handbuch zur deutschen Einheit, 1949–1989–1999* (Frankfurt and New York: Campus, 1999), pp. 285–6.

114. *DBPO*, III, VII, doc. no. 233, Mallaby to Hurd, p. 460.

115. *DBPO*, III, VII, doc. no. 238, Weston to Mallaby, pp. 470–1. The quotation is from Thomas Stearns Elliot, 'The Dry Salvages', *Four Quartets*, Canto III (San Diego, CA: Harcourt, 1943).

116. *DBPO*, III, VII, doc. no. 241, Mallaby and Eyers to Hurd, pp. 483–7 (quotation on p. 485).

117. Friedemann Buettner and Martin Landgraf, 'The European

Community's Middle Eastern Policy: The New Order of Europe and the Gulf Crisis', in Tareq Y. Ismael and Jacqueline S. Ismael (eds), *The Gulf War and the New World Order: International Relations of the Middle East* (Gainesville: Florida University Press, 1994), pp. 88, 93.

118. The text of the speech is available at <http://www.margaretthatcher.org/document/108217> (last accessed 1 October 2016).

119. See Bush's message to the Senate on 25 September in *Public Papers: George Bush, 1990, Book II*, pp. 1283–5.

120. Jeffrey A. Engel, 'Bush, Germany, and the Power of Time: How History Makes History', *Diplomatic History*, vol. 37, no. 4, 2013, p. 662.

Conclusions

Still a special relationship after unification?

As one of the Cold War triggers and in light of its persistent endurance during the East–West division, the German question undoubtedly represents a primary indicator of the vitality and strength of the special relationship in the second half of the twentieth century. While Anglo-American relations were influenced by a number of complex and diverse dynamics, the problem of Germany remained, although with varying intensity, a constant preoccupation for US and British decision-makers from Germany's unconditional surrender in May 1945 until its unification in October 1990. Nonetheless, while Washington and London regarded Germany as the centrepiece of their European policy, Anglo-American strategies did not always coincide. In the first half of the 1950s US and British decision-makers worked closely to secure the FRG's rearmament and integration into the West. However, before and after the formation of the two blocs in Europe Britain entertained hopes for an arrangement with the USSR. This desire also influenced British attitudes towards Germany during the period of East–West détente. During the late 1950s and early 1960s London struggled to adapt to the realities of its international decline. Nonetheless, British decision-makers continued to hope that their country could assert itself as a middleman between the two superpowers. As part of this strategy, London encouraged Bonn to a gradual opening up to the East in order to defuse tension between the two blocs. However, the British did not fully realise the implications that this policy would have for East–West relations.

In the same time period, the US, facing expanding budget deficits and the consequences of a protracted conflict in Vietnam, also supported the FRG's diplomatic initiatives towards the Soviet bloc. Nonetheless, both London and Washington remained suspicious of Bonn's long-term ambitions and of the repercussions of West German policy on the cohesion of the West. In the early 1970s both the Americans and the British reacted with concern when the Federal government's initiatives exceeded their expectations. Both Washington and London now resented, to a certain extent, the FRG's increasing status and growing influence on East–West relations. In the aftermath of *Ostpolitik* the special relationship was reaffirmed during the Helsinki conference by a common Anglo-American determination to emphasise the ongoing responsibilities of the Four Powers on the German question and Berlin. However, the British were unwilling to risk a new confrontation with the Soviets. Furthermore, the United Kingdom's strategic importance for the US continued to decline. This process was accelerated by Britain's entry into the EEC in 1973 and Heath's decision to concentrate on relations with Britain's European partners at the expense of the special relationship. In the second half of the 1970s the Federal Republic's importance for Washington also continued to grow as a result of a deteriorating economic situation in the United Kingdom. However, the FRG struggled to replace Britain as the most important American ally in Europe, not least due to the different views in Washington and Bonn about the process of détente and a difficult personal relationship between Carter and Schmidt.

Then in the early 1980s Anglo-American relations experienced a partial revitalisation following the Soviet invasion of Afghanistan, the INF crisis in Europe, the almost simultaneous elections of Thatcher and Reagan, and US support for Britain during the Falklands crisis. Nonetheless, the German question was not a lever of closer cooperation between Washington and London. In contrast, in the second half of the 1980s transformation in Eastern Europe and Germany triggered fundamental divergences in Anglo-American views of transition in the East. By 1989 the impending collapse of the post-Cold War European order had turned the German question into a source of attrition between the White House and Whitehall. With the advancing crisis in the Soviet bloc, Washington perceived transformation in Germany as a historic opportunity that was unlikely to reoccur to knock down the Soviet empire and to consolidate the transatlantic relationship.

In contrast, Britain feared a resurgence of German power, was reluctant to back demands for unification, and embarked on a protracted attempt to work out an arrangement with the French and the Soviets to delay it.

The achievement of German unification in such a short time period remains one of the most successful endeavours of post-War Western diplomacy. Nonetheless, its conclusion was not the product of a happy Anglo-American marriage. Rather, it was the outcome of a meticulous and at times difficult compromise between US and West German initiatives, which were often implemented at the expense of British priorities. Washington made a united Germany's ongoing commitment to the West a precondition for supporting unification. The West Germans, faced with European scepticism and distrust, acknowledged that without Washington's support and Soviet acquiescence the process of ending Germany's division would have been difficult and protracted in time.

Differences in the Anglo-American camp were evident from the late spring of 1989. Britain's views were closer to the sceptical attitude of Germany's European partners than to prevailing opinions in Washington. In the US there was a residue of apprehension about a united Germany. Former President Richard Nixon and Jimmy Carter's national security advisor, Zbigniew Brzezinski, viewed it as a threat to European stability. However, President Bush and his NSC did not share fears that unification would destabilise Europe and undermine Western cohesion. During the crisis in East Germany and in the aftermath of the Berlin Wall's collapse in November 1989, Washington consistently supported German aspirations. American diplomacy also relentlessly endeavoured to reconcile the Federal government's initiatives with the concerns of Washington's other European allies. The US government supported West German views on the condition that a united Germany remained a loyal member of NATO and the European Communities. Secretary of State Baker made this clear as early as the end of November 1989. However, the British were diffident towards Bonn's plans and American acquiescence to them. London called for reasonable periods of transition and feared that the Americans were being too conciliatory towards the West Germans.

Between the end of 1989 and the beginning of 1990 Whitehall attempted to establish a European front in order to block unification. Thatcher sought the help of the French and the Soviets and contemplated subsequent engagement with other European states, such as Italy, the Netherlands and Poland. The end result of conflicting Anglo-American priorities was a deeply riven special relationship at a fundamental crossroads of the process of transition from the East–West division to a post-Cold War European order. Whitehall's open reservations about a united Germany not only weakened notions of an Anglo-American special relationship, they also contributed to creating a negative image of Britain's role in the eyes of German decision-makers and the public at large. London appeared to the Germans, at a time when they were feeling exposed and vulnerable, as well as exultant, an obstructive and negative partner. Thatcher's intransigence, raising doubts about a forty-year-old commitment to German self-determination, harmed Britain's image. It also overshadowed the contributions of FCO diplomats to the success of the Two plus Four negotiations and to a united Germany's integration within NATO.

At the core of the prime minister's misgivings had been two fundamental considerations. First, a preference for an arrangement with Russia, which was rooted in the United Kingdom's post-War policy towards Eastern Europe and had been augmented by her personal distrust of Germany and by the fear that unification might jeopardise Gorbachev's position in Moscow. This issue became paramount once Bonn began to pursue unification, prompting Thatcher to wear the mantle of Gorbachev's protector. Second, a concern that the Federal government, together with the US, might end up destabilising the delicate network of security arrangements that had preserved the European power balance since the early stages of the Cold War. London was not alone in expressing reservations about unification and other European capitals shared Whitehall's concerns. Nonetheless, unlike Thatcher, other European leaders refrained from making them public with the same intensity.

In the US, particularly in the NSC and among Bush's closest advisors, these concerns were viewed, with a few exceptions, as exaggerated. British admonishments about a new German threat to European stability were disregarded by the White House and by the State Department. Divergences on the role of NATO and the CSCE in the unification process and on a peace settlement were particularly telling of conflicting Anglo-American priorities. Thatcher's preference for settling the German question through the involvement of the thirty-five CSCE members also revealed a misunderstanding of the American approach to unification and vision for a reformed transatlantic relationship. The results of these misperceptions were an additional chapter in a long list of failed British attempts to play the role of mediator between Washington and Moscow, a weakening of the special relationship and also Britain's estrangement from the European project. While Britain never mattered to Germany in the way that the US and France did, London feared that a reunited Germany would dominate Europe and act as 'a destabilizing rather than a stabilizing force' on the continent. Although the White House and the State Department repeatedly endeavoured to assuage these concerns, American officials had no hesitation in downplaying the special relationship in order to grasp the historic opportunity of 1989 and accomplish transformation in Germany and Europe.

Solidarity between Washington and London remained rock hard only on the issue of a united Germany's relationship with NATO. Anglo-American diplomats worked shoulder to shoulder, particularly after the Kohl–Gorbachev meetings in Moscow and Stavropol in July 1990, to defend the alliance's interests and unity. Britain's support for the US on this issue played an important role in securing that no major concessions were made to the Kremlin. Outside Europe too the British remained Washington's most reliable ally. In 1991 Anglo-American cooperation to restore Kuwaiti independence in the Gulf in part compensated for the damage caused by divergences over the German question. However, Britain's resistance to plans for closer political integration in the European Communities dealt a remarkable blow to hopes that German unification might constitute the catalyst for effective political integration in Europe and for the construction of an equal partnership across the Atlantic. Its long-term effect on the European project would be felt in the following quarter of a century, culminating in a referendum that in June 2016 signalled Britain's intention to exit the EU.

Bibliography

Primary and archival sources

US National Archives and Record Administration, College Park/Washington (NARA)
Department of State (Record Group 59 – RG 59)
Dwight D. Eisenhower Library, Dwight D. Eisenhower Papers, Abilene, KS
George Bush Presidential Library, College Station, TX
Gerald R. Ford Presidential Library, Ann Arbor, MI
Jimmy Carter Library, Atlanta, GA
John Foster Dulles Papers, Mudd Library, Princeton University, Princeton, NJ
Lyndon B. Johnson, Presidential Library, Austin, TX
Nixon Presidential Material Project, Yorba Linda, CA
Ronald Reagan Library, Simi Valley, CA

The United Kingdom National Archives, Kew
CAB   Cabinet Office records
CAB   128 Minutes 1945–74
CAB   129 Postwar memoranda 1945–73
FCO   Foreign and Commonwealth Office records
FCO   33 Western Europe
FCO   7 America and Latin America, 1967–82
FCO   14 Aviation and Telecommunications, 1967–73
FO   Records created and inherited by the Foreign Office
FO   371 Foreign Office: Political Departments: General Correspondence
FO   1042 Spandau Prison, Berlin: future of prison and treatment of remaining inmates, Nazi war criminals Rudolf Hess, Albert Speer and Baldur von Schirach
FO   408/81 Further correspondence respecting Germany: part 10
FO   408/82 Further correspondence respecting Germany: part 11

PREM   Prime Minister's Office records
PREM   11 Prime Minister's Office: Correspondence and Papers
       1951–70
PREM   13 Prime Minister's Office: Correspondence and Papers
       1964–70
PREM   15 Prime Minister's Office: Correspondence and Papers
       1970–4
PREM   19 Prime Minister's Office: Correspondence and Papers
       1979–84

Federal Republic of Germany
Politisches Archiv des Auswärtigen Amtes, Berlin (PA AA)

Official documentary collections

Foreign Relations of the United States (FRUS)
1946, vol. 5, *The British of Commonwealth, Western and Central Europe*
1946, vol. 6, *Eastern Europe, the Soviet Union*
1948, vol. 2, *Germany and Austria*
1948, vol. 3, *Western Europe*
1949, vol. 3, *Council of Foreign Ministers; Germany and Austria*
1950, vol. 1, *National Security Affairs; Foreign Economic Policy*
1950, vol. 3, *Western Europe*
1950, vol. 4, *Central and Eastern Europe; The Soviet Union*
1952–54, vol. 2, *National Security Affairs*
1952–54, vol. 5, *Western European Security*
1952–54, vol. 7, *Germany and Austria*
1955–57, vol. 27, *Western Europe and Canada*
1958–60, vol. 8, *Berlin Crisis, 1958–1959*
1961–63, vol. 14, *Berlin Crisis, 1961–1962*
1969–76, vol. 40, *Germany and Berlin, 1969–1972*
1969–76, vol. E-15, Part 1, *Documents on Eastern Europe, 1973–1976*
1969–76 vol. E-15, Part 2, *Documents on Western Europe, 1973–1976*
1977–80, vol. 20, *Eastern Europe*

Public Papers of the Presidents of the US
John F. Kennedy, 1961 (Washington, DC: Government Printing Office, 1962).
Lyndon B. Johnson, 1966, Book II (Washington, DC: Government Printing Office, 1967).
Lyndon B. Johnson, 1968–69, Book I (Washington, DC: Government Printing Office, 1970).

Ronald Reagan, 1981 (Washington, DC: Government Printing Office, 1982).

Ronald Reagan, 1983, Book I (Washington, DC: Government Printing Office, 1984).

Ronald Reagan, 1983, Book II (Washington, DC: Government Printing Office, 1984).

Ronald Reagan, 1984, Book I (Washington, DC: Government Printing Office, 1985).

Ronald Reagan, 1984, Book II (Washington, DC: Government Printing Office: 1985).

Ronald Reagan, 1985, Book I (Washington, DC: Government Printing Office, 1988).

George Bush, 1989, Book I (Washington, DC: Government Printing Office, 1990).

George Bush, 1989, Book II (Washington, DC: Government Printing Office, 1990).

George Bush, 1990, Book I (Washington, DC: Government Printing Office, 1991).

George Bush, 1990, Book II (Washington, DC: Government Printing Office, 1991).

Other official US publications

Congressional Record Index, Government Printing Office.

The Department of State Bulletin, 1947–89.

Documents on Germany, 1944–1959: Background Documents on Germany, 1944–1959, and a Chronology of Political Developments Affecting Berlin, 1945–1956 (Washington, DC: Government Printing Office, 1959).

Foreign Relations Committee, *The Future of Europe*, 101st Cong., 2nd sess., 17 January 1990.

US Arms Control and Disarmament Agency (ACDA), *Documents on Disarmament, 1967* (Washington, DC: Government Printing Office, 1968).

US Department of State Dispatch 1990

US State Department, *Germany 1947–49: The Story in Documents* (Washington, DC: Government Printing Office, 1950).

Documents on British Policy Overseas (DBPO)

Series I

vol. I, *The Conference at Potsdam, July–August 1945* (London: Her Majesty's Stationery Office, 1984)

vol. V, *Germany and Western Europe, August–December 1945* (London: Her Majesty's Stationery Office, 1990).

vol. VI, *Eastern Europe, August 1945–April 1946* (London: Her Majesty's Stationery Office, 1991).

vol. X, *The Brussels and North Atlantic Treaties, 1947–1949* (London: Her Majesty's Stationery Office, 2014).

Series II

vol. I, *The Schuman Plan, the Council of Europe and Western European Integration, May 1950–December 1952* (London: Her Majesty's Stationery Office, 1986).

vol. II, *The London Conferences, January–June 1950* (London: Her Majesty's Stationery Office, 1987).

vol. III, *German Rearmament, September–December 1950* (London: Her Majesty's Stationery Office, 1989).

Series III

vol. I, *Britain and the Soviet Union, 1968–1972* (London: Her Majesty's Stationery Office, 1997).

vol. VI, *Berlin in the Cold War, 1948–1990* (London: Her Majesty's Stationery Office, 2009).

vol. VII, *German Unification, 1989–1990* (London: Her Majesty's Stationery Office, 2009).

vol. VIII, *The Invasion of Afghanistan and UK–Soviet Relations, 1979–1982* (London and New York: Whitehall Publishing and Routledge, 2012).

Other official UK publications

Cabinet Papers: Complete Classes from the CAB and PREM Series in the Public Record Office, series 3 (Marlborough: Adam Matthew Publications, 1996).

Foreign and Commonwealth Office, *Selected Documents on Germany and the Question of Berlin, 1944–1961* (London, 1961).

House of Commons Parliamentary Debates, 5th and 6th series Margaret Thatcher Archive, Churchill College, Cambridge, digital collection, <https://www.chu.cam.ac.uk/archives/collections/thatcher-papers/> (last accessed 1 October 2016)

Statement on Defence Estimates, 1966, Command Paper 2901 (1966), 'The Defence Review'.

Federal Republic of Germany

Akten zur Auswärtigen Politik der Bundesrepublik Deutschland, 1949–53 and 1962–84.

Bundesministerium für gesamtdeutsche Fragen (ed.), *Texte zur Deutschlandpolitik*, 1967–91 (Bonn: Bundesministerium für innerdeutsche Beziehungen).

Bundesministerium für innerdeutsche Beziehungen (ed.), *Innerdeutsche Beziehungen. Die Entwicklung der Beziehungen zwischen der Bundesrepublik Deutschland und der Deutschen Demokratischen Republik 1980–1986* (Bonn: Bundesministerium für innerdeutsche Beziehungen, 1986).

Der Bundesminster des Auswärtigen informiert. *Mitteilung für die Presse.*

Deutscher Bundestag, Dokumente & Recherche, <http://www.bundestag.de/dokumente> (last accessed 29 September 2016).

Federal Law Gazette.

Press and Information Office of the Federal Government (ed.), *The Unification of Germany in 1990* (Bonn: Press and Information Office of the Federal Government, 1991).

Presse- und Informationsamt der Bundesregierung (ed.), *Bulletin des Presse- und Informationsamtes der Bundesregierung* (Bonn: Deutscher Bundesverlag).

Presse- und Informationsamt der Bundesregierung (ed.), *Bundeskanzler Helmut Kohl: Reden und Erklärungen zur Deutschlandpolitik* (Bonn: Presse- und Informationsamt der Bundesregierung, 1990).

Miscellaneous

Peter G. Boyle, *The Churchill–Eisenhower Correspondence, 1953–1955* (Chapel Hill, NC and London: University of North Carolina Press, 1990).

William Burr (ed.), *The Berlin Crisis 1958–1962*, National Security Archive Electronic Briefing Book No. 354, The National Security Archive, <http://nsarchive.gwu.edu/NSAEBB/NSAEBB354> (last accessed 28 September 2016).

Anatoly Chernyaev (compiler), *Mikhail Gorbachev i Germansky Vopros. Sbornik dokumentov 1986–1991* [Mikhail Gorbachev and the German Question 1986–1991. Collected Documents 1986–1991] (Moscow: Ves' Mir, 1996).

Anatoly Sergeevich Chernyaev, Vadim Medvedev and Georgy Shakhnazarov, *V Politburo Tsk KPSS* (Moscow: Alfaprint, 2006).

Frank Elbe and Richard E. Kiessler, *Ein runder Tisch mit scharfen Ecken: Der diplomatische Weg zur deutschen Einheit* (Baden-Baden: Nomos, 1993).

Lawrence Freedman, *Europe Transformed: Documents on the End of the Cold War – Key Treaties, Agreements, Statements, and Speeches* (New York: St. Martin's Press, 1990).

Volker Gransow and Konrad Jarausch (eds), *Die Deutsche Vereinigung: Dokumente zu Bürgerbewegung, Annäherung und Beitritt* [German Reunification: Documents on the Citizens' Movement, Rapprochement, and Accession] (Cologne: Wissenschaft und Politik, 1991).

Richard T. Gray and Sabine Wilke (eds), *German Unification and Its Discontents: Documents from the Peaceful Revolution* (Seattle: University of Washington Press, 1996).

Axel Heck, *Macht als soziale Praxis. Die Herausbildung des transatlantischen Machtverhältnisses im Krisenjahr 1989* (Wiesbaden: Springer, 2015).

Hans-Hermann Hertle, Rainer Weinert and Manfred Wilke, *Der Staatsbesuch. Honecker in Bonn: Dokumente zur deutsch-deutschen Konstellation des Jahres 1987* (Berlin: Freien Universität Berlin, 1991).

Christopher Hill and Karen Elizabeth Smith (eds), *European Foreign Policy: Key Documents* (London: Routledge, 2000).

Konrad H. Jarausch and Volker Gransow (eds), *Uniting Germany: Documents and Debates, 1944–1993* (New York and Oxford: Berghahn Books, 1994).

Nate Jones, Tom Blanton and Lauren Harper (eds), National Security Archive Electronic Briefing Book No. 533, The National Security Archive, <http://nsarchive.gwu.edu/nukevault/ebb533-The-Able-Archer-War-Scare-Declassified-PFIAB-Report-Released/> (last accessed 28 September 2016).

Burton Ira Kaufman, *Presidential Profiles: The Carter Years* (New York: Facts on File, 2006).

Hanns Jürgen Küsters and Daniel Hofmann (eds), *Dokumente zur Deutschlandpolitik, Deutsche Einheit. Sonderedition aus den Akten des Bundeskanzleramtes 1989/90* (Munich: Oldenbourg, 1998).

Vojtech Mastny, *The Helsinki Process and the Reintegration of Europe: Analysis and Documentation, 1986–1990* (New York: New York University Press, 2008).

Detlef Nakath and Gerd-Rüdiger Stephan (eds), *Die Häber-Protokolle. Schlaglichter der SED-Westpolitik 1973–1985* (Berlin: Dietz, 1999).

Gerhard Peters and John T. Woolley, *The American Presidency Project*, <http://www.presidency.ucsb.edu/ws/?pid=25964> (last accessed 29 September 2016).

Heinrich Potthoff, *Bonn und Ost-Berlin 1969–1982: Dialog auf höchster Ebene und vertrauliche Kanäle, Darstellung und Dokumente* (Bonn: Dietz, 1997).

Radio Free Europe Research, Corporate and Broadcast Archive, <http://www.rferl.org/info/archive/1854.html> (last accessed 29 September 2016).

Daniel Rotfeld and Walther Stützle (eds), *Germany and Europe in Transition* (New York: Oxford University Press, 1991).

Trevor C. Salmon and Sir William Nicoll (eds), *Building European Union: A Documentary History and Analysis* (Manchester: Manchester University Press, 1997).

Carl Christoph Schweitzer, Detlev Karsten, Robert Spencer, R. Taylor

Cole and Donald P. Kommers (eds), *Politics and Government in Germany, 1944–1994: Basic Documents* (Providence, RI and Oxford: Berghahn Books, 1995).

Svetlana Savranskaya and Thomas Blanton (eds), National Security Archive Electronic Briefing Book No. 320, *The Washington/Camp David Summit 1990: From the Secret Soviet, American and German Files*.

Simon C. Smith (ed.), *The Wilson–Johnson Correspondence, 1964–69* (Farnham: Ashgate, 2015).

North Atlantic Treaty Organization

Declaration of the Heads of State and Government Participating in the Meeting of the North Atlantic Council, Brussels 29–30 May 1989, <http://www.nato.int/docu/comm/49-95/c890530a.htm> (last accessed 30 September 2016).

North Atlantic Council, Final Communiqué, Turnberry, 7–8 June 1990, available at <http://www.nato.int/docu/comm/49-95/c900608a.htm> (last accessed 27 September 2016).

North Atlantic Council, Final Communiqué, Washington, DC, 29–31 May 1984, <http://www.nato.int/docu/comm/49-95/c840531a.htm> (last accessed 29 September 2016).

Diaries and Memoirs

Dean Acheson, *Present at the Creation: My Years in the State Department* (New York: W. W. Norton, 1969).

Konrad Adenauer, *Memoirs 1945–53* (London: Weidenfeld & Nicholson, 1966).

Jacques Attali, *Verbatim: Tome 3, Chronique des années 1988–1991* (Paris: Fayard, 1995).

James A. Baker III, *The Politics of Diplomacy: Revolution, War and Peace* (New York: G. P. Putnam's Sons, 1995).

Michael Beschloss and Strobe Talbott, *At the Highest Levels* (Boston, MA: Little, Brown, 1993).

Herbert Blankenhorn, *Verständnis und Verständigung: Blätter eines Politischen Tagebuchs 1949 bis 1979* (Frankfurt/Main: Propyläen, 1980).

Rodric Braithwaite, *Across the Moscow River: The World Turned Upside Down* (New Haven, CT and London: Yale University Press, 2002).

Zbigniew Brzezinski, *Power and Principle: Memoirs of the National Security Adviser 1977–1981* (New York: Farrar, Straus and Giroux, 1985).

G. H. W. Bush, *All the Best, George Bush: My Life in Letters and Other Writings* (New York: Scribner, 1999).

George H. W. Bush and Brent Scowcroft, *A World Transformed* (New York: Alfred A. Knopf, 1998).

Jimmy Carter, *Keeping Faith: Memoirs of a President* (New York: Bantam Books, 1983).

Alan Clark, *Diaries* (London: Weidenfeld and Nicolson, 1993).

Percy Cradock, *In Pursuit of British Interests: Reflections on British Foreign Policy under Margaret Thatcher and John Major* (London: John Murray, 1997).

Charles de Gaulle, *Discours et messages*, 5 vols (Paris: Plon, 1970), vol. 3.

Valentin Falin, *Politische Erinnerungen* (Munich: Droemer Knaur, 1993).

Gerald R. Ford, *A Time to Heal: The Autobiography of Gerald R. Ford* (New York: Harper & Row, 1979).

Hans-Dietrich Genscher, *Erinnerungen* (Berlin: Siedler, 1995).

Mikhail Sergeevich Gorbachev, *Memoirs* (New York: Doubleday, 1995).

Mikhail Sergeevich Gorbachev, *Perestroika: New Thinking in Our Country and the World* (New York: Harper & Row, 1987).

Michael Heseltine, *The Challenge of Europe: Can Britain Win?* (London: Weidenfeld and Nicolson, 1989).

Geoffrey Howe, *Europe Tomorrow: Five Speeches* (London: HMSO, 1985).

Douglas Hurd, *Memoirs* (London: Abacus, 2004).

Douglas Hurd, *The Search for Peace: A Century of Peace Diplomacy* (London: Little, Brown, 1997).

Robert L. Hutchings, *American Diplomacy and the End of the Cold War: An Insider's Account of U.S. Policy in Europe, 1989–1992* (Baltimore, MD: Johns Hopkins University Press, 1997).

Lyndon Baines Johnson, *The Vantage Point: Perspectives of the Presidency, 1963–1969* (New York: Holt, Rinehart and Winston, 1971).

Henry Kissinger, *White House Years* (Boston, MA: Little, Brown, 1979).

Helmut Kohl, *Erinnerungen 1982–1990* (Munich: Droemer, 2005).

Nigel Lawson, *The View from No. 11: Memoirs of a Tory Radical* (London: Corgi, 1993).

George C. McGhee, *On the Frontline in the Cold War: An Ambassador Reports* (Westport, CT: Praeger, 1997).

Harold Macmillan, *Pointing the Way, 1959–1961* (London: Harper & Row, 1972).

Wilfried Martens, *Europe: I Struggle, I Overcome* (Dordrecht: Springer, 2009).

François Mitterrand, *De l'Allemagne. De la France* (Paris: Odile Jacob, 1996).

Helmut Schmidt, *Menschen und Mächte* (Berlin: Siedler, 1987).

Harold Stassen and Marshall Houts, *Eisenhower: Turning the World Towards Peace* (St. Paul, MN: Merrill/Magnus Publishing, 1990).

Horst Teltschik, *329 Tage. Innenansichten der Einigung* (Berlin: Siedler, 1991).

Margaret Thatcher, *Downing Street Years* (London: Harper Perennial, 1993).

Margaret Thatcher, *The Path to Power* (London: HarperCollins, 1995).

Felix von Eckardt, *Ein unordentliches Leben* (Düsseldorf: Econ, 1967).

Harold Wilson, *The Labour Government 1964–1970: A Personal Record* (London: Weidenfeld & Nicolson and Michael Joseph, 1971).

Secondary sources

Published sources

Donald Abenheim, *Reforging the Iron Cross: The Search for Tradition in the West German Armed Forces* (Princeton, NJ: Princeton University Press, 1988).

Jefferson Adams, *Strategic Intelligence in the Cold War and Beyond* (Abingdon and New York: Routledge, 2015).

Hannes Adomeit, 'East Germany: NATO's First Eastward Enlargement', in Anton Bebler (ed.), *NATO at 60: The Post-Cold War Enlargement and the Alliance's Future* (Fairfax, VA: IOS Press, 2010), pp. 11–22.

Hannes Adomeit, 'Gorbachev, German Unification and the Collapse of Empire', *Post-Soviet Affairs*, vol. 10, no. 3, 1994, pp. 197–230.

Hannes Adomeit, 'Gorbachev's Consent to United Germany's Membership of NATO', in Frédéric Bozo, Marie-Pierre Rey, N. Piers Ludlow and Leopoldo Nuti (eds), *Europe and the End of the Cold War: A Reappraisal* (Abingdon and New York: Routledge, 2008), pp. 107–18.

Hannes Adomeit, *Imperial Overstretch: Germany in Soviet Policy from Stalin to Gorbachev* (Baden-Baden: Nomos, 1998).

Jonathan Aitken, *Margaret Thatcher: Power and Personality* (London and New York: Bloomsbury, 2013).

Richard Aldous, *Reagan and Thatcher: The Difficult Relationship* (New York: W. W. Norton, 2012).

Debra J. Allen, *The Oder–Neisse Line: The United States, Poland, and Germany in the Cold War* (Westport, CT and London: Praeger, 2003).

Stephen E. Ambrose, *Nixon: The Triumph of a Politician, 1962–1972* (New York: Simon and Schuster, 1989).

Pyeongeok An, 'Obstructive All the Way? British Policy towards

German Unification 1989–90', *German Politics*, vol. 15, no. 1, 2006, pp. 111–21.

Reinhold Andert and Wolfgang Herzberg, *Der Sturz: Honecker im Kreuzverhör* (Berlin: Aufbau, 1991).

Miriam Aziz, 'Sovereignty Über Alles: (Re)Configuring the German Legal Order', in Neil Walker (ed.), *Sovereignty in Transition* (Oxford: Hart Publishing, 2003), pp. 279–304.

Thomas F. Banchoff, *The German Problem Transformed: Institutions, Politics, and Foreign Policy, 1945–1995* (Ann Arbor, MI: University of Michigan Press, 1999).

Oliver Bange, 'Der KSZE-Prozess und die sicherheitspolitische Dynamik des Ost-West-Konflikts 1970–1990', in Oliver Bange and Bernd Lemke (eds), *Wege zur Wiedervereinigung. Die beiden deutschen Staaten in ihren Bündnissen 1970 bis 1990* (Munich: Oldenbourg, 2013), pp. 87–104.

Oliver Bange, *The EEC Crisis of 1963: Kennedy, Macmillan, de Gaulle and Adenauer in Conflict* (London: Macmillan, 2000).

Oliver Bange, 'The German Problem and Security in Europe: Hindrance or Catalyst on the Path to 1989/90?', in Mark Kramer and Vit Smetana (eds), *Imposing, Maintaining, and Tearing Open the Iron Curtain: The Cold War and East-Central Europe, 1945–1989* (Lanham, MD: Lexington Books, 2014), pp. 197–210.

Oliver Bange, '"The Greatest Happiness of the Greatest Number . . .": The FRG and the GDR and the Belgrade CSCE Conference (1977–78)', in Vladimir Bilandžic, Dittmar Dahlmann and Milan Kosanovic (eds), *From Helsinki to Belgrade: The First CSCE Follow-up Meeting and the Crisis of Détente* (Göttingen: Vandenhoeck & Ruprecht and Bonn: Bonn University Press, 2012), pp. 225–54.

Oliver Bange '"Keeping Détente Alive": Inner-German Relations under Helmut Schmidt and Erich Honecker, 1974–1982', in Leopoldo Nuti (ed.), *The Crisis of Détente in Europe: From Helsinki to Gorbachev 1975–1985* (London: Routledge, 2009), pp. 230–43.

Robert Barnes, *The US, the UN and the Korean War: Communism in the Far East and the American Struggle for Hegemony in America's Cold War* (London: I. B. Tauris, 2014).

Richard Barnet, *The Alliance: America, Europe, Japan, Makers of the Postwar World* (New York: Simon & Schuster, 1983).

Christopher John Bartlett, *'The Special Relationship': A Political History of Anglo-American Relations since 1945* (Harlow: Longman, 1992).

Michael J. Baun, 'The Maastricht Treaty as High Politics: Germany, France and European Integration', *Political Science Quarterly*, vol. 110, no. 4, 1995, pp. 605–24.

John Baylis, 'Britain and the Dunkirk Treaty: The Origins of NATO', *Journal of Strategic Studies*, vol. 5, no. 2, 1982, pp. 236–47.

John Baylis, *Anglo-American Defence Relations 1939–1984* (London: Macmillan, 1984).

John Baylis, 'Britain, the Brussels Pact and the Continental Commitment', *International Affairs*, vol. 60, 1984, pp. 615–30.

John Baylis, *The Diplomacy of Pragmatism: Britain and the Formation of NATO, 1942–1949* (Basingstoke: Macmillan, 1993).

John Baylis (ed.), *Anglo-American Relations since 1939: The Enduring Alliance* (Manchester and New York: Manchester University Press, 1997).

John Baylis, 'The 1958 Anglo-American Mutual Defence Agreement: The Search for Nuclear Interdependence', *Journal of Strategic Studies*, vol. 31, no. 3, 2008, pp. 425–66.

Robert J. Beck, *The Grenada Invasion: Politics, Law, and Foreign Policy Decisionmaking* (Boulder, CO: Westview Press, 1993).

Robert Beisner, *Dean Acheson: A Life in the Cold War* (New York: Oxford University Press, 2006).

Stefan Berger and Norman LaPorte, 'Ein zweiter Kalter Krieg? Die Beziehungen zwischen der DDR und Großbritannien, 1979–1989', in Peter Barker, Marc-Dietrich Ohse and Dennis Tate (eds), *Views from Abroad: Die DDR aus britischer Perspektive* (Bielefeld: WBV, W. Bertelsmann, 2007), pp. 163–73.

Stefan Berger and Norman LaPorte, *Friendly Enemies: Britain and the GDR, 1949–1990* (Oxford: Berghahn Books, 2010).

Henrik Bering, *Helmut Kohl: The Man Who Reunited Germany, Rebuilt Europe, and Thwarted the Soviet Empire* (Washington, DC: Regnery, 1999).

Michael R. Beschloss, *Mayday: Eisenhower, Khrushchev, and the U-2 Affair* (New York: Harper & Row, 1986).

Adolf M. Birke, *Britain and Germany: Historical Patterns of a Relationship* (London: German Historical Institute, 1987).

Günter Bischof, '"No Action": The Johnson Administration and the Warsaw Pact Invasion of Czechoslovakia in August 1968', in Günter Bischof, Stefan Karner and Peter Ruggenthaler, *The Prague Spring and the Warsaw Pact Invasion of Czechoslovakia in 1968* (New York: Lexington, 2010), pp. 215–36.

Coit D. Blacker, *Hostage to Revolution: Gorbachev and Soviet Security Policy, 1985–1991* (New York: Council on Foreign Relations, 1993).

Eugenie M. Blang, *Allies at Odds: America, Europe, and Vietnam, 1961–1968* (Lanham, MD: Rowman & Littlefield, 2011).

Thomas Blanton, 'U.S. Policy and the Revolutions of 1989', in Svetlana Savranskaya, Thomas Blanton and Vlad Zubok (eds), *Masterpieces of History: The Soviet Peaceful Withdrawal from Eastern Europe, 1989* (Budapest: Central European University Press, 2010), pp. 49–98.

Michael M. Boll, 'Superpower Diplomacy and German Unification: The Insiders' Views', *Parameters*, Winter 1996–7, pp. 109–21.

Christopher Booker and Richard North, *Great Deception: The Secret History of the European Union* (London: Continuum, 2003).

Heinrich Bortfeldt, *Washington, Bonn, Berlin: die USA und die deutsche Einheit* (Bonn: Bouvier, 1993).

Timothy J. Botti, *Ace in the Hole: Why the United States Did Not Use Nuclear Weapons in the Cold War, 1945 to 1965* (Westport, CT: Greenwood, 1996).

Robert R. Bowie and Richard H. Immerman, *Waging Peace: How Eisenhower Shaped an Enduring Cold War Strategy* (New York and Oxford: Oxford University Press, 1998).

Robert Boyce, 'In Search of the Anglo-American Special Relationship in the Economic and Financial Spheres', in Antoine Capet and Aïssatou Sy-Wonyu (eds), *The 'Special Relationship': La «relation spéciale» entre le Royaume-Uni et les Etats-Unis* (Rouen: Université de Rouen, 2003), pp. 67–88.

Frédéric Bozo, *Two Strategies for Europe: De Gaulle, the United States, and the Atlantic Alliance* (Lanham, MD: Rowman & Littlefield, 2001).

Frédéric Bozo, 'Before the Wall: French Diplomacy and the Last Decade of the Cold War, 1979–1989', in Olav Njølstad (ed.), *The Last Decade of the Cold War: From Conflict Escalation to Conflict Transformation* (London: Frank Cass, 2004), pp. 288–316.

Frédéric Bozo, 'Mitterrand's France, the End of the Cold War, and German Unification: A Reappraisal', *Cold War History*, vol. 7, no. 4, 2007, pp. 455–78.

Frédéric Bozo, 'France, German Unification and European Integration', in Frédéric Bozo, Marie-Pierre Rey, N. Piers Ludlow and Leopoldo Nuti (eds), *Europe and the End of the Cold War: A Reappraisal* (Abingdon and New York: Routledge, 2008), pp. 148–60.

Frédéric Bozo, *Mitterrand, the End of the Cold War, and German Unification* (New York: Berghahn Books, 2009).

Frédéric Bozo, 'From "Yalta" to Maastricht: Mitterrand's France and German Unification', in Frédéric Bozo, Andreas Rödder and Mary Elise Sarotte (eds), *German Reunification: A Multinational History* (London and New York: Routledge, 2017), pp. 111–32.

Frédéric Bozo, Andreas Rödder and Mary Elise Sarotte (eds), *German Reunification: A Multinational History* (London and New York: Routledge, 2017).

John W. Braasch, 'Anthony Eden's (Lord Avon) Biliary Tract Saga', *Annals of Surgery*, vol. 238, no. 5, November 2003, pp. 772–5.

Steven J. Brady, *Eisenhower and Adenauer: Alliance Maintenance under Pressure, 1953–1960* (Lanham, MD: Lexington Books, 2010).

Steven J. Brady, 'The U.S. Congress and German–American Relations', in Detlef Junker, Philipp Gassert, Wilfried Mausbach and David B. Morris (eds), *The United States and Germany in the Era of the Cold War, 1945–1990: A Handbook. Vol. 1, 1945–1968* (Washington, DC: Cambridge University Press, 2004), pp. 133–40.

Rodric Braithwaite, 'Gorbachev and Thatcher', *Journal of European Integration History*, vol. 16, no. 1, 2010, pp. 31–44.

Willy Brandt, 'Germany's "Westpolitik"', *Foreign Affairs*, vol. 50, no. 3, April 1972, pp. 416–26.

Alfredo Breccia, *L'Italia e la difesa dell'Europa. Alle origini del Piano Pleven* (Rome: I. S. E., 1984).

Steve Breyman, *Why Movements Matter: The West German Peace Movement and U.S. Arms Control Policy* (Albany: State University of New York Press, 2001).

Margaret Brodniewicz-Stawicki, *For Your Freedom and Ours: The Polish Armed Forces in the Second World War* (St. Catherines, ONT: Vanwell Publishing, 1999).

Archie Brown, 'The Change to Engagement in Britain's Cold War Policy: The Origins of the Thatcher–Gorbachev Relationship', *Journal of Cold War Studies*, vol. 10, no. 3, 2008, pp. 3–47.

Archie Brown, 'Margaret Thatcher and Perceptions of Change in the Soviet Union', *Journal of European Integration History*, vol. 16, no. 1, 2010, pp. 17–30.

Archie Brown, 'Preface: The Chequers Conference plus Ten', *Diplomacy and Statecraft*, vol. 5, no. 3, November 1994, pp. 421–510.

Martin D. Brown, 'A Very British Vision of Détente: The United Kingdom's Foreign Policy during the Helsinki Process', in Frédéric Bozo, Marie-Pierre Rey, N. Piers Ludlow and Bernd Rother (eds), *Visions of the End of the Cold War in Europe, 1945–1990* (New York and Oxford: Berghahn Books, 2012), pp. 121–33.

Suzanne Brown-Fleming, 'Personalities and Politics: The American Ambassadors to the Federal Republic', in Detlef Junker, Philipp Gassert, Wilfried Mausbach and David B. Morris (eds), *The United States and Germany in the Era of the Cold War, 1945–1990: A Handbook. Vol. 1, 1945–1968* (Washington, DC: Cambridge University Press, 2004), pp. 149–56.

Friedemann Buettner and Martin Landgraf, 'The European Community's Middle Eastern Policy: The New Order of Europe and the Gulf Crisis', in Tareq Y. Ismael and Jacqueline S. Ismael (eds), *The Gulf War and the New World Order: International Relations of the Middle East* (Gainesville: Florida University Press, 1994), pp. 77–115.

Julian Bullard, 'Great Britain and German Unification', in Jeremy Noakes, Peter Wende and Jonathan Wright (eds), *Britain and Germany in Europe, 1949–1990* (Oxford and New York: Oxford University Press, 2002), pp. 219–30.

Mark Burdman, '"Ridley Affair" Is Fiasco for British Establishment', *Executive Intelligence Review*, vol. 17, no. 30, July 1990, pp. 38–40.

Kathleen Burk, 'The Americans, the Germans, and the British: The 1976 IMF Crisis', *Twentieth Century British History*, vol. 5, no. 3, 1994, pp. 351–699.

Kathleen Burk and Alec Cairncross, *Good-bye Great Britain: The 1976 IMF Crisis* (New Haven, CT: Yale University Press, 1992).

Antoine Capet and Aïssatou Sy-Wonyu (eds), *The 'Special Relationship': La «relation spéciale» entre le Royaume-Uni et les Etats-Unis* (Rouen: Université de Rouen, 2003).

David Carlton, *Churchill and the Soviet Union* (Manchester: Manchester University Press, 2000).

Charles William Carter, 'The Evolution of US Policy toward West German–Soviet Trade Relations 1969–89', *The International History Review*, vol. 34, no. 2, 2012, pp. 221–44.

Jean Chabaud, 'The Prospects for Franco-British Co-operation', in Yves Boyer and John Roper (eds), *Franco-British Defence Co-operation: A New Entente Cordiale?* (Abingdon: Routledge, 1989), pp. 155–70.

Jeffrey L. Chidester, 'From Containment to Liberation: U.S. Strategy toward Eastern Europe', in Jeffrey L. Chidester and Paul Kengor (eds), *Reagan's Legacy in a World Transformed* (Cambridge, MA: Harvard University Press, 2015), pp. 53–75.

David Childs, *The Fall of the GDR* (Harlow: Pearson Longman, 2001).

Derek H. Chollet and James M. Goldgeier, 'Once Burned, Twice Shy? The Pause of 1989', in William C. Wohlforth (ed.), *Cold War Endgame: Oral History, Analysis, Debates* (University Park: Pennsylvania State Press, 2003), pp. 141–73.

Clay Clemens, *Reluctant Realists: The Christian Democrats and West German Ostpolitik* (Durham, NC: Duke University Press, 1989).

Michael A. Cohen, *American Maelstrom: The 1968 Election and the Politics of Division* (Oxford and New York: Oxford University Press, 2016).

Christopher Coker, 'Britain and the New World Order: The Special Relationship in the 1990s', *International Affairs*, vol. 68, no. 3, July 1992, pp. 407–21.

Alistair Cole, *François Mitterrand: A Study in Political Leadership* (Abingdon and New York: Routledge, 1997).

Jonathan Colman, *The Foreign Policy of Lyndon B. Johnson: The United States and the World, 1963–1969* (Edinburgh: Edinburgh University Press, 2010).

Jonathan Colman, *'A Special Relationship'? Harold Wilson, Lyndon B. Johnson and Anglo-American Relations 'At the Summit', 1964–68* (Manchester: Manchester University Press, 2004).

Frank Costigliola, 'An "Arm around the Shoulder": The United States, NATO and German Reunification, 1989–90', *Contemporary European History*, vol. 3, no. 1, March 1994, pp. 87–110.

Michael Cox and Steven Hurst, '"His Finest Hour"?: George Bush and the Diplomacy of German Unification', *Diplomacy and Statecraft*, vol. 13, no. 2, 2002, pp. 123–50.

Michael Creswell, *A Question of Balance: How France and the United States Created Cold War Europe* (Cambridge, MA: Harvard University Press, 2006).

Michael Creswell and Marc Trachtenberg, 'France and the German Question, 1945–55', *Journal of Cold War Studies*, vol. 5, no. 3, 2003, pp. 5–28.

Stefan Creuzberger, *Kampf für die Einheit: Das gesamtdeutsche Ministerium und die politische Kultur des Kalten Krieges 1949–1969* (Düsseldorf: Droste, 2008).

James E. Cronin, *Global Rules: America, Britain and a Disordered World* (New Haven, CT: Yale University Press, 2014).

Nicholas J. Crowson, *Britain and Europe: A Political History since 1918* (Abingdon and New York: Routledge, 2011).

Richard Davis, 'The Falkland Islands and the Special Relationship', in Carine Berbéri and Monia O'Brien Castro (eds), *30 Years After: Issues and Representations of the Falklands War* (Farnham: Ashgate, 2015), pp. 71–94.

Massimo de Leonardis, 'Defense or Liberation of Europe: The Strategies of the West against a Soviet Attack (1947–1950)', in Ennio di Nolfo (ed.), *The Atlantic Pact Forty Years Later: A Historical Reappraisal* (Berlin and New York: De Gruyter, 1991), pp. 176–206.

Anne Deighton, 'British Responses to the Polish Events, June–November 1956', in Jan Rowiński and Tytus Jaskułowski (eds), *The Polish October 1956 in World Politics* (Warsaw: PISM, 2007), pp. 239–62.

Anne Deighton, '"A Different 1956": British Responses to the Polish Events, June–November 1956', *Cold War History*, vol. 6, no. 4, 2006, pp. 455–75.

Anne Deighton, 'Germany and East-Central Europe, 1945–1990: The View from London', in Mark Kramer and Vit Smetana (eds), *Imposing, Maintaining, and Tearing Open the Iron Curtain: The Cold War and East-Central Europe, 1945–1989* (Lanham, MD: Lexington Books, 2014), pp. 211–26.

Anne Deighton, 'The Last Piece of the Jigsaw: Britain and the Creation of the Western European Union, 1954', *Contemporary European History*, no. 7, 1998, pp. 181–96.

Anne Deighton, 'Ostpolitik or Westpolitik? British Foreign Policy, 1968–75', *International Affairs*, vol. 74, no. 4, 1998, pp. 893–901.

Anne Deighton, 'Three Ministers and the World They Made: Acheson, Bevin and Schuman, and the North Atlantic Treaty, March–April 1949', in Jussi Hanhimäki, Georges-Henri Soutou and Basil Germond (eds), *The Routledge Handbook of Transatlantic Security* (Abingdon and New York: Routledge, 2010), pp. 3–16.

Mario del Pero, *The Eccentric Realist: Henry Kissinger and the Shaping of American Foreign Policy* (Ithaca, NY: Cornell University Press, 2006).

Kate Delaney, 'The Many Meanings of D-Day', *European Journal of American Studies*, vol. 7, no. 2, 2012, <http://ejas.revues.org/9544> (last accessed 29 September 2016).

Ksenia Demidova, 'The Deal of the Century: The Reagan Administration and the Soviet Pipeline', in Kiran Klaus Patel and Kenneth Weisbrode (eds), *European Integration and the Atlantic Community in the 1980s* (New York: Cambridge University Press, 2013), pp. 59–82.

Benedikt Dettling and Michael Geske, 'Helmut Kohl: Krise and Erneuerung', in Karl-Rudolf Korte (ed.), *Das Wort hat der Herr Bundeskanzler. Eine Analyse der großen Regierungserklärungen von Adenauer bis Schröder* (Wiesbaden: Westdeutscher, 2002), pp. 217–45.

John Dietrich, *The Morgenthau Plan: Soviet Influence on American Postwar Policy* (New York: Algora Publishing, 2002).

David Dilks (ed.), *The Diaries of Sir Alec Cadogan, 1938–45* (New York: G. P. Putnam and Sons, 1971).

David Dimbleby and David Reynolds, *An Ocean Apart: The Relationship between Britain and America in the 20th Century* (London and New York: Random House, 1988).

Herbert Dittgen, 'Strategy, Arms Control and Reassurance: Dilemmas in German–American Security Relations', in David Dewitt and Hans Rattinger (eds), *East–West Arms Control: Challenges for the Western Alliance* (London and New York: Routledge, 1992), pp. 3–32.

Alan P. Dobson, *Anglo-American Relations in the Twentieth Century: Of Friendship, Conflict, and the Rise and Decline of Superpowers* (New York: Routledge, 1995).

Alan P. Dobson, *US Economic Statecraft for Survival, 1933–1991: Of Sanctions, Embargoes and Economic Warfare* (London and New York: Routledge, 2002).

Alan P. Dobson and Steve Marsh (eds), *Anglo-American Relations: Contemporary Perspectives* (London and New York: Routledge, 2013).

Alan P. Dobson and Steve Marsh, 'Anglo-American Relations: End of a Special Relationship?', *The International History Review*, vol. 36, no. 4, 2014, pp. 673–97.

Alan P. Dobson and Steve Marsh, *US Foreign Policy Since 1945* (London: Routledge, 2007).

Saki Dockrill, *Britain's Policy for West German Rearmament 1950–1955* (New York: Cambridge University Press, 1991).

Klaus Dodds, *Pink Ice: Britain and the South Atlantic Empire* (New York: I. B. Tauris, 2002).

Marion Gräfin Dönhoff, 'Bonn and Washington: The Strained Relationship', *Foreign Affairs*, vol. 57, no. 5, Summer 1979, pp. 1052–64.

Frank R. Douglas, *The United States, NATO, and a New Multilateral Relationship* (Westport, CT: Praeger, 2008).

Theodore Draper, 'The Western Misalliance', in Walter Laqueur and Robert Edwards Hunter (eds), *European Peace Movements and the Future of the Western Alliance* (New Brunswick, NJ: Transaction, 1985), pp. 56–111.

Sidney David Drell and George Pratt Shultz (eds), *Implications of the Reykjavik Summit on its Twentieth Anniversary: Conference Report* (Stanford, CA: Hoover Institution Press, 2007).

John S. Duffield, *Power Rules: The Evolution of NATO's Conventional Force Posture* (Stanford, CA: Stanford University Press, 1995).

Bertrand Dufourcq, '2+4 ou la négociation atypique', *Politique étrangère*, vol. 65, no. 2, Summer 2000, pp. 467–84.

Simon Duke, *United States Military Forces and Installations in Europe* (Oxford and New York: Oxford University Press, 1989).

John Dumbrell, 'Personal Diplomacy: Relations between Prime Ministers and Presidents', in Alan P. Dobson and Steve Marsh (eds), *Anglo-American Relations: Contemporary Perspectives* (Routledge: London, 2013), pp. 82–104.

John Dumbrell, *President Lyndon Johnson and Soviet Communism* (Manchester and New York: Manchester University Press, 2004).

John Dumbrell, *Rethinking the Vietnam War* (London and New York: Palgrave Macmillan, 2012).

John Dumbrell and Sylvia Ellis, 'British Involvement in Vietnam Peace Initiatives, 1966–1967: Marigolds, Sunflowers and "Kosygin Week"', *Diplomatic History*, vol. 27, no. 1, 2003, pp. 113–49.

John P. D. Dunbabin, *The Cold War: The Great Powers and Their Allies* (London: Pearson Education, 2008).

Jean-Baptiste Duroselle, *France and the United States: From the Beginnings to the Present* (Chicago: University of Chicago Press, 1978).

Richard C. Eichenberg, 'Dual Track and Double Trouble: The Two-Level Politics of INF', in Peter B. Evans, Harold K. Jacobson and Robert D. Putnam (eds), *Double-Edged Diplomacy: International Bargaining and Domestic Politics* (Berkeley: University of California Press, 1993), pp. 45–76.

Frank Elbe, 'The Diplomatic Path to German Unity', *Bulletin of the German Historical Institute*, vol. 46, Spring 2010, pp. 33–44.

Matthew Elderfield, 'Rebuilding the Special Relationship: The 1957 Bermuda Talks', *Cambridge Review of International Affairs*, vol. 3, no. 1, 1989, pp. 14–24.

Thomas Stearns Elliot, 'The Dry Salvages', *Four Quartets*, Canto III (San Diego, CA: Harcourt, 1943).

Sylvia Ellis, *Britain, America, and the Vietnam War* (Westport, CT: Praeger, 2004).

Sylvia Ellis, *Historical Dictionary of Anglo-American Relations* (Lanham, MD: Scarecrow Press, 2009).

James Ellison, 'Dealing with de Gaulle: Anglo-American Relations, NATO and the Second Application', in Oliver J. Daddow (ed.), *Harold Wilson and European Integration: Britain's Second Application to Join the EEC* (London: Frank Cass, 2002), pp. 172–87.

James Ellison, 'Stabilising the West and Looking to the East: Anglo-American Relations, Europe and Détente, 1965–1967', in N. Piers Ludlow (ed.), *European Integration and the Cold War: Ostpolitik-Westpolitik, 1965–1973* (Abingdon: Routledge, 2007), pp. 105–27.

Jeffrey A. Engel, 'Bush, Germany, and the Power of Time: How History Makes History', *Diplomatic History*, vol. 37, no. 4, 2013, pp. 639–63.

Scott Erb, *German Foreign Policy: Navigating a New Era* (Boulder, CO and London: Lynne Rienner Publishers, 2003).

Richard A. Falkenrath, *Shaping Europe's Military Order: The Origins and Consequences of the CFE Treaty* (Cambridge, MA: MIT Press, 1995).

John E. Farquharson, 'Anglo-American Policy on German Reparations from Yalta to Potsdam', *English Historical Review*, vol. 112, no. 448, 1997, pp. 904–26.

Herbert Feis, *Between War and Peace: The Potsdam Conference* (Princeton, NJ: Princeton University Press, 1960).

Werner J. Feld, 'NATO and German Reunification', in Emil J. Kirchner and James Sperling (eds), *The Federal Republic of Germany and NATO: 40 Years After* (Basingstoke: Macmillan, 1992), pp. 75–91.

Lily Gardner Feldman, *Germany's Foreign Policy of Reconciliation: From Enmity to Amity* (Lanham, MD: Rowman & Littlefield, 2012).

Carole Fink and Bernd Schaefer, 'Ostpolitik and the World 1969–1974: Introduction', in Carole Fink and Bernd Schaefer (eds), *Ostpolitik and the World: European and Global Responses* (New York: Cambridge University Press, 2009), pp. 1–14.

Jack R. Fischel, *Historical Dictionary of the Holocaust* (Lanham, MD: Scarecrow Press, 1999).

Michael Steven Fish, 'After Stalin's Death: The Anglo-American Debate Over a New Cold War', *Diplomatic History*, vol. 10, no. 4, 1986, pp. 333–55.

Josef Foschepoth, 'Churchill, Adenauer und die Neutralisierung Deutschlands', *Deutschland Archiv*, vol. 17, no. 12, December 1984, pp. 1286–1301.

Steven Z. Freiberger, *Dawn Over Suez: The Rise of American Power in the Middle East, 1953–1957* (Chicago: Ivan Dee, 1992).

Renata Fritsch-Bournazel, 'The French View', in Edwina Moreton (ed.), *East Germany and the Warsaw Alliance: The Politics of Détente* (Boulder, CO: Westview Press, 1979), pp. 64–82.

John Lewis Gaddis, *The Cold War: A New History* (New York: Penguin Press, 2005).

John Lewis Gaddis, *Strategies of Containment: A Critical Appraisal of Postwar American National Security Policy* (New York: Oxford University Press, 1982).

John Lewis Gaddis, *We Now Know: Rethinking Cold War History* (New York: Oxford University Press, 1997).

Marilena Gala, 'From INF to SDI: How Helsinki Reshaped the Transatlantic Dimension of European Security', in Leopoldo Nuti (ed.), *The Crisis of Détente in Europe: From Helsinki to Gorbachev 1975–1985* (London: Routledge, 2009), pp. 111–23.

Mark Galeotti, *The Age of Anxiety: Security and Politics in Soviet and Post-Soviet Russia* (Harlow: Longman Higher Academic, 1995).

Raymond Garthoff, *Détente and Confrontation: American Soviet Relations from Nixon to Reagan* (Washington, DC: Brookings Institution Press, 1994).

Raymond L. Garthoff, *The Great Transition: American–Soviet Relations and the End of the Cold War* (Washington, DC: Brookings Institution Press, 1994).

Raymond L. Garthoff, *A Journey through the Cold War: A Memoir of Containment and Coexistence* (Washington, DC: Brookings Institution Press, 2001).

Francis J. Gavin, 'Nuclear Nixon: Ironies, Puzzles, and the Triumph of Realpolitik', in Fredrik Logevall and Andrew Preston (eds), *Nixon in the World: American Foreign Relations, 1969–1977* (Oxford and New York: Oxford University Press, 2008), pp. 126–45.

John P. S. Gearson, 'Britain and the Berlin Wall Crisis 1959–1962', in John Gearson and Kori Schake (eds), *The Berlin Wall Crisis: Perspectives on Cold War Alliances* (Houndmills: Palgrave Macmillan, 2002), pp. 43–72.

John P. S. Gearson, *Harold Macmillan and the Berlin Wall Crisis, 1958–1962: The Limits of Interest and Force* (Basingstoke and London: Palgrave, 1998).

Jeffrey Gedmin, *The Hidden Hand: Gorbachev and the Collapse of East Germany* (Washington, DC: AEI Press, 1992).

Michael Gehler, 'Der 17. Juni 1953 aus der Sicht des Foreign Office', *Aus Politik und Zeitgeschichte*, 25 June 1993, pp. 22–31.

Tim Geiger, 'Die Regierung Schmidt-Genscher und der NATO-Doppelbeschluss', in Philipp Gassert, Tim Geiger and Hermann Wentker (eds), *Zweiter Kalter Krieg und Friedensbewegung. Der NATO-Doppelbeschluss in deutsch-deutscher und internationaler Perspektive* (Munich: Oldenbourg, 2011), pp. 95–122.

Alain Genestar, *Les Péchés du prince* (Paris: Grasset, 1992).

Chris Gifford, *The Making of Eurosceptic Britain: Identity and Economy in a Post-imperial State* (Aldershot: Ashgate, 2008).

Mark Gilbert, *Cold War Europe: The Politics of a Contested Continent* (Lanham, MD: Rowman & Littlefield, 2014).

Martin Gilbert, *Churchill and America* (New York: Free Press, 2005).

Martin Gilbert, 'From Yalta to Bermuda and Beyond: In Search of Peace with the Soviet Union', in James W. Muller (ed.), *Churchill as Peacemaker* (New York: Woodrow Wilson Center Press and Cambridge University Press, 1997), pp. 304–32.

John Gimbell, *The Origins of the Marshall Plan* (Stanford: Stanford University Press, 1976).

James M. Goldgeier, *Not Whether but When: The U.S. Decision to Enlarge NATO* (Washington, DC: Brookings Institution Press, 1999).

Phillip H. Gordon, *A Certain Idea of France: French Security Policy and Gaullist Legacy* (Princeton, NJ: Princeton University Press, 1993).

Daniel Gossel, *Briten, Deutsche und Europa: die Deutsche Frage in der britischen Außenpolitik, 1945–1962* (Stuttgart: Steiner, 1999).

Daniel Gossel, 'Zur Innenarchitektur der westlichen Allianz: Die sicherheitspolitische Integration der Bundesrepublik als Aufgabe und Problem der Special Relationship zwischen den USA und Großbritannien (1945–1965)', in Michael Wala (ed.), *Gesellschaft und Diplomatie im transatlantischen Kontext* (Stuttgart: Steiner, 1999), pp. 273–90.

Klaus Gotto, 'Adenauers Deutschland- und Ostpolitik 1954–1963', in Rudolf Morsey and Konrad Repgen (eds), *Adenauer-Studien Bd. III. Untersuchungen und Dokumente zur Ostpolitik und Biographie* (Mainz: Matthias-Grünewald, 1974), pp. 3–91.

David Gowland and Arthur Turner (eds), *Britain and European Integration, 1945–1998: A Documentary History* (London: Routledge, 2000).

David Gowland and Arthur Turner, *Reluctant Europeans: Britain and European Integration 1945–1998* (Harlow: Longman, 2000).

David Gowland, Arthur Turner and Alex Wright, *Britain and European Integration since 1945: On the Sidelines* (Abingdon and New York: Routledge, 2010).

Andrei Grachev, 'From the Common European Home to European Confederation: François Mitterrand and Mikhail Gorbachev in Search of the Road to Greater Europe', in Frédéric Bozo, Marie-Pierre Rey, N. Piers Ludlow and Leopoldo Nuti (eds), *Europe and the End of the Cold War: A Reappraisal* (Abingdon and New York: Routledge, 2008), pp. 207–19.

Andrei Grachev, *Gorbachev's Gamble: Soviet Foreign Policy and the End of the Cold War* (Cambridge: Polity Press, 2008).

Ronald J. Granieri, 'Political Parties and German–American Relations: Politics beyond the Water's Edge', in Detlef Junker, Philipp Gassert, Wilfried Mausbach and David B. Morris (eds), *The United States and Germany in the Era of the Cold War, 1945–1990: A Handbook. Vol. 1, 1945–1968* (Washington, DC: Cambridge University Press, 2004), pp. 141–8.

Stephen R. Graubard, *Kissinger; Portrait of a Mind* (New York: W. W. Norton, 1973).

William Glenn Gray, *Germany's Cold War: The Global Campaign to Isolate East Germany, 1949–1969* (Chapel Hill, NC and London: University of North Carolina Press, 2003).

Sean Greenwood, 'Helping to Open the Door? Britain in the Last Decade of the Cold War', in Olav Njølstad (ed.), *The Last Decade of the Cold War: From Conflict Escalation to Conflict Transformation* (London: Frank Cass, 2004), pp. 265–76.

Sean Greenwood, 'Return to Dunkirk: The Origins of the Anglo-French Treaty of March 1947', *Journal of Strategic Studies*, vol. 6, no. 4, 1983, pp. 49–65.

David Gress, *Peace and Survival: West Germany, the Peace Movement, and European Security* (Stanford, CA: Hoover Institution Press, 1985).

Richard T. Griffiths, 'A Slow One Hundred and Eighty Degree Turn: British Policy towards the Common Market, 1955–61', in George Wilkes (ed.), *Britain's Failure to Enter the European Community 1961–63: The Enlargement Negotiations and Crises in European, Atlantic and Commonwealth Relations* (London: Frank Cass, 1997), pp. 35–50.

Lawrence J. Haas, *Sound the Trumpet: The United States and Human Rights Promotion* (Lanham, MD and Plymouth: Rowman & Littlefield, 2012).

Helga Haftendorn, *Coming of Age: German Foreign Policy since 1945* (Lanham, MD: Rowman & Littlefield, 2006).

Helga Haftendorn, 'German Unification and European Integration are but Two Sides of One Coin: The FRG, Europe, and the Diplomacy of German Unification', in Frédéric Bozo, Marie-Pierre Rey, Piers N. Ludlow and Leopoldo Nuti (eds), *Europe and the End of the Cold*

War: A Reappraisal (Abingdon and New York: Routledge, 2008), pp. 135–47.

Helga Haftendorn, 'The Unification of Germany, 1985–1991', in Melvyn P. Leffler and Odd Arne Westad (eds), *The Cambridge History of the Cold War. Vol. III* (Cambridge and New York: Cambridge University Press, 2010), pp. 333–55.

Kay Hailbronner and Marcel Kau, 'Constitutional Law', in Matthias Reimann and Joachim Zekoll (eds), *Introduction to German Law* (The Hague: Kluwer Law International, 2005).

Pekka Kalevi Hämäläinen, *Uniting Germany: Actions and Reactions* (Boulder, CO: Westview Press, 1994).

Mary N. Hampton, *The Wilsonian Impulse: U.S. Foreign Policy, the Alliance, and German Unification* (New York: Praeger, 1996).

Jussi M. Hanhimäki, *The Flawed Architect: Henry Kissinger and American Foreign Policy* (London and New York: Oxford University Press, 2004).

Jussi M. Hanhimäki, *The Rise and Fall of Détente: American Foreign Policy and the Transformation of the Cold War* (Washington, DC: Potomac Books, 2013).

Wolfram F. Hanrieder, *Germany, America, Europe: Forty Years of German Foreign Policy* (New Haven, CT: Yale University Press, 1989).

Joseph P. Harahan, 'The Post-Cold War Peace of Europe, 1989–1992', in Meenekshi Bose and Rosanna Perotti (eds), *From Cold War to New World Order: The Foreign Policy of George H. W. Bush* (Westport, CT: Greenwood Press, 2002), pp. 335–47.

John L. Harper, 'American Visions of Europe after 1989', in Christina V. Balis and Simon Serfaty (eds), *Visions of America and Europe: September 11, Iraq, and Transatlantic Relations* (Washington, DC: CSIS Press, 2004), pp. 23–46.

Evanthis Hatzivassiliou, *NATO and Western Perceptions of the Soviet Bloc: Alliance Analysis and Reporting, 1951–69* (London and New York: Routledge 2014).

Jarrod Hayes and Patrick James, 'Theory as Thought: Britain and German Unification', *Security Studies*, vol. 23, no. 2, 2014, pp. 399–429.

James Heartfield, *An Unpatriotic History of the Second World War* (London: John Hunt Publishing, 2012).

Kai Hebel, 'Die "Brückenbauer"? Großbritannien als transatlantischer Vermittler in der KSZE 1972–1978', in Matthias Peter and Hermann Wentker (eds), *Die KSZE im Ost-West-Konflikt. Internationale Politik und gesellschaftliche Transformation 1975–1990* (Munich: Oldenbourg, 2012), pp. 99–120.

Frank Heinlein, *British Government Policy and Decolonisation, 1945–63: Scrutinising the Official Mind* (London: Frank Cass, 2002).

Elisabeth Hellenbroich, 'Thatcher's Obsession to Block German Unity', *Executive Intelligence Review*, vol. 25, no. 32, August 1998, pp. 42–50.

Christopher Hemmer, *American Pendulum: Recurring Debates in U.S. Grand Strategy* (Ithaca, NY: Cornell University Press, 2015).

James G. Hershberg, '"Explosion in the Offing": German Rearmament and American Diplomacy', *Diplomatic History*, vol. 16, no. 4, Fall 1992, pp. 511–50.

Hans-Hermann Hertle, 'Germany in the Last Decade of the Cold War', in Olav Njølstad (ed.), *The Last Decade of the Cold War: From Conflict Escalation to Conflict Transformation* (London: Frank Cass, 2004), pp. 265–87.

Hans-Dieter Heumann, *Hans-Dietrich Genscher: Die Biographie* (Paderborn: Ferdinand Schöningh, 2012).

Beatrice Heuser, 'Britain and the Federal Republic of Germany in NATO', in Jeremy Noakes, Peter Wende and Jonathan Wright (eds), *Britain and Germany in Europe, 1949–1990* (Oxford and New York: Oxford University Press, 2002), pp. 141–62.

John Hiden and Patrick Salmon, *The Baltic Nations and Europe: Estonia, Latvia and Lithuania in the Twentieth Century* (London and New York: Longman, 1994).

Christopher Hill and Christopher Lord, 'The Foreign Policy of the Heath Government', in Stuart Ball and Anthony Seldon (eds), *The Heath Government 1970–74: A Reappraisal* (London and New York: Routledge, 1996), pp. 285–314.

William I. Hitchcock, 'The Marshall Plan and the Creation of the West', in Melvyn P. Leffler and Odd Arne Westad (eds), *The Cambridge History of the Cold War. Vol. 1: Origins* (Cambridge: Cambridge University Press, 2010), pp. 154–74.

William I. Hitchcock, *France Restored: Cold War Diplomacy and the Quest for Leadership in Europe, 1944–1954* (Chapel Hill, NC: University of North Carolina Press, 1998).

Henning Hoff, *Großbritannien und die DDR 1955–1973: Diplomatie auf Umwegen* (Munich: Oldenbourg, 2003).

Arne Hofmann, *The Emergence of Détente in Europe: Brandt, Kennedy and the Formation of Ostpolitik* (New York: Routledge, 2007).

Stephanie C. Hofmann, *European Security in NATO's Shadow: Party Ideologies and Institution Building* (Cambridge: Cambridge University Press, 2013).

Jonathan Hollowell, *Twentieth-Century Anglo-American Relations, Contemporary History in Context* (London: Palgrave Macmillan, 2001).

Andrew Holt, *The Foreign Policy of the Douglas-Home Government:*

Britain, the United States and the End of Empire (Basingstoke: Palgrave Macmillan, 2014).

Carl-Ludwig Holtfrerich, *Economic and Strategic Issues in U. S. Foreign Policy* (Berlin and New York: de Gruyter, 1989).

Alistair Horne, *Macmillan: The Official Biography* (New York: Pan Macmillan, 2008).

Jonathan M. House, *A Military History of the Cold War, 1944–1962* (Norman: University of Oklahoma Press, 2012).

Marianne Howarth, 'Vom Kalten Krieg zum "Kalten Frieden". Diplomatische Beziehungen zwischen Grossbritannien und der DDR 1972/73–1975', in Peter Barker, Marc-Dietrich Ohse and Dennis Tate (eds), *Views from Abroad: Die DDR aus britischer Perspektive* (Bielefeld: WBV, W. Bertelsmann, 2007), pp. 149–62.

Geraint Hughes, *Harold Wilson's Cold War: The Labour Government and East–West Politics, 1964–1970* (Rochester, NY: Boydell Press, 2009).

R. Gerald Hughes, *Britain, Germany and the Cold War: The Search for a European Détente 1949–1967* (London and New York: Macmillan, 2007).

R. Gerald Hughes, '"Possession is Nine Tenths of the Law": Britain and the Boundaries of Eastern Europe Since 1945', *Diplomacy and Statecraft*, vol. 16, no. 4, 2005, pp. 723–47.

R. Gerald Hughes, *The Postwar Legacy of Appeasement: British Foreign Policy since 1945* (Bloomsbury: London, 2014).

R. Gerald Hughes, 'Unfinished Business from Potsdam: Britain, West Germany, and the Oder–Neisse Line, 1945–1962', *The International History Review*, vol. 27, no. 2, June 2005, pp. 259–94.

R. Gerald Hughes and Thomas Robb, 'Kissinger and the Diplomacy of Coercive Linkage in the "Special Relationship" between the United States and Great Britain, 1969–1977', *Diplomatic History*, vol. 37, no. 4, 2013, pp. 861–905.

Robert L. Hutchings, 'The US, German unification, and European integration', in Frédéric Bozo, Marie-Pierre Rey, Piers N. Ludlow and Leopoldo Nuti (eds), *Europe and the End of the Cold War: A Reappraisal* (Abingdon and New York: Routledge, 2008), pp. 119–32.

G. John Ikenberry, *After Victory: Institutions, Strategic Restraint, and the Rebuilding of Order after Major Wars* (Princeton, NJ: Princeton University Press, 2001).

G. John Ikenberry, 'German Unification, Western Order, and the Post-Cold War Restructuring of the International System', in Peter C. Caldwell and Robert R. Shandley (eds), *German Unification: Expectations and Outcomes* (Basingstoke and New York: Palgrave Macmillan, 2011), pp. 15–39.

Maurice Isserman, *Vietnam War* (New York: Facts on File, 2003).

Jean-Paul Jacqué, 'German Unification and the European Community', *European Journal of International Law*, vol. 2, no. 1, 1991, pp. 1–16.

Harold James, *Making the European Monetary Union: The Role of the Committee of Central Bank Governors and the Origins of the European Central Bank* (Cambridge, MA and London: Harvard University Press, 2012).

Harold James and Marla Stone (eds), *When the Wall Came Down: Reactions to German Unification* (New York: Routledge, 1992).

Konrad H. Jarausch, *The Rush to German Unity* (New York: Oxford University Press, 1994).

Wanda Jarzabek, 'Polish Reactions to the West German Ostpolitik', in Poul Villaume and Odd Arne Westad (eds), *Perforating the Iron Curtain: European Détente, Transatlantic Relations, and the Cold War, 1965–1985* (Copenhagen: Museum Tusculanum Press, 2010), pp. 35–55.

Richard J. Jenses, *Reagan at Bergen-Belsen and Bitburg* (College Station: Texas A&M University Press, 2007).

Jacques Jessel, *La Double Défaite de Mitterrand. De Berlin à Moscou, les faillites d'une diplomatie* (Paris: A. Michel, 1992).

Lonnie R. Johnson, *Central Europe: Enemies, Neighbors, Friends* (New York and Oxford: Oxford University Press, 1996).

Peter Jones, *America and the British Labour Party: The Special Relationship at Work* (London: I. B. Tauris, 1997).

Peter Jones, *Open Skies: Transparency, Confidence-Building, and the End of the Cold War* (Stanford, CA: Stanford University Press, 2014).

Jean-François Juneau, 'The Limits of Linkage: The Nixon Administration and Willy Brandt's Ostpolitik, 1969–72', *The International History Review*, vol. 33, no. 2, 2011, pp. 277–97.

Sean N. Kalic, 'Reagan's SDI Announcement and the European Reaction: Diplomacy in the Last Decade of the Cold War', in Leopoldo Nuti (ed.), *The Crisis of Détente in Europe: From Helsinki to Gorbachev 1975–1985* (London: Routledge, 2009), pp. 99–110.

Lawrence S. Kaplan, *NATO Divided, NATO United: The Evolution of an Alliance* (Westport, CT: Praeger, 2004).

Lawrence S. Kaplan, *NATO and the UN: A Peculiar Relationship* (Columbia, MO: University of Missouri Press, 2010).

Tsuyoshi Kawasaki, 'The Rising Sun Was No Jackal: Japanese Grand Strategy, the Tripartite Pact, and Alliance Formation Theory', in Jeffrey W. Taliaferro, Norrin M. Ripsman and Steven E. Lobell (eds), *The Challenge of Grand Strategy: The Great Powers and the Broken Balance between the World Wars* (Cambridge and New York: Cambridge University Press, 2012), pp. 224–45.

Sean Kay, *NATO and the Future of European Security* (Lanham, MD: Rowman & Littlefield, 1998).

Caroline Kennedy-Pipe, *Stalin's Cold War: Soviet Strategies in Europe, 1943 to 1956* (Manchester: Manchester University Press, 1995).

Lothar Kettenacker, *Germany 1989: In the Aftermath of the Cold War* (Harlow: Pearson Longman, 2009).

Stephan Kieninger, 'Den status quo aufrechterhalten oder ihn langfristig überwinden? Der Wettkampf westlicher Entspannungsstrategien in den Siebzigerjahren', in Oliver Bange and Bernd Lemke (eds), *Wege zur Wiedervereinigung. Die beiden deutschen Staaten in ihren Bündnissen 1970 bis 1990* (Munich: Oldenbourg 2013), pp. 67–86.

Stephan Kieninger, *Dynamic Détente: The United States and Europe, 1964–1975* (Lanham, MD: Lexington, 2016).

Stephan Kieninger, 'Transformation or Status Quo – The Conflict of Stratagems in Washington over the Meaning and Purpose of the CSCE and MBFR, 1969–1973', in Oliver Bange and Gottfried Niedhart (eds), *Helsinki 1975 and the Transformation of Europe* (London: Berghahn Books, 2008), pp. 67–82.

Warren Kimball, 'The Anglo-American Relationship: Still Special after All These Years', in Antoine Capet and Aïssatou Sy-Wonyu (eds), *The 'Special Relationship': La «relation spéciale» entre le Royaume-Uni et les Etats-Unis* (Rouen: Université de Rouen, 2003), pp. 207–24.

Henry A. Kissinger, 'The Search for Stability', *Foreign Affairs*, vol. 37, no. 4, July 1959, pp. 537–60.

Eckart Klein, 'Deutchlands Rechtslage', in Werner Weidenfeld and Karl-Rudolf Korte (eds), *Handbuch zur deutschen Einheit, 1949–1989–1999* (Frankfurt and New York: Campus, 1999), pp. 282–91.

Yvonne Klein, 'Obstructive or Promoting? British Views on German Unification 1989/90', *German Politics*, vol. 5, no. 3, 1996, pp. 404–31.

Gerard R. Kleinfeld, 'The Genesis of American Policy toward the GDR: Some Working Hypotheses', in Reiner Pommerin (ed.), *The American Impact on Postwar Germany* (Oxford: Berghahn Books, 1995), pp. 53–64.

Joost Kleuters, *Reunification in West German Party Politics from Westbindung to Ostpolitik* (Basingstoke: Palgrave Macmillan, 2012).

Holger Klitzing, 'To Grin and Bear It: The Nixon Administration and Ostpolitik', in Carole Fink and Bernd Schaefer (eds), *Ostpolitik 1969–1974: European and Global Responses* (Washington, DC: German Historical Institute, 2009), pp. 80–110.

Hubertus Knabe, *17. Juni 1953: Der Anfang vom langen Ende der DDR* (Munich: Olzog, 2003).

Hubertus Knabe, *17. Juni 1953: Ein deutscher Aufstand* (Berlin: Propyläen, 2003).

John O. Koehler, *Stasi: The Untold Story of the East German Secret Police* (Boulder, CO: Westview Press, 1999).

Mark Kramer, 'The Demise of the Soviet Bloc', in Terry Cox (ed.),

Reflections on 1989 in Eastern Europe (London: Routledge, 2012), pp. 7–62.

Mark Kramer, 'Die Nicht-Krise um "Able Archer 1983": Fürchtete die sowjetische Führung tatsächlich einen atomaren Großangriff im Herbst 1983?', in Oliver Bange and Bernd Lemke (eds), *Wege zur Wiedervereinigung. Die beiden deutschen Staaten in ihren Bündnissen 1970 bis 1990* (Munich: Oldenbourg 2013), pp. 129–50.

Michael Kreile, 'Ostpolitik Reconsidered', in Ekkehart Krippendorf and Volker Rittberger (eds), *The Foreign Policy of West Germany: Formation and Contents* (London and Beverly Hills: Sage, 1980), pp. 123–46.

Jeffrey S. Lantis, *Domestic Constraints and the Breakdown of International Agreements* (Westport, CT: Praeger, 1997).

Ulrich Lappenküper, *Mitterrand und Deutschland: Die enträtselte Sphinx* (Munich: Oldenbourg, 2011).

Walter Laqueur and Leon Sloss, *European Security in the 1990s: Deterrence and Defense after the INF Treaty* (New York and London: Plenum Press, 1990).

David Clay Large, *Germans to the Front: West German Rearmament in the Adenauer Era* (Chapel Hill, NC: University of North Carolina Press, 1996).

F. Stephen Larrabee, 'The New Soviet Approach to Europe', in Erik P. Hoffmann, Robbin Frederick Laird and Frederic J. Fleron (eds), *Classic Issues in Soviet Foreign Policy: From Lenin to Brezhnev* (New York: A. De Gruyter, 1991), pp. 638–63.

F. Stephen Larrabee, 'The View from Moscow', in F. Stephen Larrabee, *The Two German States and European Security* (Basingstoke and London: Macmillan, 1989), pp. 182–205.

Klaus Larres, 'Britain and the GDR: Political and Economic Relations, 1949–1989', in Klaus Larres and Elizabeth Meehan (eds), *Uneasy Allies: British–German Relations and European Integration since 1945* (Oxford: Oxford University Press, 2000), pp. 63–98.

Klaus Larres, 'Britain and the GDR: The Politics of Trade and Recognition by Stealth', in Jeremy Noakes, Peter Wende and Jonathan Wright (eds), *Britain and Germany in Europe, 1949–1990* (Oxford and New York: Oxford University Press, 2002), pp. 187–217.

Klaus Larres, 'Introduction: Uneasy Allies or Genuine Partners? Britain, Germany, and European Integration', in Klaus Larres and Elizabeth Meehan (eds), *Uneasy Allies: British–German Relations and European Integration since 1945* (Oxford: Oxford University Press, 2000), pp. 1–24.

Klaus Larres, 'Neutralisierung oder Westintegration. Churchill, Adenauer, die USA und der 17. Juni 1953', *Deutschland Archiv*, vol. 26, no. 6, 1993, pp. 568–83.

Klaus W. Larres, *Politik der Illusionen. Churchill, Eisenhower und die deutsche Frage 1945–1955* (Göttingen: Vandenhoeck & Ruprecht, 1995).

Klaus Larres and Kenneth Alan Osgood (eds), *The Cold War after Stalin's Death: A Missed Opportunity for Peace?* (Lanham, MD: Rowman & Littlefield, 2006).

Henrik Larsen, *Foreign Policy and Discourse Analysis: France, Britain and Europe* (London and New York: Routledge, 1997).

Deborah Welch Larson, *Anatomy of Mistrust: U.S.–Soviet Relations during the Cold War* (Ithaca, NY: Cornell University Press, 2000).

Sabine Lee, *Victory in Europe? Britain and Germany since 1945* (Harlow: Longman, 2001).

Ursula Lehmkuhl, 'The "Ottawa Formula" and Transatlantic Relations: Politics and Diplomacy of the "Two-Plus-Four" Negotiations', *Eurostudia*, vol. 5, no. 2, 2009, pp. 1–20.

Ursula Lehmkuhl, Clemens A. Wurm and Hubert Zimmermann (eds), *Deutschland, Großbritannien, Amerika. Politik, Gesellschaft und Internationale Geschichte im 20. Jahrhundert. Festschrift für Gustav Schmidt zum 65. Geburtstag* (Stuttgart: Steiner, 2003).

Richard A. Leiby, *The Unification of Germany 1989–90* (Westport, CT: Greenwood Press, 1999).

Udo Leuschner, *Die Geschichte der FDP: Metamorphosen einer Partei zwischen rechts, sozialliberal und neokonservativ* (Münster: Edition Octopus, 2005).

Jacques Lévesque, *Fin d'un Empire, 1989* (Berkley and Los Angeles: University of California Press, 1997).

Jacques Lévesque, 'In the Name of Europe's Future: Soviet, French, and British Qualms about Kohl's rush to German unification', in Frédéric Bozo, Marie-Pierre Rey, Piers N. Ludlow and Leopoldo Nuti (eds), *Europe and the End of the Cold War: A Reappraisal* (Abingdon and New York: Routledge, 2008), pp. 95–106.

Daniel Levy, 'Integrating Ethnic Germans in West Germany: The Early Postwar Period', in David Rock and Stefan Wolff (eds), *Coming Home to Germany? The Integration of Ethnic Germans from Central and Eastern Europe in the Federal Republic* (New York and Oxford: Berghahn Books, 2002), pp. 19–37.

Margot Light, 'Anglo-Soviet Relations: Political and Diplomatic', in Alex Pravda and Peter Duncan (eds), *Soviet–British Relations since the 1970s* (Cambridge: Cambridge University Press, 1990), pp. 120–46.

Jennifer M. Lind, *Sorry States: Apologies in International Politics* (Ithaca, NY: Cornell University Press, 2012).

Julian Lindley-French, *The North Atlantic Treaty Organization: The Enduring Alliance* (London and New York: Routledge, 2007).

Werner Link, 'Détente auf deutsch und Anpassung an Amerika: Die Bonner Ostpolitik', in Detlef Junker (ed.), *Die USA und Deutschland im Zeitalter des Kalten Krieges. Ein Handbuch*, vol. 2 (Stuttgart: DVA, 2001), pp. 56–65.

Werner Lippert, *The Economic Diplomacy of Ostpolitik: Origins of NATO's Energy Dilemma* (New York: Berghahn Books, 2011).

Deborah Lipstadt, 'The Bitburg Controversy', in *American Jewish Year Book*, vol. 87, 1987, pp. 21–37.

Fredrik Logevall, *Embers of War: The Fall of an Empire and the Making of America's Vietnam* (New York: Random House, 2012).

Wilfried Loth, 'The Origins of Stalin's Note of 10 March 1952', *Cold War History*, vol. 4, no. 2, January 2004, pp. 66–88.

William Roger Louis and Hedley Bull (eds), *The Special Relationship: Anglo-American Relations since 1945* (Oxford and New York: Oxford University Press, 1986).

N. Piers Ludlow, 'The Real Years of Europe?: US–West European Relations during the Ford Administration', *Journal of Cold War Studies*, vol. 15, no. 3, 2013, pp. 136–61.

N. Piers Ludlow, 'The Unnoticed Apogee of Atlanticism? U.S.–Western European Relations during the Early Reagan Era', in Kiran Klaus Patel and Kenneth Weisbrode (eds), *European Integration and the Atlantic Community in the 1980s* (New York: Cambridge University Press, 2013), pp. 17–38.

Geir Lundestad, 'The European Role at the Beginning and Particularly at the End of the Cold War', in Olav Njølstad (ed.), *The Last Decade of the Cold War: From Conflict Escalation to Conflict Transformation* (London: Frank Cass, 2004), pp. 50–66.

Geir Lundestad, *The United States and Western Europe since 1945: From 'Empire' by Invitation to Transatlantic Drift* (Oxford: Oxford University Press, 2003).

John F. Lyons, *America in the British Imagination: 1945 to the Present* (London and New York: Palgrave Macmillan, 2013).

James McAllister, *No Exit: America and the German Problem 1943– 1954* (Ithaca, NY: Cornell University Press, 2002).

Richard McAllister, *From EC to EU: An Historical and Political Survey* (London and New York: Routledge, 1997).

Martin McCauley, *Origins of the Cold War, 1941–1949* (Harlow: Pearson Longman, 2008).

Martin McCauley, *Russia, America and the Cold War: 1949–1991* (London: Pearson, 2004).

John J. McCloy, 'The Future of Germany: Part of a Great World Problem', *The Department of State Bulletin*, vol. XXII, pp. 275–9.

Terry Macintyre, *Anglo-German Relations during the Labour*

Governments, 1964–70: NATO Strategy, Détente and European Integration (Manchester: Manchester University Press, 2007).

Lori Maguire, 'Introduction', in Lori Maguire (ed.), *The Foreign Policy Discourse in the United Kingdom and the United States in the 'New World Order'* (Newcastle upon Tyne: Cambridge Scholars Publishing, 2009), pp. 1–21.

Charles S. Maier, *Dissolution: The Crisis of Communism and the End of East Germany* (Princeton, NJ: Princeton University Press, 1997).

Patrick Major, *Behind the Berlin Wall: East Germany and the Frontiers of Power* (Oxford: Oxford University Press, 2009).

Neil Malcolm, 'The "Common European Home" and Soviet European Policy', *International Affairs*, vol. 65, no. 4, Autumn 1989, pp. 659–76.

Peter Mangold, *Almost Impossible Ally: Harold Macmillan and Charles de Gaulle* (London: I. B. Tauris, 2006).

James Mann, *The Rebellion of Ronald Reagan: A History of the End of the Cold War* (New York: Viking, 2009).

George C. Marshall, 'European Initiative Essential to Economic Recovery', 5 June 1947, *The Department of State Bulletin*, vol. XVI, no. 415, pp. 1159–60.

Garret Joseph Martin, *General de Gaulle's Cold War: Challenging American Hegemony, 1963–68* (New York: Berghahn Books, 2013).

Steve Marsh, 'The Anglo-American Defence Relationship', in Alan Dobson and Steve Marsh (eds), *Anglo-American Relations: Contemporary Perspectives* (London and New York: Routledge, 2013), pp. 179–207.

Vojtech Mastny, *The Cold War and Soviet Insecurity: The Stalin Years* (New York: Oxford University Press, 1996).

Margarita Mathiopoulos, 'The U.S. Presidency and the German Question during the Adenauer to Kohl Chancellorships', *Aussenpolitik*, vol. 39, no. 4, 1988, pp. 353–70.

Spencer Mawby, *Containing Germany: Britain and the Arming of the Federal Republic* (New York: St. Martin's Press, 2000).

Christopher Maynard, *Out of the Shadow: George H. W. Bush and the End of the Cold War* (College Station: Texas A&M University Press, 2008).

Achilleas Megas, *Soviet Foreign Policy towards East Germany* (Berlin: Springer, 2015).

Peter H. Merkl, *German Unification in the European Context* (University Park: Pennsylvania State University Press, 1993).

John J. Metzler, *Divided Dynamism: The Diplomacy of Separated Nations: Germany, Korea, China* (Lanham, MD: University Press of America, 2014).

Sigrid Meuschel, 'Auf der Suche nach Madame L'Identité? Zur Konzeption der Nation und Nationalgeschichte', in Gert-Joachim

Glaessner (ed.), *Die DDR in der Ära Honecker: Politik – Kultur – Gesellschaft* (Opladen: Westdeutscher, 1988), pp. 77–93.

Robert F. Miller, *Soviet Foreign Policy Today: Gorbachev and the New Political Thinking* (London: Routledge, 1991).

Daniel Mockli, *European Foreign Policy during the Cold War: Heath, Brandt, Pompidou and the Dream of Political Unity* (London and New York: I. B. Tauris, 2009).

Alexander Moens, 'American Diplomacy and German Unification', *Survival*, vol. 33, no. 6, November/December 1991, pp. 531–45.

Sidney Monas, 'Perestroika in Reverse Perspective: The Reforms of the 1860s', in Thomas Lahusen and Gene Kuperman (eds), *Late Soviet Culture: From Perestroika to Novostroika* (Durham, NC and London: Duke University Press, 1993), pp. 35–46.

Kenneth O. Morgan, *Callaghan: A Life* (Oxford: Oxford University Press, 1997).

Kenneth O. Morgan, 'Labour and the Anglo-American Alliance', in Antoine Capet and Aïssatou Sy-Wonyu (eds), *The 'Special Relationship': La «relation spéciale» entre le Royaume-Uni et les Etats-Unis* (Rouen: Université de Rouen, 2003), pp. 169–84.

Roger Morgan, 'The British View: West German Foreign and Security Interests', in Edwina Moreton (ed.), *Germany between East and West* (Cambridge: Cambridge University Press, 1987), pp. 83–94.

Emmanuel Mourlon-Druol, *A Europe Made of Money: The Emergence of the European Monetary System* (Ithaca, NY: Cornell University Press, 2012).

Harald Mueller and Thomas Risse-Kappen, 'Origins of Estrangement: The Peace Movement and the Changed Image of America in West Germany', *International Security*, vol. 12, no. 1, 1987, pp. 52–88.

Colin Munro, 'Britain, Berlin, German Unification, and the Fall of the Soviet Empire', *Bulletin of the German Historical Institute*, vol. 31, no. 2, November 2009, pp. 50–80.

Holger Nehring, 'Für eine andere Art von Sicherheit. Friedensbewegungen, deutsche Politik und transatlantische Beziehungen in den Achtziger Jahren', in Oliver Bange and Bernd Lemke (eds), *Wege zur Wiedervereinigung. Die beiden deutschen Staaten in ihren Bündnissen 1970 bis 1990* (Munich: Oldenbourg 2013), pp. 223–44.

Holger Nehring, *Politics of Security: British and West German Protest Movements and the Early Cold War, 1945–1970* (Oxford: Oxford University Press, 2013).

Holger Nehring, 'A Transatlantic Security Crisis? Transnational Relations between the West German and the US Peace Movements, 1977–85', in Kiran Klaus Patel and Kenneth Weisbrode (eds), *European Integration and the Atlantic Community in the 1980s* (New York: Cambridge University Press, 2013), pp. 177–200.

Michael Neiberg, *Potsdam: The End of World War II and the Remaking of Europe* (New York: Basic Books, 2015).

Iver B. Neumann, *Russia and the Idea of Europe: A Study in Identity and International Relations* (London and New York: Routledge, 1996).

Christian Nuenlist, 'Into the 1960s: NATO's Role in East–West Relations, 1958–1963', in Andreas Wenger, Christian Nuenlist and Anna Locher (eds), *Transforming NATO in the Cold War: Challenges Beyond Deterrence in the 1960s* (London and New York: Routledge, 2007), pp. 67–88.

Kitty Newman, *Macmillan, Khrushchev and the Berlin Crisis, 1958–1960* (New York: Routledge, 2007).

Randall Everest Newnham, *Deutsche Mark Diplomacy: Positive Economic Sanctions in German–Russian Relations* (University Park: Pennsylvania State University Press, 2002).

Luke A. Nichter, *Richard Nixon and Europe: The Reshaping of the Postwar Atlantic World* (Cambridge: Cambridge University Press, 2015).

Gottfried Niedhart, 'Anglo-American Relations in the Era of Détente and the Challenge of Ostpolitik', in Ursula Lehmkuhl and Gustav Schmidt (eds), *From Enmity to Friendship: Anglo-American Relations in the 19th and 20th Century* (Augsburg: Wißner, 2005), pp. 115–30.

Gottfried Niedhart, 'The British Reaction towards Ostpolitik: Anglo-West German Relations in the Era of Détente 1967–1971', in Christian Haase (ed.), *Debating Foreign Affairs – The Public and British Foreign Policy since 1867* (Berlin: Philo Fine Arts, 2003), pp. 130–52.

Gottfried Niedhart, 'Deutsch-amerikanische Beziehungen in der Anfangsphase der sozial-liberalen Ostpolitik und Differenzen in der Perzeption der Sowjetunion 1969/70', in Manfred Berg and Philipp Gassert (eds), *Deutschland und die USA in der Internationalen Geschichte des 20. Jahrhunderts: Festschrift für Detlef Junker* (Stuttgart: Steiner, 2004), pp. 505–20.

Gottfried Niedhart, 'The Federal Republic's *Ostpolitik* and the United States: Initiatives and Constraints', in Kathleen Burk and Melvyn Stokes (eds), *The United States and the European Alliance since 1945* (Oxford: Berg, 1999), pp. 289–311.

Gottfried Niedhart, 'Ostpolitik: Phases, Short-term Objectives, and Grand Design', *German Historical Institute Bulletin*, supp. no. 1, 2004, pp. 118–36.

Gottfried Niedhart, 'Zustimmung und Irritationen: Die Westmächte und die deutsche *Ostpolitik*, 1969–1970', in Ursula Lehmkuhl, Clemens A. Wurm and Hubert Zimmermann (eds), *Deutschland, Großbritannien, Amerika. Politik, Gesellschaft und Internationale Geschichte im 20. Jahrhundert. Festschrift für Gustav Schmidt zum 65. Geburtstag* (Stuttgart: Steiner, 2003), pp. 227–45.

Frank A. Ninkovich, 'The United States and the German Question, 1949–1968', in Detlef Junker, Philipp Gassert, Wilfried Mausbach and David B. Morris (eds), *The United States and Germany in the Era of the Cold War, 1945–1990: A Handbook. Vol. 1, 1945–1968* (Washington, DC: Cambridge University Press, 2004), pp. 118–24.

Leopoldo Nuti, 'Italy, German Unification and the End of the Cold War', in Frédéric Bozo, Marie-Pierre Rey, Piers N. Ludlow and Leopoldo Nuti (eds), *Europe and the End of the Cold War: A Reappraisal* (Abingdon and New York: Routledge, 2008), pp. 191–203.

Leopoldo Nuti, 'The Origins of the 1979 Dual Track Decision – A Survey', in Leopoldo Nuti (ed.), *The Crisis of Détente in Europe: From Helsinki to Gorbachev 1975–1985* (London: Routledge, 2009), pp. 57–71.

Simon J. Nuttal, *European Foreign Policy* (Oxford: Oxford University Press, 2000).

Don Oberdorfer, *Senator Mansfield: The Extraordinary Life of a Great Statesman and Diplomat* (Washington, DC: Smithsonian Books, 2003).

Christian Ostermann, '"Keeping the Pot Simmering": The United States and the East German Uprising of 1953', *German Studies Review*, vol. 19, no. 1, February 1996, pp. 61–89.

Christian F. Ostermann, 'The Role of East Germany in American Policy', in Detlef Junker, Philipp Gassert, Wilfried Mausbach and David B. Morris (eds), *The United States and Germany in the Era of the Cold War, 1945–1990: A Handbook. Vol. 2, 1968–1990* (Washington and Cambridge: Cambridge University Press, 2004), pp. 96–103.

Christian Ostermann, 'The United States, the East German Uprising of 1953, and the Limits of Rollback', *The Cold War International History Project Working Paper Series*, no. 11 (Washington, DC: Woodrow Wilson International Center for Scholars, 1994).

Christian F. Ostermann, *Uprising in East Germany 1953: The Cold War, the German Question, and the First Major Upheaval behind the Iron Curtain* (Budapest and New York: Central European University Press, 2001).

Matthew J. Ouimet, *The Rise and Fall of the Brezhnev Doctrine in Soviet Foreign Policy* (Chapel Hill, NC: University of North Carolina Press, 2003).

Ritchie Ovendale, *Anglo-American Relations in the Twentieth Century* (Basingstoke: Macmillan and New York: St. Martin's Press, 1998).

Manfred Overesch, 'The Alternative Prospect: The Plan for a Neutralized United Germany', in Ennio di Nolfo (ed.), *Great Britain, France, Germany and Italy and the Origins of the EEC, 1952–1957* (Berlin and New York: Walter de Gruyter, 1992), pp. 84–100.

Constantine A. Pagedas, *Anglo-American Strategic Relations and the French Problem, 1960–1963: A Troubled Partnership* (London: Frank Cass, 2000).

Helen Parr, *Britain's Policy towards the European Community: Harold Wilson and Britain's World Role, 1964–1967* (Abingdon: Routledge, 2005).

Craig Parsons, *A Certain Idea of Europe* (Ithaca, NY: Cornell University Press, 2003).

Michael V. Paulauskas, 'Reagan, the Soviet Union, and the Cold War, 1981–1985', in Andrew L. Johns (ed.), *A Companion to Ronald Reagan* (Oxford: John Wiley & Sons, 2015), pp. 276–94.

Vladimir O. Pechatnov and C. Earl Edmondson, 'The Russian Perspective', in Ralph B. Levering, Vladimir O. Pechatnov, Verena Botzenhart-Viehe and C. Earl Edmondson (eds), *Debating the Origins of the Cold War: American and Russian Perspectives* (Lanham, MD: Rowman & Littlefield, 2002), pp. 85–178.

P. L. Pham, *Ending 'East of Suez': The British Decision to Withdraw from Malaysia and Singapore (1964–1968)* (Oxford and New York: Oxford University Press, 2010).

Melissa Pine, *Harold Wilson and Europe: Pursuing Britain's Membership of the European Community* (London and New York: I. B. Tauris, 2007).

Avril Pittman, *From Ostpolitik to Reunification: West German–Soviet Political Relations since 1974* (New York: Cambridge University Press, 1992).

Will Podmore, *British Foreign Policy since 1870* (Bloomington, IN: Xlibris, 2008).

Ilaria Poggiolini, 'Thatcher's Double-Track Road', in Frédéric Bozo, Marie-Pierre Rey, N. Piers Ludlow and Bernd Rother (eds), *Visions of the End of the Cold War in Europe, 1945–1990* (New York and Oxford: Berghahn Books, 2012), pp. 266–79.

Ilaria Poggiolini and Alex Pravda, 'Britain in Europe in the 1980s: East & West. Introduction', *Journal of European Integration History*, vol. 16, no. 1, 2010, pp. 7–16.

Elizabeth Pond, *Beyond the Wall: Germany's Road to Unification* (Washington, DC: Brookings Institution Press, 1993).

Georgeta Pourchot, *Eurasia Rising: Democracy and Independence in the Post-Soviet Space* (London: Praeger, 2008).

Ronald E. Powaski, *The Cold War: The United States and the Soviet Union, 1917–1991* (New York: Oxford University Press, 1998).

John Prados, *How the Cold War Ended: Debating and Doing History* (Dulles, VA: Potomac Books, 2011).

Gerald Prenderghast, *Britain and the Wars in Vietnam: The Supply* of Troops, Arms and Intelligence, 1945–1975 (Jefferson, NC: McFarland, 2015).

Bill Proctor, 'We'll Always Have Grenada', *Foreign Affairs*, vol. 85, no. 6, November/December 2006, <https://www.foreignaffairs.com/articles/united-states/2006-11-01/well-always-have-grenada> (last accessed 29 September 2016).

Arch Puddington, *Broadcasting Freedom: The Cold War Triumph of Radio Free Europe and Radio Liberty* (Lexington: University Press of Kentucky, 2000).

Peter E. Quint, *The Imperfect Union: Constitutional Structures of German Unification* (Princeton, NJ: Princeton University Press, 1997).

Robert B. Rakove, *Kennedy, Johnson, and the Nonaligned World* (New York: Cambridge University Press, 2013).

Romesh Ratnesar, *Tear Down This Wall: A City, a President, and the Speech That Ended the Cold War* (New York: Simon and Schuster, 2009).

Luca Ratti, 'Britain, the German Question and the Transformation of Europe: From Ostpolitik to the Helsinki Conference (1963–1975)', in Oliver Bange and Gottfried Niedhart (eds), *Helsinki 1975 and the Transformation of Europe* (New York and Oxford: Berghahn Books, 2008), pp. 83–97.

Luca Ratti, *Britain, Ost- and Deutschlandpolitik, and the CSCE (1955–1975)* (Bern: Peter Lang, 2008).

John A. Reed, Jr., *Germany and NATO* (Washington, DC: National Defense University Press, 1987).

David Reynolds, *Britannia Overruled: British Policy and World Power in the Twentieth Century* (London: Longman, 2000).

Norrin M. Ripsman, *Peacemaking by Democracies: The Effect of State Autonomy on the Post-World War Settlements* (University Park: Pennsylvania State University Press, 2002).

Linda Risso, *Divided We Stand: The French and Italian Political Parties and the Rearmament of West Germany, 1949–1955* (Newcastle upon Tyne: Cambridge Scholars Publishing, 2007).

Gerhard A. Ritter, 'Deutschland und Europa. Grundzüge der Außenpolitik Genschers 1989 bis 1992', in Kerstin Brauckhoff and Irmgard Schwaetze (eds), *Hans-Dietrich Genschers Außenpolitik* (Wiesbaden: Springer Fachmedien, 2014), pp. 209–43.

Gerhard A. Ritter, *Hans-Dietrich Genscher, das Auswärtige Amt und die deutsche Vereinigung* (Munich: C. H. Beck, 2013).

Gerhard A. Ritter, *The Price of German Unity: Reunification and the Crisis of the Welfare State* (Oxford and New York: Oxford University Press, 2011).

Thomas Robb, 'The Power of Oil: Edward Heath, the "Year of Europe" and the Anglo-American "Special Relationship"', *Contemporary British History*, vol. 26, no. 1, 2012, pp. 73–96.

Thomas Robb, *A Strained Partnership? US–UK Relations in the Era of Détente, 1969–77* (Manchester: Manchester University Press, 2013).

Geoffrey Roberts, *Molotov: Stalin's Cold Warrior* (Washington, DC: Potomac Books, 2012).

Geoffrey Roberts, *The Soviet Union in World Politics: Coexistence, Revolution and Cold War, 1945–1991* (London and New York: Routledge, 1999).

Thomas R. Rochon, *Mobilizing for Peace: The Antinuclear Movements in Western Europe* (Princeton, NJ: Princeton University Press, 1988).

Andreas Rödder, 'Germany: Revolution and Unification', in Elisabeth Bakke and Ingo Peters (eds), *20 Years since the Fall of the Berlin Wall: Transitions, State Break-up and Democratic Politics in Central Europe and Germany* (Berlin: BWV, Berliner Wissenschafts and Cambridge: Intersentia, 2011), pp 121–38.

Sally Rohan, *The Western European Union: International Politics between Alliance and Integration* (Oxford and New York: Routledge, 2014).

Angela Romano, 'The Main Task of the European Political Cooperation: Fostering Détente in Europe', in Poul Villaume and Odd Arne Westad (eds), *Perforating the Iron Curtain: European Détente, Transatlantic Relations, and the Cold War, 1965–1985* (Copenhagen: Museum Tusculanum Press, 2010), pp. 123–41.

Angela Romano, 'More Cohesive, Still Divergent: Western Europe, the US and the Madrid CSCE Follow-up Meeting', in Kiran Klaus Patel and Kenneth Weisbrode (eds), *European Integration and the Atlantic Community in the 1980s* (New York: Cambridge University Press, 2013), pp. 39–58.

Walt W. Rostow, *Europe after Stalin* (Austin: University of Texas Press, 1982).

Margit Roth, *Innerdeutsche Bestandsaufnahme der Bundesrepublik 1969–1989: Neue Deutung* (Berlin: Springer, 2014).

Victor Rothwell, *Britain and the Cold War, 1941–1947* (London: Jonathan Cape, 1982).

Robert C. Rowland and John M. Jones, *Reagan at Westminster: Foreshadowing the End of the Cold War* (College Station: Texas A&M University Press, 2010).

Kevin Ruane, 'Agonizing Reappraisals: Anthony Eden, John Foster Dulles and the Crisis of European Defence, 1953–54', *Diplomacy and Statecraft*, vol. 13, no. 4, 2002, pp. 151–85.

Peter Ruggenthaler, 'The 1952 Stalin Note on German Unification: The

Ongoing Debate', *Journal of Cold War Studies*, vol. 13, no. 4, Fall 2011, pp. 172–212.

Hermann-Josef Rupieper, 'American Policy toward German Unification, 1949–1955', in Jeffry M. Diefendorf, Axel Frohn and Hermann-Josef Rupieper (eds), *American Policy and the Reconstruction of West Germany, 1945–1955* (Washington, DC: German Historical Institute and Cambridge University Press, 1993), pp. 45–67.

John Sakkas, 'Conflict and Détente in the Eastern Mediterranean: From the Yom Kippur War to the Cyprus Crisis, October 1973–August 1974', in Elena Calandri, Antonio Varsori and Daniele Caviglia (eds), *Détente in Cold War Europe: Politics and Diplomacy in the Mediterranean and the Middle East* (London: I. B. Tauris, 2012), pp. 141–54.

Patrick Salmon, 'The United Kingdom: divided counsels, global concerns', in Frédéric Bozo, Andreas Rödder, and Mary Elise Sarotte (eds), *German Reunification: A Multinational History* (London and New York: Routledge, 2017), pp. 153–76.

Stephanie C. Salzmann, *Great Britain, Germany and the Soviet Union: Rapallo and after, 1922–1934* (Rochester, NY: Boydell Press, 2003).

Nicholas Evan Sarantakes, *Dropping the Torch: Jimmy Carter, the Olympic Boycott, and the Cold War* (New York: Cambridge University Press, 2010).

Mary E. Sarotte, *Dealing with the Devil: East Germany, Détente, and Ostpolitik, 1969–1973* (Chapel Hill, NC: University of North Carolina Press, 2001).

Mary E. Sarotte, '"Take No Risks (Chinese)": The Basic Treaty in the Context of International Relations', *German Historical Institute Bulletin*, supp. no. 1, 2004, pp. 109–17.

Mary E. Sarotte, 'The Frailties of Grand Strategy: A Comparison of Détente and Ostpolitik', in Fredrik Logevall and Andrew Preston (eds), *Nixon in the World: American Foreign Relations, 1969–1977* (Oxford and New York: Oxford University Press, 2008), pp. 146–63.

Mary E. Sarotte, *1989: The Struggle to Create Post-Cold War Europe* (Princeton, NJ: Princeton University Press, 2009).

Mary E. Sarotte, 'Not One Inch Eastward? Bush, Baker, Kohl, Genscher, Gorbachev, and the Origin of Russian Resentment toward NATO Enlargement in February 1990', *Diplomatic History*, vol. 34, no. 1, January 2010, pp. 119–40.

Mary E. Sarotte, 'A Broken Promise? What the West Really Told Moscow about NATO Expansion', *Foreign Affairs*, vol. 93, no. 5, September/October 2014, pp. 90–7.

Mary Elise Sarotte, 'Perpetuating U.S. Preeminence: The 1990 Deals to "Bribe the Soviets Out" and Move NATO In', *International Security*, Summer 2010, vol. 35, no. 1, pp. 110–37

Mary Elise Sarotte, "His East European allies say they want to be in NATO': US foreign policy, German unification, and NATO's role in European security, 1989–90", in Frédéric Bozo, Andreas Rödder and Mary Elise Sarotte (eds), *German Reunification: A Multinational History* (London and New York: Routledge, 2017), pp. 69–87

Svetlana Savranskaya, 'The Logic of 1989: The Soviet Peaceful Withdrawal from Eastern Europe', in Svetlana Savranskaya, Thomas Blanton and Vlad Zubok (eds), *Masterpieces of History: The Soviet Peaceful Withdrawal from Eastern Europe, 1989* (Budapest: Central European University Press, 2010), pp. 1–47.

Svetlana Savranskaya, Thomas Blanton and Vlad Zubok (eds), *Masterpieces of History: The Soviet Peaceful Withdrawal from Eastern Europe, 1989* (Budapest: Central European University Press, 2010).

Tilo Schabert, *How World Politics Is Made: France and the Reunification of Germany* (Columbia, MO: University of Missouri Press, 2009).

Kori Schake, 'A Broader Range of Choice? U.S. Policy in the 1958 and 1961 Berlin Crises', in John Gearson and Kori Schake (eds), *The Berlin Wall Crisis: Perspectives on Cold War Alliances* (Houndmills: Palgrave Macmillan, 2002), pp. 22–42.

Jack M. Schick, *The Berlin Crisis, 1958–1962* (Baltimore, MD: Johns Hopkins University Press, 1963).

Helmut Schmidt, 'The 1977 Alastair Buchan Memorial Lecture', *Survival*, vol. 20, no. 1, January–February 1978, pp. 2–10.

David F. Schmitz, *Brent Scowcroft: Internationalism and Post-Vietnam War American Foreign Policy* (Lanham, MD: Rowman & Littlefield, 2011).

Susanna Schrafstetter and Stephen Twigge, *Avoiding Armageddon: Europe, the United States, and the Struggle for Nuclear Nonproliferation, 1945–1970* (Westport, CT and London: Praeger, 2004).

Thomas A. Schwartz, *America's Germany: John J. McCloy and the Federal Republic of Germany* (Cambridge, MA: Harvard University Press, 1991).

Randall L. Schweller 'Bandwagoning for Profit: Bringing the Revisionist State Back In', *International Security*, vol. 19, no. 1, 1994, pp. 72–107.

Andrew Scott, *Allies Apart: Heath, Nixon and the Anglo-American Relationship* (Basingstoke and New York: Palgrave Macmillan, 2011).

Len Scott, 'British Perspectives on the Future of European Security', in Colin McInnes (ed.), *Security and Strategy in the New Europe* (London: Routledge, 2002), pp. 178–96.

Robert Self, *British Foreign and Defence Policy since 1945: Challenges and Dilemmas in a Changing World* (London: Palgrave Macmillan, 2010).

David H. Shumaker, *Gorbachev and the German Question: Soviet–West German Relations, 1985–1990* (Westport, CT: Praeger, 1995).

John Simpson, 'The US–UK Special Relationship: The Nuclear Dimension', in Alan P. Dobson and Steve Marsh (eds), *Anglo-American Relations: Contemporary Perspectives* (London and New York: Routledge, 2013), pp. 241–62.

Filip Slaveski, *The Soviet Occupation of Germany: Hunger, Mass Violence and the Struggle for Peace, 1945–1947* (Cambridge: Cambridge University Press, 2013).

Ronald Smelser and Edward J. Davies II, *The Myth of the Eastern Front: The Nazi–Soviet War in American Popular Culture* (New York: Cambridge University Press, 2008).

Joseph Smith and Simon Davis, *Historical Dictionary of the Cold War* (Lanham, MD: Scarecrow Press, 2000).

Julie Smith and Joffrey Edwards, 'British–West German Relations, 1973–1989', in Klaus Larres and Elizabeth Meehan (eds), *Uneasy Allies: British–German Relations and European Integration since 1945* (Oxford: Oxford University Press, 2000), pp. 45–62.

Martin Smith, *Russia and NATO since 1991: From Cold War through Cold Peace to Partnership?* (New York: Routledge, 2006).

William R. Smyser, *From Yalta to Berlin: The Cold War Struggle over Germany* (New York: St. Martin's Press, 1999).

William R. Smyser, *Kennedy and the Berlin Wall: 'A Hell of a Lot Better than a War'* (Lanham, MD: Rowman & Littlefield, 2009).

Michael J. Sodaro, *Moscow, Germany and the West from Khrushchev to Gorbachev* (London: I. B. Tauris, 1991).

Carl Solberg, *Hubert Humphrey: A Biography* (New York: Norton, 1984).

Georges-Henri Sotou, 'France and the German Rearmament Problem, 1945–55', in R. Ahmann, A. M. Birke and M. Howard (eds), *The Quest for Stability: Problems of West European Security 1918–57* (London: Oxford University Press, 1993), pp. 487–512.

Stanley E. Spangler, *Force and Accommodation in World Politics* (Maxwell, AL: Air University Press, 1991).

Bartholomew Sparrow, *The Strategist: Brent Scowcroft and the Call of National Security* (New York: PublicAffairs, 2015).

Alex Spelling, 'Edward Heath and Anglo-American Relations 1970–1974: A Reappraisal', *Diplomacy & Statecraft*, vol. 20, no. 4, 2009, pp. 638–58.

Kristina Spohr, *The Global Chancellor: Helmut Schmidt and the Reshaping of the International Order* (Oxford and New York: Oxford University Press, 2016).

Kristina Spohr, 'Helmut Schmidt and the Shaping of Western Security in the Late 1970s: The Guadeloupe Summit of 1979', *The International History Review*, vol. 37, no. 1, 2015, pp. 167–92.

Kristina Spohr-Readman, 'Conflict and Cooperation in Intra-Alliance Nuclear Politics: Western Europe, the United States, and the Genesis of NATO's Dual-Track Decision, 1977–1979', in *Journal of Cold War Studies*, vol. 13, no. 2, Spring 2011, pp. 39–89.

Richard F. Staar, *USSR Foreign Policies after Détente* (Stanford, CA: Hoover Institution Press, 1987).

Gillian Staerck, 'The Role of the British Embassy in Washington', *Contemporary British History*, vol. 12, no. 3, 1998, pp. 115–38.

Gillian Staerck and Michael D. Kandiah (eds), *Anglo-German Relations and German Reunification* (London: Institute of Contemporary British History, 2003).

Rolf Steininger, *Austria, Germany, and the Cold War: From the Anschluss to the State Treaty* (New York: Berghahn Books, 2008).

Rolf Steininger, *Der Mauerbau. Die Westmächte und Adenauer in der Berlinkrise 1958–1963* (Munich: Olzog, 2001).

Rolf Steininger (ed.), *Die Ruhrfrage 1945/46 und die Entstehung des Landes Nordrhein-Westfalen: Britische, Französische und Amerikanische Akten* (Düsseldorf: Droste, 1988).

Rolf Steininger, 'Ein vereinigtes, unabhängiges Deutschland? Winston Churchill, der kalte Krieg und die deutsche Frage im Jahre 1953', *Militärgeschichtliche Mitteilungen*, vol. 36, no. 2, 1984, pp. 105–44.

Rolf Steininger, 'John Foster Dulles, the European Defense Community, and the German Question', in Richard H. Immerman (ed.), *John Foster Dulles and the Diplomacy of the Cold War* (Princeton, NJ: Princeton University Press, 1990), pp. 79–108.

Angela Stent, *From Embargo to Ostpolitik: The Political Economy of West German–Soviet Relations, 1955–1980* (Cambridge: Cambridge University Press, 1982).

Angela Stent, *Russia and Germany Reborn: Unification, the Soviet Collapse, and the New Europe* (Princeton, NJ: Princeton University Press, 1999).

Fritz Stern, *Five Germanys I Have Known* (New York: Farrar, Straus and Giroux, 2006).

Kristan Stoddart, *Facing Down the Soviet Union: Britain, the USA, NATO and Nuclear Weapons* (Basingstoke: Palgrave Macmillan, 2014).

Kristan Stoddart, *The Sword and the Shield: Britain, America, NATO and Nuclear Weapons, 1970–1976* (Basingstoke: Palgrave Macmillan, 2014).

Norman Stone, *The Atlantic and Its Enemies: A Personal History of the Cold War* (London: Allen Lane, 2010).

Walter Süß, *Staatssicherheit am Ende: Warum es den Mächtigen nicht gelang, 1989 eine Revolution zu verhindern* (Berlin: Christoph Links, 1999).

Michael Sutton, *France and the Construction of Europe, 1944–2007: The Geopolitical Imperative* (New York: Berghahn Books, 2011).

Stephen F. Szabo, *The Diplomacy of German Unification* (New York: St. Martin's Press, 1992).

William Taubman and Svetlana Savranskaya, 'If a Wall Fell in Berlin, and Moscow Hardly Noticed, Would it Still Make a Noise?', in Jeffrey A. Engel (ed.), *The Fall of the Berlin Wall: The Revolutionary Legacy of 1989* (New York: Oxford University Press, 2009), pp. 69–95.

Sara Tavani, 'British Ostpolitik and Polish Westpolitik: "Push and Pull" Diplomacy', *Journal of European Integration History*, vol. 16, no. 1, 2010, pp. 79–93.

Trevor Taylor, 'Britain's Response to the Strategic Defense Initiative', *International Affairs*, vol. 62, no. 2, Spring 1986, pp. 217–30.

Wallace J. Thies, *Why NATO Endures* (New York: Cambridge University Press, 2009).

Martin Thomas, 'From Dien Bien Phu to Evian, Anglo-French Imperial Relations, 1954–1962', in Alan Sharp and Glyn Stone (eds), *Anglo-French Relations in the Twentieth Century: Rivalry and Cooperation* (London: Routledge, 2000), pp. 310–19.

Richard C. Thornton, *The Reagan Revolution II: Rebuilding the Western Alliance* (Victoria, BC: Trafford Publishing, 2005).

Marc Trachtenberg, *The Cold War and After: History, Theory, and the Logic of International Politics* (Princeton, NY: Princeton University Press, 2012).

Marc Trachtenberg, *A Constructed Peace: The Making of the European Settlement, 1945–1963* (Princeton, NJ: Princeton University Press, 1999).

Marc Trachtenberg and Christopher Gehrz, 'America, Europe, and German Rearmament, August–September 1950', *Journal of European Integration History*, vol. 6, no. 2, December 2000, pp. 9–35.

Marc Trachtenberg and Christopher Gehrz, 'America, Europe, and German Rearmament, August–September 1950: A Critique of a Myth', in Marc Trachtenberg (ed.), *Between Empire and Alliance: America and Europe During the Cold War* (Lanham, MD: Rowman & Littlefield, 2003), pp. 1–31.

Michael J. Turner, *Britain and the World in the Twentieth Century: Ever Decreasing Circles* (London: Continuum, 2010).

Michael J. Turner, *Britain's International Role, 1970–1991* (New York: Palgrave Macmillan, 2010).

Michael J. Turner, *British Power and International Relations during the 1950s: A Tenable Position?* (Lanham, MD: Lexington Books, 2009).

John Van Oudenaren, *Détente in Europe: The Soviet Union and the West since 1953* (Durham, NC: Duke University Press, 1991).

Antonio Varsori, 'Crisis and Stabilization in Southern Europe during the 1970s: Western Strategy, European Instruments', *Journal of European Integration History*, vol. 15, no. 1, 2009, pp. 5–14.

Antonio Varsori, *Il Patto di Bruxelles (1948): Tra integrazione europea e alleanza atlantica* (Rome: Bonacci, 1988).

Antonio Varsori, *L'Italia e la fine della guerra fredda. La politica estera dei governi Andreotti (1989–1992)* (Bologna: Il Mulino, 2013).

Antonio Varsori, 'The Relaunching of Europe in the Mid-1980s', in Kiran Klaus Patel and Kenneth Weisbrode (eds), *European Integration and the Atlantic Community in the 1980s* (New York: Cambridge University Press, 2013), pp. 226–42.

Klaus Von Beyme, 'Redefining European Security: The Role of German Foreign Policy', in Carl Cavanagh Hodge (ed.), *Redefining European Security* (London and New York: Garland, 1999), pp. 165–79.

Julia Von Dannenberg, *The Foundations of Ostpolitik: The Making of the Moscow Treaty between West Germany and the USSR* (Oxford: Oxford University Press, 2008).

Alexander von Plato, *Die Vereinigung Deutschlands. Ein weltpolitisches Machtspiel: Bush, Kohl, Gorbatschow und die geheimen Moskauer Protokolle* (Berlin: Christoph Links, 2002).

Alexander von Plato, *The End of the Cold War? Bush, Kohl, Gorbachev, and the Reunification of Germany* (London and New York: Palgrave Macmillan, 2015).

Michael Wala (ed.), *Gesellschaft und Diplomatie im transatlantischen Kontext* (Stuttgart: Steiner, 1999).

Breck Walker, '"Neither Shy nor Demagogic" – The Carter Administration Goes to Belgrade', in Vladimir Bilandžic, Dittmar Dahlmann and Milan Kosanovic (eds), *From Helsinki to Belgrade: The First CSCE Follow-up Meeting and the Crisis of Détente* (Göttingen: Vandenhoeck & Ruprecht and Bonn: Bonn University Press, 2012), pp. 185–204.

Irwin M. Wall, 'The United States and Two Ostpolitiks: De Gaulle and Brandt', in Wilfried Loth and Georges-Henri Soutou (eds), *The Making of Détente: Eastern Europe and Western Europe in the Cold War, 1965–75* (London: Routledge, 2008), pp. 133–50.

William Wallace, 'British Foreign Policy after the Cold War', *International Affairs*, vol. 68, no. 3, July 1992, p. 423–42.

David Walsh, *The Military Balance in the Cold War: US Perceptions and Policy, 1976–85* (London and New York: Routledge, 2008).

Nicholas Wapshott, *Ronald Reagan and Margaret Thatcher: A Political Marriage* (New York: Sentinel, 2007).

Douglas Wass, *Decline to Fall: The Making of British Macro-economic Policy and the 1976 IMF Crisis* (Oxford and New York: Oxford University Press, 2008).

Alan Watson, 'Europe's Odd Couple', *Prospect*, no. 10, July 1996, <http://www.prospectmagazine.co.uk/features/europesoddcouple-germany-britain-thatcher-kohl-conflict> (last accessed 27 September 2016).

Donald Cameron Watt, *Succeeding John Bull: America in Britain's Place, 1900–1975* (Cambridge: Cambridge University Press, 1984).

Jürgen Weber, *Germany 1945–1990: A Parallel History* (Budapest: Central European University Press, 2004).

Janusz Józef Wec, *Socialliberale Ostpolitik: Die FDP und der Warschauer Vetrag, Die Haltung der FDP gegenüber den Verhandlungen mit Polen über den Warschauer Vertrag vom 7. Dezember 1970* (Potsdam: Friedrich-Naumann-Stiftung für die Freiheit, 2011).

Michèle Weinachter, 'Franco-German Relations in the Giscard–Schmidt Era, 1974–1981', in Carine Germond and Henning Türk (eds), *A History of Franco-German Relations in Europe: From 'Hereditary Enemies' to Partners* (New York: Palgrave Macmillan, 2008), pp. 223–33.

Samuel F. Wells, Jr., 'The Korean War: Miscalculation and Alliance Transformation', in Jussi Hanhimäki, Georges-Henri Soutou and Basil Germond (eds), *The Routledge Handbook of Transatlantic Security* (Abingdon and New York: Routledge, 2010), pp. 17–31.

Sherill Brown Wells (ed.), *American Foreign Policy Current Documents 1990* (Washington, DC: US Department of State, 1991).

Odd Arne Westad, 'The Fall of Détente and the Turning Sides of History', in Odd Arne Westad (ed.), *The Fall of Détente: Soviet–American Relations during the Carter Years* (Oslo: Scandinavian University Press, 1997), pp. 3–33.

Brian White, *Britain, Détente and Changing East–West Relations* (London and New York: Routledge, 1992).

Christian Wicke, *Helmut Kohl's Quest for Normality: His Representation of the German Nation and Himself* (Oxford and New York: Berghahn Books, 2015).

Klaus Wiegrefe, *Das Zerwürfnis: Helmut Schmidt, Jimmy Carter und die Krise der deutsch-amerikanische Beziehungen* (Berlin: Propyläen, 2005).

Geoffrey Lee Williams, *The Permanent Alliance: The European–American Partnership, 1945–1984* (Leyden: A. W. Sijthoff, 1977).

Daniel C. Williamson, *Separate Agendas: Churchill, Eisenhower, and Anglo-American Relations, 1953–1955* (Lanham, MD: Lexington Books, 2006).

Frank Roy Willis, *France, Germany, and the New Europe, 1945–1967* (Oxford: Oxford University Press, 1968).

Frank Roy Willis, *The French in Germany, 1945–1949* (Stanford, CA: Stanford University Press, 1962).

Elizabeth Wiskemann, *Germany's Eastern Neighbours: Problems Relating to the Oder–Neisse Line and the Czech Frontier Regions* (London: Oxford University Press, 1956).

Paul Wolfowitz, 'Shaping the Future: Planning at the Pentagon, 1989–93', in Melvyn P. Leffler and Jeffrey W. Legro (eds), *Uncertain Times: American Foreign Policy after the Berlin Wall and 9/11* (Ithaca, NY: Cornell University Press, 2011), pp. 44–62.

J. David Woodward, *The America That Reagan Built* (Westport, CT: Praeger, 2006).

J. David Woodward, *Ronald Reagan: A Biography* (Santa Barbara, CA: ABC-Clio and Greenwood, 2012).

Wichard Woyke, *Erfolg durch Integration: Die Europapolitik der Benelux Staaten von 1947 bis 1969* (Bochum: Brockmeyer, 1985).

Jonathan Wright, 'The Role of Britain in West German Foreign Policy since 1949', *German Politics*, vol. 5, no. 1, April 1996, pp. 26–42.

John W. Young, 'Cold War and Détente with Moscow', in John W. Young (ed.), *The Foreign Policy of Churchill's Peacetime Government, 1951–55* (Leicester: Leicester University Press, 1988), pp. 55–80.

Steven J. Zaloga, *The Kremlin's Nuclear Sword: The Rise and Fall of Russia's Strategic Nuclear Forces, 1945–2000* (Washington, DC: Smithsonian Institution Press, 2002).

Bert Zeeman, 'Britain and the Cold War: An Alternative Approach. The Treaty of Dunkirk Example', *European History Quarterly*, vol. 16, no. 3, 1986, pp. 343–67.

Philip Zelikow and Condoleezza Rice, 'German Unification', in Kiron K. Skinner (ed.), *Turning Points in Ending the Cold War* (Stanford, CA: Hoover Institution Press, 2008), pp. 229–54.

Philip Zelikow and Condoleezza Rice, *Germany Unified and Europe Transformed: A Study in Statecraft* (Cambridge, MA: Harvard University Press, 1995).

Hubert Zimmermann, 'The Improbable Permanence of a Commitment: America's Troop Presence in Europe during the Cold War', *Journal of Cold War Studies*, vol. 11, no. 1, 2009, pp. 3–27.

Hubert Zimmermann, *Money and Security: Troops, Monetary Policy and West Germany's Relations with the United States and Britain, 1950–1971* (Washington, DC: German Historical Institute and Cambridge: Cambridge University Press, 2002).

Vladislav Zubok, 'Gorbachev, German reunification, and Soviet demise, in Frédéric Bozo, Andreas Rödder and Mary Elise Sarotte (eds), *German Reunification: A Multinational History* (London and New York: Routledge, 2017), pp. 88–108.

Unpublished sources
Rodric Braithwaite, *Diary*.
Jack Cunningham, *Nuclear Sharing and Nuclear Crises: A Study in Anglo-American Relations, 1957–1963*, PhD dissertation (University of Toronto, 2010).
James D. Marchio, *Rhetoric and Reality: The Eisenhower Administration and Unrest in Eastern Europe, 1953–1959*, PhD dissertation (American University Microfilms, 1990).
Fabian Rueger, *Kennedy, Adenauer and the Making of the Berlin Wall, 1958–1961*, PhD dissertation (Stanford University, 2011).

Index

EU representative:
Easy Access System Europe
Mustamäe tee 50, 10621 Tallinn, Estonia
Gpsr.requests@easproject.com

www.ingramcontent.com/pod-product-compliance
Lightning Source LLC
Chambersburg PA
CBHW060133280326
41932CB00012B/1502